Contents

Dedication

We dedicate this book to Kenneth Janda
(Northwestern University), who taught us the power of
the Analysis of Variance.

COMPARATIVE POLITICAL ECONOMY

A Developmental Approach

Second Edition

Jan-Erik Lane and Svante Ersson

PINTER

London and Washington

PINTER
A Cassell Imprint
Wellington House, 125 Strand, London WC2R 0BB, England
PO Box 605, Herndon, VA 20172, USA

First published 1990
Reprinted with revisions 1993
Second edition 1997

British Library Cataloguing-in-Publication Data

A catalogue record for this book is available from the British Library.

ISBN   1-85567-434-3 (Hardback)
       1-85567-435-1 (Paperback)

Typeset by Ben Cracknell Studios
Printed and bound in Great Britain by Redwood Books, Trowbridge, Wiltshire

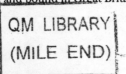

Preface

The second edition of this book is a much revised version of the first edition, which appeared in 1990. Almost the entire book has been rewritten in order to take into account the enormous changes that have occurred in the early 1990s concerning politico-economic regimes and their operations. Several entirely new chapters have been added and the remaining chapters from the first edition have been updated and rewritten. Little of what is new in the new edition has been published elsewhere. Chapter 5 has been taken from A. Leftwich (ed.) *Democracy and Development* (Cambridge: Polity Press, 1996).

The book was revised during a lengthy visit to the European Centre for Comparative Government in Berlin, where Joachim Jens Hesse provided a stimulating environment.

Berlin, autumn 1996
Jan-Erik Lane

Introduction:
the concerns of political economy

Modern political economy deals with the interaction between economics and politics by focusing upon institutions and outcomes. One of its major focuses is the economic conditions and consequences of political institutions. Thus, it asks: what is the impact of socio-economic development on democracy? Or do political institutions impact upon rates of economic growth or development? The economic consequences of political regimes are examined. Do the institutions of the welfare *states* result in better economic performance as compared with welfare *societies*? Another major focus is the interaction between political and economic institutions. The distinction between conditions and consequences on the one hand and political and economic institutions on the other hand is depicted in Figure I.1.

Figure I.1 Institutions and outcomes

	Economic outcomes	Economic institutions
Political institutions	I	II
Political outcomes	III	IV

Modern political economy focuses upon unresolved problems pertaining to categories I, II, III and IV. In category I we have a number of controversial questions concerning the economic conditions for political institutions, such as, for democratic regimes: is affluence a condition for democracy? Here also belong several much debated problems about the economic effects of political institutions. What is the economic performance record of welfare states? Do political institutions have an impact upon economic growth? Category II includes a number of puzzles about how economic and political institutions interact: is democracy necessarily connected with the market economy? Finally, category IV questions whether certain economic institutions such as private property regimes promote political outcomes such as respect for human rights.

Perhaps the most controversial question in political economy is the evaluation of the performance of various types of economic systems or so-called politico-economic regimes. Which politico-economic system is the superior one? This is a problem to be decided ultimately by values, but the deliberation about pros and cons also involves matters of fact. Does capitalism do better than socialism in terms of economic growth? How about the degree of inequality in the distribution of resources in various countries? And which type of regime is more likely to run into double digit inflation or huge national debt?

Not only are economic aspects relevant to the rise and decline of nations, but we also have to take into account how countries score on political criteria of evaluation, such as democratic values. Moreover, what about welfare effort? There are a large number of relevant evaluation criteria: which are most appropriate? And any identification of politico-economic regimes or systems faces tremendous conceptual problems in relation to real-life systems, where there is no such simple dichotomy as capitalism versus socialism.

The evaluation of existing politico-economic regimes may employ as the criteria of evaluation either output or rights. The first criterion, economic development, refers to *economic output*, or the level of national income in a country, whereas the second criterion stands for *rights*, in particular the implementation of civil and political rights, i.e. democracy. The use of these two different criteria of evaluation raises the question of the relationship between various aspects of development.

Political economy is a new field of enquiry resulting from interdisciplinary efforts between the social sciences. However, the label 'political economy' has an old history.

Old and new political economy

The term 'political economy' used to be used as synonymous with the general word 'economics' (Rothschild, 1989). The study of political economy was the analysis of the economy of a nation-state. Let us quote from *A New Dictionary of Economics*:

> political economy. This term is derived from the Greek polis, meaning a city as a political unit, and oikonomike, denoting the management of a household. The combination of words reflects how inextricably involved are the facts of production, trade and finance with those of government fiscal, monetary and commercial policy. It was not until the nineteenth century that the purely political aspects began to feature less and less in studies of economic phenomena, and ECONOMICS as it is known today developed. Since the writings of Alfred Marshall (1842–1924), notably his *Principles of Economics*, political economy, as a description of the discipline, has fallen into disuse. (Taylor, 1966: 231)

Although *A Dictionary of Economics and Commerce* simply states that political economy is the older name for economics (Hanson, 1974: 378), it should be pointed out that books by political economists like Ricardo, Marx and Stuart Mill focused on the political presuppositions of as well as the political consequences of the economy. The perspective on economic transactions was that of the political body – the state – and the basic problem concerned the understanding of how economic wealth in a society could be enhanced by the state belonging to that society. Let us quote from Adam Smith's *Wealth of Nations*, Book IV, 'Of Systems of political Oeconomy':

> Political oeconomy, considered as a branch of the science of a statesman or legislator, proposes two distinct objects; first, to provide a plentiful revenue or subsistence for the people, or more properly to enable them to provide such a revenue or subsistence for themselves; and secondly, to supply the state or commonwealth with a revenue sufficient

for the public services. It proposes to enrich both the people and the sovereign. (Smith, 1964: 375)

When 'political economy' is now brought back into circulation alongside the general term 'economics', the focus is not on economic phenomena in general but, much more specifically, on the interaction between politics and economics (Alt and Chrystal, 1983). Politico-economic interaction is conceived of in a broad fashion, as it covers both how economic factors impact upon political entities and the effects of politics upon economic entities. Modern political economy deals with the economic conditions of political events, including the impact of economic institutions. Modern political economy also discusses the consequences of political phenomena for economic outcomes, especially the impact of political institutions. Modern political economy is, though, different from macroeconomics, as political economy as a discipline is open to the employment of different approaches and not committed to the neo-classical paradigm of economics. Thus, it has raised considerable interest among political scientists and sociologists interested in economic phenomena and their social and political consequences, since the publication in 1953 of Robert A. Dahl and Charles Lindblom's *Politics, Economics and Welfare*. At the same time it has benefited much from the recent broad interest among economists in the impact of politics upon economic life, which goes beyond the concerns of macroeconomics (Barro, 1990).

Surveying the new literature in the emerging field of political economy, Martin Staniland in his *What Is Political Economy?* (1985) states that there is a special set of problems that the new discipline is interested in:

there are several kinds of political economy theory. The criterion for identifying such theory is whether or not it claims to depict a systematic relationship between economic and political processes. Such a relationship may be conceived in different ways – as a causal relationship between one process or another ('deterministic' theory), as a relationship of reciprocity ('interactive' theory), or as a behavioral continuity. Whether or not the theory in question is labeled 'political economy' is secondary: the important issue is its claim to empirical explanation. (Staniland, 1985: 5–6)

In this revised sense of 'political economy' as politico-economic interaction, it constitutes a new field of empirical research. One may follow the development of the concept of political economy by comparing the 1899 *Palgrave Dictionary of Political Economy* with the 1987 *New Palgrave Dictionary of Economics*. Let us quote from the old Palgrave (1899: vol. III): 'Originally political economy was – as its name suggests – conceived to be the common portion of two arts, 'economy in general' and the art of government.' However, the first meaning took precedence over the latter sense at the time that 'economics' began to drive out the use of 'political economy'. Yet the latter term came back in the twentieth century, but with a different and more specific meaning, as the *New Palgrave* explains:

its first modern usage in the 18th century, its demise from the end of the 19th century, when it was gradually replaced by the word 'economics', and its revival in a variety of forms, largely during the 1960s, which have altered its meaning from more traditional usage. (Eatwell *et al.*, 1987a: vol. 3: 904)

This transformation of the meaning of 'political economy' from economics to politico-economic interaction has been attended by the emergence of a variety of approaches to the study of politico-economic interaction, which are all labelled 'modern political economy' (Frey, 1978): Marxist or neo-Marxist approaches, systems theory approaches,various institutionalist approaches, as well as the public choice approach. Sometimes it is stated that modern political economy involves one method – the economic model of preferences, choice and constraint – applied to non-market behaviour (Schneider, 1989). However, such a delimitation to one approach – the neo-classical one – to the exclusion of other approaches is not fortunate (Etzioni, 1988). What is common to all kinds of modern political economy is the focus on the reciprocities between politics and economics in a wide sense, but what differs is the choice of alternative approaches.

Politico-economic theories deal with the interaction between institutions and outcomes in so far as they concern political and economic phenomena. Here, we will look at a few but certainly not all major theories about politico-economic interaction. We will discuss politico-economic models in so far as they deal with *development*, and our approach is strictly *comparative*, examining the evidence of politico-economic interaction by means of data concerning a few so-called economic and political variables for a large set of countries. One should remain open to the employment of different conceptual frameworks when modelling politico-economic interaction.

Rational choice, neo-Marxism or other approaches?

Since the mid-1960s there has been a proliferation of various approaches to the analysis of politico-economic interaction. On the one hand we have the rational choice school, which is actor-oriented and proceeds from the basic assumption about methodological individualism as well as the axiom about utility maximizing individuals. It has resulted in a number of much debated so-called public choice models: the political business cycle, the political popularity function, the Downsian model of the vote maximizing politician and the Niskanen budget maximizing bureau (Frey, 1978; Doel, 1979; Hibbs and Fassbender, 1981; Mueller, 1989). Although these public choice models have been tested in comparative research, there is nothing inherently comparative about them. They may be used to model longitudinal data in one single country. As a matter of fact, the public choice models perform differently from one country to another, which calls for more of an institutional approach (Lybeck and Henrekson, 1988).

On the other hand there is a set of Marxist or neo-Marxist models which are holistic and emphasize macro aspects of political and economic systems; for instance, the dependency models and world systems (Frank, 1967; Wallerstein, 1979; Szentes, 1983). These political economy models have a more clear comparative edge than the public choice models, as they explicitly model country differences in welfare, economic growth and structural dependence. In order to test the idea that there is a world capitalist system that keeps various countries in different relations of autonomy and heteronomy one needs to turn to cross-sectional data about politico-economic performance.

It has been argued that the neo-Marxist political economy models referring to world system modelling are weak because of a lack of empirical evidence, or even in terms of their capacity to be put to a systematic empirical test (Taylor, 1987). Be that as it may, these neo-Marxist models have stimulated one special branch of political economy, i.e. the comparative approach to country differences in political system and economic system properties.

The competition between public choice models and Marxist political economy has been fierce, but here we will focus on a few models concerning politico-economic interaction that are distinctly comparative. Some distinctive hypotheses deal with system questions about how economics and politics or vice versa are related: the affluence hypothesis concerns the relationship between economic affluence and democracy as a type of polity, arguing that wealth is a necessary or sufficient condition for the persistence of a democracy; the 'politics matters' theory claims that politics matters for policy outputs and outcomes, rejecting economic determinism which states that public policies are a function of wealth; and one economic growth hypothesis argues that economic development is conditioned not only by economic and social factors but also by politics in a wide sense. All three hypotheses crop up in various approaches or schools, such as policy analysis, public choice and political economy; and they touch upon problems that are extremely value ingrained and policy relevant. In this book, we analyse and test these three models or three sets of hypotheses, because they are truly complex. No attempt will be made to force the findings into one or the other school in modern political economy. Albert Hirschman claimed in *A Bias for Hope* (1971) that much remains to be done before we reach a basic understanding of how politics and economics relate to each other. What follows below is an attempt to contribute to the creation of a theory of politico-economic interaction by means of country comparative analysis.

The distinction between a public choice or rational choice approach and a neo-Marxist or radical political economy approach bears on the separation between micro and macro theory, between a focus on microscopic entities and macroscopic units. Rational choice theory intrinsically favours micro theory, as it is claimed that actor-oriented theories based on microscopic entities are superior to structural theory – often denounced as functionalism. Although the predictive power and formal elegance of rational choice approaches must be acknowledged, as must the often severe methodological problems inherent in some systems approaches (Barry, 1970), it is difficult to do without macrotheoretical constructs when one is interested in wholes or macroscopic events.

By-passing the clash between rational choice and structural approaches as well as the gulf between micro and macro theory, we focus on middle range theories about politico-economic interaction. Any understanding of how the political system relates to the economic system of a country would have to be founded on an identification of political and economic structures and their properties. The crucial question in a middle range approach is not whether political and economic structures may be ultimately analysed with a micro theory (reductionism) or require a macro theory (holism). More important is the problem: if one takes a middle range perspective on the states and economies of the post Second World War period, then what concepts are adequate for the analysis of politico-economic data? We need theoretical constructs, but which ones are the most promising?

How political institutions affect a country's social and economic development has been much debated. It has been argued that politics matters, either in the form of political institutions or in the form of public policies having an impact on

economic growth. John Zysman (1983) stated that industrial policies matter for
initiating and sustaining the so-called Rostow take-off stage, and that the financial
market institutions impact upon economic growth. One much debated hypothesis
argues that so-called institutional sclerosis in the societal fabric of a country reduces
average economic growth (Olsen, 1982). And there is the Eric Weede hypothesis,
which claims that democracy as a regime type negatively affects economic
development (Weede, 1984b).

There is a cluster of questions about how politics conditions economic growth
in the long run. Does the structure of political institutions matter? Let us look at
whether some significant relationship exists between economic development and
types of polities, like democracy or authoritarianism. Is it simply the length of time
of institutionalization that has elapsed since the introduction of a modern state
that accounts for the variation in economic growth rates? Perhaps public policies
promote or reduce economic growth; or it could simply be a matter of the less
affluent countries catching up with the rich countries (Dowrick and Nguyen, 1987;
Castles, 1990, 1991), the level of affluence reducing the amount of change in the
economy.

Some of the questions in categories I, II and IV can be examined by means of a
comparative approach using the country as the basic unit of analysis. This is what
we will attempt to do, including as many countries as possible for which
information is available about political and economic factors and institutions. The
problems in political economy that may be handled by means of a comparative
approach often refer to questions of development – i.e. economic, social or political
development. More specifically, we will deal with three puzzles that were much
debated in the early 1990s.

Three basic puzzles in political economy

The general concept of development – economic, social and political – has no doubt
offered a challenging perspective for the analysis of countries. The concept of
development could be employed not only to approach change within these countries
over time, but also as a conceptual tool to handle the differences between countries.
Thus, the concept of development may be employed for both longitudinal and
cross-sectional purposes.

The study of economic change resulted in a number of different theories about
the sources of economic growth in less advanced economies, from purely economic
theories to broad social theories, including political institutions – see Peter Hall's
Growth and Development (1983). There is perhaps still no consensus as to the
relative weight to be given to various factors that are conducive to economic growth.
It used to be believed that economic growth could be understood mainly in terms
of economic variables like levels or rate of growth in investments, or the quantity
or quality of human capital or technology (Solow, 1988; Chauduri, 1989). As interest
began to focus on economic development in poor countries, broader social forces
were considered – for example, agriculture by Lewis and religion by Myrdal
(Thirlwall, 1986; Chenery and Srinivasan, 1988). Thus, one may ask what the impact
of the structure of agriculture, the level of urbanization and religion, as well as
political institutions, is upon economic growth (Chenery and Srinivasan, 1988).

There are several relevant ways of classifying systems from a politico-economic perspective. In the mainstream economics literature the focus is on the concept of an economic system, and a few key kinds of economic system are identified and evaluated. A definition of 'economic system' may look as follows: 'An economic system is a set of mechanisms and institutions for decision making and the implementation of decisions concerning production, income, and consumption within a given territorial area' (Lindbeck, 1977: 214). It follows from such an identification of the economic system in a country that it covers not only what traditionally counts as economic institutions, like property and the market. Any description of an economic system would have to include a statement of the place of the state and the range of mechanisms for public resource allocation and income redistribution, i.e. political institutions. Thus, we may speak of *politico-economic regimes* in order to denote the various ways in which the market, the state, property institutions and public systems for budget allocation and redistribution are mixed in different countries (Bromley, 1989).

It is possible to classify economic systems institutionally. The basic distinction used to be the separation between market-oriented and planned economies, following John M. Montias's work *The Structure of Economic Systems* (1976). Its relevance has, however, declined sharply with the system transitions initiated in 1989, involving the dismantling of the command economy in many countries. It is impossible to speak of economic systems without bringing up the state and the role it plays in economic life. The capitalist economy has a specific set of state institutions. Such a combination of economic and political institutions regulating economic life we call a 'politico-economic regime'.

If the simple distinction between socialism and capitalism was never adequate to capture the variety of economic system institutions, then this is even more so the case today after the demise of most of the command economies. Here, we have the *first* of the three key questions that we wish to answer: *what are the basic types of politico-economic system today*? If there is more than one non-socialist regime, which one comes closest to the ideal model of capitalism or the market economy? And what is the overall performance of various economic regimes in terms of not only, for instance, affluence and economic growth but also social and political criteria?

The term 'capitalism' has a negative connotation to many people, which is the reason why some scholars speak instead of the 'market economy'. However, in 1985 Oliver Williamson associated positively with 'capitalism' in his *The Economic Institutions of Capitalism*, claiming that a decentralized market economy promotes economic efficiency in both the short and the long run. Yet the market economy in the classical Adam Smith interpretation is not the only capitalist system, as one must also take the Friedrich List state-capitalist model into account, as well as the Adolf Wagner model of a mixed economy, the capitalist welfare state.

Which countries practise the institutions of the market economy and what difference does it make in terms of outcomes when compared with the outcomes of the other politico-economic regimes? It is not enough only to examine economic growth rates, as there is a long-standing criticism of the economic development concept as neglecting social development aspects. One needs to take social development indicators into account in addition. What matters for quality of life? Affluence? Economic system? Will economic development in the form of a sustained process of economic growth over a number of decades automatically bring about a more just distribution of income?

In *The Rise and Decline of Nations* (1982), Mancur Olson identifies the fortunes of a nation with economic growth. There is no question that material prosperity as measured by the rate of growth of the economy is important, but when one is considering the fate of a nation, equal weight should be given to the political situation. Liberty and equality may be as relevant as economic growth when one is appraising whether nations rise, decline or develop politically. However, whereas the concept of economic development is a rather clear one, the notion of political development is far more ambiguous.

In many development studies there was an implicit assumption about mono-causation, with socio-economic change determining political development. Although there was promising work oriented towards the concept of political modernization (see Myrion Weiner and Samuel P. Huntington's *Understanding Political Development*, 1987), in the end there was an uncomfortable feeling that severe methodological problems had been left unresolved. No doubt the concept of development was much more successful in the field of social studies and development economics.

The political development theme has attracted considerable attention. Yet, despite much research, political science lacks a concept of political development comparable to the notion of economic development as measured by rates of growth in overall output or income. The attempt to replace a multidimensional conception of political change with some specific notion of political development has not been successful, as the concept of political development is surrounded by ambiguity. In fact, it is an essentially contested notion. We will speak of political development as 'democratization' and enquire at great length into the links between democracy and socio-economic development.

Modernization theory, evolving around 1960 and receiving renewed attention today, contained a hypothesis about linear causality between socio-economic development on the one hand and political development on the other. Political systems would move from a primitive stage towards a developed stage, reflecting the seminal trend of social change offset by economic development away from an agricultural economy, as if there existed an objective criterion on what is politically developed and not developed. But how could one be sure that what was developed in one context, e.g. in the OECD nations, would also constitute development in another context, e.g. the Third World?

At times, political systems experience large-scale changes. The structural changes in Portugal, Spain and Greece by which authoritarian structures were dismantled constitute macro changes. The ongoing processes of change within the former communist world introducing democratic institutions and making room for markets and private initiative is another example of macropolitical or structural change in polities. The comparative study of political systems contains plenty of conceptual distinctions between various kinds of systems, as well as between various aspects of political systems. Perhaps the most prevalent is that between democracy and dictatorship. Although the concept of democracy may be delineated in various ways, the distinction appears to have a clear empirical foundation, as we may separate a set of democratic countries and a set of authoritarian countries without too much argument about borderline cases. This distinction may be buttressed by the employment of indicators which allow the specification of when a political system has undergone a regime change, from democracy to dictatorship or from authoritarianism to democracy.

A basic problem in modernization theory, raised by Seymour Martin Lipset in *Political Man* (1960) and by Dan Usher in *The Economic Prerequisite to Democracy* (1981), is whether there is any relationship between the democratic organization of the regime and the level of affluence in a country. The fundamental problem of the social and economic sources of democracy involves a number of questions. What is the surface correlation between levels of affluence and democratic regime properties? And how do we account theoretically for such a statistical association? According to the well known study by Irma Adelman and Cynthia T. Morris, *Society, Politics and Economic Development* (1967), there is a strong correlation between various indicators of material affluence and the typical expressions of a democratic regime. Is this still true today; and what about the Third World countries as well as the emerging new democracies?

What is the connection between affluence, economic growth and democracy? This is the *second* of our three fundamental questions concerning institutions and outcomes. If development consists of both economic and political development, then it must be vital to understand how they are interrelated. Why is democratic stability to be found in countries with an advanced capitalist economy? Is it the institutions of the market economy that are critical for democracy or is it affluence in general that promotes democratic stability? Studies on the connection between affluence and democracy start off from the Cutright finding in 1963 of an association between the two of about $r = 0.67$ (Diamond, 1992). One may also ask whether democracy promotes economic development (Pourgerami, 1991). Are there any links between democracy and social development?

Whereas it used to be clear which countries predominantly employed the state as the mechanism of allocation and which countries based the allocation of resources on markets, developments since the Second World War have resulted in mixtures of capitalism and socialism. Charles Lindblom in *Politics and Markets* (1977) called for new combinations of capitalism and socialism, arguing that market regimes are biased towards the interests of the owners of capital. But is market socialism really feasible? This has become a highly relevant question in the 1990s, as the Eastern European countries began searching for a new identity both politically and economically in the autumn of 1989 and the welfare states attempt economic reforms. Removing the planned economy, several Eastern European countries have opted for the market economy.

When examining development strategies, one needs to look at how countries vary not only in economic growth records but also in terms of quality of life indicators or income distribution measures. Does state involvement or intervention enhance a country's position on economic or social development indices? The economic policies recommended by the International Monetary Fund under the heading of structural adjustment programmes entail that the size of the state should be reduced in order to attain a vibrant civil society. Perhaps an open economy is more conducive to economic growth than is high public expenditure.

In relation to the peculiar type of mixed economy blending private ownership and markets with extensive budget-making, one may ask: what accounts for cross-country variation in the size and orientation of mixed economies? Harold Wilensky's *The Welfare State and Equality* opened up the debate in 1975 on whether politics really matters for the determination of national policies. Wilensky emphasized the level of economic affluence as the explanation of country variation in public policies, but should not other factors also be included (Tarschys, 1975; Castles, 1982)? In *Budgeting* (1986), Aaron Wildavsky examines the large number of factors that have been suggested as sources of expenditure variations in the public budget. What would an empirical test of these public sector growth hypotheses amount to? There is the seminal process of public sector growth in the set of democratic regimes which rely upon markets to a large extent. One may research the major factors behind this process – the public budget driving out the market mechanism. We may ask what accounts for the similarities and dissimilarities between the rich countries with regard to the structure of their public sectors.

Here, we face the *third* of our three key questions. *Is the welfare state the best politico-economic regime*? The main competitor of the welfare state regime is the welfare society regime. What is the performance record of welfare states looking at economic and social outcomes? This again brings us to the question of the performance of alternative politico-economic regimes. Does a large public sector promote socio-economic development?

To sum up: in the literature there are two basic distinctions, one in relation to political systems and another in relation to economic systems. The first refers to capitalism versus socialism, whereas the second involves democracy versus dictatorship. Crossing these two distinctions one arrives at the standard typology of politico-economic regimes in Figure I.2.

Figure I.2 Politico-economic regimes

	Democracy	Dictatorship
Capitalism	I	II
Socialism	III	IV

However, after the dismantling of the command economies and the massive move towards democracy in the early 1990s, this scheme is not particularly valid. We need new basic categories in order to describe and evaluate politico-economic regimes.

If 'socialism' stands for public ownership of the means of production, then there are few socialist economies today. And the trend is not towards more of socialism. The interesting two categories in Figure I.2 are I (capitalism and democracy) and II (capitalism and dictatorship). Elaborating on these two categories, one may distinguish between various types of capitalism and investigate their possible connections with democracy and dictatorship. One may thus identify three types of capitalist regimes: decentralized market regimes, state-capitalist systems and welfare state regimes. What is their overall performance record in terms of development criteria?

According to one theory, the decentralized market economies will outperform the other types of politico-economic regime (Friedman, 1962). Contradicting the so-called marketers is the opposite theory that more state involvement in the economy will improve developmental outcomes. What does the evidence today imply concerning these two alternative theories, taking into account economic, social and political development criteria?

Data, countries and indicators

In this book, we attempt an empirical analysis of politico-economic interaction in the rich world, the communist world as it existed up to 1990 and Third World countries, evaluating a few theories of how political institutions and public policy interact with socio-economic development in a reciprocal fashion. More specifically, we focus on some questions about development – economic as well as political – and the socio-economic determinants of polities, the pattern of public policies in various political systems and their explanation, as well as the impact of political institutions and public policy on economic growth.

An attempt will be made to classify countries in various parts of the world according to a set of politico-economic concepts. A number of indices will be employed in order to render a quantitative statement possible. The study comprises various sets of countries, in each case selected for the main problems dealt with in each chapter, and the OECD nations, several former communist countries and at least forty Third World countries are included. The social and economic correlates of polities will be sought in order to find out how political structure is conditioned by the social and economic structure on the macro level. The indicators employed and the data sources used are stated in each chapter. It hardly needs to be pointed out that there are great problems in finding reliable information about some of the countries. How these problems are to be resolved is an open question. Thus, the statistics on economic growth within communist countries are probably not strictly reliable. And often no data at all are available on Third World countries, particularly for the 1950s and 1960s. In whatever way these difficulties are met, the solutions to the problems of data validity and reliability are bound to have an impact on the substantive findings.

Two different data sets are employed in the empirical analyses. One set consists of data for the time period 1950 to 1989, when command economies were significant. The other set covers data for the 1990s, when the emphasis is upon the various types of capitalist politico-economic systems.

Contents of the book

The first five chapters describe how far development has come around the world, looking at the three aspects of development: economic, social and political development. In Chapter 1 the development perspective is introduced and the difficulties in the concept of development are presented. Chapter 2 enquires into economic development, focusing upon affluence and economic growth, whereas Chapter 3 looks at social development. The troublesome concept of political development is covered in Chapter 4. The development focus that we have chosen for our comparative analysis of a few key problems in political economy entails that we have to investigate the links between economic, social and political aspects of development. If economic development results in affluence and political development enhances democracy, then is there any link between affluence and democracy?

Chapter 5 examines the link between affluence and democracy that has been discussed by political scientists, sociologists and economists in an effort to explain why there is a positive – though not perfect – correlation between the two entities.

One may point out that affluence and democracy are distinct from an analytic point of view, the first referring to output and the second to rights. Surely, it is conceivable that output may be high in a country at the same time that human rights are not enforced. Evidently, the direction of causality between output and rights must in the short run be that the former comes first and the latter after, because the mere introduction of civil and political rights will not bring about affluence, as many countries have experienced since 1989. In the long run things may prove to be different. Can politics have an impact upon economic development?

Chapter 6 starts the discussion of development strategies. Chapters 7, 8 and 9 discuss the political aspects of economic development, first by means of a general analysis of the politics of economic growth and then by an examination of one case, South Africa.

In the remaining chapters development ideals are examined. Which is the best politico-economic regime? In the debate about public sector reform it is argued that there are two fundamental alternatives for countries with an advanced economy: the welfare state, with its mixed economy; or the welfare society, which is anchored in the decentralized market economy. Which performs best on a number of evaluation criteria of politico-economic regimes? This question is looked at through both a general analysis covering the OECD countries and a case study of Sweden.

The focus of this book on development reflects a value orientation that guides our selection of the topics or problems. Prosperity or decline of a country involves more than simply growth rates in the economy. Besides economic development there is social and political development. Many countries in the world are committed to development in the sense of promoting socio-economic objectives, but what are their actual accomplishments with regard to developmental objectives? And how do countries score on political development interpreted as the implementation of civil and political rights?

Does development imply that the Third World should simply become identical with the rich world? In which respects? The concept of development seems to contain a teleological bias, as if there were some goal towards which political change should evolve – the advanced capitalist democracies perhaps. What if change processes moved in a different direction – perhaps this would constitute retro- or underdevelopment? Would or should socio-economic or political development always result in modernization? We examine these philosophical problems concerning development in the next chapter.

Part I

Developmental Outcomes

1   The concept of development: Myrdal's analysis

Introduction

Development is a key word when one is comparing nations. Some countries are said to be highly developed, some rapidly developing, others underdeveloped. Even if these words are not used, similar distinctions are singled out by means of other more diplomatically phrased terms. In the official statistics we find the following categories: low-income economies, middle-income economies and high-income economies; industrial market economies and non-market economies (World Bank). Sometimes developed market economies are distinguished from developing countries and centrally planned economies (World Economic Survey).

At the same time, the notion of development is an essentially contested conception (Sen, 1988). It has been argued that the concept of development is a value-loaded notion, expressing Western preconceptions about basic values in social life. It presupposes or requires that the non-Western world adheres to a similar culture to that of the advanced economies, giving priority to economic growth and its derivatives. Moreover, it has also been claimed that there could be no general concept of development, as the country-specific patterns of evolution are simply too diverse (Meier, 1984).

Two main problems in the development concept

The concept of development is a multidimensional concept. It stands for a set of properties that refer to economic, political or social aspects of life. Theories about development may focus on various aspects of development (Bardhan, 1988; Lewis, 1988). *An Asian Drama* (1968), a treatise on development by Gunnar Myrdal, focuses on the social and economic aspects of the phenomenon:

> What is actually meant in characterizing a country as 'underdeveloped' is that there is in that country a constellation of numerous undesirable conditions for work and life: outputs, incomes and levels of living are low; many modes of production, attitudes, and behavioral patterns are disadvantageous; and there are unfavorable institutions, ranging from those

at the state level to those governing social and economic relations in the family and the neighborhood. (Myrdal, 1968: 1840)

One of the most debated problems in development theory is the extent to which social and economic indicators on the level of development of a country tend to covary. Thus it has been argued that a simple economic indicator on development like gross domestic product (GDP) per capita does not tap the social aspects of development (Adelman and Morris, 1972; Morris, 1979). The level of social development involves more than just an average income measure such as the extent of inequality in the distribution of income and wealth or the real-life access to basic necessities like food, physicians and shelter. We will look at the hypothesis that social and economic aspects of development are related, as, for instance, Myrdal (1968: 1840) argues that there exists a 'general causal relationship among all these conditions, so that they form a social system. It is the task of the study of underdevelopment and development to determine this relationship within the social system'. Myrdal emphasizes the orientation of development towards economy in particular and social well-being in general, but we may ask if there is not also a political aspect of development: political development. Thus, within the field of comparative politics in political science there has been a search for a counterpart to the notion of socio-economic development, namely political development. With the aid of such a concept one would understand the transition from a so-called primitive political system to what is called a 'modern' one, not only in terms of economic change but also as political change.

The first much debated issue in comparative research concerns the possibility of a causal relationship between socio-economic development and political development (Rustow, 1970; Huntington, 1984; Laband, 1984). Or perhaps political development conditions economic and social development (Goldsmith, 1987; Pourgerami, 1988).

The second much debated problem in development theory concerns the value-loaded character of the concept. Again, Myrdal (1968: 1840) raises this issue, when talking in the following manner about the constellation of development attributes: 'They are evaluated undesirable – or low or disadvantageous or unfavorable – from the standpoint of the desirability of "development" – a characterization afflicted with vagueness but definite enough to permit its use.' When the implicit values hidden in the development notion are made explicit, it is often claimed that there are alternative routes to development. Whereas there is at least some agreement about what socio-economic development amounts to, it is an ideological task to define the ends and means of political development.

The concept of development presents two difficulties. On the one hand, it seems feasible to make a distinction between development in general and political development in particular. On the other hand, there is every reason to suspect that the notion of development or political development is a so-called value-loaded concept (Myrdal, 1961). Both problems – how to separate a neutral concept of political change from a normative notion of political development, and how to distinguish between general social development and political development in particular – reflect the genesis of theories of change or development in the grand sociological theories of the coming of a Western society (Higgott, 1983).

The emergence of the occidental type of society and polity is described with pairs of polar concepts: community versus society (Tönnies), mechanical versus organic solidarity (Durkheim), rationality versus traditionalism (Weber), primary versus secondary social attachment (Cooley), status versus contract (Maine), folk versus urban culture (Redfield) and sacred versus secular social orders (Becker).

The first difficulty means that one faces a severe problem as to how to model the relationship between development in general and political development in particular. One may distinguish between economic, social and cultural development (Portes, 1976). Are we to believe that political development is some function of social development? Or is a modern polity an aspect of the phenomenon of social development? If one allows for the possibility that the relation between social development and political development is an empirical one – a so-called synthetical problem and not an analytical one – then we may approach either phenomenon as the dependent variable, recognizing that political development may not only reflect but also trigger social development. In any case, we need to sort out theories of political development from general theories of social and economic transformation. Here we focus primarily upon what theories of development amount to with regard to politics, government, the state or the political system, whichever concept one may prefer.

The second difficulty concerns the direction of change involved in the notion of national development or political development. Sometimes it is admitted that we may talk about both positive and negative development, but the overall impression is that political development is something inherently valuable, i.e. the opposite of political development is political decline or decay. If this is correct, then a theory of political change would have to be far more encompassing than a theory of political development. It has been argued that the value component in theories of development reflects a Western bias (Wiarda, 1983).

The word 'development' is both an ordinary term in everyday language and a technical term in several scientific theories. It may be interesting to map some of its usages in these two contexts before we outline an institutional approach to development, focusing upon the evaluation of politico-economic regimes by means of criteria taken from development studies.

Semantics of 'development'

In ordinary language there is a basic meaning of 'develop' as 'unfold' that lies behind the various connotations that we are interested in when talking about country development. Let us quote from some standard dictionaries. The Oxford English Dictionary (1961) contains the following entries, among others, on 'development'.

1. A gradual unfolding, a bringing into fuller view. 2. Evolution or bringing out from a latent or elementary condition. 3. The growth and unfolding of what is in the germ; evolution. 4. Gradual advancement through progressive stages, growth from within. 5. A developed or well-grown condition; a state in which anything is in vigorous life or action. 6. The developed result or product; a developed form of some earlier and more rudimentary organism, structure, or system.

Testifying to the complexity of the notion of development, Webster's Third New International Dictionary (1965) has a heavy set of entries on 'develop', some of which we quote to convey how difficult the concept is to handle. Thus we have:

De-vel-op also de-vel-ope. 1a: unfold, unfurl; b: to change the form of (a surface) by applying point by point to a specified surface; c: to lay out or evolve into a clear, full, and explicit presentation. 4: to open up: cause to become more completely unfolded so as to reveal hidden or unexpected qualities or potentialities. 5a: to make (something latent) active: cause to increase or improve: promote the growth of; b: to make actually available or usable; 6a: to cause to unfold gradually: conduct through a succession of states or changes each of which is preparatory for the next; b: to expand by a process of growth. 7: 1a: to go through a process of natural growth, differentiation, or evolution by successive changes from a less perfect to a more perfect or more highly organized state.

Evidently, development relates to a process in time of some kind. In scientific usage development is often qualified by 'economic', 'social' or 'political'. We may then expect more substantive definitions.

Scientific usage

Fred W. Riggs points out that the concept of development occurs in several disciplines. Thus one talks about individual, attitudinal, cultural, group, organizational, social, community, urban, global and model development. It must by no means to be taken for granted that 'development' in these contexts has the same meaning (Riggs, 1984: 132–3). Sometimes the word is employed in relation to improvements (land, capital), sometimes to activities (plans, projects), sometimes to agents (persons, organizations) or parameters (resources), sometimes to Third World countries (developing countries) or industrialized areas (developed areas) or sometimes in relation to studies (development studies) (Riggs, 1984: 131–2). Moreover, the word 'development' may denote a process or a state of affairs – a condition. It is important to keep this distinction in mind when one proceeds to the phenomenon of development in the context that interests us, i.e. the seminal trends of Third World countries. Riggs presents a picture of this distinction between process and condition, which is reproduced in Figure 1.1.

In social science contexts a number of treatises on development may be found. What are the major connotations of this word when used by economists, sociologists and political scientists? We now present some quotations from leading scholars in the fields of development studies and the analysis of development processes.

Economics

'Economic development' used to be synonymous with 'economic growth' or even 'economic progress' in general (Sen, 1988). It was measured by the rate of expansion in GDP per capita. The difficulty was not the meaning of the term, nor how it was to be measured in aggregate national statistics, but how to account for economic development, i.e. to identify the forces that were conducive to a rapid expansion of income per capita. There was sharp disagreement between alternative theories or approaches to economic development: neo-classical, Keynesian, institutionalist, dualist, dependence and neo-liberal schools (Thirlwall, 1983; Todaro, 1985; Bardhan, 1988).

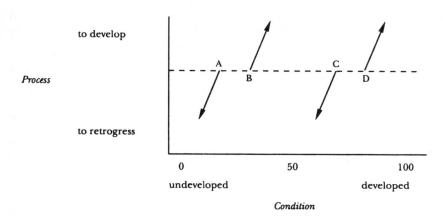

Figure 1.1 A model for the concept of development

Source: Riggs (1984: 134).

During recent years this solid foundation for the concept of economic development has been eroded, as the development notion has come to be more and more an essentially contested one *per se* (see Chenery and Srinivasan, 1988, 1989). It has been argued against a simple notion of economic development that 'economic development' refers to more than simply growth in national income per capita. One has to consider broad welfare indicators – the so-called *social indicator approach*. Moreover, the handy equation, economic development equals economic growth, by-passes the distributional problem of how national income is divided among social groups or in general how the resources are allocated to various collective or individual purposes. Finally, it is argued that the implicit value bias in economic development as economic growth should be brought out explicitly, as one cannot take for granted that economic growth is under all circumstances something positive. It may even be the case that what is labelled economic development is conducive to underdevelopment of a country within the confines of a world capitalist system (Streeten, 1972; Toye, 1987; Sen, 1988; Syrquin, 1988).

It is no doubt easy to find references to economic development where it is regarded as the key to human progress. Look at the following:

> Most would agree that development implies more than just a rise in real national income; that it must be a sustained, secular rise in real income accompanied by changes in social attitudes and customs which have in the past impeded economic advance. But at this point agreement on what constitutes development would probably end. (Thirlwall, 1983: 22)

> Development must, therefore, be conceived as a multidimensional process involving major changes in social structures, popular attitudes, and national institutions, as well as the acceleration of economic growth, the reduction of inequality, and the eradication of absolute poverty. (Todaro, 1985: 85)

What can be done here is to make some distinctions without any claim as to the true meaning of 'economic development'. It seems important to separate the following: (a) level or rate of growth in GDP total or per capita; (b) level or rate of change in a set of social indicators measuring individual well-being on average or quality of life; (c) the distribution of income or wealth and measures of skewness in relation to these.

We may then approach the problematic nature of economic development as two hypotheses as to whether higher levels of national income per capita also mean greater welfare or a more equal distribution of income. The traditional approach to economic development by-passes the simple fact that a larger GDP may be spent on purposes other than the reduction of poverty: defence, national symbols or conspicuous consumption. In Chapter 3 we will approach economic development in such an open-ended fashion. In *The Odyssey of Rationality* (1989), Albert Lauterbach summarizes the debate on the concept of development in the field of economics, stating:

> instead of the manifold and fluctuating meanings of 'development' in general, perhaps the following concept could be agreed upon for the basic aim concerned: 'Striving for the better in the condition of the general population groups concerned in line with their own felt needs and without sudden disruption of their established value systems and ways of life'. (Lauterbach, 1989: 221)

Such an approach to the development concept implies a broadening of the perspective from economic indicators to social indices. However, it seems to be a good strategy to associate the analysis of economic development with the test of established growth theory. As A. P. Thirlwall underlines in his *Growth and Development* (1983), it is possible to conceive of economic growth without economic development taking place at the same time, but it is hardly conceivable that there may be a process of economic development without a basis in sustained economic growth.

Sociology

Sociologists tend to take a broader view on development than economists, generally speaking. The term 'development' appears to denote a major process of social transition or transformation, from some earlier stage called 'primitive society' or 'traditional society' to some later stage referred to as 'modern society' or simply 'modernity'. What kinds of social change are involved here? Let us look at some quotations:

> Development takes two forms, industrialization, which is dynamic and innovative as a consequence of the allocation of new information to technology, and modernization, which is derivative. (Apter, 1971)

> The process of social change whereby less developed societies acquire characteristics common to more developed societies. (Lerner, 1968)

> Economic diversification within an advanced industrial technology; heightened social mobility and the movement toward impersonal and rationalized social relationships; a concentration of the population in cities and in more comprehensive social units generally; and the mobilization of persons en masse through popular education, organization, and communication. (Scalapino, 1964)

Advanced, non-traditional practices in culture, technology and economic life are introduced and accepted on a considerable scale. (Deutsch, 1961)

The model of a kind of broad social transformation often called 'modernization', which recurs in the quotations above, may be illuminating when one speaks generally about problems in Third World countries, but it may be highly misleading if one looks in particular at a specific country and its social transformation.

Countries differ in terms of social change. We must therefore be aware of the possibility that some countries may display some, but not all, of the properties typical of modernization, while other countries display other properties. In fact, the idea of a model of social transformation implies a number of empirical hypotheses about the relationships between various aspects of social systems. Perhaps the notion of modernity replacing tradition (Eisenstadt, 1973) was less deficient because of its Western value biases than weak in terms of actual empirical research conducted on the ways in which social change takes place in Third World countries.

The concept of social development should be broadened to include all aspects pertaining to the quality of life, and not simply industrialization and urbanization. One may also wish to take equality into account; for example, when one examines how the fruits from a sustained process of economic growth are distributed among the broad layers of the population.

Political Science

Basically, there are two different approaches to development among political scientists. First, there is the derivative approach, focusing on the political consequences of socio-economic transformation on the political system. Second, there is the non-derivative approach, trying to identify a path of political change that would be more or less self-sufficient.

The derivative approach focuses on political development as an aspect or effect of socio-economic development. It is thus committed to the belief that such a general phenomenon exists and that political factors are truly determined by socio-economic ones. Let us offer quotations of this theory of political development as the adaptation to profound social and economic change – the coming of modernity.

The expansion of roles, increased functional specificity, and the concomitant construction and/or reconstruction of social, economic, and political institutions to reflect, cope with, and channel this expansion. (Benjamin, 1972)

The elaboration of new and more complex forms of politics and government as societies restructure themselves so as to absorb progressively the stock and flow of modern technology which is, essentially, uniform. (Rostow, 1971)

a time sense that makes men more interested in the present and future than in the past; a better sense of punctuality; a greater concern for planning, organization and efficiency; a tendency to see the world as calculable; a faith in science and technology; and, finally, a belief in distributive justice. (Weiner, 1965)

Although it must be important to look at the political implications or consequences of social or economic change, particularly so when it is a matter of the broad movement from the agrarian society to the industrial society, there is the basic problem that these political effects may be very different from one country to another. Is there really a general phenomenon of socio-economic development which causes the same kind of major political changes?

It is far from certain that we will be able to identify these consequences for the political system under one single concept: the notion of political development. It is obvious from the above quotations that the concept of political development tends to be a highly general one, with little specific content. Actually, this conception of political development as the adaptation to socio-economic transformation on a large scale is essentially a set of hypotheses that need elaboration and testing.

The non-derivative conception of political development claims that there is a single path of political change that implies development of the polity, but that it cannot be modelled as uniformly caused by socio-economic factors. How is the political change conceived? A few quotations suggest what constitutes a process of political development:

Any two political systems [may be compared with respect to] capabilities, performance of process functions, and performance of socialization and recruitment. (Almond and Powell, 1966)

No longer implies democracy as much as a stable system of authority promoting a favorable climate for investment, and infrastructure growth. (Apter, 1977)

The new requirements which are demanded of institutions if they are to maintain stability and cope responsibly with social conflict. (Binder, 1972)

The level of ... adaptability, complexity, autonomy, and coherence of [any political system's] organization and procedures. The rationalization of authority, the differentiation of structures, and the expansion of political participation. (Huntington, 1965)

Increasing governmental efficiency in utilizing the human and material resources of the nation for national goals. (Organski, 1965)

Four dimensions: stability, legitimacy, participation, and capacity; within a certain unspecified range, development along any one of these dimensions can vary independently of the other three. (Sigelman, 1971)

A process whose goal is a political system which can provide for the functional requirements of long-term persistence ... the capacity to direct the course and rate of social and economic change. (Von Vorys, 1973).

The common core of these definitions of 'political development' is that political system change is a process with a logic of its own, and not just the automatic impact of socio-economic transformation. What the more specific content of this type of political change that implies political development may be is very much up in the air considering the above quotations. A variety of phenomena are mentioned as the content of political development: structural differentiation, functional performance, institutionalization, adaptation, increased governmental capacity, stability and legitimacy, as well as democratization. The abstract nature of these definitions of 'political development' calls for a more concrete approach that searches for empirical variables that somehow measure these dimensions.

It may be the case that a certain kind of macropolitical change process is caused by social structure change, but that is an empirical question to be answered by investigating the various sources of such a political development. However, what unites these various definitions is much less than what divides them, as it is far from obvious that 'political development' stands for one and the same process in these quotations. The semantic ambiguity surrounding the concept of political development makes it imperative that we take a closer look at the various properties or dimensions identified with political development.

Summing up

The semantic inquiry above leads one to the conclusion that there is so much uncertainty and ambiguity surrounding the notion of development that one had better make a preliminary distinction between economic, social and political development. Although there are ties between these aspects of development, they should be handled as hypotheses about relationships that need corroboration from empirical research, using a variety of indicators on each aspect. Further distinctions are preferably made within each of these three separate aspects of development between different manifestations of development, as the empirical analysis of various manifestations of development proceeds.

All the time it is recognized that the word 'development' is highly ingrained with value notions, as it pictures a macro process of change to be something desirable. Amartya Sen (1988: 20) argues that 'What is or is not regarded as a case of "development" depends inescapably on the notion of what things are valuable to promote.' He separates between two types of value dependence: value heterogeneity and value endogenity. It is not only the case that economic change may be valued differently by various people; economic change may also bring about alterations in the values of those involved in economic development. How is such a value-ingrained concept to be handled in neutral and objective social science research?

By separating the factual component from the value-loaded element in the concept of development, we wish to make an empirical inquiry into the variety of phenomena denoted by the term 'development' without any commitment as to whether any such phenomenon is intrinsically good or just. But how are we going to approach the many aspects of development, which is a truly multifaceted phenomenon? A complete study of development would require a handbook with many volumes. Here, we can only choose one angle, and that is for us to examine whether there are institutional effects in economic, social and political development.

An institutional approach to development

There is much debate about politico-economic regimes in the 1990s. The former command economies are searching for institutional alternatives to the Leninist-Stalinist framework. The welfare states attempt large-scale public sector reform, where some countries have moved from the welfare state camp towards the welfare society scheme. And many Third World countries seek to reform their politico-economic institutions, enhancing market operations as well as democracy. A politico-economic regime is a set of institutions mixing the public and the private sectors.

Let us start from the latter and talk about the concept of a capitalist economic system. After 1989 few countries have any other economic system than capitalism, as the number of countries with a genuine planned economy is marginal. One may discuss how some of the former command economies are to be classified, but perhaps North Korea and Cuba are the only true examples of a communist economy left today. What is a capitalist economic system and are there different types of capitalist economies?

There is a whole literature on what the characteristic features of the capitalist economy are. Several scholars have battled with the question of defining a 'capitalist' economy, from Werner Sombart's large-scale study of the evolution of the capitalist economy in the late medieval period in *Der moderne Kapitalismus* (1924–7) to Oliver Williamson's examination of what 'capitalism' stands for in the late twentieth century (1985). Let us quote from Joseph Schumpeter's article 'Capitalism' from 1946:

> A society is called capitalist if it entrusts its economic process to the guidance of the private businessman. This may be said to imply, first, private ownership of nonpersonal means of production, such as land, mines, industrial plant and equipment; and second, production for private account, i.e. production by private incentive for private profit. But, third, the institution of bank credit is so essential to the functioning of the capitalist system that, though not strictly implied in the definition, it should be added to the other two criteria. (Schumpeter, 1989: 189)

Such a general definition of 'capitalism' allows for a couple of specific alternative ways of institutional identification, especially when one takes into account how the public sector is to be combined with the institutions of capitalism. No capitalist economy can exist without state institutions. The critical question is how much the state should intervene in the economy, as there is bound to be at least a minimum state involvement in order to guarantee that the presuppositions of the market economy are fulfilled.

A system of capitalist institutions focuses upon private property rights and the existence of markets for both the real and the financial economies. Thus, a capitalist economy is different from a socialist one, as the means of production are not owned by the state and the allocation of goods and services is not handled through a plan. These minimum characteristics may be combined with a variety of state institutions, which creates the possibility of different politico-economic regimes.

Any economic system needs a state framework. The state may relate to a capitalist economy in three ways. First, there is the decentralized market economy, where state intervention is low, especially in relation to redistribution. Second, we have the state-capitalist regimes, where state intervention tends to be high, mainly by state ownership of key industries or by state regulation of markets. Third, there is the welfare state, where state intervention is again high, but in the form of public provision of certain goods and services in combination with extensive redistribution, rather than through ownership.

It is a central concern for political economy to understand how these three politico-economic regimes result in various development outcomes. Thus, we will evaluate how decentralized capitalism, state-capitalism and the welfare state perform on three kinds of development criteria: economic development, social development and political development.

Each of these economic systems has its own problem when evaluated by means of development criteria. Decentralized capitalist systems are not all democracies; state-capitalist systems tend to be dictatorships and welfare states display nice social development outcomes but tend to be mediocre in terms of economic growth. What guidance can one get from evaluating the evidence about existing politico-economic regimes?

These observations call for a theory about politico-economic regimes which could answer strategy questions about the developmental outcomes of various combinations of capitalism and the state. Chapter 6 outlines such a theory, but before we make predictions about the workings of alternative mixes of the state and a capitalist economy, we will discuss the concept of development and measure its various actual modes.

Conclusion

The concept of development has many aspects. Myrdal underlined two, one dealing with the nature of real-life development and the other referring to the study of development in research. First, he emphasized that development is a process involving circular causation between economic, social and political aspects of development. Second, he pointed out that development is a value-loaded concept, which entails a danger of a bias in the research approaches to all its variety of aspects.

In this chapter we have separated the economic, social and political aspects and formulated the perspective from which we will analyse development, namely the search for links between politico-economic regimes and development. There are, of course, many other relevant perspectives, because development is an enormous field of research. Our bias is that we wish to see development not simply as affluence and economic growth but also as quality of life and democracy.

Development is a major goal for most if not all Third World nations. It is believed to be the key to solving social problems and a necessary condition for not having to face even greater difficulties. Various methods have been tried in order to promote development, from central planning and coordination to the introduction of market capitalism. Usually development is interpreted as an economic target, although one must remember that development is more than gross national product growth.

A fundamental issue in political economy is the problem of priority as regards economic factors and politics with regard to causality. Precedence is often given to economic variables which, according to several well known hypotheses, are claimed to explain political phenomena. At the same time, economic determinism in whatever shape it may come has been challenged by the opposite hypotheses, which attribute economic phenomena to political factors. We will evaluate these contrary claims in the chapters to come.

2 Economic development: the gap model

Introduction

In this chapter we wish to present an overview of the differences in economic output between major countries in the world by taking up one well-known development theory (Lal, 1983; Jones and Kenen, 1984; Chenery and Srinivasan, 1988). The so-called gap theory figures prominently in the interpretation of development data (Thirlwall, 1983). The hypothesis states that the income differences between a set of rich countries and a set of poor countries are tremendous and tend to increase over time. The hypothesis is pessimistic about development as it predicts that the differences in affluence between countries will increase. We will question whether the gap theory is confirmed when a large number of countries, rich as well as poor, are included in the analysis of development data.

It is often stated that the income gap between rich and poor countries is increasing and that there is a North–South divide hidden behind these sets of countries (Brandt Report, 1980). This trend, if true, is certainly a cause of concern, since it would counteract important ambitions behind the development ideology as interpreted by the United Nations (UN). The quest for development has no doubt dominated much of the politics in several Third World countries and it has inspired the UN to initiate its programmes for developmental decades and call for a new international economic order.

We will look into how valid these statements are to the effect that the so-called developing countries are not only not catching up but also lagging behind even more than before. The set of developing countries is not a homogeneous one, which implies that we need to look at the variation in levels and rates of development not only between rich and poor countries but also within different sets of so-called less developed countries or LDCs (Syrquin, 1988). There may also exist a variation within the set of rich countries that needs to be pinpointed, as this set covers not only the rich market economies but also some communist systems or former communist countries. The use of the concept of newly industrializing countries – the NICs – seems to imply that the identification of rich and poor countries may change over time. In order to pinpoint the issue it is necessary to consider how the concept of economic development is to be measured.

Indicators and data

GDP measures the total final output of goods and services produced in an economy by residents and non-residents, regardless of the allocation to domestic and foreign claims. It is calculated without making deductions for depreciation. Let us start from this rather simple but helpful indicator, turning to more complex measures of well-being later on. GDP per capita may be employed to measure the level of economic affluence. It is an open question whether other indicators on social welfare covary considerably with the GDP per capita indicator. The GDP per capita indicator displays problems concerning both validity and reliability. In terms of indicator validity, GDP per capita measures are sensitive to the size of the money economy, the price level and the currency exchange rate. With regard to reliability, the national income accounts of various countries have been estimated using different procedures, which affects the comparability of the information (Kuznets, 1965, 1966, 1968; Streeten, 1972; Little, 1982).

The raw data about GDP rendered by various countries have to be examined and recalculated in order to remove a number of errors and make the data series comparable between nations. If a GDP per capita index is constructed from such a cautious procedure, then it may be used to arrive at a crude but informative picture of economic differences between various countries.

First we have employed one standardized series – real GDP per capita in international prices relative to the US dollar – compiled by Summers and Heston (1994). The data series give annually, in addition to population and exchange rates, real product and price level estimates for four different national income concepts estimated for some 130 countries from 1950 to 1992. From the Summers and Heston data set, where several of the problems of indicator validity and reliability have been taken into account, a sample selection has been made, dividing the countries into subsets corresponding to the OECD countries, Latin American countries, African countries, Asian countries and communist countries (post-communist). The classification has been chosen in an attempt to evaluate the gap theory, looking at both the between- and the within-set differences and how they have developed during the post-war period. Average growth rates may also be calculated with regard to these countries or sets of countries for various time periods.

Here the set of rich countries would consist of the set of OECD nations with the exception of Mexico. The set of socialist systems would consist of the Eastern European countries and not cover Third World communist countries like China. Mainland China may be properly classified in the set of Asian countries as it has been an LDC and never entered the Comecon bloc.

The second data set covers the most recent years and employs data from the World Bank, covering some 140 countries, focusing upon a slightly different income concept, namely purchasing power parity (PPP). It would strengthen the argument put forward below if the overall tendency was the same in two data series measuring affluence in different ways.

The gap theory

First, the gap theory implies that there was a sharp gulf in economic affluence between a set of rich countries and another set of poor countries at the end of the

Second World War. Second, the gap theory suggests that this gap has increased during the entire post-war period, not only during the 1950s and the 1960s but also during the 1970s and the 1980s. Third, the gap theory claims that this unbridgeable gulf coincides roughly with a major geographical separation between the northern and southern parts of the world. Fourth, the gap theory predicts that the income differences within the sets of rich countries and the sets of poor countries are less than the differences between these sets.

The Summers and Heston data series allow us to evaluate these implications of the gap theory by taking a close look at the variation in levels of overall economic well-being between and within sets of countries from 1950 to 1992. An analysis of the growth differentials in real GDP per capita complements the study of levels of average GDP per capita. The differences between the five sets of countries are as important as the variation in real GDP per capita income within these sets of countries. The coefficient of variation (CV) may be employed to indicate the within-group differences, where a CV score of more than roughly 0.20 may be said to indicate substantial variation.

Affluence levels 1950 and 1990

Allowing for all the objections to the use of a GDP per capita indicator on the average economic affluence in a country, we may establish that this measure really indicates profound between- and within-country set differences. Let us start with the year 1950 and look at national averages between the different sets of countries as well as the variation within these sets themselves (Table 2.1).

Table 2.1 GDP per capita in 1950 (international US dollars)

	Mean	Max.	Min.	CV
OECD (n = 24)	4243	8772	1065	0.50
Latin America (n = 19)	1923	4799	949	0.58
Asia (n = 6)	686	1058	228	0.41
Africa (n = 9)	994	3295	221	1.00
Mean (n = 58)	2611	8772	221	0.80

Source: Summers and Heston (1994).

The average income per capita in the set of OECD countries amounted to $4243, which was double that of the average income in Latin America. No figure is available for the average income in the communist systems, but one estimate is at a lower level than that of Latin America given the devastating effects of the Second World War. The average economic affluence would, according to these data, be higher in Africa than Asia, which partly reflects the small number of countries covered around 1950. However, we must note the substantial variation within the OECD set. In the United States, which fought in the war mainly outside its borders, the average income (8772) was about six times higher than in Japan (1430).

Around 1950 the level of affluence in the OECD countries was clearly higher than in the Third World. This is true in relation to the average income scores for

African countries (994) and Asian countries (686). But the set of Latin American countries that also did not have to fight a war within their borders constitute an exception, as the average for the OECD countries is only double that of Latin America, whereas it is four times that of Africa and five times that of Asia.

Not only is the Latin American mean real GDP per capita of $1923 substantially higher than that in most other Third World countries, but the maximum score in Venezuela (4799) surpasses the country scores for several OECD countries. Had one looked only at the data for 1950, it would be far from obvious that the gap interpretation could be proposed at all. Considering the GDP per capita income in Argentina (4032) and Uruguay (3451), it remains a fact that Latin America does not fit the simple classification: rich versus poor or North versus South.

Thus, in 1950 the average income of the OECD countries was about five times higher than that of African and Asian countries but only roughly twice as high as that of Latin American countries. In order to indicate somewhat more extensively the country differences at the beginning of a long period of overall economic growth and of staggering expansion in world trade, we will look at the variation within these three sets of countries. Let us consider Table 2.2.

The gap theory is based on a hypothesis about a North–South divide in the separation between rich and poor countries. Yet we see from Table 2.2 that geographical situation does not coincide with the division into rich and poor countries. Australia (6678) and New Zealand (6667) were among the most well-off countries in 1950, second only to the United States (8772) and Switzerland (6813). In addition, there was a rather sharp North–South division within rich Western Europe, as Italy, Greece and Spain scored lower than Venezuela, Uruguay and Trinidad. In fact, both Turkey and Portugal were closer to the average values for the Third World than for the OECD set.

As we turn to country data for the developing nations a lot of variation is to be expected, since we know that the countries in the Third World have walked along different paths of economic development since 1850 (Reynolds, 1985). Table 2.2 indicates that the country variation within the three subsets of developing nations was larger than within the two subsets of rich countries.

Although not very many countries in Asia, Africa and Latin America can be compared at this time owing to problems with reliable data, what is most striking is not the general poverty in the Third World but the substantial variation. There was in the 1950s a clear and wide gulf between Latin America and the other parts of the Third World, which hardly fits in with the gap theory. Clearly, it must be misleading to designate Mexico (2198), India (590) and Ethiopia (221) as underdeveloped countries, as if they were of one kind or on a similar level.

The country differences between the set of African and Asian countries were not pronounced in 1950. Myanmar (228), Pakistan (602) and the Philippines (778) had a low GDP per capita, as had Nigeria (456), Kenya (590) and Egypt (751). There were extremely poor countries in Africa: Zaire (332) and Uganda (543). Mauritius (3295) and Sri Lanka (1058) did better. Had information about more countries been available, this gloomy picture of Africa may well have been more pronounced. In order to find out whether these country differences are stable or change as the gap theory predicts, we compare the 1950 data with similar information for 1960 (Table 2.3).

The overall developments of the 1950s corroborate the gap theory in so far as the distance between the OECD countries and two of the three sets of Third World countries increased. The gap model is only true with regard to how average per

Table 2.2 GDP per capita in 1950 (international US dollars)

OECD		Latin America		Africa		Asia	
Australia	6678	Argentina	4032	Egypt	751	India	590
Austria	2930	Bolivia	1274	Ethiopia	221	Myanmar	228
Belgium	4433	Brazil	1265	Kenya	590	Pakistan	602
Canada	6380	Chile	2431	Mauritius	3295	Philippines	778
Denmark	5263	Colombia	1503	Morocco	821	Sri Lanka	1058
Finland	3506	Costa Rica	1457	Nigeria	456	Thailand	857
France	4045	Dominican		South Africa	1941		
Germany	3421	Republic	949	Uganda	543		
Greece	1409	Ecuador	1194	Zaire	332		
Iceland	3808	El Salvador	1206				
Ireland	2730	Guatemala	1532				
Italy	2743	Honduras	981				
Japan	1430	Mexico	2198				
Luxembourg	6534	Nicaragua	1152				
Netherlands	4532	Panama	1309				
New Zealand	6667	Paraguay	1253				
Norway	4358	Peru	1504				
Portugal	1208	Trinidad	3046				
Spain	1913	Uruguay	3451				
Sweden	5807	Venezuela	4799				
Switzerland	6813						
Turkey	1065						
United							
Kingdom	5395						
United States	8772						

Source: Summers and Heston (1994).

Table 2.3 GDP per capita in 1960 (international US dollars)

	Mean	Max.	Min.	CV
OECD ($n = 24$)	5663	9895	1622	0.41
Communist ($n = 4$)	1588	2397	431	0.53
Latin America ($n = 21$)	2318	6338	924	0.66
Asia ($n = 22$)	1501	3884	316	0.69
Africa ($n = 40$)	901	2862	257	0.60
Mean ($n = 111$)	2343	9895	257	0.97

Source: Summers and Heston (1994).

Table 2.4 GDP per capita in 1960 (international US dollars)

OECD		Latin America		Africa		Asia	
Australia	7782	Argentina	4462	Algeria	1723	Bangladesh	952
Austria	5143	Bolivia	1148	Angola	931	China	567
Belgium	5495	Brazil	1784	Benin	1100	Hong Kong	2247
Canada	7258	Chile	2885	Botswana	535	India	766
Denmark	6760	Colombia	1684	Burkina Faso	456	Indonesia	638
Finland	5291	Costa Rica	2096	Burundi	640	Iran	2946
France	5823	Dominican		Cameroon	641	Iraq	3427
Germany	6570	Republic	1195	Central		Israel	3477
Greece	2093	Ecuador	1461	African Republic	704	Jordan	1162
Iceland	4964	El Salvador	1427	Chad	756	Korea, South	904
Ireland	3311	Guatemala	1660	Congo	1123	Malaysia	1420
Italy	4564	Haiti	924	Côte d'Ivoire	1120	Myanmar	316
Japan	2954	Honduras	1039	Egypt	809	Nepal	628
Luxembourg	7921	Jamaica	1773	Ethiopia	257	Pakistan	638
Netherlands	6077	Mexico	2836	Gabon	1789	Papua	
New Zealand	7960	Nicaragua	1606	Ghana	894	New Guinea	1235
Norway	5610	Panama	1575	Guinea	559	Philippines	1133
Portugal	1869	Paraguay	1177	Kenya	659	Saudi	
Spain	3123	Peru	2019	Lesotho	313	Arabia	3884
Sweden	7592	Trinidad	5627	Liberia	717	Singapore	1658
Switzerland	9409	Uruguay	3968	Madagascar	1191	Sri Lanka	1259
Turkey	1622	Venezuela	6338	Malawi	380	Syria	1575
United Kingdom	6823			Mali	535	Taiwan	1256
United States	9895			Mauritania	780	Thailand	943
				Mauritius	2862		
				Morocco	815		
		Communist		Mozambique	1153		
				Namibia	1790		
		Czechoslovakia	1603	Niger	532		
		Romania	431	Nigeria	567		
		USSR	2397	Rwanda	537		
		Yugoslavia	1921	Senegal	1047		
				Somalia	1103		
				South Africa	2191		
				Tanzania	319		
				Togo	367		
				Tunisia	1101		
				Uganda	598		
				Zaire	489		
				Zambia	965		
				Zimbabwe	989		

Source: Summers and Heston (1994).

capita income developed in the OECD on the one hand and in Latin America and Africa on the other hand. As the world economy entered a long period of staggering growth in output and trade, the mean average income in African countries did not increase between 1950 and 1960, whereas that of the set of Latin American countries increased slowly. The beginnings of the enormous economic expansion in Asia is already evident in the 1960 figures.

The differences between the 1950 and 1960 data may partly reflect the simple fact that we cover more countries in 1960. Thus, when the communist countries are included, we see that the difference between them and the OECD amounts to a factor of roughly 3. Although we find in the data for 1960 signs that indicate the gap theory, not all the facts confirm the gap theory. Let us take a closer look at the variation within our subsets (Table 2.4).

During the 1950s all the so-called rich countries benefited from high levels of economic activity. The increase in GDP per capita in Japan was a high 100 per cent in this decade, but other rich countries also expanded their national income rapidly: the Federal Republic of Germany, Spain, Portugal and Italy.

Several countries in Asia hardly increased their average income per capita at all during the 1950s, mainly as a result of sharp increases in population. Some Asian countries faced a severe poverty problem around 1960, although it is somewhat arbitrary to identify a poverty line: China (567), Indonesia (638) and Pakistan (638) are all nations with very high populations. However, in the set of Asian countries there were also some examples of an average GDP per capita higher than the minimum value in the OECD set: Iran (2946), Iraq (3427), Saudi Arabia (3884) and Hong Kong (2247).

By 1960 Africa was already different from Asia and Latin America, as dismal poverty was much more prevalent. The set of African countries really constituted a special Third World set of countries where the average income always tended to be much below that of the mean income in the other two sets of Third World countries. The standard predicament in Africa was one of extreme poverty: Malawi (380), Rwanda (537), Mali (535), Zaire (489) and Niger (532). In the northern countries and in the Portuguese colonies there was a more decent level of income: Algeria (1723), Tunisia (1101), Angola (931) and Mozambique (1153). Gabon (1789), South Africa (2191) and Madagascar (1191) scored much higher than Tanzania (319) and Togo (367).

Table 2.5 GDP per capita in 1970 (international US dollars)

	Mean	Max.	Min.	CV
OECD ($n = 24$)	8208	12963	2202	0.33
Communist ($n = 7$)	3120	4825	809	0.41
Latin America ($n = 21$)	2952	7753	834	0.62
Asia ($n = 24$)	2479	7838	418	0.84
Africa ($n = 42$)	1104	3704	296	0.68
Mean ($n = 118$)	3277	12963	296	0.96

Source: Summers and Heston (1994).

Table 2.6 GDP per capita in 1970 (international US dollars)

OECD		Latin America		Africa		Asia	
Australia	10756	Argentina	5637	Algeria	1826	Bangladesh	1280
Austria	7510	Bolivia	1661	Angola	1165	China	696
Belgium	8331	Brazil	2434	Benin	1118	Hong Kong	4502
Canada	10124	Chile	3605	Botswana	823	India	802
Denmark	9670	Colombia	2140	Burkina Faso	374	Indonesia	715
Finland	8108	Costa Rica	2904	Burundi	341	Iran	4796
France	9200	Dominican		Cameroon	804	Iraq	4409
Germany	9425	Republic	1536	Central		Israel	6004
Greece	4224	Ecuador	1789	African Republic	747	Jordan	1422
Iceland	6772	El Salvador	1810	Chad	660	Korea, South	1680
Ireland	5015	Guatemala	2028	Congo	1670	Malaysia	2154
Italy	7568	Haiti	834	Côte d'Ivoire	1615	Myanmar	418
Japan	7307	Honduras	1237	Egypt	1163	Nepal	670
Luxembourg	9782	Jamaica	2645	Ethiopia	296	Oman	6633
Netherlands	9199	Mexico	3987	Gabon	3704	Pakistan	1029
New Zealand	9392	Nicaragua	2359	Ghana	1059	Papua New	
Norway	8034	Panama	2584	Guinea	467	Guinea	1896
Portugal	3306	Paraguay	1394	Kenya	586	Philippines	1403
Spain	5861	Peru	2736	Lesotho	419	Saudi Arabia	7838
Sweden	10766	Trinidad	6795	Liberia	982	Singapore	3017
Switzerland	12942	Uruguay	4121	Madagascar	1146	Sri Lanka	1243
Turkey	2202	Venezuela	7753	Malawi	440	Syria	2294
United				Mali	419	Taiwan	2188
Kingdom	8537			Mauritania	872	Thailand	1526
United States	12963			Mauritius	2398	Yemen	879
				Morocco	1342		
				Mozambique	1497		
				Namibia	2642		
				Niger	805		
				Nigeria	767		
				Rwanda	647		
		Communist		Senegal	1146		
				Sierra Leone	1435		
		Czechoslovakia	2520	Somalia	921		
		GDR	4825	South Africa	3254		
		Hungary	3358	Sudan	817		
		Poland	2941	Tanzania	424		
		Romania	809	Togo	618		
		USSR	4088	Tunisia	1442		
		Yugoslavia	3297	Uganda	647		
				Zaire	686		
				Zambia	1117		
				Zimbabwe	1082		

Source: Summers and Heston (1994).

In relation to the 1950 and 1960 data the gap theory fails to recognize the significant difference between Africa and Latin America. Some countries in Latin America did fairly well around 1960, even when compared not only with communist systems but also with some OECD nations. High average income scores were found in Venezuela (6338) and in Uruguay (3968), as well as in Argentina (4462), Chile (2885) and Mexico (2836) – above the minimum value for the OECD set.

The 1960s was again a decade with strong expansion in the world economy, and several countries achieved high yearly growth rates in their economies. Yearly growth rates of about 3 to 4 per cent were not uncommon and some countries accomplished even more. What was the impact of a decade of high levels of economic activity on the global income distribution between countries? Does the gap theory prediction of larger differentials between the rich countries and the Third World hold true? We can see this in Table 2.5.

The gap theory prediction of a widening gap between the rich and the poor countries only partly fits the data from around 1970. The decade of strong economic growth around the world benefited some countries more than others. The income gap between Latin America and Africa on the one hand, and the OECD nations and the communist systems except China on the other hand, increased considerably. The already dismal development in Africa continued, especially with sub-Saharan Africa doing much worse than northern Africa. The economic advances in Asia are clearly apparent in the data (Table 2.6).

However, the gap theory is not validated owing to the developments in a few Asian countries; the so-called baby tigers of Singapore (3017), South Korea (1680) and Taiwan (2188). These countries entered what Rostow referred to as the take-off stage in the 1950s, which resulted in growth rates that bridged the gap to the affluent world (Rostow, 1960). Perhaps Japan should be included among these aggressive new industrializing countries, as the average income per capita in Japan grew from US$2954 in 1960 to a staggering $7307 in 1970. A number of communist countries had incomes far above the minimum value of the OECD set: USSR (4088), the German Democratic Republic (4825) and Hungary (3358).

How does the mixed picture of 1970 compare with data for 1980, which indicate how the gap theory fared when the world economy went into a sustained period of recession? Table 2.7 contains the information about mean average country values for the five sets of countries around 1980.

Table 2.7 GDP per capita in 1980 (international US dollars)

	Mean	Max.	Min.	CV
OECD (n = 24)	10499	15295	2874	0.28
Communist (n = 8)	4727	7638	1422	0.39
Latin America (n = 21)	3737	11262	1033	0.64
Asia (n = 24)	5435	31969	505	1.29
Africa (n = 42)	1306	4797	322	0.77
Mean (n = 121)	4668	31969	322	1.06

Source: Summers and Heston (1994).

Table 2.8 GDP per capita in 1980 (international US dollars)

OECD		Latin America		Africa		Asia	
Australia	12520	Argentina	6506	Algeria	2758	Bangladesh	1085
Austria	10509	Bolivia	1989	Angola	675	China	972
Belgium	11109	Brazil	4303	Benin	1114	Hong Kong	8719
Canada	14133	Chile	3892	Botswana	1940	India	882
Denmark	11342	Colombia	2946	Burkina Faso	457	Indonesia	1281
Finland	10851	Costa Rica	3717	Burundi	480	Iran	3434
France	11756	Dominican		Cameroon	1194	Iraq	7242
Germany	11920	Republic	2343	Central		Israel	7895
Greece	5901	Ecuador	3238	African Republic	706	Jordan	3384
Iceland	11566	El Salvador	2014	Chad	528	Korea, South	3093
Ireland	6823	Guatemala	2574	Congo	1931	Kuwait	20018
Italy	10323	Haiti	1033	Côte d'Ivoire	1790	Malaysia	3799
Japan	10072	Honduras	1519	Egypt	1645	Myanmar	505
Luxembourg	11893	Jamaica	2362	Ethiopia	322	Nepal	892
Netherlands	11284	Mexico	6054	Gabon	4797	Oman	6521
New Zealand	10362	Nicaragua	1853	Ghana	976	Pakistan	1110
Norway	12141	Panama	3392	Guinea	817	Papua	
Portugal	4982	Paraguay	2534	Kenya	911	New Guinea	1779
Spain	7390	Peru	2875	Lesotho	994	Philippines	1879
Sweden	12456	Trinidad	11262	Liberia	927	Saudi	
Switzerland	14301	Uruguay	5091	Madagascar	984	Arabia	13750
Turkey	2874	Venezuela	7401	Malawi	554	Singapore	7053
United				Mali	532	Sri Lanka	1635
Kingdom	10167			Mauritania	885	Syria	4467
United States	15295			Mauritius	3988	Taiwan	4459
				Morocco	1941	Thailand	2178
				Mozambique	923	United Arab	
				Namibia	2904	Emirates	31969
				Niger	717	Yemen	1313
				Nigeria	1438		
				Rwanda	757		

Communist

Bulgaria	3926	Senegal	1134
Czechoslovakia	3731	Sierra Leone	1139
GDR	7638	Somalia	744
Hungary	4992	South Africa	3496
Poland	4419	Sudan	866
Romania	1422	Tanzania	480
USSR	6119	Togo	731
Yugoslavia	5565	Tunisia	2527
		Uganda	534
		Zaire	476
		Zambia	971
		Zimbabwe	1206

Source: Summers and Heston (1994).

Table 2.9 GDP per capita in 1990 (international US dollars)

	Mean	Max.	Min.	CV
OECD (n = 24)	12877	18054	3741	0.26
Post-communist (n = 5)	4805	6203	3820	0.20
Latin America (n = 20)	3354	7764	1294	0.52
Asia (n = 20)	4268	14849	1264	0.91
Africa (n = 34)	1403	5838	399	0.86
Mean (n = 103)	5177	18054	399	0.99

Source: Summers and Heston (1994).

Table 2.10 GDP per capita in 1992 (international US dollars)

	Mean	Max.	Min.	CV
OECD (n = 22)	13325	17954	3807	0.22
Post-communist (n = 3)	4559	5208	3826	0.15
Latin America (n = 16)	3384	7082	1385	0.50
Asia (n = 14)	4690	16471	1282	1.03
Africa (n = 29)	1474	6167	408	0.88
Mean (n = 84)	5589	17954	408	0.98

Source: Summers and Heston (1994).

The recession in the world economy in connection with the oil crises did not break the pattern that emerges when data about levels of average income per capita since 1950 are compared. The increase in the mean value for the OECD, the communist systems and the Asian countries continued during the 1970s, whereas the average scores for Latin America and Africa changed little.

The trends of the early 1980s implied a break with the seminal tendencies from 1950 to 1980. Several countries suffered real setbacks in their average GDP per capita, in particular Latin American and African, but also the communist systems. And the variation within all the five sets of countries increased, suggesting that the setback in the world economy hit countries differently. Table 2.8 shows the country data for 1980.

The development pace among the Asian countries was far higher than that of the Latin American countries and that of African countries. The gulf between the rich world and the world of LDCs increased with regard to Africa and Latin America but not in relation to Asia. More recent data are presented in Table 2.9, which allow us to take into account developments during the 1980s which proved very turbulent for many countries.

One can see that the 1980s was a lost decade for both the communist countries and many Third World countries, especially in Latin America and Africa. The basic implication of a widening gulf between the rich sets of countries or the North and the sets of Third World countries or the South holds only with regard to the comparison between the OECD countries on the one hand and countries in Africa and Latin America on the other. Until 1980 the planned economies were not outdistanced by the OECD countries. When later data became available, the decline of the command economies became apparent. Poland going from $4419 per capita in 1980 to $3826 in 1992 was not a single phenomenon among the Eastern European economies during the 1980s: the setbacks were showing up in a striking manner by 1990. It is not, however, generally true in relation to all parts of the Third World. Looking at the data for 1992 we can make a more definitive evaluation of the gap theory (Table 2.10).

By comparing the 1992 average scores with the 1960 average scores it may be established that the distance between the rich countries and the poor countries has not generally increased. On the contrary, the difference between the OECD countries and the Asian countries has decreased. Let us examine the most recent individual country information more closely (Table 2.11).

Among the OECD countries there is a sort of north–south division, as the northern parts had a higher level of economic affluence than the southern parts, with the exception of United Kingdom and Ireland. Japan (15 105) had by 1992 passed Australia (14 458) and New Zealand (11 363) despite the fact that in 1950 the gap was quite wide, as Australia and New Zealand had a per capita income four times higher than that of Japan (1430). Had Japan been classified as a Third World country, then there would have been one major exception to the gap theory.

Economic development among many African countries has been negative since 1970. The average income among the African countries included in this analysis almost stood still between 1980 and 1992. The variation is immense on the African continent, from Mauritius (6167) to Central African Republic (514) and Burkina Faso (514), the northern and southern parts doing better than the central parts. The trend was the same among the Latin American countries, where average income per capita hardly changed between 1980 and 1992. However, the shift to a lower level of economic activity in the world economy in the 1980s hit some parts of the Third World more harshly than others.

What invalidates the gap theory is the continued strong increase in real GDP per capita in several Asian countries. Even when the world economy went into slump, the average income per capita among the set of Asian countries grew, from $2479 in 1970 to $4690 in 1992. Whereas in 1950 the average income per capita was six times larger in the set of OECD countries than among the set of Asian countries, the same gap had narrowed to a 3 : 1 ratio in 1990. The sharp advance in this part of the Third World was not, however, evenly distributed within that set.

In the set of Asian countries we note the so-called NICs and NECs: Singapore (12 653), Thailand (3942), Malaysia (5746) and Hong Kong (16 471). How precarious it is to generalize about a development pattern in the Third World appears evident from a comparison between these aggressive growth nations and the more populous countries. Thirty years of development in India (1282), Pakistan (1432) and the Philippines (1689) has enabled these countries to increase their living standards only marginally in excess of the income implication of their strong population growth. The gap theory fails to take into account the tremendous income differences within the Asian part of the Third World.

The same objection to the gap theory may be made with regard to the set of Latin American countries and the set of African countries. It is true that there was little progress between 1960 and 1992 in countries like Zaire, Zambia and Nigeria, as well as in Argentina, Venezuela and Uruguay. But on the other hand there are

Table 2.11 GDP per capita (international US dollars) 1992

OECD		Latin America		Africa		Asia	
Australia	14458	Bolivia	1721	Algeria	2719	Bangladesh	1510
Austria	12955	Brazil	3882	Burkina Faso	514	China	1493
Belgium	13484	Chile	4890	Burundi	569	Hong Kong	16471
Canada	16362	Columbia	3380	Cameroon	1029	India	1282
Denmark	14091	Costa Rica	3569	Central		Indonesia	2102
Finland	12000	Dominican		African Republic	514	Iran	3685
France	13918	Republic	2250	Chad	408	Israel	9843
Germany	14709	Ecuador	2830	Congo	2240	Malaysia	5746
Iceland	12618	El Salvador	1876	Côte d'Ivoire	1104	Pakistan	1432
Ireland	9637	Guatemala	2247	Egypt	1869	Papua	
Italy	12721	Honduras	1385	Gabon	3622	New Guinea	1606
Japan	15105	Mexico	6253	Ghana	956	Philippines	1689
Luxembourg	16798	Panama	3332	Guinea	740	Singapore	12653
Netherlands	13281	Paraguay	2178	Kenya	914	Sri Lanka	2215
New Zealand	11363	Peru	2092	Lesotho	952	Thailand	3942
Norway	15518	Uruguay	5185	Madagascar	608		
Spain	9802	Venezuela	7082	Malawi	496		
Sweden	13986			Mauritania	837		
Switzerland	15887			Mauritius	6167		
Turkey	3807			Morocco	2173		
United				Mozambique	711		
Kingdom	12724			Namibia	2774		
United States	17945			Nigeria	978		
				Rwanda	762		
		Post-communist		Sierra Leone	734		
				South Africa	3068		
		Bulgaria	5208	Togo	530		
		Hungary	4645	Tunisia	3075		
		Poland	3826	Uganda	547		
				Zimbabwe	1162		

Source: Summers and Heston (1994).

Table 2.12 Average growth rates in GNP per capita

	1965–85			1985–94		
	Mean	Max.	Min.	Mean	Max.	Min.
OECD (n = 22)	2.6	4.7	1.4	1.6	5.2	−0.3 (n = 24)
Communist (n = 8)	5.0	5.8	4.1	−5.9	0.9	−18.6 (n = 21)
Latin America (n = 21)	1.3	4.3	−2.1	0.5	6.2	−6.4 (n = 21)
Asia (n = 14)	3.9	7.6	1.0	2.2	8.2	−6.3 (n = 24)
Africa (n = 32)	0.5	4.0	−2.6	−0.2	6.6	−6.6 (n = 41)

Sources: Economic growth 1965–85, World Development Report (1987); 1985–94, World Development Report (1987), World Bank (1996).

countries with exceptional economic progress in the same sets of countries: Tunisia and Botswana in Africa, and Brazil and Chile in Latin America. The country differences in development pace are most substantial in the Third World; as a matter of fact, they are so large that the general notion of a set of rich countries becoming richer than a set of poor countries is more confusing than clarifying, at least as long as it has the connotation of the North versus the South or the OECD versus the Third World generally.

Growth rates

An analysis of average growth rates in the economy may complement the focus above on country differences in levels of affluence. The pace of economic development may be measured by various indicators. We will employ the real GDP per capita measures or GNP per capita and calculate average growth rates for the sets of countries specified above for various time periods. It should be pointed out that using output per capita data for measuring economic growth means that we take the population change directly into account. A country may have a strong increase in total production, yet show little economic growth owing to strong population increase.

The gap theory implies a definitive country pattern with regard to average growth rates. The yearly growth rates of the economy of a country may hover owing to short-term factors. However, here we focus on seminal growth trends over long time periods. If it were true that the overall income differences between the sets of rich countries on the one hand and the sets of Third World countries on the other were increasing over time, then there would be higher average growth rates in the economies of the rich countries than in the economies of the Third World countries. Is this true? Let us look at Table 2.12, which shows gross national product (GNP) per capita data. GNP measures the total domestic and foreign output claimed by residents. It comprises GDP plus net factor income from abroad.

Economic growth from one year to another reflects a number of temporary factors which increase or decrease the pace of economic development. The average growth rates over longer periods of time, i.e. the speed of economic expansion when the yearly economic fluctuations have been taken into account, are of interest here. Countries differ considerably in terms of average growth rates, but is the variation in accordance with the prediction of the gap theory?

The mean average growth rates between 1965 and 1995 differ among the five sets of countries. It is true that the mean average growth rates in the sets of OECD countries are higher than that of the set of Latin American countries or that of the African countries – as the gap theory implies. However, the mean average growth rate among the Asian countries is larger than that of the OECD countries, which is exactly where the gap theory falters.

Developing countries are not of one kind, as if there were one single average growth rate for all Third World countries. On the contrary, there are considerable differences in economic growth over time within all five sets of countries. Let us look at the country variation within the Third World countries with regard to 1970 and 1995, including the post-communist countries (Table 2.13).

Table 2.13 Percentage increase in GDP and GNP per capita

	1970–85 (GDP)				1985–94 (GNP)			
Rapid increase		*Decrease*		*Rapid increase*		*Decrease*	
Singapore	15.2	Mozambique	−3.1	Thailand	8.2	Georgia	−18.6
South Korea	9.8	Angola	−2.9	South Korea	7.8	Armenia	−12.9
China	8.8	Venezuela	−2.9	China	6.9	Lithuania	−7.8
Taiwan	8.5	Chad	−2.8	Singapore	6.9	Cameroon	−6.6
Indonesia	7.8	Zaire	−2.6	Botswana	6.6	Estonia	−6.4
Malaysia	7.8	Ghana	−2.4	Chile	6.2	Nicaragua	−6.4
Tunisia	5.7	Liberia	−1.9	Indonesia	6.0	Jordan	−6.3
Brazil	5.3	Jamaica	−1.8	Malaysia	5.7	Romania	−6.2
Syria	5.2	Madagascar	−1.6	Mauritius	5.6	Albania	−6.0
Thailand	4.9	Argentina	−0.8	Hong Kong	5.3	Côte d'Ivoire	−5.2
Egypt	4.8	Bolivia	−0.8	Ireland	5.2	Ukraine	−5.1
Cyprus	4.7	Sudan	−1.3	Portugal	4.0	Russia	−4.4
Ecuador	4.4	Ethiopia	−0.6	Mozambique	3.5	Slovakia	−3.3
Paraguay	4.2	Nigeria	−0.5	Namibia	3.4	Mongolia	−3.3
Barbados	4.1	Peru	−0.5	Japan	3.2	Bulgaria	−3.2
Cameroon	3.5	Chile	−0.3	Uganda	3.0	Central	
Colombia	3.2	Uruguay	0.2	Uruguay	3.0	African	
Sri Lanka	3.2	Kenya	0.5	India	2.9	Republic	−2.8
Gabon	3.1			Costa Rica	2.9	Peru	−2.5
Jordan	3.0			Sri Lanka	2.8	Syria	−2.4
Morocco	2.5			Spain	2.7	Algeria	−2.4
Algeria	2.4			Israel	2.5	Trinidad	−2.3
						Gabon	−2.3
						Rwanda	−2.2

Sources: Summers and Heston (1988), World Bank (1996).

Table 2.14 Real GDP per capita 1900–1992

	1900	1913	1970	1980	1992
OECD	2867 (20)	3285 (22)	10126 (22)	12930 (22)	15835 (22)
Latin America	1311 (7)	1733 (7)	5300 (7)	6129 (7)	5949 (7)
Africa	486 (2)	869 (3)	1288 (10)	1449 (10)	1331 (10)
Asia	739 (10)	826 (10)	1368 (10)	2136 (10)	3881 (10)
Communist	1543 (3)	1642 (5)	4681 (7)	6070 (7)	4626 (7)
Mean	1892 (42)	2201 (47)	5700 (56)	7245 (56)	8474 (56)

Note: Numbers of countries are shown in parentheses.

Source: Maddison (1995).

The average mean country growth rate among the OECD countries was 2.6 per cent between 1970 and 1985. The finding is again that there are several Third World countries that have been successful in bridging the gulf between themselves and the rich countries. There are also several countries that have fallen behind even more, but that does not change the fact that the gap theory implication is not confirmed. Besides the gap theory we need a theory about the so-called NICs and NECs that develop in a manner different from the pattern of the gap theory. Economic development after 1989 is characterized by the advance of China and South East Asia.

Additional evidence: other series

In order to map the recent trend in economic development one may consult a few other series of data concerning real GDP per capita or purchasing power parities. Can we detect any evidence of the workings of the gap model mechanism in these different data series? Maddison (1995) presents a long series for a sample of countries. Table 2.14 shows the huge increase in affluence in Asian countries between 1970 and 1992.

Although the average income in the rich OECD countries increased considerably during the twenty years or so covered in Table 2.14, one also observes the sharp rise in affluence among Asian countries, amounting to almost a tripling. The data indicate a sharp decline in the former communist countries after the system transition, as well as a serious stagnation for Latin America and Africa.

Around 1900 to 1913, among the richest countries of the world we find the United Kingdom, Australia, New Zealand and Argentina, all of which had fallen back considerably by 1992, as had other rich Latin American countries. Rich countries do not necessarily maintain their edge and poor countries can close the gap.

The real GDP figures may be complemented by measuring affluence in another way: purchasing power parity. This takes into account the prices of various goods in order to establish how much an income can really buy. Table 2.15 shows these data for the early 1990s.

Table 2.15 Purchasing power parities (PPPs) 1990 to 1994

	PPP 90	PPP 94
OECD	15404 (24)	18629 (24)
Latin America	3495 (22)	4915 (22)
Africa	1580 (43)	2155 (32)
Asia	4684 (33)	7563 (20)
Post-communist	4762 (21)	3806 (18)
Mean	5378 (143)	7296 (115)

Note: Numbers of countries are shown in parentheses.

Sources: PPP 90, World Development Report (1993); PPP 94, World Bank (1996).

This evidence points to affluence growing more quickly outside the rich set of countries, with the exception of the former communist countries, where the data clearly indicate continued decline. The increase in average affluence in Asia is staggering, considering the short time period. But Latin America and even Africa seem to have picked up in the early 1990s.

Is the gap model true?

We can now make a final assessment of the gap model. Let us quote from Kuznets, who stated in 1966:

> It follows that the current international difference in per capita product, which is roughly between fifteen and twenty to one (based on the average for the developed countries and that for the populous Asian countries with per capita GDP in the early 1960s of below $100), results partly from differences in growth rates over the nineteenth and twentieth centuries, and partly from disparities in initial per capita product.

This was at the time a factually correct assessment of long-term developments, but he also partly made a prediction about the trends after the Second World War. He went on to claim: 'Furthermore, since most countries that have enjoyed modern economic growth had initially high per capita product, international differences have grown wider and have continued to do so even in the post-World War II years' (Kuznets, 1966: 304–5).

This is not generally true any longer. Since 1960 the traditionally sharp distinction between poor and rich countries has lost its discriminating power. The well known gap theory about development implies a pessimistic view of what future economic development may bring about. The gap theory argues that there was a wide gulf between a set of rich countries and a set of poor countries at the end of the Second World War, and that this gap has tended to increase during the post-war period.

It was believed that this separation between rich and poor countries coincided with the distinction between OECD countries and communist countries, with the exception of China on the one hand and the Third World countries on the other, or with a divide between the North and the South. Looking at the real GDP data, we cannot confirm the gap theory, as it is not true that this sharp gulf already existed in 1950 or that the gap between the OECD countries and all sets of Third World countries continues to grow over time. Figure 2.1 shows the relation between level of affluence in 1970 and the average rate of economic growth between 1965 and 1980 ($r = 0.19$, $n = 107$).

There is not the kind of relationship between level of economic affluence and average economic growth that the gap theory implies. There is an important set of Third World countries that have been able to close the gap with the OECD countries during the post-war period. Some countries have moved out of poverty. It is not the case that the level of affluence in a country determines the average rate of economic growth, which suggests that the gap can be closed. Let us look at a similar figure for a recent decade. Figure 2.2 contains a scatter plot of economic affluence around 1980 and economic growth between 1985 and 1994 ($r = 0.06$, $n = 111$). Again there is no connection between level of affluence and average growth rates, many poor countries growing quicker than rich ones.

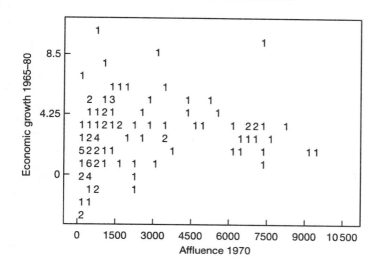

Figure 2.1 Affluence 1970 and economic growth 1965–80

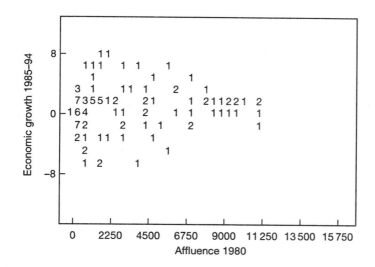

Figure 2.2 Affluence 1980 and economic growth 1985–94

Conclusion

It is a widely held belief that the distance between the rich OECD nations and the poor Third World countries is increasing: in spite of several decades of various kinds of efforts at development the gap has not been closed, nor is it narrowing. It is true that there were substantial country differences in income per capita around 1960, reflecting a distinction between a rich Occident and a poor South, but it is not true that the same country differences are simply maintained or even increase.

To emphasize the major finding: there is no relation between level of affluence and rate of change in affluence on a per capita basis. This means that the development alternative is a real one. Some countries have moved out of poverty during the post-war period. The developmental process displays such considerable variation among the countries of the world that the traditional separation between rich and poor countries in terms of the distinction between industrialized OECD nations and non-industrialized Third World countries is inadequate.

One may give a most concrete example of the tremendous increase in affluence in some Asian countries by looking at Hong Kong, although it is not a state. GDP per capita in this British crown colony started at $2247 in 1960 and stood at $16 471 in 1992, which latter figure ranks Hong Kong higher than Sweden, while Sweden in 1960 was four times more affluent than Hong Kong.

Now, development may mean several things. If the concept of development refers to economic change in particular and social welfare in general, then one would want to know if and to what extent the developmental process may bring about considerable social change as a result of economic growth. But how close is the connection between economic development and social development? The next chapter deals with this problem. We will look at social development by focusing on the concepts of quality of life and of equality in income distribution.

The development process among various sets of countries displays so much variation both between and within these sets – OECD, communist or post-communist countries, Latin America, Asia and Africa – that the traditional separation between rich and poor countries, the northern versus the southern hemisphere, or affluent countries and Third World countries, is more confusing than illuminating, especially if one takes into account the enormous economic growth in the Asian NICs and NECs as well as in China in the 1990s.

3 Social development: the Kuznets curve

Introduction

There is no single unanimously accepted definition of development in the literature (Todaro, 1985; Thirlwall, 1986; Sen, 1988). When some national income statistic is mentioned in relation to development it is clearly understood that it is only one among several possible indicators. Myrdal approached the concept of development as multidimensional, referring to production output and incomes, conditions of production, levels of living, attitudes towards life and work, institutions and policies (Myrdal, 1968: 1860). Although Myrdal treated these aspects of development as separate from each other, he also claimed that they covary, each reinforcing the others in a process of circular causation (Myrdal, 1968: 1859–66). No doubt income measures are given priority in the development literature, in particular GDP per capita (Gersovitz et al., 1982).

Economic or socio-economic development typically relates to a positive change – a real increase – in total output or in the well-being or material welfare of the citizens of a country. The value component of the concept of development is here quite explicit and straightforward: a developing nation is a country that is becoming better off and a developed country is one that is well off. But here the agreement between scholars also ends. What is contested is how to measure the extent of welfare of a nation as well as how to explain which factors are conducive to development as increased well-being. We will deal with the two counter-arguments one at a time.

Often a simple economic indicator such as level or rate of growth of GDP is considered a tool for analysing welfare in a society. There are basically two counter-arguments: on the one hand, it has been claimed that an indicator like GDP per capita does not adequately map individual welfare, which includes other things like health, employment, housing and so forth, meaning that we have to pay attention to broad social indicators; on the other hand, we have the argument that what matters is not the overall size or growth rate of GDP but its distribution among various social groups. Attempts have been made to construct more complex indices measuring more generally social welfare, such as the Physical Quality of Life Index and the Disparity Reduction Rate, which taps the change in physical quality of life over time (Morris, 1979; Pourgerami, 1989). A rising national income may be used for many purposes besides raising the level of affluence among the poor. Thus we have to look at the extent of inequality in the distribution of income.

It is not necessary, however, to commit oneself to any of these positions, as one may approach socio-economic development in an open fashion. To what extent do various measures – economic or social – covary in a data set covering some seventy-five nations in various parts of the world? What is the main relationship between affluence on the aggregate level and the distribution of income?

Quality of life

The problems of comparing countries in relation to the general notion of affluence or rate of change in affluence are well known (Kuznets, 1966). First, there are difficulties in obtaining access to data; for some countries this has been the case up to the past ten years. Generally, longitudinal data series are more problematic than cross-sectional data. Second, there are severe problems of interpretation and comparability (Meier, 1984; Thirlwall, 1986). How can we know that the indicators measure the same phenomenon? Problems of indicator validity and reliability are confounded by culture barriers: indicators that tap one dimension in one context cannot be transferred to another context with a similar interpretation. These data problems impose limits on what can be achieved in terms of country comparison, but they do not exclude an analysis of levels or rates of development.

It may be worthwhile to penetrate the extent to which the above picture about differences in affluence is generally true when alternative indicators of affluence are resorted to. Are we to conclude that the per capita differences in income as measured by GDP covary with similar country differences in standards of living? Material well-being or social welfare is a difficult notion to pin down in measurement indices. A number of social indicators are relevant for consideration in the measurement of welfare. We include the following indicators: infant mortality, number of doctors, energy consumption, life expectancy, literacy, school enrolments, telephone, radio, TV, real GDP per capita in 1980 and calories per capita.

Table 3.1 Factor analysis of welfare indicators around 1980 ($n = 75$)

Indicators	Factor 1	Factor 2
Life expectancy	0.884	0.357
Literacy	0.875	0.338
School enrolment ratio	0.860	0.308
Infant mortality	−0.850	−0.359
Number of physicians	0.775	0.450
Calories per capita	0.728	0.521
Real GDP per capita 1980	0.610	0.740
Television	0.542	0.817
Energy consumption	0.396	0.802
Telephones	0.387	0.817
Radio	0.208	0.841
Explained variance (per cent)	75.8	9.4

Source: Taylor and Jodice (1983).

The claim that underdevelopment is a general predicament that distinguishes between countries implies that these social indicators covary to a high extent. Moreover, development theory also implies that the per capita income indicator covaries strongly with each of the social indicators. Table 3.1 comprises a factor analysis, with findings that are relevant for these beliefs.

The findings of the factor analysis offer substantial evidence that there is a general predicament of underdevelopment because there is strong covariation between the indicators. Countries that have a low level of affluence as measured by the GDP per capita indicator tend consistently to score low on the most basic indicators of material well-being, but there seems to be also a more luxurious aspect to welfare that these basic indicators do not covary with. The fact that underdevelopment is a general social predicament does not imply, however, that there are two homogeneous sets of countries, developed and underdeveloped.

The Human Development Index (HDI), employed in the UNDP statistics, may be used to map the average country variations in quality of life. It is based upon a composite index with indicators similar to those of factor 1 in Table 3.1. The variation in the HDI is shown in Table 3.2 with regard to the 1990s.

Table 3.2 Quality of life: human development index

	1993	1995
OECD ($n = 24$)	0.942	0.918
Post-communist ($n = 21$)	0.802	0.782
Latin America ($n = 22$)	0.669	0.742
Africa ($n = 43$)	0.284	0.430
Asia ($n = 33$)	0.531	0.629
Mean ($n = 143$)	0.587	0.658

Source: UNDP (1993, 1995).

The connection between quality of life and affluence as measured by economic output is not linear, as quality of life first rises proportionately with affluence but then levels off. Thus, the country differences in quality of life are not that pronounced, except with regard to Africa, where the human condition is in many places dismal. Quality of life has gone down in the post-communist countries but is advancing steadily in Asia, generally speaking.

One major developmental trend affecting quality of life is the rapid urbanization process in Third World countries. In 1975, 66 per cent of the world population lived in the countryside, with the remaining 34 per cent in urban areas – 18 per cent in industrialized countries and 16 per cent in the developing countries. By the year 2000, it is predicted 52 per cent will live in rural areas and 48 per cent in urban areas, with 15 per cent in industrialized countries and 33 per cent in the developing world. However, around 2025 only 39 per cent will live in rural areas, as 48 per cent will live in urban areas in the developing world and 13 per cent in the industrialized world. The majority of the world's population will live in cities for the first time in history, and many in so-called megacities. There are now 12 of them: Mexico City, Los Angeles, New York, Buenos Aires, São Paulo, Bombay, Calcutta, Beijing, Shanghai, Seoul, Osaka and Tokyo – all having more than 10 million inhabitants. By 2000 there will be many more: Rio de Janeiro, Paris, Moscow, Manila, London, Lagos, Karachi, Johannesburg, Jakarta, Dhaka, Delhi, Cairo and Bangkok. The political implications of massive urbanization are not clearly understood, neither for democracy nor for political stability.

Income distribution

A fundamental objection to the use of the standard GDP or GDP per capita indicator of economic affluence is that it says nothing about the distribution of affluence in a country. This is a real limitation of this indicator as a growth in total output or overall national income over and above the population increase does not necessarily imply that poverty has been reduced for all social groups. Economic growth in poor countries implies that there are more resources to be distributed among various social strata, but which groups benefit is an open question.

The GDP per capita indicator needs to be complemented with an index that measures the extent of inequality of income distribution. The literature contains a few indices measuring the variation in income between households or regions: the Gini index or some kind of Lorenz curve or measures of the share of either the top 10 or 20 per cent or the bottom 10 per cent. It should be pointed out that there is a reliability problem when one is handling income distribution data for a large set of countries. In some countries the statistical information is not quite accurate and the definitions of income or economic affluence vary from one country to another, which reduces the comparability of such data. It is, of course, interesting to observe whether income differences increase or decrease as the world economy expands. Table 3.3 presents the situation around 1990.

Table 3.3 Income inequality around 1990

	Low[1]	Ratio[2]
OECD	18.5 ($n = 17$)	6.6 ($n = 17$)
Post-communist	24.4 ($n = 2$)	3.6 ($n = 2$)
Latin America	11.4 ($n = 12$)	17.9 ($n = 12$)
Asia	18.0 ($n = 13$)	7.2 ($n = 13$)
Africa	15.4 ($n = 11$)	9.8 ($n = 13$)
Mean	16.4 ($n = 55$)	9.7 ($n = 55$)

Note:
1 Low indicates the share of income of the lowest 40 per cent of households.
2 Ratio indicates the income of the highest 20 per cent of households in relation to that of the lowest 20 per cent of households.

Source: UNDP (1994).

Income inequalities are huge in Latin America, whereas they are not pronounced in the post-communist countries. Income equality seems to be higher in the rich OECD countries than in the developing world, which indicates the existence of a

Kuznets effect (see below). What about income inequality in the 1970s? Table 3.4 shows the data.

Table 3.4 Income inequality around 1970: percentage share of top 20 per cent

OECD (n = 20)	43.9
Communist (n = 4)	34.4
Latin America (n = 17)	58.3
Asia (n = 13)	47.6
Africa (n = 19)	53.8
Mean (n = 73)	50.0

Sources: Muller (1985), World Bank (1991a).

Although these data series are not strictly comparable, one may observe the same country pattern in the 1970 data as in the 1990 information. Communist countries score lower on income inequality than the other country sets, where Latin America in particular displays huge income differences. In Africa, South Africa has shown the most pronounced income differences, reflecting its racial tensions.

It may be interesting to look more closely at the country variation in income inequality. Table 3.5 lists the country scores on one such measure, ratio (see Table 3.3, note 2), for roughly 1990.

Table 3.5 Income inequality around 1990: country scores (ratio)

OECD countries		Non-OECD countries			
Australia	9.6	Bangladesh	4.1	Pakistan	4.7
Belgium	4.6	Botswana	4.7	Panama	29.9
Canada	7.1	Brazil	32.1	Peru	10.5
Denmark	7.1	Chile	17.0	Philippines	7.4
Finland	6.0	China	6.5	Poland	3.9
France	6.5	Colombia	13.3	Rwanda	4.0
Germany	5.7	Costa Rica	12.7	Singapore	9.6
Italy	6.0	Ghana	6.3	Sri Lanka	11.5
Japan	4.1	Honduras	23.5	Tanzania	26.1
Netherlands	5.6	Hungary	3.2	Thailand	8.3
New Zealand	8.8	India	4.7	Tunisia	7.8
Norway	5.9	Indonesia	4.9	Uganda	4.9
Spain	5.8	Israel	6.6	Venezuela	10.3
Sweden	4.6	Jamaica	8.1		
Switzerland	8.6	Kenya	22.6		
UK	6.8	Malaysia	11.7		
USA	8.9	Mexico	13.6		
		Morocco	7.0		
		Nepal	4.3		

Source: UNDP (1994).

The country differences are sometimes so huge that one must question the validity or reliability of the data. But the overall pattern is that Latin American countries are characterized by extreme income differences. Some African countries also display such huge differentials. Japan shows the greatest equality. Why? The basic model linking income distribution to affluence is the Kuznets curve.

The Kuznets curve

A higher average GDP per capita does not imply a higher standard of living for the entire population. The standard indicator on levels of economic affluence says nothing about the distribution of economic affluence. The Kuznets theory proposed in 1955 suggested that a rise in economic affluence had a somewhat contradictory impact on the pattern of distribution (Kuznets, 1955). At first the income differences would increase, but later these differentials would decrease. Thus, there would be something like an inverted U-shaped curve linking levels of affluence with some measure of the extent of inequality in the distribution of incomes. A similar hypothesis was suggested by Myrdal (1957) and Hirschman (1958).

There has been a lot of research on the Kuznets theory, but so far there has been no conclusive answer (McCormick, 1988). Some of the difficulties in testing theories about income distribution arise from the lack of reliable data for a large number of countries. Various indicators may be employed, but there are not enough cross-sectional or longitudinal data for more refined tests. Part of the confusion also stems from the interaction between the two entities. A low or high level of economic affluence may have one kind of impact on the income distribution, whereas the income distribution may have another kind of impact on levels of economic affluence. Moreover, other factors, like public policy, may change the impact of the two variables on each other. It is also an open question whether the Kuznets theory should be tested by means of cross-sectional or longitudinal data (Bigsten, 1987).

The data set employed allows us to examine the Kuznets curve at different points of time, as the relationship between income distribution and levels of economic affluence need not be stable. Even if Kuznets was correct in linking a reduction in income differences with growing affluence, the magnitude of the impact of affluence upon income equality may differ at various points of time, reflecting, for instance, how the division of the national income between labour and capital changes.

Looking at the relationship between average real GDP per capita in a country around 1980 and the degree of inequality in its income distribution between households, we have a negative relationship between level of affluence and income inequality ($r = -0.66$), although a non-linear test would be more appropriate (Ahluwalia, 1976a; Weede, 1980). Whether the finding that income inequality is reduced as the income per capita of a country increases is in accordance with an inverted U-curve may be discussed, but the Kuznets effect is there.

Even if it is true that income inequality may vary considerably between Third World countries like Brazil and Pakistan, it is still the case that income inequality decreases the larger the average GDP per capita in a country. It is true that income inequality rises somewhat as we move from very poor countries to countries with a higher level of affluence, but in general, the richer a country the larger the probability that its income distribution is more equal. The Kuznets curve suggested in the 1950s may be traced in the data from the 1970s (Figure 3.1).

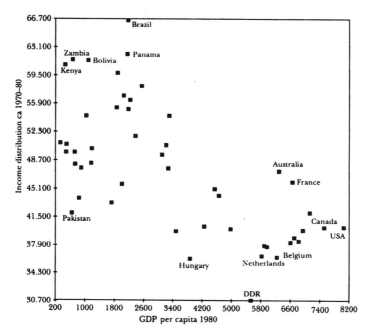

Figure 3.1 GDP per capita 1980 and income distribution 1970–80

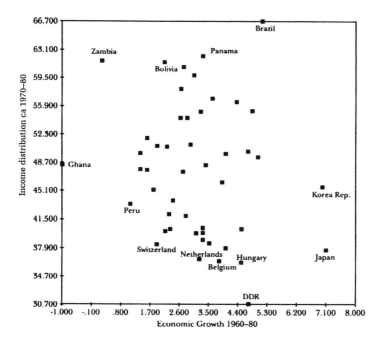

Figure 3.2 Economic growth 1960–80 and income distribution 1970–80

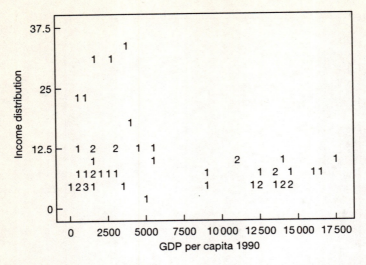

Figure 3.3 Interaction between income distribution and real GDP per capita 1990

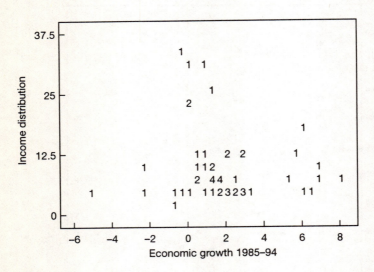

Figure 3.4 Income distribution and economic growth 1985–94

The cross-sectional test of the Kuznets hypothesis may be complemented by a longitudinal test. It is often argued that the extent of income inequality in countries like India or Brazil has increased over time (de Carvalho and Wood, 1980; Mathur, 1983). Since there has also been some economic development during the same time period, it may be argued that the Kuznets curve fits longitudinal data about an association between economic growth and income inequality. Figure 3.2 relates the degree of income inequality to average rates of economic growth between 1960 and 1980.

The hypothesis of a Kuznets curve is not strictly validated. The amount of income inequality varies independently of the rate of growth in the economy. It is not possible to predict the variation in income inequality knowing the average country growth rates in the economy between 1960 and 1980. There are cases of all conceivable extremes: a low growth rate and much inequality (Zambia) or more equality (Peru) versus a high rate of growth and much inequality (Brazil) or more equality (Japan). But it is now possible to trace out something like a Kuznets curve around an inverted U-shaped curve linking income inequality with level of affluence.

Let us look at more recent data. Figures 3.3 and 3.4 may be consulted, the first showing the interaction between income distribution and real GDP per capita 1990 and the other, income distribution and economic growth from 1985 to 1994.

It appears from Figures 3.3 and 3.4 that the Kuznets effect is considerably weaker in the 1990s than earlier. The correlation (r) between ratio and real GDP per capita equals -0.29 and between ratio and economic growth 1984 to 1995 amounts to -0.13. Could it reflect the triumph of a market ideology since 1989?

A cautious interpretation of more recent data suggests that there is a probability that at first the extent of income inequality increases as the level of affluence rises, but the overall relationship between income inequality and level of affluence remains negative. There is cause for more optimism with regard to the impact of economic development upon economic equality, despite everything. Whether a rise in economic output will bring about a higher standard of living depends on how the overall developmental process evolves.

The developmental process

Developmental theory designates some countries as developed and others as underdeveloped, or the former as highly developed and the latter as less developed. The advanced industrial nations have passed through the process of social change, taking them out of agrarian poverty, into industrial affluence and further on to the post-industrial condition. Such a pattern of social change is considered the main objective for the poor countries according to the theory and practice of the modernization theme. The basic policy problem is to identify the strategy of modernization: planning- or market-induced change? The historical experiences of the market economies and the lessons from the Soviet Union and China suggest two ideal types which may be combined in practice in various ways. The Japanese development is often referred to as state-led market capitalism, whereas China appears to be moving towards so-called market socialism or some new mixture of communism and capitalism.

Although there is considerable disagreement about the means and goals of development, it can be stated that the zest for modernization may meet with success. Developing countries are not of one kind. Some have developed very quickly, accomplishing vast social change, whereas other countries have hardly modernized at all. Even if it is true that generally the gap between rich and poor countries has not been reduced, it is also not the case that it is impossible for countries in the Third World to close that distance.

Development has a dynamic connotation. It singles out a set of countries that try to find the path from poverty to affluence. Developmental countries are those countries that are moving at varying rates of speed from a low level to a higher level of social welfare. Sometimes the ambition is high, as the rich countries are depicted as models of what the developmental process should result in. Sometimes the modernization zeal is more realistic, as the goal of the developmental process is only to move the countries out of poverty.

Table 3.6 Average growth rates in GNP per capita

	1960–80	1985–94
OECD	3.6 ($n = 22$)	1.6 ($n = 24$)
Post-communist	5.3 ($n = 8$)	−5.9 ($n = 21$)
Latin America	2.7 ($n = 15$)	0.5 ($n = 21$)
Asia	4.3 ($n = 12$)	2.2 ($n = 24$)
Africa	1.7 ($n = 15$)	−0.2 ($n = 41$)
Third World	2.8 ($n = 43$)	0.7 ($n = 75$)
Sample	3.3 ($n = 72$)	−0.2 ($n = 131$)

Sources: Economic growth 1960–80, World Bank (1982); 1985–94, World Bank (1996).

Let us consider an economic indicator, GNP growth per capita as measured by data collected by the World Bank (Table 3.6). Growth in the economy varies from one year to another and reflects a number of factors that are not related to development. What is of interest here is the average growth rate in different countries, i.e. the speed of the developmental process after accounting for economic fluctuations from one year to another. Countries differ substantially in so far as the long-term per capita growth rates between 1960 and 1994 are concerned.

Growth rates have in general been lower in Third World countries than in the rich countries. The exception is to be found among the Asian countries, where the mean growth rate exceeds that of the OECD countries. The growth in the economies in Africa has been particularly weak, whereas the average growth rate in Central and Latin America is not that low. The mean growth rate of the communist systems for 1960–80 is quite high at 5 per cent, which seems an exaggeration. When data for 1985–94 are included the picture is not that bright for these countries. The severe pollution problems in Eastern Europe are not captured by this measure, which reveals that it is not a perfect indicator of well-being. GNP fell by 6 per cent yearly between 1985 and 1994.

There are two possible explanations of the pattern in GNP growth per capita: output or population. Either the rate of increase in production in the Third World has been weak or the rate of population growth has been very strong. Let us look at some data that may shed light on this question. Table 3.7 presents information about the growth in aggregate GDP for the 1960s, 1970s and 1980s.

Table 3.7 Average growth rates in GDP

	1960–70	1970–80	1980–93
OECD	5.3 (n = 22)	3.3 (n = 22)	2.6 (n = 22)
Post-communist	7.2 (n = 2)	6.5 (n = 7)	−0.6 (n = 20)
Latin America	5.2 (n = 14)	5.2 (n = 15)	1.7 (n = 20)
Asia	6.5 (n = 12)	6.8 (n = 15)	4.6 (n = 23)
Africa	4.2 (n = 15)	3.8 (n = 15)	2.6 (n = 37)
Third World	5.2 (n = 41)	5.2 (n = 42)	2.9 (n = 70)
Mean	5.3 (n = 65)	4.7 (n = 71)	2.3 (n = 122)

Sources: Economic growth 1960–80, World Bank (1982); 1980–93, World Bank (1995).

It is not primarily the dynamism in the economies of the Third World that is at fault. Actually, the average increase in output in Third World countries is as good as that of the rich countries. With regard to the Asian world it may even be stated that the rate of economic growth is higher. What accounts for the low increase in income per capita in LDCs is the rapid rise in the population (Bairoch, 1975). Table 3.8 reveals that the expansion of the population is almost as large as the increase in output, indicating that the overall change in level of affluence per capita will not be enough to bridge the gap between the rich countries and the poor, except in a few rapidly developing countries.

Table 3.8 Average population growth rates

	1960–70	1970–80	1980–94
OECD	0.99 (n = 22)	0.77 (n = 22)	0.7 (n = 24)
Post-communist	0.87 (n = 9)	0.72 (n = 9)	0.8 (n = 27)
Latin America	2.53 (n = 15)	2.34 (n = 15)	2.4 (n = 22)
Asia	2.65 (n = 13)	2.45 (n = 13)	3.0 (n = 34)
Africa	2.65 (n = 15)	2.81 (n = 15)	3.3 (n = 43)
Third World	2.60 (n = 43)	2.57 (n = 43)	3.0 (n = 82)
Mean	1.91 (n = 74)	1.81 (n = 74)	2.2 (n = 150)

Sources: Economic growth 1960–80, World Bank (1982); 1980–94, Encyclopaedia Britannica (1995).

Economic development, for example in Japan, South Korea, Singapore, Malaysia, China, Chile and Botswana, with high rates of economic growth, has meant a strong expansion in the level of affluence between 1960 and 1994. The figures for GDP per capita in some of these countries are comparable to those of some of the OECD countries. The level of affluence in Japan is higher than that of the Netherlands. Singapore is comparable with the UK, and South Korea and Malaysia with Turkey.

Trade patterns

A seminal hypothesis in development theory argues that foreign trade is characteristic of advanced or developing countries. The theory of international trade implies that the more a country engages in trade with other countries, the more likely it is that it will benefit from the consequences of an open economy in a way which improves the prospects for rapid socio-economic expansion at home. The basic Ricardian theory of comparative advantages claims high gains for all the interacting countries from productive specialization and trade (Yarbrough and Yarbrough, 1988). Although the debate on the potential benefits and costs of extensive international trade between countries has developed far beyond the simple Ricardian model (Lal, 1983; World Development Report, 1987), there is still the fundamental notion that trade or openness of the economy is typical of countries with a high level of affluence or with a high level of average economic growth (Bhagwati and Ruggie, 1984; Caves and Jones, 1985; Chacholiades, 1985; Choksi and Papageorghiou, 1986).

Is it true that extensive international trade always characterizes rich countries and that a heavy concentration on the home market is typical of poor countries? Let us test this idea in relation to an indicator of the scope of trade in an economy: the *impex index* or the sum of exports and imports in relation to GNP. Table 3.9 shows the variation for the country sets.

The increasing integration of the world economy has made all countries more or less open. The variation in openness is not that pronounced. Table 3.10 covers the cross-country variation in the degree of openness of the economy since 1960. There is a quite substantial variation in the extent to which the economy of a so-called rich country is an open one. The small affluent countries in Western Europe have considerably more open economies than the United States and Japan, where the domestic market is very large. A very high degree of openness is characteristic of the Dutch, Belgian and Irish economies. The so-called Third World countries differ even more in terms of openness of the economy (Table 3.11).

Again we find that small countries tend to have a more open economy than large countries, all other things equal (Katzenstein, 1985). The very high score of Singapore must be pointed out, as it exemplifies how export-led capitalism may lead a country on to a path of staggering economic growth. Not all countries have augmented the openness of their economies, although the overall trend is development towards increased openness in the economies of a dynamic world-wide international trade.

Is there a clear relationship between the openness of the economy and basic indicators on economic growth and average level of affluence? On the one hand, Bela Balassa argues strongly for the existence of a causal connection between foreign trade and economic growth – see *Comparative Advantage, Trade Policy and Economic Development* (1989). One may speak of a so-called trade theory of economic growth, which argues that the trade patterns of a country are of decisive importance for its dynamism (Nurkse, 1961; Little *et al.*, 1970; Kreuger, 1978). On

Table 3.9 Openness of the economy

	1980	1990
OECD	66.6 (n = 24)	62.4 (n = 24)
Post-communist	58.9 (n = 8)	69.6 (n = 5)
Latin America	52.8 (n = 22)	55.1 (n = 20)
Asia	89.1 (n = 26)	90.2 (n = 20)
Africa	70.5 (n = 42)	64.0 (n = 34)
Mean	69.9 (n = 121)	67.3 (n = 103)

Source: Summers and Heston (1994).

Table 3.10 Openness of the economy: OECD and communist (post-communist) countries

	1960	1970	1980	1992		1960	1970	1980	1992
Australia	31.5	28.9	33.9	37.9	Algeria	56.0	51.2	64.7	51.2
Austria	48.4	61.2	75.6	77.9	Angola	37.6	51.4	81.2	–
Belgium	78.5	101.3	128.3	137.1	Benin	24.0	50.4	66.0	–
Canada	36.0	42.9	55.1	54.0	Bulgaria	–	–	66.4	97.1
Denmark	65.8	58.8	66.5	66.4	Burkina Faso	9.3	27.3	50.6	42.6
Finland	45.0	52.6	66.7	52.6	China	9.0	5.0	20.2	33.5
France	26.9	31.1	44.3	44.9	Czechoslovakia	27.6	30.6	67.7	–
Germany	35.2	40.4	53.3	60.0	Ethiopia	19.5	21.7	32.9	–
Greece	25.1	28.4	47.1	–	Hungary	–	62.6	80.3	67.4
Iceland	92.8	92.3	72.6	64.2	Mozambique	50.2	65.8	51.4	124.3
Ireland	68.9	81.9	112.6	117.2	Nicaragua	47.5	55.3	67.5	–
Italy	25.8	32.8	46.5	39.6	Poland	–	40.3	59.2	40.4
Japan	21.1	20.3	28.3	18.0	Romania	24.5	28.0	75.3	57.7
Luxembourg	160.1	164.6	177.6	181.3	Russia	5.2	5.7	15.2	–
Netherlands	90.3	87.4	100.9	100.1	Tanzania	64.4	54.2	39.5	–
New Zealand	47.9	48.3	61.8	60.4	Yugoslavia	32.6	42.0	41.6	–
Norway	87.0	84.9	88.5	79.1					
Portugal	40.9	56.2	72.6	–					
Spain	17.5	27.5	33.8	38.0					
Sweden	45.7	48.2	60.8	54.1					
Switzerland	58.9	67.3	77.0	68.5					
Turkey	9.9	14.6	20.6	44.4					
UK	43.5	45.3	52.3	48.9					
USA	9.4	11.4	21.1	21.9					

Source: Summers and Heston (1994).

Table 3.11 The impex indicator of economic openness: Third World countries

	1960	1970	1980	1992		1960	1970	1980	1992
Argentina	17.6	13.5	11.5	–	Malaysia	88.2	79.9	112.6	155.8
Bangladesh	25.7	20.8	24.1	26.7	Mali	24.1	32.5	51.1	–
Bolivia	50.5	48.9	37.7	40.5	Mauritania	60.0	74.0	104.6	90.9
Botswana	52.9	86.0	116.4	–	Mauritius	68.7	85.1	112.6	129.9
Brazil	11.8	14.5	20.4	16.6	Mexico	20.2	15.4	23.7	31.7
Burundi	22.6	22.3	32.1	39.3	Morocco	45.5	39.2	45.3	51.6
Cameroon	52.2	50.9	51.3	40.9	Myanmar	48.2	15.6	20.2	–
Central					Namibia	73.3	63.1	151.8	124.7
African					Nepal	16.5	12.8	30.3	–
Republic	59.3	70.9	68.8	33.6	Niger	21.9	28.9	61.7	–
Chad	33.1	54.4	48.4	56.4	Nigeria	21.7	19.6	48.0	73.7
Chile	31.1	28.6	49.8	59.9	Oman	–	93.4	100.3	–
Colombia	30.6	29.8	31.8	35.4	Pakistan	25.7	22.4	36.6	41.7
Congo	107.5	92.6	120.2	75.3	Panama	68.8	79.6	91.9	75.7
Costa Rica	48.1	63.2	63.3	83.5	Papua New				
Côte					Guinea	44.5	72.4	96.5	97.4
d'Ivoire	61.9	64.9	76.2	62.1	Paraguay	33.2	31.1	44.0	54.3
Dominican					Peru	40.2	33.9	41.6	22.4
Republic	40.6	41.8	48.1	64.6	Philippines	22.8	42.6	52.0	62.7
Ecuador	34.0	33.0	50.6	58.9	Rwanda	24.1	26.8	40.8	29.5
Egypt	39.7	32.9	73.4	65.1	Saudi Arabia	68.7	87.9	101.3	–
El Salvador	44.9	49.7	67.4	43.0	Senegal	66.4	59.4	72.3	–
Gabon	83.4	89.8	96.6	73.3	Sierra Leone	–	61.1	65.7	50.5
Ghana	52.3	44.0	17.6	42.9	Singapore	360.9	224.6	423.4	341.0
Guatemala	28.7	36.4	47.1	45.0	Somalia	28.3	28.3	121.7	–
Guinea	30.4	28.8	64.3	49.5	South Africa	57.1	47.6	64.7	43.8
Haiti	37.5	31.5	52.1	–	Sri Lanka	94.8	54.1	87.0	72.2
Honduras	45.0	62.0	80.3	65.5	Sudan	–	31.4	35.6	–
Hong Kong	190.0	180.9	180.7	285.8	Syria	52.4	38.6	53.7	–
India	12.7	8.2	16.7	21.4	Taiwan	30.2	60.7	106.4	–
Indonesia	24.8	28.0	53.3	55.8	Thailand	37.2	34.4	54.8	76.7
Iran	35.6	44.7	29.8	31.1	Togo	65.9	88.3	107.5	74.2
Iraq	69.7	53.9	94.7	–	Trinidad	114.3	84.4	89.4	–
Israel	38.5	69.3	90.4	64.4	Tunisia	53.0	48.5	85.9	80.9
Jamaica	74.2	70.7	105.3	–	Uganda	22.6	20.9	29.3	27.8
Jordan	57.5	43.0	115.7	–	United Arab				
Kenya	59.4	60.5	67.0	55.2	Emirates	–	–	112.4	–
Korea					Uruguay	33.9	26.7	35.7	42.8
South	15.9	37.9	75.5	–	Venezuela	45.9	37.8	50.6	54.0
Kuwait	–	–	112.6	–	Yemen	–	39.4	116.8	–
Lesotho	58.9	65.2	142.6	155.9	Zaire	22.7	33.7	32.8	–
Liberia	72.1	97.7	109.9	–	Zambia	93.1	90.5	86.8	–
Madagascar	30.5	40.7	43.1	41.8	Zimbabwe	82.9	59.4	63.6	74.8
Malawi	61.3	63.4	63.7	62.2					

Source: Summers and Heston (1994).

the other hand, there is the opposite argument that economic growth influences the trade pattern (Johnson, 1958, 1975; Södersten, 1965).

Table 3.12 presents simple correlation data about the relationship between socio-economic development and trade. A strict test of various alternative theories about the causal relationships and reciprocities between trade and growth would require a more sophisticated econometric analysis.

Table 3.12 Impex, affluence and economic growth: correlations

	Impex 1960	Impex 1970	Impex 1985	Impex 1990
Real GDP/capita 1960	0.07	0.12	0.16	–
Real GDP/capita 1970	0.08	0.16	0.18	–
Real GDP/capita 1985	0.20	0.23	0.18	–
Growth real GDP/capita 1965–85	0.13	0.07	0.11	–
Real GDP/capita 1990	–	–	–	0.22
Growth 1985–94	–	–	–	0.20
	$(n = 84)$	$(n = 92)$	$(n = 88)$	$(n = 103)$

Sources: Summers and Heston (1994), World Bank (1984, 1987).

If we look only at simple measures of association between indices that measure trade and affluence, we can note that there is hardly any indication of a relationship at all. However, if one resorts to a regression analysis where more factors are taken into account, the picture may look different. This is a task that is beyond the aims of this book. One may note finally that the openness of the economy reflects more the size of the country, large countries having more closed economies. Thus, we have the following correlation between the degree of openness of the economy and LNpopulation (natural logarithm of population) 1990 = -0.44 $(n = 103)$.

Conclusion

The human development index may be employed to probe the social consequences of economic development. It takes living conditions into account and not simply economic output. After all, the national income can be used for other purposes than raising the living standards. Figure 3.5 shows the relationship between affluence and the HDI for 1995, where $r = 0.72$.

One may establish that as it is absolutely essential to raise living standards from very low levels to moderate levels, one needs only rather modest increases in affluence. After a certain level, a higher level of affluence does not translate into a proportional increase in quality of life, as high levels of affluence may be expressed in conspicuous consumption.

Income equality is another vital objective when one moves from economic development to social development. There is evidence to the effect that higher levels of affluence are conducive to more income equality. But the so-called Kuznets effect is not as pronounced today as it used to be. Generally speaking, richer countries have more equal distribution of income, but several poor countries exist

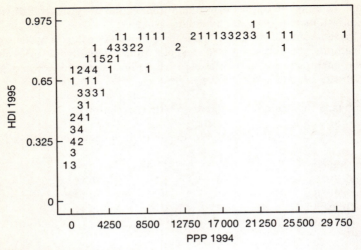

Figure 3.5 Affluence and HDI

where the income distribution is also rather equal, simply because almost all are poor. A few poor countries like those in Latin America, and South Africa, Kenya and Tanzania in Africa have extreme income differentials; Japan does not.

We have now examined economic development and its social correlates in two chapters. Before we turn to the more amorphous concept of political development, we underline once again that economic development is not deterministically bound by the past. Countries may move out of the poverty trap, as the first move to a higher level of affluence implies a substantial rise in quality of life. On the other hand, we do not observe the workings of the so-called Barro mechanism in the world economy. The Barro growth theory argues that country levels of affluence will equalize in the long run, poor countries catching up when trade takes place or labour and capital move between countries (Barro, 1991). The correlation between PPP in 1990 and economic growth from 1985 to 1994 is $r = 0.25$, which is in line with the argument launched here that affluence and economic growth are independent of each other, suggesting a bias in favour of a hope that poverty can be reduced.

4 Political development: institutionalization or democratization?

Introduction

The literature on macropolitical change has focused much on political development, in particular some desired process of transformation of the Third World polities. The basic problem, however, is whether there is an identifiable entity to be denoted by such a concept. A survey of various theories of political development provides a way to outline some conceptions of political change. As the theory of political development is in reality a set of theories of political and social change, an overview of the literature on political development provides a rich view of the interaction between economic and social development on the one hand and political development on the other.

In 1971, Samuel Huntington described the state of the concept of political development as one of confusion, or 'of dubious usefulness': 'To the extent that political development is thought of as an umbrella concept encompassing a multiplicity of different processes ... these often turn out to have little in common except the label which is attached to them.' Conceptual confusion may be a source of clarity, if one makes distinctions between various phenomena of political development and studies their interrelationships by means of empirical methods. Huntington went on:

> No one has yet been able to say of the various elements subsumed under the label of political development what Lerner, at a different level, was able to say about the broader processes subsumed under the label modernization: that they hang together because 'in some historical sense, they *had* to go together'. (Huntington, 1971: 304)

Is it really the case that the various phenomena denoted by 'political development' covary?

A basic problem in the study of political development is how it relates to general processes of social and economic development. Some look upon political development as a function of social change, whereas others examine the extent to which political change is conducive to economic development and social transformation. The literature on political development is amorphous in another sense, i.e. the wide variety of modes of presentation concerning the various phenomena of development (Leftwich, 1990).

Starting from these deliberations, we pose two problems that we will examine as far as possible given the present state of data. On the one hand, we wish to derive a set of indicators or ways of measuring the various dimensions in the concept of political development. On the other hand, we want to know whether the concept of political development is truly multidimensional: given the derivation of a set of indicators, what is the covariation between them?

Political development as democracy

If political development is some process of change that is also ethically appealing, then perhaps it is democratization? Some theories of political development explicitly state that the end of the change process is democracy, whereas other theories of change implicitly imply democratization.

The idea that political development would result in a democratic regime was first suggested in a succinct form by Seymour Martin Lipset in a famous 1959 article, 'Some social requisites of democracy: economic development and political legitimacy'. Criticizing the Lipset approach for its lack of measurement quality, Bollen suggested an index of democracy which could be used in quantitative analyses of political development. And Bollen was successful in confirming the Lipset hypothesis about a close association between the introduction of democracy and high levels of socio-economic development. The famous Cutright analysis of 1963 is a version of the same theme, as is the work by Russett (1964) and Dahl (1971). The study of Adelman and Morris (1967) points in the same direction, but how valid are these findings if one looks at more recent data? It is recognized that the problem of the conditions for democracy is a complex one (Rustow, 1970).

The theory about an almost direct link between economic growth and the strengthening of democratic regimes was severely questioned in Guillermo O'Donnell's *Modernization and Bureaucratic-authoritarianism: Studies in South American Politics* (1973). Contrary to the Lipset and Cutright hypothesis, O'Donnell showed that high levels of modernization in Latin America coincide with various types of authoritarian rule. In fact, it has stimulated a whole new inquiry into the relationships between capitalism and right-wing authoritarianism, searching for a theory explaining these unrecognized data (Collier, 1978).

The democracy approach looks upon the political system as the dependent variable, whereas socio-economic development is considered as the independent variable. However, it is possible to reverse the relationship and consider in particular economic development as the dependent variable. A number of attempts have also been made to look for determinants of economic growth among political variables, such as the introduction of a democratic regime (Weede, 1983, 1984b) or the length of time of institutionalization (Olson, 1982).

The functional approach

One may question whether democratization is the only valuable form of political change. Perhaps a modern polity implies more than democracy, or democratization reflects more valuable change processes? It is no exaggeration to state that *The Politics of Developing Areas* (1960), edited by Gabriel Almond and James S. Coleman, is the basic book in the functionalist tradition. Since it has been used as a textbook, its view of political development and change, presented in the introductory chapter by Almond, have become widely known and at times much accepted.

A multidimensional model of political development would start from the Almond conception of the political system as fulfilling functions in terms of structures. On the one hand, we have the input functions: political socialization and recruitment, interest articulation, interest aggregation and political communication. On the other hand, there is the set of output functions: rule-making, rule application and rule adjudication (Almond and Coleman, 1960: 17).

Political development is specified as the degree of specificity with which structures fulfil functions, as well as the extent to which political structures are separated out of each other. Almond claims:

> In our presentation of the functional theory, we have continually stressed the point that all political structure is multifunctional, and all political culture is dualistic. The peculiar properties of 'modernity' of structure and culture are a particular mode of solution to the problems of multifunctionality and cultural dualism. (Almond and Coleman, 1960: 63)

One may reply that equating political development with such a general phenomenon as structural specificity amounts to very little. One may wish to know a little more about this structural specificity, what it looks like and how it comes about.

The answer was given in the major elaboration of the functionalist approach to politics: *Comparative Politics* (Almond and Powell, 1966). It had the subtitle *A Developmental Approach*, and it focused in particular on a special type of political change: the increase in system capabilities, in conversion processes and in adaptation functions. The 1966 model, though basically functionalist, is different from the 1960 model in that it incorporates a systems approach as well. Influenced by David Easton's *A Systems Analysis of Political Life* (1965), Almond and Powell speak of inputs and outputs as well as demand and support. Political systems have a varied capacity for handling inputs and outputs, as conceptualized in the idea of system capacity: regulative, extractive, distributive and responsive capability (Almond and Powell, 1966: 29).

Moreover, political systems vary with regard to the internal functioning of the system in terms of conversion processes: 'the ways in which demands and supports are transformed into authoritative decisions and are implemented' (Almond and Powell, 1966: 29). Lastly, we have the system maintenance and adaptation functions. Thus, political development refers to the following basic functions: capabilities, conversion processes, system maintenance and adaptation functions. The concept of development has two modes: positive or negative development, depending on the direction of change in these basic functions.

Almond and Powell then propose their theory of political development, which has been the target of much criticism. The crucial notion of level of development refers to three aspects of structure: differentiation, autonomy and secularization. The basic theoretical proposition claims that the more modern or developed a polity is, the more it is characterized by differentiation, autonomy and secularization. Almond and Powell state 'that the development of higher levels of system capabilities is dependent upon the development of greater structural differentiation and cultural secularization' (Almond and Powell, 1966: 323).

The 1966 theory aroused two kinds of reaction: an acceptance that sometimes led to dogma or a rejection that was sometimes sharp. The Almond conception of political development was much influenced by the general theory of structural-functionalism, as interpreted, for example, by Frances X. Sutton in 'Social theory and comparative politics' (1963), building on the several volumes of Talcott Parsons and his associates in the late 1940s and the 1950s (Parsons, 1951; Parsons and Shils, 1951; Levy, 1952; Parsons and Smelser, 1956). The general rebuttal of sociological functionalism contributed to the severe reaction against the Almond framework.

To sum up, the structural-functional approach to political development focused on the notion of system capacity and structural differentiation and its modes. Modern political systems are more developed because they have more differentiated structures. But this is all that the functionalist approach has to say about political development – and it is not terribly striking or surprising. Moreover, how is this concept of political development to be measured? A number of interesting change phenomena that fall outside the scope of the functionalist approach seem to exist.

The idea that political development has something to do with system capacity and structural differentiation may be taken out of its functionalist webs. A number of scholars include these two concepts when defining the concept of political development, without adhering to functionalism.

The typical approach to political development has been to mention more than one defining characteristic, while leaving it open as to whether or not the various definition properties covary or not. In his *Aspects of Political Development* (1966), Lucien Pye surveyed the literature to find no fewer than ten key properties: (a) the political prerequisites of economic development; (b) the politics typical of industrial societies; (c) political modernization; (d) the operation of a nation-state; (e) administrative and legal development; (f) mass mobilization and participation; (g) the building of democracy; (h) stability and orderly change; (i) mobilization and power; and (j) one aspect of a multidimensional process of social change.

How could so many dimensions of a complex process of political change be reduced to manageable proportions? Pye states that the '*capacity* of a political system ... is related to the outputs of a political system and the extent to which the political system can affect the rest of society and economy', and that 'running through much of the discussion of political development is that of *differentiation* and specialization', implying that 'offices and agencies tend to have their distinct and limited functions, and there is an equivalent of a division of labor within the realm of government' (Pye, 1966: 46–7). It is easier to measure political system capacity than political system differentiation in terms of empirical indicators.

James S. Coleman singles out integration and capacity besides equality as typical of political development. He writes about political development as 'the successful institutionalization of (1) new patterns of integration regulating and containing the tensions and conflicts produced by increased differentiation, and (2) new patterns of participation and resource distribution adequately responsive to the demands generated by the imperatives of equality' (Coleman, 1965: 15).

It seems obvious that the Coleman addition of equality and participation to capacity and differentiation implies a risk, as they need not go together with the other two aspects of development. The tie between capacity and differentiation is far stronger than between these two and participation. However, even the association between capacity and differentiation may be doubted, as the first refers more to the output side of the political system, whereas the second stands for some property of the structure of the system. In any case, it remains to be clarified how capacity and differentiation are to be measured empirically.

To identify political development with system capacity implies that political development is somehow a function of an increase in state involvement: the stronger the state the greater political development. However, when political development is identified with autonomy and system differentiation it seems as if it implies less state involvement. The less encompassing the nature of the state and the more subsystem autonomy there is, the more political development we have. To allow for this possibility of a contradiction in the concept of political development the set of indicators measuring the increase in state involvement should be separated from the set of indices measuring the decrease.

If political development is identified with participation or equality, one seems to move along a different line of argument from when one talks about state involvement. At the same time, one should beware of a distinction between participation and equality, as they need not go together. If political development does mean both state involvement and autonomy, this simply reflects the fact that both processes of change may be considered valuable. If this is so, then perhaps what matters is modernization in general. We must take up the general approach to political development in the form of modernization, as Samuel Eisenstadt defined it, as a transformation towards the type of 'social, economic and political systems that have developed in Western Europe and North America from the seventeenth century to the nineteenth', spreading later to the South American, Asian and African continents (Eisenstadt, 1966: 1).

Social process approach

It is quite plausible to regard political development as a reflection of more general processes of social development. The theory of modernization states that political development is an offspring of more general developmental trends – industrialization, urbanization and mass literacy – moving a society from a traditional state to a modern one. There are a number of alternative versions of the modernization theme (Binder, 1986).

Marion J. Levy's *Modernization and the Structure of Societies* (1966) takes a broad approach to modernization and its modes. Levy states: 'A society will be considered more or less modernized to the extent that its members use inanimate sources of power and/or use tools to multiply the effects of their efforts' (Levy, 1966:1). Such a broad definition of modernization turns the theme into a general account of the evolution of culture and civilization. It is no wonder that Levy offers little in terms of middle-range hypotheses about the interaction between political change and more specific processes of socio-economic transformations. The modernization theme includes efforts to be more specific. Often the modernization theme was more oriented towards a static comparison of two kinds of society or polity – traditional or modern – than towards the process of change from one to the other.

One famous book on the modernization theme was *The Passing of Traditional Society: Modernizing the Middle East* by David Lerner (1958). Lerner presented a model distinguishing between three ideal types of orientation – modern, transitional and traditional – on the basis of the following criteria: literacy, urbanism, media participation and empathy (Lerner, 1958: 71). The process of modernization is the movement away from traditional society, which involves three basic phases: urbanization, literacy and media participation. The special contribution of Lerner to the modernization theme is the emphasis on communication mechanisms which mould the transition process. Political development refers to mass participation, involving the use of modern media systems which have replaced the old oral systems.

Lerner identifies four dimensions in modernization, which are correlated to a considerable extent: urbanization, literacy, media participation and political participation. These findings refer to the 1950s, and it may be questioned whether the phenomena really are interrelated today. It is an open question whether extensive political participation typical of democracies does indeed always follow from or is accompanied by high levels of literacy. Moreover, it is possible to look for expressions of modernization other than political participation, and we may regard other types of political change as equally basic.

In Lerner's work the concept of transitionals plays a major role. They stand between modern man and traditional man and they face the serious task of defining the process of modernization. They may constitute an elite that specifies the goals and means of the process of modernization – spokesperson and administrator. For an interpretation reminiscent of the Lerner distinctions, see Pye's (1958) separation between administrator, agitator and broker.

An article by Karl Deutsch, 'Social mobilization and political development' (1961) was an attempt to quantify the often diffuse concepts in the modernization theme. Frequently, modernization theory simply employs a pure distinction between two ideal types to portray the meaning of modernization. However, some authors adopting this approach attempted to model the modernization process by means of quantitative equations. Two different models were employed. One described the general process of modernization or the coming of a Western-type society: industrialization, urbanization and mass mobilization. The other model placed the modern polity in a context where it was preceded by the process of social modernization. Typically, political development is looked upon as a reflection of more basic socio-economic transformations. Social mobilization denotes, as Deutsch writes,

> a concept which brackets together a number of more specific processes of change, such as changes of residence, of occupation, of social setting, of face-to-face associates, of institutions, roles, and ways of acting, of experiences and expectations, and finally of personal memories, habits and needs, including the need for new patterns of group affiliation and new images of personal identity. (Deutsch, 1961: 493)

Like Myrdal, he conceived of these changes as interacting, resulting in a 'cumulative impact', which tends to transform political behaviour.

Whereas functionalism focused on the static differences between two types of society or two kinds of polity, the modernization approach emphasized the dynamic processes of change from one type of society to another. However, the exact implications of social change for political change remained to be specified. Now, developments in both the Muslim world and the Buddhist world show that rapid socio-economic change may trigger various kinds of authoritarian responses in state and society.

In *The Politics of Modernization*, David Apter (1965) elaborated on qualitative modernization theory by explicitly focusing on the variety of political system responses to the problems of the transformation from traditional to modern society characterizing Third World events. These polity-type responses include a neo-mercantilist state, a mobilization state and a reconciliation state (Apter, 1965: 420).

Modernization

Some authors really tried to specify more definitely what modernization was all about. The problem involved two fundamental questions. On the one hand, there is the interpretation of the transformation of European society from feudalism to industrial life. On the other hand, we have the statement of the major differences between the industrialized world – the OECD countries as well as the communist world – and the Third World LDC countries. A model was searched for that would solve these two different problems simultaneously. Sutton (1963) identified the following characteristics of a traditional society versus a modern society:

Agricultural society: 1. A predominance of ascriptive, particularistic, diffuse patterns. 2. Stable local groups and limited spatial mobility. 3. Relatively simple and 'occupational' differentiation. 4. A 'deferential' stratification system of diffuse impact.

Modern industrial society: 1. A predominance of universalistic, specific, achievement norms. 2. A high degree of social mobility. 3. A well developed occupational system, insulated from other social systems. 4. An egalitarian class system based on generalized patterns of achievement. 5. A prevalence of associations, i.e. functionally specific non-ascriptive structures.

Modernization theorists argued that the transition from one kind of society to another kind implies a radically different polity. In *Political Modernization in Japan and Turkey* (1964), Rustow and Ward identified a list of properties of the so-called modern polity: (a) a highly differentiated and functionally specific system of governmental organization; (b) a high degree of integration within this governmental structure; (c) the prevalence of rational and secular procedures for the making of political decisions; (d) the large volume, wide range and high efficacy of its political and administrative decisions; (e) a widespread and effective sense of popular identification with the history, territory and national identity of the state; (f) widespread popular interest and involvement in the political system, though not necessarily in the decision-making aspects thereof; (g) the allocation of political roles by achievement rather than ascription; and (h) judicial and regulatory techniques based upon a predominantly secular and impersonal system of law (Rustow and Ward, 1964: 6–7).

Although the Rustow and Ward identification was a substantial effort at making development theory more concrete and less abstruse, a number of questions remain unanswered. There is the problem of change: how is a modern polity typically introduced? There is also the problem of causality: is political modernization determined by socio-economic transformation? Moreover, there was the problem of classification: did communist systems have modern polities? In order to approach these problems, development theory turned to comparative history.

Political development as institutionalization

What is truly modern? Are modernity and tradition always mutually exclusive? If modernization is what political change is all about, especially if it is conducive to a morally appealing condition – political development – then we need to know what a modern society or polity amounts to. Capitalism or socialism? Public sector expansion or market values? Occidental rationalism or oriental rejection of mechanistic atomism? Since it is difficult to identify what change is truly development – conducive to modernity – then perhaps political development is the capacity to cope with processes of development, whatever modernism may amount to. Samuel Huntington broke the spell of the modernization theme by equating valuable political change with growth of order or of distinctness and firmness of political institutions (O'Brien, 1972).

The idea that institutionalization is basic to political development has been advanced by Huntington in a number of articles. Let us follow the presentation in Huntington's article 'Political development and political decay' (1965). He states that it is useful to distinguish political development from modernization and 'to identify political development with the institutionalization of political organizations and procedures' (Huntington, 1965: 386). Rapid increases in mobilization and participation could actually undermine political institutions. Fast modernization produces political decay and not political development, argued Huntington.

This is a straightforward criticism of the modernization theme, but we must take a close look at what Huntington puts in the place of modernization: what is institutionalization? Huntington (1965: 394) writes: 'Institutionalization is the process by which organizations and processes acquire value and stability. The level of institutionalization of any political system can be defined by the adaptability, complexity, autonomy and coherence of its organizations and procedures.' These defining concepts – adaptability, complexity, autonomy and coherence – are very abstract and we need more information about how they are measured and then how these measures may be added together into a single index of institutionalization as political development. Is it really the case that increased institutionalization must result in more adaptability or autonomy? Huntington states about adaptability and complexity: 'Adaptability can be measured by chronological age, leadership successions, generational changes, and functional changes. Complexity can be measured by the number and diversity of organizational subunits and by the number and diversity of functions performed by the organizations.'

To measure autonomy is more difficult, states Huntington, but it can be measured by the distinctiveness of the norms and values of the organization, by the personnel controls – co-optation, penetration, purging – between the organization and other groups and by the extent to which the organization controls material resources. Coherence also seems to be complex as Huntington requires a lot of information to be available. It could be measured by the number of contested successions in relation to total successions, by the number of splits among leaders and members, by the occurrence of alienation and dissent within the organization and by the loyalty of organization members (Huntington, 1965: 404–5).

Following this suggestion as to the measurement of political development as institutionalization, it is no exaggeration to state that it entails a complex procedure. And we still need more information about how these four measures are to be combined into a single measure: simple addition or perhaps some other mathematical procedure.

Reviewing the literature on political development in 1975 (Huntington and Dominguez, 1975), Huntington seems to have become aware of the difficulties with the proposed approach to political development. He declares that not much could be gained by trying to identify one diffuse and value-laden concept like political development with a more analytical and value-free concept like institutionalization (Huntington and Dominguez, 1975: 47). Instead Huntington formulates a number of hypotheses about the linkages between socio-economic modernization and political development. The process of modernization is assumed to have an impact on the level of institutionalization, the degree of modernity or tradition of the political system and the concentration or pluralism in the distribution of power.

Huntington here comes close to a repetition of some of the basic ideas of the modernization approach. The emergence of a modern polity implies the rationalization of authority, the expansion of political participation and the differentiation of structures. However, Huntington also argues that socio-economic modernization implies the destruction of the traditional political system, meaning that we have to recognize both political decay and political birth. Institutionalization is but one pattern of political change and Huntington is clearly aware of the possibility that political change may imply the failure to develop proper institutions. He states:

> Thus, as socio-economic modernization takes place, either the existing political institutions adapt to meet the new needs, or the political institutions are themselves changed into or replaced by new political institutions more capable of meeting those needs, or the modernization of the political system grinds to a halt and severe stresses develop as a result of the gap between continuing socio-economic modernization and aborted political modernization. (Huntington and Dominguez, 1975: 54)

Although Huntington still conceived of political development as related to modernization, he approached modernization as presenting a set of major challenges to the political system instead of looking at political development as a derivative of socio-economic modernization. And successful modernization requires the institutionalization of patterns of behaviour that introduce a modern polity to replace a traditional one. The idea that political development is related to crisis phenomena has stimulated a so-called crisis approach to political development.

The crisis approach

Political development may not be interpreted as deterministic change towards some desirable end state, but as the successful path to some temporary condition. Basic social change means unrest and reorientation; perhaps political development is the polity's response to these various crisis phenomena, as Almond *et al.* argue in *Crisis, Choice and Change: Historical Studies of Political Development* (1973).

This novel theory of political development was elaborated by Binder *et al.* in *Crises and Sequences in Political Development* (1971), summarizing some of the volumes of a major research project on political development conducted by the American Social Science Research Council in the 1960s. They state:

> If we re-examine these five areas of critical change, or these five crises of political development, the crisis of identity, the crisis of legitimacy, the crisis of participation, the crisis of distribution, and the crisis of penetration, we will find that all five types of change may occur without any concomitant strengthening of the political institutions of the country affected. (Binder *et al.*, 1971: 65)

Thus political development may not be order or institutionalization *per se*, but it is related to a successful institutional response where elites cope with challenges, maintaining the valuable entity of order, whether rightist or leftist.

Brunner's and Brewer's *Organized Complexity: Empirical Theories of Political Development* (1971) explains processes of change in modern Turkey and the Philippines, where Brunner and Brewer focused on factors which the political elite could manipulate, again underlining choice and response to political system crisis. Almond and Rustow also suggested a new approach to political development, underlining choice and response by actors, and identifying various kinds of processes of change involving political unrest and the conscious response to political instability by leaders and institutions (Rustow, 1970; Almond *et al.*, 1973).

Binder points out in a 1986 article that the concept of political development tends to differ as a function of how one perceives the institutional response to crisis. He separates between: (a) the liberal theory of development (democracy and equality as systems response); (b) the state theory (increased control, planning and technology); (c) the revolutionary theory (mobilization of the masses and socialist transformation); and (d) the dependence theory (increased centre-periphery dependency). Some identify the concept of political development with democracy, others with étatism, and still others with revolution and socialism.

Political development as underdevelopment

There are two main implications arising from the consequences of socio-economic changes such as modernization of society for the stability of the polity. One popular theme implies that political development leads to more stability as political systems adapt to the new exigencies. Thus we find attempts to measure political development by various indicators of political stability (Sigelman, 1971: 36–7): government stability, interest articulation by anomic groups, political leadership, interest articulation by associational groups and the character of bureaucracy.

Alternatively, another major theme implies that instability is typical of political development, as there is a search for indicators of political development in phenomena of political instability: *coups d'état*, major constitutional changes, cabinet changes and changes in effective executive (Banks, 1972a and b). There is no doubt that the state of the concept of political development is bewildering. No less conspicuous is the 180-degree reversal of development as conducive to underdevelopment. If political development is the outcome of processes of change that present real challenges to political elites, then could it be that these social and economic change processes result in undesirable outcomes? Perhaps the overall movement is towards political underdevelopment.

In *Capitalism and Underdevelopment in Latin America* (1967), André Gunder Frank introduced a quite novel paradigm for interpreting broad processes of social, economic and political change, partly inspired by earlier Marxist interpretations by Baran and Sweezy, among others. The crucial distinctions in the Frank framework are between undeveloped and underdeveloped and between centre and periphery. The transition from traditionalism to modernism is one of movement from an undeveloped stage towards underdevelopment – the opposite theme to that of the modernization theorists. The process of underdevelopment is governed by the logic of the interaction between a world capitalist centre and Third World periphery, in terms of which the predicament of the so-called developing nations becomes worse. How do we test this new radical theory of development as underdevelopment? Does it imply something more specific about political change?

According to the theory of world system analysis proposed by Immanuel Wallerstein (1974, 1979), processes of change in various parts of the world are interdependent in terms of a more or less zero-sum game. The centre of the capitalist world, including the Eastern European countries, is the winner in this world system interaction, and the poor Third World countries are the losers. The basic criterion of change is the increase in inequality between these nations and within the peripheral countries. Wallerstein looks upon development as being determined by commodity production for profit in a world market which is characterized by various forms of labour exploitation based on asymmetrical power relations between powerful states and peripheral areas.

Thus development results in inequality, inflation and unemployment in the Third World. What are the implications for political development? Although the radical approach to development has resulted in an abundant literature about capitalism and the Third World (Chilcote and Johnson, 1983), there is perhaps not a distinct radical theory about political development. In it we still find the same hope for some kind of desirable political change process.

Thus far, the radical theory of development as the underdevelopment of an undeveloped area has offered little in terms of suggestions about the political implications of this process of underdevelopment. The Frank–Wallerstein theme is mainly a socio-economic theory. When political development is discussed along the lines of this theme the approach is exclusively normative. Ocampo and Johnson, on the other hand, define political development in the following way, without tying it to ideas about how to reverse the trend towards development: 'Development involves the liberation of man from conditions of exploitation and oppression. Politics is the means of human liberation' (Ocampo and Johnson, 1972: 424). However, underdevelopment theory has been criticized as being too deterministic and general in describing everything with the centre–periphery concepts, as well as being too little action-oriented (Phillips, 1978; Taylor, 1987).

Dimensions and indicators of political development

It may be stated that the concept of political development appears to be ambiguous. It remains to be asked whether it is multidimensional, what the various dimensions are and how these could be employed for further inquiry into political change. It may refer to both social and political phenomena or only to political phenomena. Rich in a value-loaded sense, it may refer to some desirable pattern of poltical change, e.g. towards democracy. Or it may mean some general institutional pattern or institutional response. It may cover both successful institutional change and institutional failure. More neutrally, it may refer to both political stability and political instability. How the radical approach to development is to be handled in terms of indicators is an open question.

It may be worthwhile to introduce some distinctions and then to try to elaborate on how these distinctions relate to each other at the measurement level. Thus we have a large number of variables related to the four aspects of development derived from the literature.

1 Democratic development: democracy score, human rights, political role of the military, party system fractionalization or pluralism, political or economic discrimination and party system functions.
2 Capacity: government consumption, general or central government expenditure, military personnel and military expenditure, war involvement post-Second World War.
3 Institutionalization: institutional sclerosis, year of introduction of modern leadership, years in effect, state status.
4 Stability: political strikes, violence and protests.

These variables may be measured by means of a number of indicators. If data for the variables listed above for some seventy countries in a cross-section referring roughly to the 1970s are examined, can we identify one concept of political development? We have not included any of the former Eastern European communist systems, since the focus is on the nature of the overall political change involved in moving from an undeveloped to a developed situation as this is conceived in the analysis of the Third World countries.

Democracy

Since there is much ambiguity as well as controversy surrounding the concept of democracy, stating a proper set of indicators for the measurement of various levels of democracy is no easy task. In the literature there are several attempts at deriving indices measuring various aspects of the democratic nature of a polity. They range from discrimination indices over human and civil rights indices to party system indices, including a measure of the overall role of the military establishment in national politics (Table 4.1). In order to reduce the amount of information about this aspect of political development we have used a standard data reduction technique.

Table 4.1 Factor analysis of democracy indicators ($n = 67$)

Indicators	Factor loadings		Communality
	Factor 1	Factor 2	
Political discrimination	−0.01	0.94	0.88
Economic discrimination	0.08	0.92	0.86
Human rights c.1980	0.81	−0.05	0.66
Democracy c.1965	0.87	0.05	0.76
Democracy c.1960	0.81	0.07	0.65
Party system functions	0.81	0.03	0.66
Role of military	−0.71	0.21	0.54
Political rights	−0.91	−0.13	0.85
Civil rights	−0.92	−0.12	0.86
Party system fractionalization 1970s	0.66	0.17	0.46
Party system fractionalization 1960s	0.68	0.42	0.64
Explained variance (per cent)	53.6	17.5	

Sources: political discrimination, economic discrimination, Taylor and Jodice (1983); human rights 1980, Humana (1983); democracy 1965, 1960, Bollen (1980); Party systems functions, role of military, Estes (1984); political rights, civil rights, party system fractionalization 1970s, Taylor and Jodice (1983); party systems fractionalization 1960s, Banks (1971).

Most of the indicators on the extent of democracy of a political system identify one single dimension. The exceptions are the discrimination indices, which appear to vary somewhat independently of the democracy scores. The explanation is that the political as well as the economic discrimination indices measure the intensity of discrimination, which means that countries with large immigrant groups will score high on these indices, though they may also score high on the number of political and human rights for the citizens of these countries.

State capacity

Political system capacity is expressed in various ways, or may constitute a potential that can be drawn upon in times of exceptional events. Different factors in a society may be conducive to polity strength or state capacity. The indicators of political capacity range from the size of the population − a source of great power ambitions − over actual involvement in war activities − one traditional expression of political ambition to display strength − to ordinary measures of the size of the state or the public sector. Since small states and peaceful societies that are welfare states have 'big governments' we should expect to find that the capacity indicators do not covary (Table 4.2).

As expected, capacity in a political context may mean two very different things: welfare spending or military effort, for instance as war involvement.

Table 4.2 Factor analysis of capacity indicators ($n = 67$)

Indicators	Factor loadings		Communality
	Factor 1	Factor 2	
Military personnel	0.16	0.65	0.45
Military expenditure	0.28	0.80	0.72
War involvement	0.05	0.79	0.62
Central government expenditure 1970s[a]	0.79	0.45	0.83
Central government expenditure 1970s[b]	0.83	0.45	0.89
General government expenditure 1970s	0.92	0.09	0.85
Public consumption	0.88	0.05	0.78
Explained variance (per cent)	55.5	18.1	

Sources: military personnel 1975, Taylor and Jodice (1983); military expenditure 1970s, Sivard (1980); war involvement after 1945, Weede (1984a); central government expenditure 1970s[a], Sivard (1980); central government expenditure 1970s[b], Taylor and Jodice (1983); general government expenditure 1970s, IMF (1982); public consumption, World Bank (1980b).

Institutionalization

The concept of institutionalization may appear to be abstract, but the truth is that it is generally agreed that the measurement of the concept refers to state consolidation and nation building (Rokkan *et al.*, 1970; Tilly, 1975). On the one hand, there is the introduction of modernized leadership at a crucial point of time in the history of a country. On the other hand, we have the official recognition of the state in international affairs. The general index of institutional sclerosis is a recent attempt to measure the period of time of uninterrupted organizational growth in a society, in order to tap the strength of so-called distributional coalitions or special interest organizations (Olson, 1982) (Table 4.3).

Table 4.3 Factor analysis of institutionalization indicators ($n = 67$)

Indicators	Factor loading	Communality
	Factor 1	
Modernized leadership: introduction	0.94	0.88
Modernized leadership: in effect	0.84	0.71
Institutional sclerosis	0.93	0.87
Qualified as a state	0.82	0.68
Member of international system	0.84	0.71
Explained variance (per cent)	76.9	

Sources: modernized leadership, Taylor and Hudson (1972); institutional sclerosis, Choi (1983); year qualified as state, year member of the international system: Banks (1971).

The finding is that institutionalization is a rather simple phenomenon that may be tapped by the employment of one institutionalization score; for instance, modernized leadership.

Stability

Political development would necessarily imply political change, but the opposite is not true. And where there is polity change there may also be the typical expressions of political instability: protest or violent protest as well as the occurrence of violence in state and society in general. Of course, the first type of phenomenon may be accompanied by the second kind and vice versa (Table 4.4).

Table 4.4 Factor analysis of stability indicators $(n = 67)$

Indicators	Factor loadings		Communality
	Factor 1	Factor 2	
Protest demonstrations	0.73	0.30	0.62
Riots	0.83	0.27	0.76
Political strikes	0.82	−0.06	0.67
Armed attacks	0.54	0.72	0.81
Assassinations	0.03	0.87	0.76
Deaths from domestic violence	0.18	0.83	0.72
Explained variance (per cent)	52.4	20.3	

Source: Taylor and Jodice (1983).

The various indicators on protest and violence are both interrelated and independent to some extent. We may distinguish between two rather distinct factors: non-violent protest and the occurrence of violence.

To what extent are the indices now derived really independent in relation to data about some seventy countries for the 1970s? Table 4.5 presents some clues as to the answer to the problem of multidimensionality of the political development concept.

Table 4.5 Correlation matrix for derived political development dimensions

	(1)	(2)	(3)	(4)	(5)	(6)
Democracy (1)	1.00	0.44	−0.35	−0.62	0.09	−0.22
Polity capacity (2)		1.00	0.03	−0.26	−0.07	−0.17
Military involvement (3)			1.00	−0.02	0.16	0.22
Institutionalization (4)				1.00	−0.41	−0.14
Protest (5)					1.00	0.48
Violence (6)						1.00

Note: $n = 67$.

The overall finding is that it is striking how little the six indices on various aspects of political development correlate. There is hardly any evidence of the notion of some general concept of political development that would constitute the common core of the various polity characteristics listed as development in the literature. This means that one faces the decision as to whether or not 'political development' as a key term should be replaced by a whole set of different words, one for each of the separate dimensions identified. Actually, there are one or two cases of moderate interaction: violence and protest on the one hand, as stated above, and on the other democracy and institutionalization, reflecting the long lifetime of the regimes of the Western political systems that survived the authoritarian challenge during the Second World War.

We will now go on to look at the variation in the scores on democracy, state capacity, institutionalization, protest and violence, in five subsets of nations: the OECD world, the Central and South American world, the post-communist countries and the sets of African and Asian countries. How do these countries vary between and within the sets when data for the late 1980s and early 1990s are examined?

Comparative analysis of political development

Any interpretation of the concept of political development may combine factual and normative elements. To some scholars political development means a desirable condition, whatever the likelihood of its occurrence; for example, a dominant position of the left as the starting point for real development of an undeveloped or underdeveloped country. To others there is a balance between feasibility and desirability, as, for example, in the argument that democracy is the result of true political development. Or such a balance identifying recurrent matters of fact with political ideology values may be expressed in the notion that political development implies increased state involvement in the form of 'big' government or strength in military ventures. Finally, the conception of political development may be almost exclusively oriented towards factual matters, whatever their intrinsic value may be; for example, the institutionalization interpretation or the instability–stability theme.

The mix of fact and value in the concept of political development may appear troublesome but it does not preclude that the various dimensions included in the umbrella idea of political development may be used to point out some pertinent country differences. Table 4.6 reports on an analysis of variance of one of the six political development indices, that is, democracy.

Politically developed countries in the sense of democratic regimes are not unsurprisingly to be found in the set of OECD countries. The experience of democracy is particularly low in the sets of African and Asian countries, whereas some Central and Latin American countries hover between authoritarianism and democracy in a circular time frame. The high eta-coefficient indicates that the differences between these categories of countries are larger than the differences within the same categories. Let us take a closer look at the occurrence of democratic regime characteristics in the world around 1991 (Table 4.7).

Table 4.6 Average democracy scores 1983, 1986 and 1991

	1983	1986	1991
OECD	88.8 ($n = 22$)	91.5 ($n = 22$)	91.4 ($n = 22$)
Latin America	64.9 ($n = 10$)	66.9 ($n = 17$)	71.0 ($n = 21$)
Africa	55.3 ($n = 15$)	46.8 ($n = 22$)	52.6 ($n = 26$)
Asia	53.2 ($n = 20$)	48.0 ($n = 20$)	45.9 ($n = 28$)
Post-communist	39.0 ($n = 8$)	34.8 ($n = 8$)	78.7 ($n = 7$)
Mean	64.1 ($n = 75$)	60.9 ($n = 89$)	64.5 ($n = 104$)
Eta-squared	0.53	0.57	0.55

Source: The democracy score is based upon Humana (1983, 1986, 1992).

Table 4.7 Democracy 1991

OECD		Latin America		Africa		Asia	
Australia	91	Argentina	84	Algeria	66	Afghanistan	28
Austria	95	Bolivia	71	Angola	27	Bangladesh	59
Belgium	96	Brazil	69	Benin	90	China	21
Canada	94	Chile	80	Botswana	79	Hong Kong	79
Denmark	98	Colombia	60	Cameroon	56	India	54
Finland	99	Costa Rica	90	Côte d'Ivoire	75	Indonesia	34
France	94	Cuba	30	Egypt	50	Iran	22
Germany	98	Dominican		Ghana	53	Iraq	17
Greece	87	Republic	78	Kenya	46	Israel	76
Ireland	94	Ecuador	83	Libya	24	Jordan	65
Italy	90	El Salvador	53	Malawi	33	Cambodia	33
Japan	82	Guatemala	62	Morocco	56	Korea, North	20
Netherlands	98	Honduras	65	Mozambique	53	Korea, South	59
New Zealand	98	Jamaica	72	Nigeria	49	Kuwait	33
Norway	97	Mexico	64	Rwanda	48	Malaysia	61
Portugal	92	Nicaragua	75	Senegal	71	Myanmar	17
Spain	87	Panama	81	Sierra Leone	67	Nepal	69
Sweden	98	Paraguay	70	South Africa	50	Oman	49
Switzerland	96	Peru	54	Sudan	18	Pakistan	42
Turkey	44	Trinidad	84	Tanzania	41	Papua New	
United		Uruguay	90	Togo	48	Guinea	70
Kingdom	93	Venezuela	75	Tunisia	60	Philippines	72
United States	90			Uganda	46	Saudi Arabia	29
				Zaire	40	Singapore	60
				Zambia	57	Sri Lanka	47
				Zimbabwe	65	Syria	30

Post-communist

Bulgaria	83
Czechoslovakia	97
Hungary	97
Poland	83
Romania	82
Russia	54
Yugoslavia	55

Thailand	62
Vietnam	27
Yemen	49

Source: Humana (1992).

Table 4.8 Average polity capacity scores 1992

OECD ($n = 24$)	46.8
Latin America ($n = 18$)	21.8
Africa ($n = 21$)	29.4
Asia ($n = 21$)	25.4
Post-communist ($n = 3$)	49.2
Eta-squared	0.51

Note: The polity capacity score is based upon the indicator general government expenditures 1992 from IMF (1994).

Table 4.9 Polity capacity around 1992

OECD		*Latin America*		*Africa*		*Asia*	
Australia	41.2	Argentina	16.9	Botswana	35.4	Bhutan	42.4
Austria	54.0	Bolivia	18.9	Cameroon	19.2	China	9.9
Belgium	54.1	Brazil	38.5	Chad	31.3	India	30.0
Canada	49.4	Chile	29.1	Egypt	39.3	Indonesia	20.0
Denmark	60.6	Colombia	15.3	Ethiopia	26.7	Iran	18.6
Finland	45.3	Costa Rica	23.9	Gabon	30.4	Israel	52.5
France	51.5	Dominican		Ghana	16.6	Jordan	33.4
Germany	48.4	Republic	10.8	Kenya	28.0	Korea, South	17.0
Greece	33.6	Ecuador	14.7	Lesotho	55.8	Malaysia	31.5
Iceland	42.9	El Salvador	11.1	Madagascar	15.1	Myanmar	11.3
Ireland	53.0	Guatemala	11.7	Malawi	25.0	Nepal	18.3
Italy	50.6	Mexico	33.4	Mauritius	25.5	Oman	43.0
Japan	22.9	Nicaragua	30.0	Morocco	28.7	Pakistan	24.3
Luxembourg	57.6	Panama	31.2	Namibia	44.2	Papua New	
Netherlands	57.7	Paraguay	13.8	Rwanda	25.3	Guinea	32.3
New Zealand	38.7	Peru	12.9	Sierra Leone	21.9	Philippines	20.0
Norway	56.7	Trinidad	31.9	South Africa	34.1	Singapore	19.4
Portugal	46.9	Uruguay	28.8	Tunisia	31.9	Sri Lanka	26.9
Spain	43.8	Venezuela	20.0	Zaire	15.3	Syria	23.1
Sweden	65.0			Zambia	21.7	Thailand	16.8
Switzerland	39.5			Zimbabwe	45.5	United Arab	
Turkey	24.2					Emirates	12.1
United			*Post-communist*			Yemen	31.4
Kingdom	47.4						
United States	39.1	Czechoslovakia	48.2				
		Hungary	58.0				
		Romania	41.4				

Source: IMF (1994).

Countries that score low on the democracy index within the OECD set of nations are the ones that have recently experienced the dismantling of an authoritarian regime: Spain in 1975, Portugal in 1975 and Greece in 1973. The status of democratic institutions in Turkey is still precarious, to say the least. In Asia there are a few countries which have a democratic tradition, though not a long one: India, Nepal and Malaysia. There is hardly any country in Africa that could qualify as a democracy, whereas there are a few cases in Central and Latin America: Costa Rica and Uruguay, for example.

The hypothesis that political development is political system capacity implies that countries with large public sectors are the developed nations (Table 4.8). Extensive public expenditure patterns are to be found either in welfare states providing citizens with the public provision of a number of services, including social security, or in those leviathan states where for one reason or another military expenditure is the reason for comprehensive public budgets. Let us look more closely at country variations (Table 4.9). Not surprisingly, Sweden scores highest in the OECD set, as it has sometimes been considered the OECD model for a future welfare state. The Scandinavian countries score high generally, whereas Southern European nations score lower. The score of the United States reflects its military commitment rather than high welfare spending. As we move on to consider political system capacity in the Third World, it must be recognized that military spending is often the cause of big budgets as a percentage of overall national resources in Egypt, Israel, Jordan, Morocco, Tunisia, India and Pakistan. Let us consider military effort (Table 4.10).

Table 4.10 Military effort scores 1992

OECD (n = 24)	2.4
Latin America (n = 22)	2.4
Africa (n = 38)	4.8
Asia (n = 29)	7.8
Post-communist (n = 17)	2.7
Mean (n = 130)	4.3
Eta-squared	0.17

Note: The military effort score is based upon the indicator military expenditures as a percentage of GDP 1992 from UNDP (1995).

One may raise objections in relation to the interpretation of state capacity as military effort. However, states may use their capacity to mobilize resources and employ modern techniques in warfare in order to promote various state-related objectives, including, for example, national aggrandizement. The military effort index differentiates between the five categories of nations as well as within these subsets (Table 4.11).

Table 4.11 Military effort 1992

OECD		Latin America		Africa		Asia	
Australia	2.4	Argentina	1.7	Algeria	2.7	Bangladesh	1.3
Austria	0.9	Bolivia	1.9	Angola	35.5	China	5.0
Belgium	1.8	Brazil	0.7	Benin	1.3	India	2.5
Canada	2.0	Chile	2.7	Botswana	3.1	Indonesia	1.4
Denmark	2.0	Colombia	2.4	Burkina Faso	4.3	Iran	7.1
Finland	1.9	Costa Rica	0.9	Cameroon	1.6	Iraq	21.1
France	3.4	Cuba	5.0	Central African		Israel	11.1
Germany	2.4	Dominican		Republic	2.0	Jordan	11.2
Greece	5.6	Republic	1.4	Chad	2.6	Cambodia	4.8
Iceland	0.0	Ecuador	2.2	Congo	3.8	Korea, North	25.7
Ireland	1.2	El Salvador	1.7	Côte d'Ivoire	0.8	Korea, South	3.8
Italy	2.0	Guatemala	1.1	Egypt	6.0	Laos	6.1
Japan	1.0	Haiti	2.1	Ethiopia	20.1	Lebanon	5.0
Luxembourg	1.2	Honduras	1.5	Gabon	3.7	Malaysia	4.8
Netherlands	2.4	Jamaica	0.7	Ghana	0.8	Mongolia	5.9
New Zealand	1.6	Mexico	0.5	Kenya	2.8	Myanmar	3.1
Norway	3.3	Nicaragua	10.9	Lesotho	5.3	Nepal	1.1
Portugal	2.9	Panama	1.2	Libya	6.3	Oman	17.5
Spain	1.7	Paraguay	2.0	Madagascar	1.1	Pakistan	7.7
Sweden	2.5	Peru	3.8	Malawi	1.4	Papua New	
Switzerland	1.6	Trinidad	1.3	Mali	2.9	Guinea	1.8
Turkey	4.7	Uruguay	2.7	Mauritania	3.1	Philippines	2.2
United		Venezuela	3.6	Mauritius	0.4	Saudi Arabia	11.8
Kingdom	4.0			Morocco	4.0	Singapore	5.4
United States	5.3			Mozambique	10.2	Sri Lanka	4.9
				Namibia	2.9	Syria	16.6
		Post-communist		Niger	1.0	Thailand	2.7
		Albania	2.3	Nigeria	0.7	United Arab	
		Armenia	2.5	Rwanda	6.8	Emirates	14.6
		Azerbaijan	1.9	Senegal	2.1	Vietnam	11.0
		Belarus	4.5	South Africa	3.0	Yemen	9.3
		Bulgaria	5.7	Sudan	15.8		
		Estonia	0.6	Tanzania	3.6		
		Georgia	3.2	Togo	3.1		
		Hungary	3.5	Tunisia	3.3		
		Kazakhstan	3.8	Uganda	2.9		
		Kyrgyzstan	0.7	Zaire	2.9		
		Latvia	0.5	Zambia	2.6		
		Lithuania	0.7	Zimbabwe	4.3		
		Moldova	2.1				
		Poland	2.3				
		Tajikistan	3.7				
		Turkmenistan	4.8				
		Ukraine	3.8				

Source: UNDP (1995).

Table 4.12 Institutionalization

OECD	1815 ($n = 25$)
Latin America	1884 ($n = 22$)
Africa	1951 ($n = 43$)
Asia	1936 ($n = 34$)
Post-communist	1863 ($n = 29$)
Mean	1899 ($n = 153$)

Eta squared = 0.73

Note: The institutionalization score is based on the following indicator: modernized leadership from Black (1966).

Table 4.13 Institutionalization

OECD		Latin America		Africa		Asia	
Australia	1801	Argentina	1853	Algeria	1847	Afghanistan	1923
Austria	1848	Bolivia	1880	Angola	1975	Bangladesh	1971
Belgium	1795	Brazil	1850	Benin	1960	Bhutan	1975
Canada	1791	Chile	1861	Botswana	1966	China	1905
Denmark	1807	Colombia	1863	Burkina Faso	1960	Hong Kong	1936
Finland	1863	Costa Rica	1889	Burundi	1962	India	1919
France	1789	Cuba	1898	Cameroon	1960	Indonesia	1922
Germany	1803	Dominican		Central		Iran	1906
Greece	1863	Republic	1881	African		Iraq	1921
Iceland	1874	Ecuador	1875	Republic	1960	Israel	1920
Ireland	1870	El Salvador	1939	Chad	1960	Jordan	1923
Italy	1805	Guatemala	1881	Congo	1960	Cambodia	1949
Japan	1868	Haiti	1879	Côte d'Ivoire	1960	Korea, North	1910
Luxembourg	1795	Honduras	1919	Egypt	1922	Korea, South	1910
Netherlands	1795	Jamaica	1924	Ethiopia	1924	Kuwait	1961
New Zealand	1826	Mexico	1867	Gabon	1960	Laos	1949
Norway	1809	Nicaragua	1909	Ghana	1957	Lebanon	1920
Portugal	1822	Panama	1903	Guinea	1958	Malaysia	1963
Spain	1812	Paraguay	1841	Kenya	1963	Mongolia	1921
Sweden	1809	Peru	1879	Lesotho	1966	Myanmar	1923
Switzerland	1798	Trinidad	1959	Liberia	1847	Nepal	1975
Turkey	1908	Uruguay	1828	Libya	1952	Oman	1975
United		Venezuela	1870	Madagascar	1960	Pakistan	1919
Kingdom	1649			Malawi	1964	Papua New	
United States	1776			Mali	1960	Guinea	1975
				Mauritania	1960	Philippines	1899
				Mauritius	1968	Saudi Arabia	1964
				Morocco	1934	Singapore	1965
				Mozambique	1975	Sri Lanka	1920
				Namibia	1990	Syria	1920
				Niger	1960	Taiwan	1895
				Nigeria	1960	Thailand	1932

Post-communist				Africa (cont.)		Asia (cont.)	
Albania	1912	Lithuania	1861	Rwanda	1962	United Arab	
Armenia	1861	Macedonia	1878	Senegal	1960	Emirates	1971
Azerbaijan	1861	Moldova	1861	Sierra Leone	1961	Vietnam	1949
Belarus	1861	Poland	1863	Somalia	1960	Yemen	1963
Bosnia	1878	Romania	1878	South Africa	1910		
Bulgaria	1878	Russia	1861	Sudan	1924		
Croatia	1878	Slovakia	1848	Tanzania	1961		
Czech		Slovenia	1878	Togo	1960		
Republic	1848	Tajikstan	1861	Tunisia	1922		
Estonia	1861	Turkmenistan	1861	Uganda	1962		
Georgia	1861	Ukraine	1861	Zaire	1960		
Hungary	1848	USSR	1861	Zambia	1965		
Kazakhstan	1861	Uzbekistan	1861	Zimbabwe	1965		
Kyrgyzstan	1861	Yugoslavia	1878				
Latvia	1861						

Source: Black (1966).

Among the OECD nations Greece and the United States are really the only countries with a high score on this political development dimension. Notice the very low scores for Iceland, Luxembourg and Switzerland. Outside the OECD framework the situation is very different, in Asia in particular but also in Africa, as we find a large number of countries with extensive experience of war: Israel, Iraq, Saudi Arabia, Sudan, Angola and Ethiopia.

The institutionalization index is scored in such a way that low scores mean a lengthy time period of institutionalization and high scores stand for recent institutionalization (Table 4.12). Those countries where a modernized leadership or a process of nation-building was introduced in the late nineteenth or early twentieth centuries are politically developed in this interpretation of the concept. Let us look more closely at the country variation within the five categories of countries (Table 4.13).

The developed nations in this interpretation are to be found in the rich world and in Central and Latin America. Very low scores are to be found for the United Kingdom, the United States, Switzerland, France, Belgium and Denmark, as well as for Uruguay, Mexico and Brazil. Less institutionalized are the countries in Asia and Africa. Several of these nations date their birth to the post-Second World War period: Zambia, Malawi, Zaire, Kenya and Madagascar in Africa, for example, as well as Singapore and Malaysia in Asia.

The institutionalization scores basically measure state longevity, where a state is dated to the introduction of modernized leadership, which in some cases may come before the actual declaration of formal independence. They reflect to some extent political stability, since statehood often requires time in order to function in a predictable fashion. Yet institutionalization does not entail democracy, and Table 4.13 indicates that whereas some democracies are young states like Botswana and Mauritius, there are some authoritarian states which score high on the index of state institutionalization, such as Peru and Jordan.

Similarly, early state institutionalization does not entail social order or the absence of political protest and the occurrence of political violence. Table 4.14 maps the existence of political protest phenomena per 1000 population.

Table 4.14 Protest scores 1980–9, 1991–3

	1980–9	1991–3
OECD countries	0.68 ($n = 24$)	0.10 ($n = 24$)
Latin America	2.34 ($n = 22$)	0.89 ($n = 22$)
Africa	0.46 ($n = 41$)	0.34 ($n = 42$)
Asia	1.08 ($n = 31$)	0.25 ($n = 30$)
Post-communist	1.25 ($n = 8$)	0.51 ($n = 26$)
Mean	1.03 ($n = 126$)	0.38 ($n = 144$)
Eta-squared	0.11	0.08

Source: Banks (1994).

It appears that political protest occurred more often in the 1980s than in the early 1990s. Protest phenomena like strikes and popular demonstrations are very country-specific phenomena, reflecting political instability. This can be seen from the country scores in Table 4.15.

When one talks about protest as a country characteristic, one can refer to a few countries that are highly politically unstable: Central America, West Africa, the Middle East and the former Soviet Central Asia. One cannot, however, draw the conclusion that the occurrence of political violence is the same thing as protest phenomena. Table 4.16 shows the country scores on political violence.

One notes the same trend in these data, i.e. the level of political violence is low in the early 1990s compared with the 1980s. Table 4.17 shows the individual country scores for violence phenomena per 1000 population.

Table 4.15 Protest 1991–3

OECD		Latin America		Africa		Asia	
Australia	0.06	Argentina	0.06	Algeria	0.52	Afghanistan	0.00
Austria	0.00	Bolivia	0.84	Angola	0.00	Bangladesh	0.06
Belgium	0.20	Brazil	0.01	Benin	0.43	China	0.00
Canada	0.00	Chile	0.00	Botswana	0.78	India	0.04
Denmark	0.39	Colombia	0.06	Burkina Faso	0.11	Indonesia	0.00
Finland	0.20	Costa Rica	1.67	Burundi	0.00	Iran	0.07
France	0.21	Cuba	0.00	Cameroon	0.52	Iraq	0.17
Germany	0.26	Dominican		Central African		Israel	2.17
Greece	0.30	Republic	1.40	Republic	0.00	Jordan	0.00
Iceland	0.00	Ecuador	0.78	Chad	0.00	Cambodia	0.00
Ireland	0.28	El Salvador	0.00	Congo	0.88	Korea, North	0.00
Italy	0.11	Guatemala	0.76	Côte d'Ivoire	0.25	Korea, South	0.61
Japan	0.01	Haiti	1.32	Egypt	0.11	Kuwait	0.94
Luxembourg	0.00	Honduras	0.85	Ethiopia	0.00	Laos	0.00

OECD (cont.)		Latin America (cont.)		Africa (cont.)		Asia (cont.)	
Netherlands	0.00	Jamaica	0.83	Gabon	0.93	Lebanon	1.82
New Zealand	0.00	Mexico	0.05	Ghana	0.00	Malaysia	0.00
Norway	0.00	Nicaragua	2.84	Guinea	0.35	Mongolia	0.00
Portugal	0.00	Panama	3.75	Kenya	0.38	Myanmar	0.02
Spain	0.13	Paraguay	0.00	Lesotho	0.00	Nepal	0.77
Sweden	0.00	Peru	0.00	Liberia	0.00	Oman	0.00
Switzerland	0.15	Trinidad	0.81	Libya	0.00	Pakistan	0.03
Turkey	0.00	Uruguay	0.97	Madagascar	1.00	Papua New	
United		Venezuela	0.57	Malawi	0.32	Guinea	0.52
Kingdom	0.12			Mali	0.62	Philippines	0.00
United States	0.04			Mauritania	0.00	Saudi Arabia	0.00
				Mauritius	0.93	Singapore	0.00
				Morocco	0.08	Sri Lanka	0.06

Post-communist

				Africa (cont.)		Asia (cont.)	
Albania	5.22	Latvia	0.00	Mozambique	0.00	Syria	0.00
Armenia	0.90	Lithuania	0.00	Namibia	0.00	Thailand	0.11
Azerbaijan	0.98	Macedonia	0.49	Niger	0.13	United Arab	
Belarus	0.00	Moldova	0.46	Nigeria	0.15	Emirates	0.00
Bosnia	0.00	Poland	0.03	Rwanda	0.29	Vietnam	0.02
Bulgaria	0.22	Romania	0.39	Senegal	0.00		
Croatia	0.21	Russia	0.13	Sierra Leone	0.00		
Czechoslovak.	0.19	Slovenia	0.00	Somalia	0.59		
Estonia	0.00	Tajikistan	1.70	South Africa	0.76		
Georgia	0.18	Turkmenistan	0.00	Sudan	0.00		
Hungary	0.10	Ukraine	0.04	Tanzania	0.00		
Kazakhstan	0.06	Uzbekistan	0.19	Togo	3.44		
Kyrgyzstan	0.00	Yugoslavia	1.80	Tunisia	0.00		
				Uganda	0.00		
				Zaire	0.44		
				Zambia	0.12		

Source: Banks (1994).

Table 4.16 Violence scores 1980–9, 1991–3

	1980–9	1991–3
OECD countries	0.07 ($n = 24$)	0.04 ($n = 24$)
Latin America	1.3 ($n = 22$)	0.60 ($n = 22$)
Africa	0.53 ($n = 41$)	0.28 ($n = 42$)
Asia	0.71 ($n = 31$)	0.26 ($n = 30$)
Post-communist	0.05 ($n = 8$)	0.19 ($n = 26$)
Mean	0.59 ($n = 126$)	0.27 ($n = 144$)
Eta-squared	0.06	0.09

Source: Banks (1994).

Table 4.17 Violence 1991–3

OECD		Latin America		Africa		Asia	
Australia	0.00	Argentina	0.00	Algeria	0.20	Afghanistan	0.59
Austria	0.13	Bolivia	0.42	Angola	0.30	Bangladesh	0.00
Belgium	0.10	Brazil	0.03	Benin	0.00	China	0.00
Canada	0.00	Chile	0.23	Botswana	0.00	India	0.02
Denmark	0.00	Colombia	0.19	Burkina Faso	0.22	Indonesia	0.01
Finland	0.00	Costa Rica	0.00	Burundi	0.76	Iran	0.00
France	0.05	Cuba	0.00	Cameroon	0.00	Iraq	0.51
Germany	0.01	Dominican		Central		Israel	0.65
Greece	0.30	Republic	0.00	African		Jordan	0.00
Iceland	0.00	Ecuador	0.00	Republic	0.00	Cambodia	0.35
Ireland	0.00	El Salvador	2.71	Chad	0.34	Korea, North	0.00
Italy	0.07	Guatemala	1.52	Congo	0.88	Korea, South	0.00
Japan	0.00	Haiti	1.32	Côte d'Ivoire	0.00	Kuwait	0.47
Luxembourg	0.00	Honduras	2.56	Egypt	0.13	Laos	0.00
Netherlands	0.00	Jamaica	0.00	Ethiopia	0.06	Lebanon	2.92
New Zealand	0.00	Mexico	0.04	Gabon	0.93	Malaysia	0.00
Norway	0.00	Nicaragua	1.29	Ghana	0.00	Mongolia	0.00
Portugal	0.00	Panama	1.67	Guinea	0.00	Myanmar	0.14
Spain	0.05	Paraguay	0.23	Kenya	0.00	Nepal	0.00
Sweden	0.00	Peru	0.46	Lesotho	0.00	Oman	0.00
Switzerland	0.00	Trinidad	0.00	Liberia	2.54	Pakistan	0.02
Turkey	0.11	Uruguay	0.32	Libya	0.22	Papua New	
United		Venezuela	0.26	Madagascar	0.17	Guinea	1.29
Kingdom	0.10			Malawi	0.00	Philippines	0.13
United States	0.00			Mali	0.12	Saudi Arabia	0.00
				Mauritania	0.00	Singapore	0.00
				Mauritius	0.00	Sri Lanka	0.71
				Morocco	0.16	Syria	0.00
		Post-communist		Mozambique	0.21	Thailand	0.02
				Namibia	0.00	United Arab	
Albania	0.00	Latvia	0.00	Niger	0.26	Emirates	0.00
Armenia	0.60	Lithuania	0.00	Nigeria	0.01	Vietnam	0.00
Azerbaijan	0.42	Macedonia	0.00	Rwanda	0.72		
Belarus	0.00	Moldova	0.46	Senegal	0.00		
Bosnia	0.46	Poland	0.03	Sierra Leone	0.24		
Bulgaria	0.00	Romania	0.00	Somalia	1.33		
Croatia	0.42	Russia	0.00	South Africa	0.13		
Czechoslovak.	0.00	Slovenia	0.00	Sudan	0.25		
Estonia	0.00	Tajikistan	1.13	Tanzania	0.00		
Georgia	1.10	Turkmenistan	0.00	Togo	1.43		
Hungary	0.00	Ukraine	0.00	Tunisia	0.00		
Kazakhstan	0.00	Uzbekistan	0.00	Uganda	0.06		
Kyrgyzstan	0.00	Yugoslavia	0.28	Zaire	0.08		
				Zambia	0.00		

Source: Banks (1994).

Countries characterized by civil war or the collapse of civil society score high on this indicator: Rwanda, Burundi, Somalia, Togo, Liberia, Sri Lanka, Central America, Lebanon, Papua New Guinea, Tajikistan and Georgia.

The hypothesis that political instability is a typical concomitant event to political change follows from the interpretation of development as crisis-conducive processes. However, the overall finding is that the variation in the two main expressions of political instability does not follow the variation in the other aspects of political development.

Conclusion

The theme of political development aroused interest in the late 1950s among political scientists who were moving away from a particularistic concern with occidental political systems on the basis of a mainly legalistic approach. The new theme soon generated a vast literature. There were so many attempts at interpreting desirable political change stemming from the grand socio-economic transition from agraria to industria (Riggs, 1964), and the variety of theoretical models shifted so much, that a final statement fitting all the hypotheses into the theory of political development was needed (Pye, 1987). It would have given to political science what economic growth theory gave to economics. We all know that this did not happen. The theme fell apart, rejected as methodologically flawed owing to its unrecognized Western value biases (Leftwich, 1990).

However, whatever the scientific value of the set of theories of political development may be, it is impossible to disregard vital phenomena of political change. A fresh start may be made where the elusive concept of political development is left off. When the crucial part played by so-called value premises (Weber, 1949; Myrdal, 1970) is recognized, the political development concept may be unpacked into manageable dimensions. Explicit multidimensionality is substituted for implicit ambiguity. The derivation of different aspects of political development may be substantiated by the interpretation of data for a selection of countries of the world, thus validating the theoretical distinctions that are derived.

The various aspects of political development do not hang together. At present, the use of clear-cut indices for six dimensions of political development does discriminate between categories of countries as well as between countries within the sets of OECD, Central and South American, African and Asian, and post-communist countries. Table 4.18 confirms the result from Table 4.5, namely that the six dimensions are independent of each other when recent data for the 1980s and 1990s are utilized.

Whether each and any of these dimensions constitutes political development in a real sense is a question to be resolved by semantic argument. But having recourse to some measurable aspects of political development is a necessary condition for moving ahead to analyse the causes and effects of political development. Let us proceed to an analysis of the social and economic sources of one prominent type of political development: democratization. We will come back to institutionalization in Chapter 8. How valid is the hypothesis that there is a connection between economic development and democracy?

Table 4.18 Correlation matrix of political development dimensions

	Humana			GGEXP	MIL	SCLER	PRO8	PRO0	VIO8	VIO0
	1983	1986	1991							
Humana 1983	1.00	0.94	0.70	0.53	−0.56	−0.46	0.00	0.11	−0.09	0.18
Humana 1986		1.00	0.78	0.50	−0.52	−0.50	0.06	0.14	−0.18	−0.09
Humana 1991			1.00	0.66	−0.50	−0.64	0.18	0.12	−0.12	−0.10
GGEXP				1.00	−0.05	−0.48	0.04	−0.10	−0.19	−0.22
MIL					1.00	0.24	−0.04	−0.10	0.04	−0.01
SCLER						1.00	−0.10	0.08	0.11	0.09
PRO8							1.00	0.41	0.29	0.34
PRO0								1.00	0.10	0.37
VIO8									1.00	0.70
VIO0										1.00

Note: *n* varies from 71 to 144 depending upon which variable is referred to; Humana 1983, 1986, 1991 = Humana's indices of democracy; GGEXP = general government expenditure/GDP; MIL = military expenditure/GDP; SCLER = institutional sclerosis or starting-point in time of modernized leadership; PRO8, PRO0 = protest scores 1980–9, 1991–3; VIO8, VIO0 = violence scores 1980–9, 1991–3.

5 Democracy and socio-economic development: the Lipset model

Introduction

In the literature on political development, democracy has been one of the key connotations. A democratic regime has an intrinsic value in itself, because its political norms cherish the active participation of the people in government. Moreover, democratic states meet certain criteria of political decency, such as the institutionalization of human rights, considered to be intrinsically valuable in international law as well as in a number of constitutions.

In the 1990s democracy is widely recognized as the best political regime yet invented, because its citizens are treated with respect or dignity and have some say in political decision-making. But we must also consider the extrinsic value of democratic rule. Do democracies in the long run tend to deliver other favourable outcomes, e.g. presenting their citizens with a high level of social and economic development? If this is not the case, people could start searching for other types of regime which could lead to a higher level of affluence or sustained economic growth over a longer time period.

In this chapter we wish to enter the discussion of the second part of the argument favouring democratic regime, the extrinsic merits of democracy. Is it true that democracies generally deliver better outcomes than other kinds of political system? Is social or economic development more favourable in democracies than in non-democracies?

It is not enough merely to look at the overall performance of democratic states. One must also try to pin down the causal link between democracy and development, if indeed there is such a connection. The occurrence of a democratic regime in an affluent society could be accidental, or it could result from the impact of socio-economic development upon democracy. Is income equality higher in democratic countries than in authoritarian regimes and, if so, why?

The discourse

One may identify different approaches focusing on the relation between democracy and development. One tradition starts with the concept of democracy, asking first how to measure democracy and then ranking regimes as more or less democratic, in order to look finally at what consequences democracy may have for development. This position has been taken by political scientists or sociologists (Bollen, 1980; Bollen and Jackman, 1985, 1989; Muller, 1988). Another tradition looks at a variety of factors which may have an impact on development, among which institutional factors in politics are included. Here we mostly find economists or political economists (Scully, 1988, 1992; Pourgerami, 1988; Grier and Tullock, 1989).

Starting from the recognition of a factual association between levels of affluence and degrees of democracy, the problem was defined as to how to interpret such an empirically given relationship. Development as conducive to democracy was the classical argument put forward by Seymour Martin Lipset (1959; see also Rueschemeyer et al., 1992; Diamond, 1992; Lipset et al., 1993; Lipset, 1994). 'Development' here usually means the level of affluence, as measured, for instance, in terms of GNP per capita. A high level of affluence would enhance democratic institutions by creating a broad middle class with cross-cutting cleavages, thus tempering conflicts and enhancing the practical politics of bargaining. However, nothing excluded the contrary hypothesis that democracy could foster economic development. Still another possible interpretation was that democracy and affluence could accompany each other or interact, reinforcing each other reciprocally.

What is at stake here is the precise question about politico-economic causality; that is, whether democracy is conducive or not to social and economic development (Pourgerami, 1988; Sirowy and Inkeles, 1990). We will test a number of models that claim that democracy has direct consequences for socio-economic development. 'Development' is a general concept that stands for various things, such as economic growth and level of affluence or even social development as measured by a complex set of indicators. We are particularly interested in any evidence that supports the hypothesis that the direction of causality is from democracy to development, and not the other way around.

In the social science debate about democracy and development one finds three different arguments about their relationship (Sirowy and Inkeles, 1990). Let us look at three sets of relevant models that advance such theoretical arguments. After that we will look more closely at the measurement of the key concepts: economic growth, affluence, quality of life or human development, income inequality and democracy.

Conflict models

One set of arguments states that democracy is not conducive to development, interpreted as either economic growth or improvements in quality of life. This position not only claims that democracy has no positive impact upon development, but in addition states that democracy has a negative impact upon socio-economic development. It seems to receive considerable support from developments in South-East and East Asia, where rapid economic development has taken place within three more or less authoritarian regimes, in South Korea, Taiwan and Singapore. There are two versions of this negative argument.

First, it is underlined that democracies have a lot of dysfunctions, in particular new democracies. They face problems in establishing stable government that may pursue effective and consistent policies. In particular, political instability can hamper economic and social development in the new democracies in the Third World (Myrdal, 1957, 1968).

Second, there is another argument, relevant for older democracies, that takes as its starting point the need for governments in countries with a democractic regime to win support from a majority of the voters. In order to secure such popularity they must respond with policies that meet demands for more welfare spending in the form of transfer payments that are not conducive to economic growth. Democracies harbour strongly organized groups which tend to take care of their own special interests at the expense of the general interests of the nation or public interests such as economic growth (Olson, 1982). The stronger the positions of the organized interest groups, the less favourable are the conditions for economic development (Olson, 1990).

The different conflict models argue that democratic regimes are forced to focus almost exclusively on questions of redistribution at the expense of matters related to investments and capital accumulation. Democracy is based on pork-barrel 'politicking', resulting in myopic policies that reduce overall effectiveness in the economy. Democracies tend to favour equality over efficiency in the trade-off between public spending which enhances growth and policies with redistributive aims. An empirical test supporting the conflict model is provided by Weede, who concludes: 'The overall effect of political democracy on economic growth is negative, but rather weak' (Weede, 1983: 35).

Compatibility models

The compatibility models put forward two kinds of argument for the hypothesis that democracy is conducive to development, or, in a softer version, that democracy at least does not decrease affluence or economic growth. On the one hand, it is stressed that a market economy, involving special institutions, tends to go hand in hand with institutions that safeguard civil and political rights, i.e. with political democracy (Olson, 1993). If a market economy is expected to operate well, then it requires the kind of social institutions that tend to be available only in democracies. If democracy is a precondition for a functioning market economy, then it may also be conducive to development in the form of economic growth.

Thus, democracy indirectly promotes economic development, because it strengthens the market economy, which tends to outperform other economic systems, such as the planned economy, on development criteria such as growth, quality of life or level of human development (Vorhies and Glahe, 1988; Scully and Slottje, 1991; Spindler, 1991).

On the other hand, one finds an argument that starts from the tendency of a democracy to rely on the cooperation of the people (Wittman, 1989). In order to achieve such broadly based cooperation among citizens, it is necessary to develop social conditions that meet the needs of the population. This would imply that social inequalities tend to be less pronounced in societies with a democratic regime.

In the long run, democracies enhance economic development and promote social equality, since they act to foster a community of well educated citizens, who in turn produce highly qualified industrial outputs, further strengthening both cooperation and growth. A study supporting this version of the compatibility model is to be found in the *World Development Report* of 1991: 'The results of regression analysis do not go as far as to suggest that liberties contribute positively to income growth, but they imply that they do not hold growth back' (World Bank, 1991a: 50; see also Bhalla, 1994).

Sceptical models

The sceptical argument admits that it may well be the case that democracy and development could go together in the long run, but it stresses that democracy in itself has little direct impact upon development. It stresses that there are many intervening factors that may have an impact upon the interaction between these two entities. This sceptical view is strengthened by the fact that several emipirical studies on the relationships between democracy and development are inconclusive, some of them supporting the conflict model while others support the compatibility model (Przeworski, 1992).

This sceptical standpoint is to be found in many studies (Sørensen, 1992). For example, Barsh concludes an article as follows: 'Democracy does not appear to "cause" growth, but economic differentiation certainly creates demands for democratic participation, which governments must then meet in the interests of further economic growth and political stability. Democracy is neither a "quick fix" for development problems, nor a substitute for resources. Over the long run, however, democracy and development can become reinforcing' (Barsh, 1992: 133). The same conclusion is to be found in Levine and Renelt, who state: 'We find that indexes of revolutions and coups (REVC) and civil liberties (CIVL) are not robustly correlated with GYP (i.e. average annual growth rate of GDP per capita)' (Levine and Renelt, 1992: 957). In a recent article, Przeworski and Limongi (1993: 64) say that we simply do not know 'whether democracy fosters or hinders economic growth'. A similar message is launched by Weede (1993), Helliwell (1994) and Burkhart and Lewis-Beck (1994).

We will evaluate the evidence for these three models in this chapter. The conflict model argues that democracy and development tend to clash; the compatibility model states that democracy may enhance social and economic development; and finally the sceptical model hints that democracy and development may accompany each other, but that it is hardly the case that democracy is a major cause of socio-economic development, at least not in the short run. First, we introduce our empirical tools; second, we test a number of models related to the three arguments rendered above.

Method and data

In order to be able to elaborate more on the relationship between democracy and development, we will rely on a data set covering states with a population of more than one million in 1990. This means that we cover some 130 states; in some instances we will also look at the new states created after 1990, but our analysis will mainly focus on the period prior to 1990.

The states included may be divided into different groups and our choice is the following five groups: (a) OECD plus Israel, (b) former socialist states, (c) the Americas, (d) Africa and (e) Asia. The rationale for this classification is that we wish to inquire into the stability of estimates over various parts of the world, divided into sets of states.

The same rationale explains our choice of different time periods. Our main analysis will focus on relationships during the 1980s, but in order to test for the stability over time of our estimates, we will also cover time periods from the early 1950s onwards.

As a starting point for our analysis we will rely on correlation analyses and regression analyses using OLS (ordinary least-squares regression) estimates; in order to test for the robustness of the estimates made they will be applied to various measures for different periods of time. Thus, in our analysis, we try to enquire into the stability and robustness of estimated relations between democracy and development that take into account possible variations in space and in time. Our choice of variables and indicators included in the analyses is presented in the following sections.

Democracy

The term 'democracy' may be defined in various ways. One may stress political democracy, economic democracy or social democracy. In our context, we focus on what is most commonly labelled 'political democracy', which implies the existence of extensive political rights and civil liberties, as suggested by Dahl in his discussion of polyarchy (Dahl, 1971; Bollen, 1990). Although there is some consensus on what this interpretation implies with regard to the referents of the concept, i.e. the countries that are to be designated as 'democracies', there remain issues where opinions differ, e.g. what the concept implies outside of the political sphere.

When one is mapping democracy in the present world, one crucial issue is to decide whether it is possible to characterize democracy in terms of properties that are categorical or continuous. One line of argument is that democracy is an inherently categorical variable: it is only meaningful to distinguish between democracies and non-democracies. Democracy in this sense is indivisible; a state is either democratic or non-democratic. There may also be something called a 'semi-democracy' (Huntington, 1991: 11).

The other line states that it is meaningful to distinguish between states that are more or less democratic, meaning thus that democracy is a measurable property (Bollen, 1981, 1990; Bollen and Jackman, 1989). Following this idea, a series of indicators on democracy or proxies for democracy have been constructed, from Lerner (1958) and Lipset (1959) to Bollen (1980) and Humana (1992).

We adhere to the latter standpoint, arguing for the utility of constructing continuous measures of democracy, which make it possible to map the variation in democracy between nations, in space as well as time. This does not mean that it is an easy task; some may even argue that it is more or less impossible, since such indicators tend to be inherently culturally biased towards the Western political culture (Barsh, 1993). Even though it is problematic to use such measures, we find that they allow for a much more systematic analysis of problems related to democracy that are highly relevant today.

We focus explicitly on indicators of political democracy that try to capture the extent of political rights and civil liberties available to the citizens of a given polity. This means that we reject the inclusion of measures referring to economic democracy or economic freedom (Spindler, 1991). At a conceptual level, political democracy must be distinguished from economic democracy or economic freedom, although empirically there may be interrelations between indicators of these concepts.

Measures of democracy

There are now a lot of measures available on democracy, human rights or similar concepts (Bollen, 1986). The first systematic attempt at measuring democracy was made by Bollen (1979, 1980), constructing widely used scores for the years 1960 and 1965. He was preceded by others: Cutright (1963), Neubauer (1967), Adelman and Morris (1967), Smith (1969) and Jackman (1975). Gastil and Freedom House have worked on such measures from 1973 and other attempts in this direction have been reported by Perry (1980), Humana (1983, 1986, 1992), Pourgerami (1988), Coppedge and Reinecke (1990), Gurr (1990), Vanhanen (1990, 1992), Arat (1991) and Hadenius (1992). Most of the measures cited are only available for one or two different periods of time, but there are two exceptions: Gurr (1990) and the Gastil/Freedom House contribution.

The time period covered by Gurr is considerable, since it starts with 1800 and ends with 1986. Gurr employs two indicators that are relevant for measuring democracy, namely AUTOC (institutionalized autocracy) and DEMOC (institutionalized democracy). These two indicators covary, yet they are not identical, which means that combining the two indicators (DEMOC minus AUTOC) results in a measure that allows for more variation in the low range as well as the high range of democracy; this new measure has then been normalized, meaning that a highly democratic regime has a score of 10 and a highly non-democratic regime has a score of 0.

The indexes constructed by Gastil and Freedom House cover the period from 1973 up to the present, and they give yearly scores for two indexes, one for political rights and one for civil liberties. Analyses of these indexes have proved that they are highly correlated; therefore one of them may be said to be redundant (Banks, 1989). This fact makes it reasonable to add the two scores and combine them to one democracy score, since the two main components of political democracy are political rights and civil liberties. This new democracy measure has been arrived at through adding the scores, and normalizing the democracy scores so that a highly democratic regime scores 10 and a highly non-democratic regime scores 0.

Thus, we have access to different sets of measures for democracies; Gurr and Gastil/Freedom House cover longer periods, while others (Bollen, Perry, Vanhanen, Coppedge and Reinecke, Hadenius) cover only short time periods. The next step is to test the reliability of these indexes by means of a series of correlation analyses. Do they roughly measure similar phenomena that might be called 'democracy', or the extent of democracy?

Correlating indexes of democracy

The most useful indexes are the Gurr and Gastil/Freedom House measures, because together they cover the post-war period to now. How well do they match other indexes? And how well do they covary themselves? In order to clarify this, a set of correlations are explored. First, there are tests for different periods of time from 1960 up to 1990. The Gurr measures and the Gastil/Freedom House measures are correlated with the measures constructed by Bollen, Perry, Vanhanen, Coppedge and Reinecke, and Hadenius, as well as with each other. Second, these correlations are tested for the five subsets of nations outlined earlier. Is there an internal consistency between the different measures when applied to the same periods of time and tested on the total set and the various subsets?

Looking at the total set, the correlations are generally high enough to warrant the finding that these indicators measure similar phenomena. It is important to note that the Gurr index correlates quite well with the Bollen index for both 1960 and 1965; Gurr's index also correlates highly with the Coppedge and Reinecke index for 1985; the Gastil/Freedom House index covaries highly with the Hadenius index for 1988; the correlations with the Perry index and the Vanhanen index are somewhat lower, but still acceptable. The Gurr index and the Gastil/Freedom House index also coincide strongly for the years 1975, 1980 and 1985, with a lowest correlation coefficient of 0.87.

The overall finding is the same if one looks into the five subsets, but there are some exceptions. The African political systems are not as easy to classify as the systems on other continents. This also applies to the socialist political systems. To sum up, it seems reasonable to conclude that the Gurr index and the Gastil/Freedom House index measure similar phenomena that we can interpret as democracy. These indexes seem to be reliable in terms of different time periods as well as in terms of different subsets. Consequently, these two indexes will be used as our indicators to measure the degree of democracy in the post-war world.

Variation in democracy in time and space

Using these two democracy indexes, it is now possible to present an overview of the variation in democracy in time and in space. Let us first look at the scores for the two indexes over time and variations for the different subsets. These data are reported in Table 5.1.

The scores for the two indexes differ somewhat, depending on the number of countries included and the particular time point looked at. However, the rankings of the subsets are similar, and very stable. The OECD countries come out first, followed by the Americas, Asia, Africa and the socialist states. This pattern holds true for all periods of time except the first (1950) and the last (1992), where the socialist subset has risen from last position to third position. This is also the case when one looks at development over time. Democracy has been on the rise from the mid-1970s to now, whereas it went down from a higher level in 1950 to the lowest level in 1975. This pattern differs from one subset to another. That this is the case is also apparent from a correlation analysis where developments over time are estimated.

In general, the correlation coefficients for the total set are high, from lowest 0.68 (GU50–GU80, GU50–GU85 and DEM75–DEM92) to highest 0.97 (DEM85–DEM88) and 0.92 (GU80–GU85). The larger the time interval covered, the lower the coefficients owing to changes taking place between. The rise of the Castro regime as well as the transition process following 1989 is evident when one looks at the socialist subset. In a similar manner the transition from authoritarian regimes to democratic regimes in the Mediterranean in the mid-1970s is displayed in the OECD subset.

So far we have mapped one crucial independent variable: democracy. The next step is devoted to the analysis of the dependent variable: development.

Table 5.1 Democracy scores

Index	n	Total	Africa	Americas	Asia	Socialist	OECD	Eta²
GU50	82	5.21	4.75	4.18	4.26	2.04	8.85	0.50
GU60	101	5.08	3.63	5.48	4.12	2.04	8.78	0.40
GU70	124	4.55	3.00	5.29	4.04	1.73	8.76	0.41
GU80	128	4.66	3.00	5.55	3.81	1.92	9.50	0.50
GU85	128	4.86	2.89	6.64	3.84	1.88	9.76	0.61
DEM80	129	4.21	2.46	5.48	3.17	1.15	9.35	0.64
DEM85	129	4.27	2.12	6.51	3.17	1.03	9.42	0.69
DEM88	129	4.48	2.26	6.79	3.47	1.35	9.53	0.69
DEM92	128	5.26	3.47	6.75	3.56	4.93	9.57	0.50

Note: The set of socialist countries covers the former communist states before and after the 1989 regime transformations. GU = Gurr's index; DEM = Gastil/Freedom House index; 50, 60 and so on refer to estimates for 1950, 1960 and so on. The indices are normalized: 0 (minimum) means non-democracy and 10 (maximum) stands for democracy.

Development

The concept of development can be given various meanings. It is relevant to distinguish between development as a process (rate of change) and development as a condition (or level) (Riggs, 1984: 133). When democracy is considered a cause or partially a cause of development, then the way in which the concept is being used must be clarified. Development either describes some rate of change, like economic growth, or stands for a general level of socio-economic welfare or social equality. Both interpretations require the construction of indices that measure economic growth, quality of life and income inequality. Let us look into these two meanings of 'development': process versus condition.

Development as economic growth

Within mainstream economics, development stands for economic growth, i.e. growth in output as indicated by standard measures like GNP/GDP, often expressed on a per capita basis. As these measures can cover longer or shorter time periods, we rely on two different sets of data in order to map economic growth. One set refers to estimates of average annual growth rate of GDP per capita in various editions of the *World Development Report* covering the periods 1950–60, 1960–70, 1970–81 and 1965–89 (World Bank, 1983, 1991a).

The other set refers to estimates constructed from Summer and Heston's data bank, covering roughly the same periods of time from 1950 to 1985 (Summers and Heston, 1988). Growth rates are computed for the relevant time period and averaged by the number of years included. This data set is preferred to the later 1991 data set, because it includes estimates for the former communist states. The data refer to growth per capita and the time periods covered include three short-term periods (1950–60, 1960–70 and 1970–80) and one long-term period (1960–85).

In order to test the reliability of these measures, a new set of correlation analyses has been devised. These correlations refer to four different time periods and two sets of economic growth data.

These two measures of economic growth do covary, although there is a distinct difference between the period 1950–60, with $r = 0.90$, and the periods 1965–89 and 1960–85, with $r = 0.76$. This also holds true for the subsets, but there are instances where the reliability is low, as within the OECD subset for the periods 1965–89 and 1960–85. The discrepancies may be explained by differences in the measurement procedure and the time periods covered. These differences are also displayed when the records of economic growth for the various time periods and the different sets of nations are mapped.

Table 5.2 Economic growth rates (percentages)

Time	n	Total	Africa	Americas	Asia	Socialist	OECD	Eta^2
EG50/60	81	2.30	1.51	2.08	2.39	4.40	3.33	0.11
EG60/70	103	2.80	1.83	2.41	3.13	5.23	4.34	0.29
EG70/81	114	1.80	0.58	1.95	2.92	4.43	2.34	0.13
EG65/89	97	1.62	0.86	1.01	2.43	4.45	2.60	0.17
G50/60	64	3.60	1.17	2.39	4.15	5.98	4.30	0.29
G60/70	112	3.65	2.48	3.33	3.97	4.55	5.36	0.14
G70/80	116	2.72	1.43	2.58	4.26	3.80	3.26	0.11
G60/85	111	3.40	2.08	2.08	5.24	5.02	4.81	0.13

Note: Growth rates refer to per capita growth; G = Summers and Heston's series; EG = World Bank series of yearly growth rates reported in *World Development Report*; 50/60, 60/70, etc. = growth rates for 1950–60, 1960–70, etc.; n = number of countries included in the calculation of average growth rates for the various subsets.

The figures based on the *World Development Report* exhibit in general lower estimates than the figures based on Summers and Heston (1988) – see Table 5.2. The growth figures for the socialist states reported are high, probably too high. Excluding these states, the pattern is fairly clear. In the 1950s and the 1960s the OECD countries in general, and Japan in particular, experienced the highest economic growth, while other Asian states took the lead during the 1970s and 1980s. The African states had the lowest growth rates, while the Americas come somewhere in between.

The pattern of economic growth over time is not stable. The 1950s come close to the 1960s but the 1970s differ from the 1960s, and growth in the 1950s has no implications for growth between 1960 and 1985, while this long-term growth goes hand in hand with growth in the 1960s and the 1970s. The conclusion that might be drawn from these findings is that high economic growth during one period of time does not imply a high growth rate during another period.

Development as human development

One criticism forwarded against the interpretation of development as economic growth is that it only captures an economic dimension. Development is something else or something more complex that ought to be related to the quality of life of mankind (Doyal and Gough, 1991; Inkeles, 1993). As a response to this criticism, a lot of indexes have been constructed that try to cover these complex aspects of human development and human well-being.

One of the innovators of this field is Morris (1979), who invented a Physical Quality of Life (PQL) index that took account of life expectancy and infant mortality. Since 1990 the United Nations Development Programme has presented a Human Development Index (HDI) that combines an adjusted GDP/capita estimate, life expectancy, infant mortality and level of literacy. Slottje (1991) and Slottje et al. (1991) have constructed rankings of indexes of quality of life that capture a wide range of indicators, from socio-economic ones to political ones. The problem with these rankings is that they often come to highly counter-intuitive conclusions. Although there are a lot of other indexes suggested in the literature (DasGupta and Weale, 1992; Lind, 1993), we will rely on PQL and HDI as measures of human development.

It is evident that these indexes measure similar phenomena. Although they cover various periods of time, they do covary to a very high degree. This is also true if one looks into the five subsets, even though the covariation is somewhat lower for Africa, Asia and the socialist subsets. The level of human development differs quite sharply between the five subsets. As may be expected, the highest level is to be found in the OECD subset, while the socialist states rank second, although a decrease is noticeable there in the 1990 scores; among the other subsets America ranks third, Asia fourth and Africa last. This is detailed in Table 5.3.

Table 5.3 Human development scores

Index	n	Total	Africa	Americas	Asia	Socialist	OECD	Eta²
HDI70	107	0.485	0.211	0.600	0.385	0.812	0.823	0.79
PQL	125	57.8	31.0	68.8	50.8	86.5	91.4	0.74
HDI87	127	0.574	0.296	0.694	0.505	0.801	0.950	0.66
HDI90	125	0.553	0.284	0.667	0.495	0.737	0.941	0.66

Note: HDI = Human Development Index (UNDP, 1990, 1991, 1993); PQL = Physical Quality of Life (Morris, 1979); 70, 87, 90 = years 1970, 1987, 1990.

Development as income equality

Another aspect of development that has been related to democracy in many analyses is the degree of income equality within a society (Hewitt, 1977; Simpson, 1990). Low or moderate inequalities are associated with a higher level of development, while large inequalities go hand in hand with lower levels of development (Kuznets, 1955).

A lot of measures are available on income distribution. The data we rely on refer to total household income for various income groups (World Bank, 1991b). We mainly use estimates of the income share of the top 20 per cent of households, i.e. the larger the share of incomes of this group, the more unequal the income distribution tends to be. These distributions are reported for three different periods of time, roughly equal to 1960, 1970 and the late 1980s. In addition, two summary measures have been created in order to increase the number of cases, one for the top 10 per cent of households, and another for the top 20 per cent of households. As might be expected, these measures on income inequality covary to a rather high degree.

These measures do covary quite well for the whole set, indicating that they isolate a similar phenomenon. The low number of cases makes some of the correlations for the subsets irrelevant, but it is important to note that the two summary measures (TOP10 and TOP20) correlate well for the whole set as well as for all the subsets.

The pattern of income distribution disclosed in Table 5.4 indicates that the most even income distribution was found in the former communist states. Even though one may raise some question marks around this fact, there are reports that give this picture a certain plausibility (Alexeev and Gaddy, 1993). Disregarding the socialist states, it is evident that the OECD states reveal the most equal distribution, while inequalities seem be most pronounced in the Americas.

Table 5.4 Income inequality

Index	n	Total	Africa	Americas	Asia	Socialist	OECD	Eta^2
TOP2060	29	48.8	45.6	59.6	49.2	38.5	46.9	0.51
TOP2070	46	50.9	54.9	59.8	48.8	35.7	44.0	0.54
TOP2089	33	44.9	49.0	52.7	45.1	36.7	40.6	0.57
TOP10	48	29.8	32.1	36.8	32.5	22.3	24.9	0.53
TOP20	62	48.3	51.7	56.2	46.3	36.7	42.9	0.41

Note: TOP2060 = share of total income of the rich 20 per cent of the population around 1960; (World Bank, 1991b); TOP10 = share of total income of the rich 10 per cent of the population (World Bank, 1991b).

The data indicate that income inequalities have hardly changed over a period of roughly thirty years since the early 1960s. For Africa, the data indicate an increase in income inequality, which reflects the overall weak economic performance of this continent.

Democracy and development

Thus far, we have presented a few apparently reliable measures of democracy and such different aspects of development as economic growth, human development and income distribution. In order to be able to say something about which effect, if any, democracy has on development, we adopt the following path of analysis. First, we establish the bivariate or surface relations between these two phenomena, with no conclusion about the direction of the interaction; second, we try to model the deeper interaction between democracy and development, taking into account some of the factors generally suggested in the literature as relevant for explaining the variation in socio-economic development.

Democracy and development: the bivariate case

Speaking generally, one may argue that a simple model of a bivariate relation between two phenomena tends to be underspecified. Still, it is also the case that the bivariate relation disclosed tends to remain valid in other better specified models. To look at the bivariate relation is thus a relevant step in the inquiry into a causal relationship, if indeed one exists. The correlation analyses commented upon below will cover several periods of time and involve one total set of states and five subsets of states.

Democracy and economic growth

Two democracy indexes (Gurr, Gastil/Freedom House) will be relied upon, as well as two different estimates of economic growth (World Bank, Summers and Heston). A correlation analysis of the relation between these measures has been made.

Criteria for a robust relation between democracy and economic development would be that the different measures show significant relations for the whole set as well as for the different subsets. There is no instance where these criteria are met. However, it is evident that in the short-run periods, i.e. the 1950s, the 1960s and the 1970s the covariation is weak and most often not statistically significant for the whole set.

Significant and weakly positive relations are to be found only when looking at the long-run periods. In particular, this is true when the democracy scores are averaged for longer periods of time. This is, however, not the case when we go into the different subsets. Thus, one may conclude that this relation is not invariant over time or in space. Thus, looking only at the whole set of nations, one may conclude that there seems to be a positive but weak relation between democracy and economic development in the long run. The data so far support the argument that democracy has little impact upon economic growth.

Democracy and human development

The next step in the analysis of bivariate relations concerns another aspect of development that treats development as a more complex phenomenon, i.e. human development. A correlation analysis following the same outline as that in the preceeding analysis has been employed.

Whatever the democracy index used, the time period chosen and the subset of nation selected, there seems to be a stable positive relationship between democracy and human development. There are some deviations from this general pattern, such as the OECD nations in the early 1970s, the socialist states in the early 1980s and Asia in the 1980s. Still, one may conclude that there is a robust positive relationship between democracy and human development. The data support the compatibility argument.

Democracy and income distribution

The third aspect of development to be scrutinized is income distribution. One problem with the analysis of income distribution, neglecting for the moment the problems of measurement, is the lack of estimates for most nations of the world. This means that breaking down an analysis for the different subsets of nations is not always meaningful. A correlation matrix of the relation between democracy and measures on income distribution has to take into account that the low number of cases makes such an undertaking precarious. In most instances it is evident that no significant relations are available. One of the exceptions refers to the relation between the averaged democracy scores (GU, DEM) and the summarized measure of income of the top 20 per cent of households (TOP20), where for the whole set a significant negative relation is to be reported, while the African subset has another sign. Democracy seems to covary positively with an equal income distribution if one takes a long-run perspective; the data supporting the compatibility argument.

Modelling democracy and development

Moving from bivariate relationships to model estimations, it is important to specify models that satisfy reasonable demands for theoretical relevance. Let us first look at models relating democracy and economic development.

Models of democracy and economic development

When the sources of economic growth have been researched within a cross-sectional framework, a set of important factors having clear impact has been identified (Kormendi and Meguire, 1985; Barro, 1991; Levine and Renelt, 1992; Mankiew et al., 1992). The so-called convergence theme emphasizes the starting point or the initial per capita income, as countries with a low output at an early stage tend to catch up with rich countries, given the same growth potential as determined by access to human capital (enrolment in secondary schools), physical capital and technology. Other relevant economic factors include the size of the public sector, the growth of the working-age population and the openness of the economy or the economic system. Non-economic factors considered are cultural factors like religion, age of political regimes and the character of the political regime, such as the degree of democracy.

We try to estimate models relevant for explaining the variation in the long-term economic growth, i.e. for 1960–85 (G6085) and for 1965–89 (EG6589). Four measures are used to capture the impact of democracy on economic development: two average measures and two measures referring to the mid-1980s. Two of the models estimated are presented in Table 5.5.

Table 5.5 Two models to explain variation in long-term economic growth

	Model 1: growth 60–85 (G6085)			Model 2: growth 65–89 (EG6589)		
	B	t	Beta	B	t	Beta
AVEDEM	0.285	1.58	0.26	0.074	0.66	0.22
LNGNPC60	−6.098	−0.85	−1.63	−3.791	−0.85	−1.83
LNGNPC60sq	0.193	0.38	0.74	0.214	0.68	1.49
INVEST	0.214	3.67	0.47	0.128	3.48	0.51
SECSCO	0.421	2.80	0.41	0.085	0.88	0.15
OPEN80	−0.006	−0.56	−0.06	0.003	0.48	0.06
ECOSYST	−0.496	−1.71	−0.16	−0.398	−2.14	−0.23
CORE	0.627	0.64	0.13	−0.663	−1.10	−0.25
PROT	−1.590	−1.09	−0.12	−1.740	−1.94	−0.23
SCLER	−0.007	−0.78	−0.12	−0.009	−1.58	−0.29
CONSTANT	42.304	1.35		32.081	1.59	
R2a		0.36 (n = 91)			0.25 (n = 86)	

Note: We have included potentially relevant explanatory variables in the model (the original model). Another model (the modified model) has been estimated that includes the democracy index together with those variables that meet the criteria of statistical significance at a reasonable level, i.e. the t-statistics should roughly be ±2 or larger. This adds up to a total of sixteen models estimated, since they are applied to two measures of economic growth and four measures of democracy; only two of them are reported in detail here.

Sources: AVEDEM = average of democracy scores 1973–88 (Gastil/Freedom House); LNGNPC60 = the logarithm for GNP per capita in international US dollars 1960 (Summers and Heston, 1988); LNGNPC60sq = the square of the logarithm for GNP per capita in international US dollars 1960; INVEST = investments as a percentage of GDP on an average 1960–85 (Mankiew *et al.*, 1992); SECSCO = share of working-age population in secondary school on an average 1960–85 (Mankiew *et al.*, 1992); OPEN80 = import and export as a percentage of GDP in 1980 (Summers and Heston, 1988); ECOSYST = type of economic system, ranging from free market to planned economy (Gastil, 1987); CORE = position in the world economy (Terlouw, 1989); PROT = percentage of the population with Protestant creed (Barrett, 1982); SCLER = consolidation of modernized leadership (Black, 1966).

It is striking that economic factors like investment in physical capital and access to human capital have a positive impact on economic development. Economic growth is also negatively related to the initial per capita income, as predicted by the convergence or maturity hypothesis. This is more or less the general pattern, but our interest is primarily focused on the impact of democracy. What is the finding with regard to this factor?

Among sixteen parameters estimated, four meet our criteria of statistical significance, while one comes very close. Among the other eleven, ten show the expected sign, but they are not significant, meaning that chance factors may have influenced the estimates. There are also differences depending upon choice of dependent variable, since in no instance is the variable EG6589 associated with a significant effect from the democracy variable. That is, the differences in estimates are primarily owing to the choice of the dependent variable and not caused by the choice of democracy measure. However, the conclusion one may draw from this is that there is no robust significant positive relationship between economic growth in the long run and the degree of democracy in a nation. To claim a robust relationship would imply significant estimates irrespective of the choice of the crucial dependent and independent variables.

The preceding analysis will now be applied to economic growth in the 1950s, the 1960s and the 1970s. Similar models will be tested, but somewhat modified owing to availability of relevant data. The purpose of the analysis is once again to inquire into the robustness of the impact of the democracy variable within various model specifications. In Table 5.6 only the estimates of the democratic variables are displayed.

Table 5.6 Regression models for economic growth 1950–80

	B	t	Beta	R2A	n
EG50–60					
(1) GU50	0.217	2.05	0.41	0.07	42
(2) GU50	0.206	2.05	0.38	0.13	42
G50-60					
(1) GU50	0.307	2.31	0.44	0.13	42
(2) GU50	0.293	2.31	0.42	0.18	42
EG60-70					
(1) GU60	−0.087	−1.07	−0.16	0.34	66
(2) GU60	−0.094	−1.18	−0.17	0.33	66
EG70-81					
(1) DEM75	0.106	0.89	0.14	0.13	95
(2) DEM75	0.148	1.30	0.19	0.14	95
G70-80					
(1) DEM75	0.106	0.69	0.11	0.12	95
(2) DEM75	0.107	0.69	0.11	0.13	95

Note: See Tables 5.1 and 5.2 for abbreviations. Original model (1), and modified model (2).

Three periods of time are selected with various specifications of the models: (1) the original model and (2) the modified model. Looking to the 1950s, one can establish that there is a robust positive relation between democracy and economic development. However, this is the only set of robust estimates arrived at. For the 1960s and 1970s there are no such significant relationships to report, and this is so irrespective of what measures are used for the independent or the dependent variables. Thus, only for the 1950s is it possible to say that the impact of democracy on economic development is positive. In most other instances there is no significant relationship between democracy and economic development.

The finding is that democracy has no stable impact upon economic development: it is neither negative nor positive for economic growth. Other factors are of much greater importance: investment in physical capital and access to human capital, on the one hand, and the starting point of economic development, on the other hand. Thus, we may also conclude that it is not the case that democracy is an obstacle to economic development.

Models of democracy and human development

If development is given a more complex meaning it might equal human development. According to the bivariate analyses reported on earlier, democracy seems to be positively related with human development. Is this also true when this relation is tested within the framework of different model specifications?

The general model attempted is roughly the same as the ones attempted in the analysis of economic growth, i.e. in addition to democracy measures the independent variables contain information on investment in human capital, level of economic development, economic system, openness of the economy and non-economic factors like strength of Protestantism and time of political modernization. Two measures of human development are used as the dependent

Table 5.7 Regression models for human development level

	B	t	Beta	R2A	n
HUMD90					
(1) AVEDEM	20.86	3.16	0.22	0.88	90
(2) AVEDEM	22.09	3.67	0.24	0.88	90
(1) AVEGU	16.30	3.20	0.18	0.88	90
(2) AVEGU	17.77	3.63	0.20	0.88	90
(1) DEM80	11.23	2.04	0.12	0.87	93
(2) DEM80	13.44	2.60	0.15	0.87	93
(1) GU80	10.18	2.32	0.12	0.87	93
(2) GU80	11.85	2.83	0.14	0.87	93
PQL					
(1) AVEDEM	3.13	5.65	0.37	0.89	90
(2) AVEDEM	3.19	6.15	0.38	0.89	90
(1) AVEGU	2.14	4.81	0.27	0.88	90
(2) AVEGU	2.16	5.08	0.27	0.88	90
(1) DEM80	1.79	3.71	0.27	0.88	93
(2) DEM80	1.92	4.25	0.24	0.87	93
(1) GU80	1.44	3.71	0.19	0.87	93
(2) GU80	1.46	3.98	0.20	0.87	93

Note: AVEDEM = the average score for the Gastil/Freedom House index measures 1973–88; AVEGU = the average score of the Gurr index measures 1973–86.

variables, i.e. the Human Development Index of 1990, and the Physical Quality of Life index of around 1980. Four measures of democracy are used, two average measures and two measures referring to 1980. The findings of these estimations with respect to the democracy measures are reported in Table 5.7.

Even when we take into account the effect of the level of initial economic development and access to human capital, there remains a stable positive relationship between democracy and human development. This holds true, independent of which human development measure is used or which democracy measure it is tested against. This seems to be a case of a robust positive relationship. Democracies are to be found in societies where the human development scores are high and vice versa. Which is cause and which is effect?

Models of democracy and income distribution

Our final indicator of development is income distribution. One may expect a negative relationship between democracy and our measures of income distribution: the more democracy, the more equal the distribution of income, i.e. the lower scores on our measures TOP10 and TOP20. The form of presentation of the analysis follows the same pattern as in the preceding analyses, i.e. only estimates for the democracy measures are reported in Table 5.8.

Table 5.8 Regression models for income inequality

	B	t	Beta	R2A	n
TOP10					
(1) AVEDEM	0.695	1.14	0.31	0.36	40
(2) AVEDEM	0.380	0.64	0.17	0.34	40
(1) AVEGU	0.351	0.68	0.13	0.34	40
(2) AVEGU	0.254	0.68	0.13	0.34	40
(1) DEM80	−0.194	−0.38	−0.09	0.34	41
(2) DEM80	−0.504	−1.05	−0.23	0.25	41
(1) GU80	0.079	0.22	0.04	0.26	41
(2) GU80	0.050	0.15	0.03	0.29	41
TOP20					
(1) AVEDEM	−0.24	−0.32	−0.08	0.32	53
(2) AVEDEM	−0.20	−0.29	−0.06	0.32	53
(1) AVEGU	−0.37	−0.77	−0.14	0.32	53
(2) AVEGU	−0.27	−0.61	−0.10	0.33	53
(1) DEM80	−0.24	−0.42	−0.08	0.29	54
(2) DEM80	−0.13	−0.24	−0.04	0.29	54
(1) GU80	−0.30	−0.73	−0.12	0.30	54
(2) GU80	−0.19	−0.48	−0.08	0.30	54

Note: Data used in this chapter were made available by the Inter-university Consortium for Political and Social Research. The data for Polity II: Political Structures and Regime Change, 1800–1986 were prepared by Ted Robert Gurr. Neither the collector nor the consortium bears any responsibility for the analysis presented here.

There are some differences between the two independent variables, the impact of democracy being positive on TOP10 and negative on TOP20. However, none of these estimates is significant. All the democracy measures meet with insignificant estimates, irrespective of what model specification is chosen. It is thus not possible to say that democracy is conducive to a more equal income distribution, but neither can one say that inequality is a consequence of democracy. The relations estimated simply say that democracy is more or less irrelevant for the kind of income distribution found in a society.

Conclusion: democracy and development

When inquiring into the relationship between democracy and development we have tried to use reliable measures on democracy and on development that are available for different periods of time after the Second World War. We have also identified three dimensions of development, namely economic development, human development and income distribution. The purpose of the inquiry is to evaluate whether democracy is conducive or not conducive to development. We are looking for a robust relationship, meaning a relationship that is stable over time and valid irrespective of reliable measures that are used.

The findings imply that the answer to the democracy–development causation problem depends upon what is meant by 'development'. There is only one robust relationship that we have been able to identify, and it concerns democracy and human development. The positive finding concerns the interaction between democracy and quality of life, which is stable over time and also independent of what measures we have relied upon.

The negative findings mean that it has not been possible to establish a stable relation between democracy and economic growth or between democracy and degree of income equality. For certain measures and for certain periods there is evidence for the existence of a positive relation between democracy and economic growth, but it is not stable. The same applies even more to evidence of an impact of democracy upon income distribution.

The first positive conclusion that we may draw is that democracy tends to go together with human development. Thus, democracy is strongly connected with human development. But it is premature to conclude that this is a one-way causal relationship, since we have not excluded the possibility that the level of human development may be conducive to democracy. The second positive conclusion is that democracy is not an obstacle to economic growth or a fair income distribution.

Part II

Development Strategies

6 Smith, Marx, List and Wagner

Introduction

A principal focus in political economy is the distinction between the public and the private sectors and its implications for the polity and the economy. This deals with how the state is involved in the economy of a society and what the short-term and long-term economic consequences of the size and structure of the public sector are (Palgrave, 1899: vol. III; Eatwell *et al.*, 1987a: vol. 3).

In this chapter we will introduce some basic concepts pertaining to the public–private sector distinction, by means of which one may identify the types of politico-economic regimes evaluated in Chapter 7. These terms refer to mechanisms for the allocation of resources, to the size and orientation of the public redistribution of income and wealth, and to structures of ownership of the means of production (Margolis and Guitton, 1969; Stiglitz, 1988).

The political economies of the countries of the world differ along these three dimensions: mechanism of allocation, extent of redistribution and ownership structure. One of the chief questions in political economy, old or new, is whether economic development is related to how the basic politico-economic system is built up around the allocative, distributive and ownership structures (Pryor, 1968; Eckstein, 1971; Kornai, 1986). We have here a whole set of problems for comparative research into how development is effected by the public–private sector distinction, which we will look at in the ensuing empirical chapters. In this chapter we examine this question from a theoretical point of view.

Four ideal types

One basic problem in any society is how to allocate the resources in an efficient manner. A second fundamental problem is the ownership question, or how the means of production are to be owned. The efficiency question is how to devise a system whereby the resources are allocated to various uses in such a way that it would not be possible to achieve a better result had the resources been allocated differently. The ownership problem relates to basic questions about equity and power in society.

In any society, resources or different factors of production have to be allocated among various usages and income as well as wealth have to be distributed to the households (Musgrave and Musgrave, 1980). Overlooking such phenomena as gift exchange and heritage, there are in principle only two mechanisms for deciding allocative and distributive matters: markets or politics (Arrow, 1963; Akerloff, 1970; Alchian, 1988). The use of politics as the mechanism of allocation implies budget-making and planning as well as the resort to hierarchies to implement the budget document or plan. When markets are trusted with allocating resources, the basic mechanism of choice is individual agreement or voluntary exchange (Buchanan, 1967, 1986).

Allocative questions may be handled to a considerable extent by markets, but the results of or the preconditions for voluntary exchange may be the target of public policy-making, the state attempting redistribution of income and wealth by means of the budget (Binder et al., 1974). It is not always easy to distinguish between allocative and redistributive programmes in the public sector, as redistribution does not have to be in money but may involve goods and services – redistribution in kind. The welfare state, with its huge public budget, mixes allocative and redistributive programmes to such an extent that it is difficult to tell which programme is which (Atkinson and Stiglitz, 1980; Musgrave and Musgrave, 1980).

In any society the means of production may be owned by the state or the society. Questions about the ownership of the means of production used to be framed as capitalism versus socialism. The ownership problem remains central in the political economy approach, but this distinction between two polar types of ownership of the means of production, either exclusively private or public, is too simple in relation to present-day realities, given much state intervention into the market economy in terms of taxation or regulation.

One fundamental type of resource allocation system employs competitive prices as the tool for allocating resources to producers and consumers. It presupposes the existence of markets where scarcity prices are determined by the interaction between demand and supply. The other fundamental type of resource allocation system employs planning and central coordination. The government decides how resources are to be allocated among alternative employments – budget allocation.

Resources or the means of production could be owned predominantly by the public or the private sectors. The prevailing ownership institution may be various private property regimes, or the state may be heavily involved in the control of economic resources, either through public enterprises or through the large tax state.

Market allocation or budget allocation? Private property regimes or state control or intervention? Real-life politico-economic regimes are combinations of these distinctions, involving mixtures and hybrid examples. In political economy, one finds four ideal types modelling how allocation mechanisms may be combined with ownership structure:

1 Adam Smith: market allocation based upon private property regimes.
2 Karl Marx: budget allocation with public ownership.
3 Friedrich List: state intervention into markets with state control of key industries but with little redistribution.
4 Adolf Wagner: market allocation in combination with budget allocation and state intervention for redistributional purposes.

The traditional contradiction between capitalism and socialism captures only two of these four politico-economic models. Besides Adam Smith's market regime – decentralized capitalism – and Karl Marx's command economy, there are two other ideal types which are highly relevant for the comparative analysis of politico-economic systems, namely Friedrich List's economic nationalism and Adolf Wagner's welfare state.

In the Western World, developments in politico-economic systems since the Second World War have meant that more and more of the budget allocation has been inserted into an economic system that used to be very much based on market allocation and private ownership, as predicted by Wagner (Galbraith, 1962; Johansen, 1977).

Two different reasons lie behind the seminal process of public sector growth among the rich market economies: public policy in relation to so-called market failures and policy-making with regard to income redistribution (Head, 1974; Wolf, 1988). Budget allocation and market allocation have been combined in more equal doses than envisaged in the pure model of decentralized capitalism – the so-called mixed economy of the welfare states (Brown and Jackson, 1978; Lybeck, 1986; Lybeck and Henrekson, 1988). At the same time, the seminal development in the OECD countries of a process of public sector growth has meant that public ownership of resources has increased.

The major development in the socialist world up to the collapse of the command economy in 1989 has been the opposite one, to try to insert more market allocation into a system of public ownership of the means of production (Lindblom, 1977). Is it possible to achieve an introduction of markets into an economic system based on public ownership of the means of production? This is the question about the possibility of so-called market socialism.

All four models are of relevance to countries in the Third World. The developmental success of the countries in South-East Asia is often attributed to their adherence to the state-capitalist model of List. The basic problem of development administration is to make crucial choices about allocation mechanism and ownership structure in order to promote development goals (Hirschman, 1958; Verma and Sharma, 1984). Which politico-economic regime is the best one in promoting development? Are welfare regimes possible outside rich countries?

Smith: the market economy and efficiency

The concept of efficiency in resource allocation has a precise and specific meaning (Layard and Walters, 1978; Bohm, 1986). Three conditions are sufficient and necessary for an allocation system to be efficient:

1 Efficiency in consumption: on the demand side of the economy, consumers trade with each other in order to maximize their individual utilities. An allocation is efficient if it is not possible after a trade to retrade and arrive at a position where the utility of at least one consumer can be increased and the utility of no other consumer be decreased.
2 Efficiency in production: on the supply side of the economy producers deliver goods and services. An allocation is efficient if it is not possible to increase the supply of at least one good while the supply of other goods remains constant. Efficiency in production means that it is not possible to increase output by changing the composition of the factors of production employed. Overall efficiency also requires that efficiency in consumption matches efficiency in production; hence we have condition 3.

3   Product-mix efficiency: the value to the consumer of a good equals its marginal cost.

It is possible to show that a market economy may under certain conditions fulfil these efficiency requirements by the employment of the price mechanism as the allocation instrument (Arrow and Scitovsky, 1972; Mishan, 1981; Eatwell *et al.*, 1989a). Given a set of competitive prices concerning goods and factors of production, the market mechanism will arrive at a situation where there is efficiency in consumption and in production, as well as in the overall economic sense (Debreu, 1959; Samuelson, 1971; Lachman, 1986).

These efficiency conditions apply under certain conditions which render the market appropriate for certain types of goods and not others. The market is suitable for the allocation of private consumer goods, i.e. divisible goods that have few externalities and are characterized by rivalry or no jointness (Bator, 1958; Head, 1974; Musgrave and Musgrave, 1980). The market economy faces severe problems when it comes to indivisible goods or public goods and externalities. Moreover, the market is not able to handle overall macroeconomic decisions, like consumption versus investment. Finally, the problem of determining the distribution of incomes is not solved. We may apply an independent criterion of justice to the outcomes of the operation of market forces (Nath, 1969; Rawls, 1971).

The basic problem in a market economy is not its internal functioning. On the contrary, if the conditions for market allocation are satisfied, there is no cause for hesitation, as the efficiency requirement is met. Problematic in relation to market allocation is the applicability of the 'invisible hand', as the conditions for a perfectly functioning market economy are narrow (Eatwell *et al.*, 1987b). Wolf identifies four sources of so-called market failure or situations where the typical conditions for the successful operation of markets do not apply: (a) externalities and public goods; (b) increasing returns to scale or jointness; (c) market imperfections in terms of actor misinformation or factor inflexibility, often called internalities; (d) distributional equity (Wolf, 1988: 20–9). The situation with regard to a command economy is the very opposite one, as it is the internal mechanics of such a resource allocation system that are problematic.

Theoretically, it is possible to prove that the employment of competitive prices in markets with perfect competition and adequate production technology results in allocative outcomes that satisfy the necessary and sufficient conditions for efficiency. But this is all just theory. The practical institutions of market regimes – capitalism – involve much more than simply perfectly competitive markets. In his *The Economic Institutions of Capitalism* (1985), Oliver E. Williamson states:

> Firms, markets, and relational contracting are important economic institutions. They are also the evolutionary product of a fascinating series of organizational innovations. The study of the economic institutions of capitalism has not, however, occupied a position of importance on the social science research agenda. (Williamson, 1985: 15)

The practical feasibility of market allocation is bound together with the occurrence of market failure. The new transaction costs approach within economics emphasizes that basic contractual problems of asymmetrical information, moral hazard and adverse selection limit the applicability of market exchange, and that they may be handled in terms of a variety of institutional responses (Akerloff, 1970; Mueller, 1986; Williamson, 1986; Ricketts, 1987; Alchian, 1988).

How widespread market failure is depends on both the evaluation of externalities and inequities in market outcomes and the occurrence of internalities and inefficiencies in market operations, but also on the probability that government action and bureaucratic implementation constitute a real alternative to market failure. The Coase theorem implies that market failure may not be a condition for state intervention, if the likelihood of government failure is even larger (Buchanan, 1986). Thus the practicality of a market-oriented society is tied into the fundamental problem of a demarcation line between the private and the public sectors in societies with extensive private property institutions. Budget allocation of resources or budget redistribution of income may ameliorate market failure, but there are limits to the size of the public sector when economic efficiency is considered.

Marx: the command economy and inefficiency

The allocation mechanism in a command economy is the command or directive stemming from the authority of the state. The ministry of production in a command economy faces the same requirements for efficiency in consumption and production which the market handles by the invisible hand. How is it possible for a command economy to meet the efficiency requirement in consumption and production? It is necessary to distinguish between two problems in relation to a command economy. The first problem is one of *theoretical possibility*: could a command economy satisfy the general conditions for efficiency in resource allocation? The second problem concerns *practical feasibility*: is it possible in a real world sense to devise a system of resource allocation that satisfies the efficiency conditions although it allocates resources by command?

It has been argued that the ministry of production could create such an information system and such an allocation system that it would be able to allocate goods and factors of production to consumers and producers in such a way that the efficiency criteria were met (Barone, 1935). However, although this may be theoretically possible, the basic problems concern its practical feasibility (Hayek, 1935; Bergson, 1981). When looking at the existing examples of command economies it seems as if the practical problems are enormous. Before we begin the empirical evaluation of the model of a command economy, we will look at some of the difficulties from a theoretical point of view.

The practical problem for the central planning board in a command economy is to build up an information system so vast that allocation becomes efficient (Kornai and Liptak, 1962; Heal, 1973; Eatwell *et al.*, 1990). The basic idea is that government proposes an allocation of all the goods and services in the economy among various uses – the plan. Then it collects information to make it possible to assess the marginal contribution to social welfare that a good or service makes in each of its uses, but according to whose preferences – the consumers' or the planners'? The next step would be that, having derived these marginal contributions, government calculates a new plan in which inputs have been shifted from uses where their marginal values are low to those where they are high (Heal, 1973: 156).

Grave doubts have always been raised as to the practical feasibility of this planning model. How could any central authority store or master knowledge about the marginal productivities in a total economy? This is not possible in a changing world (von Mises, 1936; Caiden and Wildavsky, 1974). Even if the *information problem* could be solved in a small economy, the *incentive problem* would still remain. Since it would be rational for each producer to disguise its information about technologies, a strategic game would result. Participants would try to promote their interests by biased information. If the ministry of production attempted to force the directives on producers, then there would be no incentive to search for a rational technology.

A command economy may use prices instead of explicit commands as in a war economy, but these prices would not constitute market prices. Prices may be employed for several purposes (Johansen, 1977–8). They may reflect the interaction between demand and supply, but they may also express central authority directives. In a command economy, prices have the function of conveying to the participants in the economy the conditions for their activity as the central authority considers the situation. The prices of goods and services as well as of the factors of production are strictly controlled, meaning that they express the intentions of the central planning board, not the demand and supply of consumers and producers – administrative prices. It has been suggested that efficiency problems could be resolved by a sort of Groves–Ledyard mechanism (Varian, 1984; Eatwell *et al.*, 1989b), but whether it is practical remains to be seen.

The advantage of a command economy is that it may make certain types of planning easy. The state can decide the overall direction of the economy. Macroeconomic planning that made distinctions between consumption and investment as well as between collective goods and consumer goods would become much easier, as the amount of central control would be so much larger. The central planning model emphasizes knowledge of technological factors for the governance of the economy in accordance with the preferences of the central planning board (Dobb, 1940).

The disadvantages of the command economy derive from the fact that it tends to be badly inefficient with regard to the allocation of consumer goods or capital. Although it is true that the ministry of finance or the budgetary authority could, in principle, employ efficient shadow prices or exchange ratios between different kinds of resources or production factors, the practical feasibility of such a mechanism is open to doubt. Controlling prices and employing them as tools for commanding the economic decisions of consumers and producers means most probably that neither efficiency in consumption nor efficiency in production will be met. In practical situations we find the curious expressions of a command economy: severe shortages for some goods, enormous overproduction of other goods, mismanagement of capital resources and a peculiar allocation of the labour force (Zaleski, 1980; Kornai, 1986).

These difficulties are well known from studies of the Eastern European systems (Ellman, 1979; Nove, 1986; Åslund, 1989). A huge planning bureau used prices to allocate resources, but these prices did not reflect changes in demand and supply. They were cost-plus prices, meaning that they were based on the average unit production cost in enterprises producing a good (Eidem and Viotti, 1978). The planning bureaus based their administrative decisions on available technology in terms of how much of the input resources were needed to produce an output unit given the existing knowledge about production functions. Moreover, the planning bureaus were able to adjust these prices in accordance with national priorities concerning the goods that should be produced, replacing consumer sovereignty with collective preferences interpreted by a group of planners (Spulber, 1969; Bergson and Levine, 1983; Eatwell *et al.*, 1990; Brus and Laski, 1990).

In an ideal command economy there would be no need for prices. The state would know the relative value of each good in terms of preferences. No existing economy could, however, be governed in this way. Although, for example, the Soviet economy was basically run by means of a large planning framework – allocating resources to various regions, factories and consumers – it employed some sort of prices: administrative prices (McAuley, 1979; Dyker, 1985). The single units in the Soviet economy were given a budget within which to make economic decisions about resources. This does not mean that these decisions guided resource allocation, but simply that there was a limit as to how far planning could proceed. The economic decisions of consumers and producers were still largely determined by the plan.

Major economic changes, then, also have to come from the plan. The administrators of the economy must employ various devices in order to gather information about how to increase efficiency. The state has to remain alert to various signals from producers and consumers that the allocation of resources must be changed – queues, overproduction, misallocation, wastage. On the one hand, the state must be able to coordinate and process a vast amount of knowledge. The problems with a planning system are that the state may not get the right information from producers and consumers, and that the state may not be able to process such a vast amount of information. There are limits to the capacity of any group of actors to control social systems, in particular economic ones. On the other hand, there is the serious incentive problem: what is the reward for the various participants in a planned economy – consumers, producers and administrators – when they search for and transmit the best available knowledge?

Change in production and management becomes particularly difficult in a command economy, as there is little scope for innovation and few rewards for individual initiatives. To devise a number of performance indicators does not help, as they may be strategically manipulated in a system based on hierarchical control (Leeman, 1963). The sudden and dramatic collapse of the Eastern European command economies in the late 1980s appears to have been a mature reaction to long-term system problems of the kind outlined above (Davis and Scase, 1985).

The serious problem of efficiency in a command economy resulted in a search for another resource allocation model that is based less on planning and recognizes the fundamental importance of scarcity prices (see Brus and Laski, 1990). The socialist models of Lange, Taylor and Lehner are based on an attempt to combine public ownership with market prices (Lange, 1936–7; Lippincott, 1938; Lerner, 1944; Lange and Taylor, 1964; Mandel, 1986).

The competitive socialist model

The Lange–Taylor model is interesting, as it explicitly tries to accommodate a socialist system of resource allocation within the standard efficiency criteria. It is not based on the notion of a command economy with a huge planning office directing the economy by means of state authority.

The Lange–Taylor model attempts to combine the trial and error procedure of a competitive price mechanism with public ownership of production. The assumptions of the model include: (a) the allocation of capital is to be based on administrative criteria; (b) the allocation of labour and consumption goods is to be determined by the interaction between demand and supply in free markets;(c) the producers of goods are to be instructed to obey the following rules: (i) to choose the combination of factors which minimize the average cost of production; (ii) the scale of output is to be determined where marginal cost is equal to the price of the product (Lange and Taylor, 1964).

Given these initial conditions, the state authorities are to start the trial and error process by arbitrarily setting the prices for goods and labour. The interaction between consumers and producers on various markets will then in successive stages lead to a state where the prices are adjusted by the price board until the efficiency conditions are met. Thus, a socialist economy could be using real prices and achieve an efficient allocation of resources.

Two detailed models of resource allocation in a socialist economy employing scarcity prices have been developed. The Lange–Arrow–Hurwicz (LAH) model is an attempt to copy the competitive mechanism of a market economy in a socialist system (Arrow and Hurwicz, 1960). The LAH planning procedure may be outlined as a replica of Walras's *tatonnement* process:

> At a given distribution of resources amongst consumers, the central planning board (CPB) quotes a vector of prices. Producers then calculate the production programmes that would maximize profits at these prices, and inform the centre of the supplies, demands and profits that would result. The profits are distributed as the centre may see fit amongst consumers, who then, facing given profit shares and wage rates, choose their most preferred consumption bundles, and inform the CPB of these. The centre now acts as an auctioneer, raising prices of goods in excess demand, and vice versa: and so the process continues. (Heal, 1973: 79)

An alternative to the LAH model is the Malinvaud process, where the centre employs a competitive price mechanism in order to arrive at knowledge about the production possibilities of the firms, which may be used to determine an efficiency locus. The Malinvaud model places a much stronger role with the central planning board (Malinvaud, 1967).

It has been argued that the trial and error method suggested in the LAH model of a socialist system of resource allocation will face severe practical information problems. Will the successive reconsideration of prices by a state board really work? Would there not be too slow a process of price adaptation to information about the relationship between demand and supply? How is the remuneration to labour to be decided? Is it really possible to have an equal distribution of income when wages are to be determined in the market? According to Hayek, the iterative revision of prices to be fed into market operations would require a board of supermen, with perfect knowledge about all production technologies and the behaviour of managers (Hayek, 1940). It has also been argued that the so-called competitive solution would not handle macroeconomic disturbances well (Dobb, 1940; Wright, 1947). The Malinvaud process has been criticized as requiring too much coordination between producers.

Another basic problem in the competitive solution remains to be pointed out: the incentive problem. Why would managers in the various production units follow the assumptions of the model, meaning that they would be socially rational without any remuneration? Why would it not be possible that the managers of production might try to influence the price board to set the prices in such a way that any losses will be recovered? Why would managers attempt to minimize costs if they are not allowed to capitalize on the profits? If the profits are to be returned to the price board, why would managers care about production costs?

The socialist bias in the LAH model is apparent in the restrictions on capital. Capital would be owned and controlled by the state and profits, interests and rents earned in government enterprises would be distributed as a sort of social dividend unrelated to labour income. But how could there be efficiency in capital allocation given these restrictions?

What is the exact meaning of competition in the LAH model? Could there really be competition on either side of the economy if severe socialist restrictions concerning wages and ownership were upheld? It may be argued that from a static point of view the competitive solution might achieve efficiency, but what about a dynamic perspective? Why would managers care about the introduction of new technology if the profits were not to be capitalized in one way or another? According to the Austrian school, there is no stationary solution, as the economy is always in a process of change and adaptation. If risk and uncertainty is inherent in management, then the incentive problem would be most severe, as there would be no reward for embarkment on a process of innovation (Schumpeter, 1944). What really is the difference between the central planning solution and the competitive solution?

The competitive solution suggested by Lange, Taylor and Lehner is an attempt to solve the efficiency equations by means of the market mechanism instead of the administrative solution in the central planning model. The administrative solution is deficient because there is no vast and reliable information system available as required. The competitive solution aims at replacing the administrative mechanism with a trial and error mechanism in combination with some severe socialist restrictions. What is the difference in reality?

It would seem that the competitive solution reduces the tasks of the ministry of production from a giant comprehensive planning body to a small price board making adjustments here and there. This is not so, however. The price board in the competitive solution would need extensive knowledge – pure information undisturbed by tactical considerations – in order to control the behaviour of managers. Is average cost really minimized? Is price really equal to marginal cost? Why could not various managers cooperate and try to influence the price or hide information about the cost function? Who could judge whether there really is free entry to the market in a socialist state, where the state controls access to capital? Is it not conceivable that it would be difficult to operate markets where the availability of capital is not free?

Some goods may display economies of scale, meaning that there will be losses for the managers when price is set equal to marginal costs. If the price board is asked to change the price so that losses are eliminated, then why could not the board be equally willing to change the prices for other goods? Would it not require the same amount of extensive information as in the command economy to be able to judge the cost function of various enterprises? It seems as if the competitive solution also requires a central planning board.

The information requirements are no less formidable in the competitive solution than in the central planning solution. And both face the same incentive problem: how could the participants in this type of resource allocation be trusted with an ambition to act according to the rules? Just as there would be an advantage for managers in a command economy to misrepresent costs in order to maximize their own advantage, so there would be no incentive for managers in the competitive solution to minimize costs, if they could not count on some of the profits being made available to them.

The difference between a central planning board and a price board would in effect be marginal. No central planning board would ever be able to allocate all resources without the use of some price mechanism. And no price board would ever reach an efficient allocative state if it did not have access to comprehensive knowledge about production possibilities and make correct decisions about the release of the socially owned capital resources.

The zest for a fundamental but still socialist reform of the command economies in Eastern Europe and in mainland China has cropped up now and then as a reaction to the rigidities, shortages and inefficiencies of the command economies (Ellman, 1979; Kornai, 1980; Åslund, 1989). However, these reform movements in the command economies accomplished less than was hoped for and this is the reason why the Eastern European countries decided in 1989 to look for alternative economic systems outside the various socialist models. What is the basic difficulty in the theoretical argument for a new kind of socialist politico-economic regime: market socialism (Nove, 1983; Le Grand and Estrin, 1989)?

Market socialism

The idea of market socialism was launched as a result of the inefficiency problems of a centrally planned economy. The informational requirements of a central planning board would simply be too great to handle by any social organization. However, proposals for or models of a combination of markets and a socialist economy are ambiguous with regard to two basic problems: the position of a coordinating body and the range of the use of markets to allocate resources. From a theoretical point of view, we may predict serious difficulties in implementing market socialism in an existing politico-economic system. Let us pinpoint these problems before we look at attempts at other socialist models.

All models of market socialism assume some coordinating board, but the scope of its operations and power differs. Given the fact that the coordinating board has the responsibility for allocative efficiency, it seems difficult to restrict its operations. Even if it employed competitive prices it would still face the requirement that it itself operates rationally. What mechanism in market socialism would guarantee that the coordinators make the correct decisions? It seems as if the theories of market socialism simply assume that the coordinating board will consist of highly competent people who are unambiguously devoted to the efficiency goal. But why would this be the case? *Sed quis custodiet ipsos custodes*?

The incentive problem recurs at the management level (Bergson, 1981). There is no mechanism that will reward the managers to act in a way that is socially productive as long as profits cannot be capitalized by the managers. The same problem appears again with regard to labour. If wages are to be set on the basis of an equality requirement, then it is difficult to see why labour would behave in a way that is conducive to collective rationality.

On the consumption side, market socialism was meant to strengthen the principle of consumer sovereignty in socialist economies. The use of administrative prices in command economies means that effective demand may show up in ways other than via the price mechanism. There is a constant danger in a command economy of replacing consumer preferences with the preferences of the coordinators. Not even market socialism could accept the principle of consumer sovereignty, as the coordinators would make crucial choices about the division between consumption and investment as well as the long-range orientation of the overall economy. What would be the incentives for coordinators to make the correct decisions?

The incentive problem is the most difficult problem that market socialism faces. How is it to be solved, given the tension between the use of market prices on the one hand and the restrictions of a socialist economy on the other? The literature on capitalism versus socialism tends to focus on the information problem that arises as markets are replaced by planning, but the incentive problem is more severe. It accounts for the widespread feeling of apathy in several socialist countries, where reforms aiming at market socialism have been tried but where the incentive problem has not reached a satisfactory solution. It also explains the development of a sharp tension between the official economy and the unofficial or black economy in socialist systems.

Could a socialist production system be efficient? What amount of market-type operations and mechanisms could be inserted into a socialist economy in order to raise productivity and affluence? These questions have been much debated by economists over the past fifty years. The debate is clearly relevant to the recent attempts in the communist world to promote efficiency in their economies. The practical lessons are that a command economy is possible but not efficient. In order to promote efficiency the price mechanism has to be resorted to, in the sense that prices reflect scarcity of values. This in turn requires that the reward function of the price system is recognized in the *incentive system* of the society, meaning that it will pay for the participants to communicate truthfully and behave rationally in relation to economic parameters.

Only if a socialist state allows private incentives is it possible to employ the price system to allocate resources in an efficient way. The socialist restrictions of the Lange–Taylor model mean that the competitive solution will be a variant of the command economy model. How could there be efficiency in production if managers were not allowed access to a capital market as well as being permitted to capitalize profits without the intervention of the state?

How far is it possible to accommodate private incentives without breaking the socialist assumptions of the economic system? The debate about the possibility and efficiency of a socialist economy has focused far too much on abstract equilibrium conditions and by-passed crucial institutional problems. The basic difficulty in a socialist economy is not to derive a set of solutions to the standard efficiency conditions but to devise and maintain institutions that implement these solutions in the short run as well as in the long run. It seems that the two models of a socialist economy – the competitive model and the central planning model – make far too strong or simplistic institutional assumptions about the practicability of managing a large economy along socialist lines.

It is impossible to discuss the possibility of change in allocation mechanisms without taking the institutional structure for ownership into account. If market mechanisms are to be employed instead of planning or administration, then private ownership must be allowed. If one favours efficiency in resource allocation, then one has to accept the institutional requirements and consequences of the working of the market. The fact that a country has an ownership structure that is fundamentally public implies that there are definite limits to the scope for the operation of the market mechanism.

The introduction of market socialism in communist systems is always of limited significance and restricted to a few types of divisible goods. Often it is accompanied by a process in which attempts to broaden the relevance of the market mechanism are curtailed by a fear of the consequences for the structure of ownership and property rights. Public ownership limits the use of the market mechanism to such an extent as to make the whole idea of market socialism superficial.

Looking at the various attempts at some type of market socialism in what used to be the communist world – in the Soviet Union, Hungary, Yugoslavia, China – we may predict on theoretical grounds that these reforms will pass through an ambiguous process of implementation characterized by opposite forces. The reforms will be either curtailed after a while or restricted to a narrow sector of the economy. Or there will be a severe incentive problem, as apathy will be the response to a situation where private initiatives are allowed but not rewarded. Or, finally, the communist state will have to recognize private initiative to an extent that must have system power implications which call for a very delicate balance between the established order and the new initiatives.

The relevance of market socialism to developing countries is limited, owing to the fundamental contradictions between the need to maintain control and the pressure to extend market operations. It is symptomatic that the economies characterized by rapid and steady growth have not attempted to adopt the model of market socialism. On the contrary, the economies of the Pacific area have successfully tried a model of capitalism introduced and supervised by government (Zysman, 1983).

It is often stated that Yugoslavia and Hungary are the only countries where market socialism was tried on a significant scale (Brus and Laski, 1990). There was a mix of regime reforms in Yugoslavia, not all of which can be subsumed under the label of market socialism (Singleton and Carter, 1982; Estrin, 1983; Lydall, 1986). Participatory schemes for workers attracted international attention as a way to reform the rigid bureaucratic nature of the command economy (Dahl, 1985), but to what extent these participatory reforms imply market socialism is an open question. The reform of the Hungarian economy away from the command model and towards the market socialism model never managed to introduce real market mechanisms, as the enterprises remained dependent on the state.

Wagner: budget allocation, redistribution and the mixed economy

Extensive budget allocation instead of market allocation in a system with considerable private ownership of the means of production and consumption has become typical in the OECD countries. The relevance of budget allocation has been on the increase in capitalist systems for several decades, transforming these private societies to mixed economies, although the seminal process of public sector expansion has now come to a halt (Webber and Wildavsky, 1986; Wildavsky, 1986). It would appear that there is a limit to the process of public sector growth. The distinction between a mixed economy and a command economy is a qualitative one, and the transformation of a society with strong private ownership and existing market mechanisms into a system oriented towards the planning mechanism would require structural changes that are far more encompassing than yearly increments in a slow process of public sector growth.

Budget allocation takes place in the yearly budgetary process, where requests seek appropriations and appropriations result from the consideration of competing requests (Wildavsky, 1984, 1988). The principal tool for deciding which requests will be which appropriations is the authority of government, not the voluntary agreement between producers and consumers. Budget allocation is characterized by considerable stability, in that there is a short-term plan, which is of a determinate form about how resources are to be employed and for what purposes.

The mechanism of allocation in the budgetary process is not based on competition and exchange, but rests on the authority of government to decide on the basis of cost calculations from one supplier, the bureau. Budget allocation is a strategic game between two actors, the government demanding a service and the bureau supplying the service on the condition that total costs will be covered. Thus, we have the typical feature of the budgetary process that programme quantity will be set where marginal value equals marginal cost (Niskanen, 1971).

Budget allocation is based on monopoly and hierarchy. Goods and services are produced by one supplier and consumed by the citizens without any choice of an alternative. Quantity is determined by the authorities on the basis of various considerations, including citizen preferences as revealed in some political process or collective preferences as defined by some authority. The programme is uniformly provided by the authority to be consumed in equal ways by its clients. Quantity is determined in the budgetary process as a result of the interaction between government demanding a programme and the bureau supplying the programme. There is large scope for negotiation and strategic behaviour in the budgetary process, as described by Aaron Wildavsky in a series of studies of the budgetary process (Wildavsky, 1984, 1986, 1988).

Price and cost in budget allocation serve administrative functions. On the one hand, the appropriation informs bureaus about the amount of resources they are entitled to use. On the other hand, the authority mobilizes resources in the form of either taxes or charges. Producer costs are the appropriations which reflect the bargaining power of the two principal actors in the budgetary process. Consumer prices may be fixed on a variety of grounds, from allocative efficiency to redistributional criteria. The remunerations to labour and capital are largely based on administrative prices. Labour costs are a function of the bargaining power of the public employees in relation to government, whereas capital costs are handled by means of various administrative criteria.

The basic principles of public administration structure budget allocation. The means and ends of programmes are determined in a plan document which singles out the supplier and identifies the production functions. There is a predetermined structure of monopoly suppliers, the bureaucracy. There is no competition between the bureaus, as they have been assigned long-term tasks which are unique for each bureau. Clear standards for the operation of the bureaus are laid down and the output of the bureaus is regulated by means of technical and legal criteria. Complaint is expressed by means of voice, not exit.

As Albert Hirschman argued in *Exit, Voice and Loyalty* (1970), the difference between budget and market allocation appears most clearly in the handling of allocation failures and the expression of dissatisfaction. Whereas the consumer may exit from the market when faced with a product or service he or she dislikes, the citizen in a voting context has no such powerful tool at his or her disposal. Instead, the dissatisfied citizen has to go through the tiresome and lengthy process of complaining to those responsible for the provision of the good or the service, which is a lot less efficient than simply turning to a competitor in the market.

Long-term planning in a mixed economy is of a different nature. It is also based on a plan document but it lacks the determinate form. It is more of a projection and a guess than a real commitment to the path to be travelled. Short-term budget allocation and long-term planning have certain advantages which may make them attractive alternatives to market allocation. However, there are certain disadvantages which have become more apparent in the era of big government.

The government budget is a promise about who can expect what money. It is a real commitment that there is a high probability that resources will be forthcoming, particularly in rich countries. In his comparative model of the budgetary process, Wildavsky employs two conceptual pairs in order to derive four ideal types. On the one hand, we have the predictability of the budgetary process as to whether its appropriations will lead to safe expenditure in accordance with what was planned, or the state budget is characterized by instability in that budgets are remade continuously. On the other hand, there is the environment of budget-making – how rich or poor the economy is that supports the public sector. Typical of the *incremental* budgetary fashion that has been prevalent in the mixed economies is the combination of stability and affluence, whereas *repetitive* budgeting typical of Third World countries takes place in a poor environment where the budgetary process tends towards instability (Wildavsky, 1986).

The variation among the so-called rich market economies may be further explained by looking more closely at the budgetary contexts in the leading OECD countries. Wildavsky explains the variation in budget size by the interaction between the containment of conflict and the support on spending, where the first factor reduces and the second factor enhances budget-making (Wildavsky, 1986). The question of variation in public finances is one of the core problems of political economy. We will deal with this problem of the size and orientation of the public budget in empirical analyses of both the variation within the OECD set of countries and the variation between rich market economies, communist systems and Third World countries, in Chapter 10.

Budgetary stability has a one-year periodicity. It is typical of short-term budget allocation, however, that the one-year periodicity tends to extend to a long-term stability, as stated in the theory about incrementalism. Once appropriations are fixed they are non-negotiable. People can predict what services and goods are forthcoming and employees may trust that their salaries will be paid (Rose, 1989). The budget document is transformed into expenditure decisions which may be called upon in due time. Uncertainty is minimized, predictability maximized.

Stability, when considered advantageous, tends to characterize the development of the budget, meaning that yearly changes will be only marginal. The theory of incrementalism used to be the established explanation of the short-term budgetary process. It was considered valid until budget-making became more erratic and shifting as a reaction to a more volatile environment. Yearly changes became non-marginal and programmes were really extinguished. It remains to be seen whether non-marginal budget-making amounts to a real change or if it is simply the exception that confirms the rule. The relevance of incrementalism hinges on the interpretation of the concept of marginal changes as well as the occurrence of changes in appropriations. It could be the case that incrementalism overemphasized the extent of stability that used to take place before the turmoil of the early 1980s or that the 1980s really meant a decisive break with the past.

A society that trusts budget allocation for a large number of services and goods values control and predictability highly. Government lays down what to expect for one year for a wide variety of utilities. This enhances security of employment and makes it possible to control outputs in accordance with regulations. Short-term cost efficiency is traded for long-term stability and predictability. Budget allocation is the attempt to make the future controllable and predictable in terms of predetermined criteria. The information contained in the budget is a one-way communication that states what will take place and how. Budget allocation is the authoritative allocation of values for a society. And authority, if benevolent, may accomplish beneficial outcomes.

Budget allocation enhances similarity. The emphasis on similarity follows from two sources: technical rationality and a preference for equality. Budget allocation is a method to inform on how resources are to be used to accomplish a number of goals. And such information has its own requirements. In a system of big government it becomes impossible to take each and every factor into account and to treat each appropriation differently – hence the need for standardization and similarity. To allocate by means of a budget is to employ rules, and rules are expedient if they are universal with as few exceptions as possible.

The drive for similarity is further strengthened by the preference for similarity in societies with big government. Big government is both an effect and a cause of the trend towards similarity. In relation to the set of public goods, there can be no choice between budget and market allocation, because there is so-called market failure. However, in relation to other kinds of goods and services, there is a real choice between politics or markets. Often budget allocation is preferred to market allocation because it makes possible the control of outputs, which in turn makes standardization possible at the same time as further enhancing similarity for its own reasons.

Budget allocation initiates a need for yet more budget allocation. Budget allocation creates clients who tend to hang on to their appropriations and if possible extend them further. And people are always looking for new appropriations to become clients of budgetary programmes. Budget allocation has its adherents among those who favour stability and value predictability. Once an item of expenditure is accepted on the budget it has a strong probability of remaining there for a long period of time. A variety of arguments have been put forward to account for the expansion of budget allocation (Tarschys, 1975; Larkey et al., 1981; Rose, 1984; Wildavsky, 1985).

The growth of the state is essentially a political process through which the budget has driven out the market as the mechanism of allocation. The process is a universal one in systems with a structure of predominantly privately owned means of production. It is considered that a number of problems and deficiencies may be better attacked by the use of the budget instrument – public policy solutions to market failure. Essentially, it is a preference for stability and predictability as well as similarity. The mixed economy or the bargaining society (Johansen, 1979) means that allocative processes comprise a limited number of choice participants as well as that allocation decisions may be predicted and controlled by government and its bureaus. It also involves the Schumpeterian tax state.

Whereas there is a search in communist systems for more market allocation and its derivatives – rapid adjustment, flexibility and mutual adaption – the opposite tendency has characterized the development of the political economies of the OECD countries. One has resorted to government in order to allocate the welfare state goods and services, although neither could these goods and services be classified as pure public goods nor is budget allocation often based on the occurrence of externalities or economies of scale. The budget instrument has been considered superior to market allocation in relation to a number of basically private goods and services, where the elements of jointness and non-excludability have not been conspicuous. In relation to health, social services and education, predictability and similarity have been deemed more important than flexibility or efficiency.

Hierarchy has replaced markets in economies with extensive private ownership. The budget instrument appears to handle the transaction costs in a complex society, characterized by bounded rationality and opportunism with a small number of powerful actors, better than the market. Internal organization will drive out market exchange systems when these conditions obtain (Williamson, 1975), whether in the private sector or in society in general. Combining the transaction argument with the stability and similarity argument, there is a strong case for budget allocation in relation to semi-public goods.

However, there are institutional limits to the expansion of the budget. The structure of privately owned means of production implies some amount of individual choice which works against the expansion of budget allocation. Budget expansion may be conducive to individual freedom, but it basically means that resources are allocated by one actor in accordance with standardized rules. Regulation is typical of budget allocation, but there is a limit to the regulative capacity of government in systems with private ownership. When take-home pay goes down, the period of budget expansion is bound to come to an end in systems with private ownership (Rose, 1985). The larger the budget the more serious are the efficiency problems – excess burdens (tax wedges) occur.

On the one hand, governments may regulate the private sector in a way that restricts competition (Buchanan et al., 1980; Spulber, 1989). On the other hand, budget allocation of resources may involve budget-maximizing bureaucrats (Niskanen, 1971). A large public sector may involve both extensive regulation and huge public resource allocation by means of bureaus.

Budget allocation presupposes bureaucracy or structures of public administration. And the problem of efficiency and productivity in budget allocation is very much tied up with the problem of bureaucracy. The distrust of the early 1990s in bureaus as producers of goods and services applies not only to the rich market economies or the so-called mixed economies but equally to the Third World countries where there has been a reassessment of planning and bureaucracy as the tool for managing development objectives.

It has been argued that the welfare state could be dismantled in favour of market allocation with regard to welfare state goods and services (Buchanan, 1986). This presupposes considerable transfer payments in order to maintain a minimum level of income equality. Such a society would constitute a market society that would maximize individual choice and preferences if transaction costs were not to become staggering. Taxes would be reduced considerably, and thereby also the occurrence of the so-called 'tax wedges' that are so typical of the mixed economy. This is the problem of excess burden (see Rosen, 1988).

A very salient problem in political economy is to identify criteria for the determination of the size of the allocative and redistributive budget. Such criteria may be either normative, looking for an optimal size of budget allocation and budget redistribution (Margolis and Guitton, 1969), or empirical, i.e. the actual factors that explain the variation in the size of the public sector and the welfare state commitments among the nations in the world (Wilensky, 1975; Castles, 1982; Wildavsky, 1986).

The mixed economies of the OECD countries differ, however, in terms of both size and orientation. Why? How can we account for the strong variation in welfare state commitments among rich and Third World countries in terms of an empirical analysis? The convergence hypothesis was suggested in the 1960s as a prediction to the effect that welfare state expenditures between market countries and communist systems would become more and more similar (Tinbergen, 1967; Galbraith, 1969). Is it really true that public policies tend to grow more similar between countries as the level of affluence increases? Perhaps politics matters for public policy outputs or outcomes, as discussed in the literature on policy determinants (Danziger, 1978; Sharpe and Newton, 1984)?

A number of important questions for research may be identified in relation to Wagner's model of the welfare state. Is public sector growth related somehow to the state of the economy or to the structure of the polity (Wilensky, 1975)? How far is it possible to expand budget allocation within the confines of extensive private ownership of the means of production? How does public sector expansion affect economic growth?

List: development planning

The model of economic development suggested by Friedrich List in 1837 designs a major role for the state, but more in terms of guidance or planning than ownership, with the exception of key industries which should be controlled by the state (List, 1983). It has been claimed that the List model played an important role not only in European countries such as Germany and France but also in Japan (Gerschenkron, 1962; Johnson, 1982; Okimoto, 1989) and South-East Asia in general, with the exception of Hong Kong – what is referred to as the 'governed market theory of East Asian success' (GM theory) (Wade, 1990). What, then, is developmental planning?

Planning is typically resorted to for a reason other than to keep the public household going, namely to plan the overall development of resources in society. Planning for the long-term development of the economy is a mixture of projection and decision. Planning attempts both to predict the future development of markets and their outcomes, and to influence the working of markets in a manner that is conducive to macroeconomic objectives. Short-term planning of the economy or budget allocation is often based on long-run planning, though the link is far less tight than was once expected. Planning is considered advantageous because it could contribute to stability and predictability. And planning procedures are strong in societies where stability and predictability are highly valued. There is, however, a limit to how much planning can be combined with a structure of private ownership.

The concept of planning is often employed in discussions about politico-economic systems. How does it relate to the concepts discussed so far? Actually, it is far from clear what is meant by 'planning' (Wildavsky, 1973). Several distinctions may be made between different kinds of planning (Johansen, 1977–8): macroeconomic planning is the regulation by the state of fiscal, monetary and trade parameters in order to influence macroeconomic targets; microeconomic planning is the control by the state of basic decision parameters; comprehensive planning is the attempt to control the whole economy in more or less detail; indicative planning is the effort to influence the economy by means of selective measures that work out their own consequences.

In a market economy, some kinds of macroeconomic planning by means of indicative planning mechanisms had been considered relevant after the great depression in the 1930s. Yet macroeconomic planning began to be questioned in the 1970s, as there was a reaction in several OECD nations against a too optimistic and perhaps naive adherence to Keynesian macroeconomic principles (Sawyer, 1989). Microeconomic planning is not in agreement with a market economy, as it is characteristic of budget allocation. Comprehensive planning is typical of command economies.

Whereas planning may be employed both in systems based on market allocation and in command economies, although differently, the distinction between competition and budget allocation as the medium of allocation is a sharp one. Budget allocation occurs in both command and market economies although in quite different amounts. Whereas budget allocation in socialist systems covers all types of goods, in market economies it used to be confined to the provision of public goods. In a system where the state or the public owns only key industries, it is not necessary to resort to a command economy.

Is it possible to employ market-type decision mechanisms and achieve planning, albeit different from comprehensive planning in a command economy (Tinbergen, 1952; 1967)? In any economic structure the role of prices is crucial, but we must distinguish between competitive prices and administrative prices. To what extent may various ownership structures be combined with different allocation mechanisms? The Indian debate, for example, about the place of planning in an economy with large-scale private ownership is highly relevant in this context (Bardhan, 1984; Mareshwari, 1984).

Planning may be increased to a certain extent within a system of privately owned resources. In a process of public sector growth where more and more resources are allocated by government, planning is bound to increase. There is a need for planning the development of the public household above and beyond what is possible in budget allocation, and the strong increase in the public sector calls for a coordinating mechanism in relation to the market system. However, there comes a point when planning takes over the basic decision functions of the market. Markets and planning may coexist to some degree only. The continued existence of privately owned means of production presents a challenge to planning systems as they reject the drive for control and predictability. The tension between planning and markets implies that either there will be even more planning or one has to accept that planning may not work efficiently owing to the unpredictable and uncontrollable interaction with markets.

Planning became as popular in rich as in poor countries after the Second World War, when almost all kinds of budget-making and administration were identified with planning (Wildavsky, 1973). In the Third World outside the communist systems there was a strong belief in combining planning with market allocation as a way to by-pass the conflict between capitalism and communism (Caiden and Wildavsky,

1974). Developmental planning was the technique to steer the economy towards the goals of five-year plans stating collective objectives. It motivated the expansion of the role of the state in society, calling for a number of political and administrative measures. Not only would the economy grow but developmental planning would assure the right kind of economic growth. The strength of these planning techniques varied from country to country. India is perhaps the most well known example of developmental planning with a strong socialist dose, though maintaining a structure of private ownership (Little, 1982). Its role in the South-East Asian 'miracles' has been a contested issue (Krugman, 1994).

The many failures of developmental planning have resulted in a reconsideration of the place of market forces in processes of development and as a strategic instrument to bring about economic growth (Toye, 1987; Balassa, 1989). The List model of economic nationalism provides the state with an activist role in promoting economic growth within a capitalist economy, i.e. with private property institutions. The state shall guide economic development by targeting special growth sectors, either owning key industries in these sectors or helping private firms to expand in these sectors by special inducements such as cheap loans or low interest rates. The List model is a version of the infant industries argument or the industrial policy thesis. State-capitalism accepts the institutions of capitalism but restricts their operation through government intervention by means of the ownership of key enterprises or through guidance and control of investments by private firms in the form of state-led industrialization – see Wade's analysis of East Asian industrialization in *Governing the Market* (1990) and *The Industrial Policy Debate* (Johnson, 1984).

Conclusion

Competitive prices in markets have several advantages over administrative prices in a planned economy. They are conducive to efficiency in resource allocation. They enhance flexibility and rapid adjustment. They reveal the value of goods and services momentarily and serve as an optimum medium for communicating preferences. Their weakness is a lack of stability and predictability (Stigler, 1966).

Competitive prices presuppose the operation of markets with numerous suppliers and demanders. Producer and consumer differences are to be reflected in the market by means of price and quantity. This model may operate well in a society with capitalist institutions including private ownership and a variety of incentive mechanisms, where individuals may express preferences in the form of possessions as long as the problems in relation to externalities, economies of scale and distributional equity have been resolved somehow. If, however, the emphasis is on control and predictability, then market allocation may be questioned as the appropriate medium of communication.

Theoretically speaking, in any society resources have to be allocated between alternative uses. There are, basically, two institutional mechanisms for the allocation of resources: markets and budgets (Borcherding, 1977). They complement each other only to a limited extent, as stated in the theory of public goods (Baumol, 1965; Samuelson, 1971; Arrow, 1980). Resources may be owned in two basic ways, publicly or privately. The structure of ownership sets limits on the employment of the two mechanisms of allocation. It may be derived from political economy theory that there is a definite limit on the tendency of publicly dominated ownership structures to move towards the use of markets. Similarly, the continued existence of private ownership means that there is a boundary for the growth of government or the expansion of the scope of budget allocation. The so-called mixed economy is a hybrid of market and budget allocation.

We now turn to data about existing politico-economic regimes in order to determine whether some or all of these theoretical notes hold up in the face of empirical evidence. In a comparative perspective it seems important to separate between various kinds of capitalist regimes and to attempt to evaluate how they perform on political economy criteria. Thus the so-called rich market economies perform very differently in terms of such a crucial criterion of evaluation as average economic growth. How can we explain performance differences among different existing capitalist systems?

We need to proceed from the pure theoretical argument about the pros and cons of four ideal types of economic regime connected with different schools of thought on the possible combinations of state and market, public and private, to empirical research into the similarities and differences between various politico-economic systems. One tentative distinction is that between decentralized capitalist, capitalist-state and mixed-capitalist systems on the one hand, and socialist regimes on the other hand (Chapter 7). A step forward may be taken by an empirical analysis of the performance variations both *between* these categories and *within* each category itself. Such a research programme involves an analysis of other performance dimensions besides the differential rates of economic development of politico-economic systems.

It should be pointed out that we have been talking about four ideal types of politico-economic regime. In reality there are mixtures and borderline cases. Many welfare states have, for example, partly accepted the quest for privatization typical of decentralized capitalism.

7 Politico-economic regimes: an evaluation

Introduction

In *Comparative Economic Systems* (1989), Gregory and Stuart employ a framework for the analysis of economic systems comprising four basic features, each of which has two modes: (a) organization of decision-making (centralization and decentralization); (b) provision of information and coordination (market or plan); (c) property rights (private or cooperative and public); (d) the incentive system (moral or material). Gregory and Stuart use these categories to derive three main types of politico-economic regime: capitalism, market socialism and planned socialism.

Gregory and Stuart evaluate the performance of their three types of economic systems by means of a set of outcomes – economic growth, efficiency, income distribution, stability, development objectives and national existence – where the overall finding is the precedence of the capitalist type on these evaluation criteria in relation to the others. Is it really true that capitalist politico-economic regimes outperform other types? There are a few problems in the Gregory and Stuart argument that may be highlighted in a comparative analysis.

Can we really speak of actually existing market socialist regimes? Is there some kind of pure model of capitalism which contains the essence of all non-socialist systems, or should we recognize the existence of different kinds of capitalist politico-economic regimes? Why should we focus on the evaluation criteria that Gregory and Stuart employ? In order to evaluate how various types of politico-economic systems do in the real world, one could employ both economic and political evaluation criteria.

In this chapter we evaluate politico-economic regimes by means of developmental criteria derived from the distinction between economic output and rights. We make two analyses, one covering the pre-1989 world and the other the early 1990s, in order to take into account the extensive changes taking place in the structure of the political economies after 1989 as part of the general move towards more markets and less state intervention. And we will consider the following performance dimensions of a politico-economic regime: economic growth, inflation, civil and political rights and the extent of inequality in the distribution of income.

Regimes, evaluation criteria and the data

It is interesting to relate the Gregory and Stuart categories to Gastil's (1987) framework, as it is a more refined one. Gastil categorizes politico-economic systems in the following way:

1 *Capitalist*: a high degree of economic freedom and relatively little market intervention by the state.
2 *Capitalist-statist*: substantial state intervention in markets and large public sectors, although the state remains committed to the institutions of private property.
3 *Mixed capitalist*: an activist state with income redistribution, market intervention and regulation, although the size of direct budget allocation of resources is not that large.
4 *Mixed socialist*: some economic freedom, private property and individual initiative within the framework of a socialist economy.
5 *Socialist*: basically command economies with little economic freedom, private property and individual initiative.

Gastil classified a large number of countries with the following politico-economic categories:

1 *Capitalist*: USA, Canada, Dominican Republic, El Salvador, Costa Rica, Colombia, Ecuador, Chile, Ireland, Belgium, Luxembourg, Switzerland, Spain, FR Germany, Iceland, Liberia, Cameroon, Kenya, Malawi, Jordan, South Korea, Japan, Thailand, Malaysia, Australia, New Zealand, Haiti, Barbados, Guatemala, Honduras, Cyprus, Niger, Côte d'Ivoire, Sierra Leone, Gabon, Chad, Lebanon and Nepal.
2 *Capitalist-statist*: Mexico, Panama, Venezuela, Peru, Brazil, Bolivia, Paraguay, Argentina, Italy, Ghana, Nigeria, Zaire, South Africa, Morocco, Iran, Turkey, India, Pakistan, Sri Lanka, Philippines, Indonesia, Jamaica, Trinidad, Mauritania, Central African Republic, Uganda, Saudia Arabia and Taiwan.
3 *Mixed capitalist*: Uruguay, United Kingdom, Netherlands, France, Portugal, Austria, Greece, Finland, Sweden, Norway, Denmark, Senegal, Tunisia, Israel, Singapore, Nicaragua, Guinea, Burundi, Sudan and Egypt.
4 *Mixed socialist*: Yugoslavia, Zambia, Madagascar, Guyana, Mali, Burkina Faso, Togo, Congo, Rwanda, Somalia, Libya, Syria, China and Burma.
5 *Socialist*: GDR, Hungary, Soviet Union, Bulgaria, Romania, Czechoslovakia, Tanzania, Ethiopia, Algeria, Iraq, Albania, Benin, Angola, Mozambique, Afghanistan, Mongolia, North Korea, Cambodia, Laos and Cuba.

There are problems in relation to the Gastil framework, even when one recognizes that he deals with the realities of the early 1980s. First, are the categories really conceptually distinct? Whereas it may be empirically feasible to distinguish the decentralized capitalist systems from the mixed capitalist ones, the distinction between mixed socialist and socialist is troublesome to apply. Similarly, the separation between pure capitalist and capitalist-statist is not easy to handle.

Second, any classification of countries into types of politico-economic regimes is bound to be time-dependent. Gastil's classification refers to the late 1970s and early 1980s, but politico-economic structures are not invariant over time. If the object is to evaluate the performance of politico-economic regimes over time during the post-Second World War period, then the classification has to be reworked for the time period after 1989, which sees the dismantling of the command economies.

The evaluation of politico-economic regimes below will be made using evaluation criteria that can be derived from the developmental perspective that runs through the entire book: economic development, social development and political development.

The average rate of economic growth over a number of years taps a dynamic aspect of politico-economic regimes, whereas the average yearly rate of inflation captures a stability aspect. The evaluation criteria in a democracy index identify several crucial performance aspects in relation to human rights, such as freedom and equality before the law. Finally, there is the inequality dimension to be measured by an indicator on the skewness in the distribution of income, which is a standard criterion of social development. These evaluation criteria – economic, political and social – have been measured using various data sources.

We now turn to an analysis of variance in order to find out whether it is true that one kind of politico-economic regime – capitalism – performed better than its main competitor – socialism – as long as the command economies were in place. How can we test this hypothesis? If it were true that capitalism did better than socialism, then performance data – economic growth and inflation, human rights and inequality – would differentiate between regimes. Is this the case? Since the dichotomy between capitalism and socialism is too crude, we compare three types of captalist regimes with the socialist type of politico-economic system in relation to performance data covering the post-war period up until about 1989. We finish this chapter by looking at an evaluation from the 1990s, but then we must employ a different method of classifying economic regimes.

Politico-economic evaluation pre-1989

Table 7.1 presents a tentative classification of politico-economic types that suits the world before the 1989 downfall of the command economies. Since politico-economic regimes tend to remain fairly stable over long periods of time, one may dare to suggest that these categories cover the 1960s, 1970s and 1980s. By examining whether different policy outputs and outcomes measured by means of average scores characterize these politico-economic regimes, one could gain indications about which regimes are attended by what results.

Starting from the Gastil framework, we have made some changes when classifying countries into sets of politico-economic regimes. On the one hand, a few countries have been classified somewhat differently; Italy, for example, has been placed among the mixed capitalist systems and not as a capitalist-statist system. On the other hand, the two categories of mixed socialist and socialist have been combined into one single category. The set of socialist regimes includes countries that have had a planned economy and a one-party state for a long period during the post-war period, although some of these countries abandoned the communist regime type in 1989 or 1990. We have reduced the number of countries (n = 84) included in the analysis of variance of the performance scores, concentrating mainly on large countries. The classification has been checked with *The Economist Atlas* and *Political Systems of the World*.

Table 7.1 Classification of politico-economic regimes 1960–85

Capitalist	Capitalist-statist	Mixed capitalist	Socialist
USA	Mexico	Ireland	GDR
Canada	Panama	UK	Yugoslavia
Dominican Rep.	Venezuela	Netherlands	Hungary
El Salvador	Peru	France	Czechoslovakia
Costa Rica	Brazil	Italy	Bulgaria
Guatemala	Bolivia	Austria	Romania
Honduras	Paraguay	GFR	Soviet Union
Ecuador	Argentina	Sweden	China
Colombia	Ghana	Denmark	Zambia
Chile	Nigeria	Finland	Madagascar
Switzerland	Zaire	Norway	Burkina Faso
Greece	Morocco	Belgium	Egypt
Niger	Iran		Sudan
Kenya	Portugal		Libya
Malawi	India		Myanmar
Liberia	Pakistan		Tanzania
Cameroon	Sri Lanka		Algeria
Taiwan	Philippines		Iraq
Jordan	Indonesia		Benin
South Korea	Uganda		Afghanistan
Japan	Spain		North Korea
Thailand	Turkey		Poland
Singapore			
Malaysia			
Australia			
New Zealand			
Côte d'Ivoire			
Sierra Leone			
Gabon			
Chad			

Gastil's description of the Federal Republic of Germany as only capitalist must be questioned, given the strong tradition towards the welfare state in the 1949 constitution. Similarly, Portugal and Spain should be regrouped in the light of the strong state involvement in these societies, at least during the fascist period. The more detailed description of some African and Asian countries is open to discussion.

Among the *capitalist* systems we find both OECD countries and Third World countries. This category is to be found in all the continents, as it includes the United States and Canada, Ecuador and Chile, Greece and Switzerland, Niger, Côte d'Ivoire and Kenya, Jordan, Thailand, Malaysia and Japan and finally Australia and New Zealand.

The *capitalist-statist* type covers politico-economic regimes where the state plays a large role within the framework of an extensive private property system and market allocation. This category includes mainly Third World countries in Latin America (Argentina, Brazil, Mexico and Venezuela), or in Africa (Uganda, Morocco and Nigeria), as well as some in Asia (the Philippines and Indonesia). The critical question in relation to this category is whether the Baby Tigers of South-East Asia are to be placed here (Wade, 1990; Chowdhury and Iyanatul, 1993; Krugman, 1994). Since South Korea, Taiwan and Singapore left import substitution rather early in favour of an export orientation we place them in the capitalist camp. How to apply this category to OECD countries is debatable. Turkey is often designated as capitalist-statist, but what about Spain and Portugal with regard to their fascist heritage, meaning here economic nationalism?

There are several OECD countries in the set of *mixed capitalist* systems. Actually, most of the Western European nations enter this category because of their welfare state orientation. Whether we also find some Third World countries in this category is to be doubted, as welfare state spending is low among poor countries.

The category of *socialist* countries covers a few Third World communist regimes besides the Eastern European countries that adhered to a Leninist model of a politico-economic regime until 1989–90. Thus all politico-economic regime types except the mixed capitalist category include both rich and poor countries. A necessary but not sufficient condition for welfare state spending on a grand scale – big government without socialism – is a rich economy, as is argued in Chapter 10.

We will start with the economic dimension, including indices that measure the level of affluence and the average economic growth for various time periods during the post Second World War period as well as an indicator of the extent of inflation between 1980 and 1985. Then we will bring in the political and social evaluation criteria.

Below we report on findings from an analysis of variance of the performance data on these four sets of regimes. Some statistics are rendered for each of the evaluation criteria: mean values, maxima and minima as well as CV scores and the eta-squared statistic. We are interested in how these different groups of politico-economic regimes perform in relation to each other, as well as how much variation there is within the various groups of regimes. The basic question is this: is there more variation *between* the four sets of regimes than *within* the four subsets themselves? If the eta-squared statistic shows scores that are larger than 0.5, then we may conclude that the distinctions between the four politico-economic regimes are real. If, on the contrary, the eta-squared statistic is lower than 0.5, then there is more variation within these categories, meaning that the regime property itself does not account for the variation in performance.

Level of affluence

Tables 7.2 and 7.3 partly confirm the general impression that capitalism performs better than socialism in terms of economic prosperity, but we must take a closer look at various kinds of capitalist regimes comparing each of them with the socialist regimes. Let us begin back in 1960 (Table 7.2).

Fifteen years after the end of the Second World War the capitalist and mixed capitalist regimes had a higher level of affluence on average than the socialist type regimes. Since the mixed capitalist type does not cover any Third World country, the distance between the average score for the mixed capitalist regime is far higher than the average affluence scores of the capitalist and the socialist regimes. Yet the average real GDP per capita was higher in the capitalist set of countries than in the set of socialist countries. The difference was not striking, or $1872 versus $1708 on average. The variation as measured by the CV scores was quite extensive among both captalist and socialist regimes, as opposed to the fairly homogeneous set of mixed capitalist regimes, which are welfare states in Western Europe.

Table 7.2 Real GDP per capita in regime sets, 1960

	Mean	Max.	Min.	CV	Eta^2
Capitalist (n = 30)	1872	7380	237	1.11	
Capitalist-statist (n = 22)	1319	5308	314	0.87	
Mixed capitalist (n = 12)	4427	5490	2545	0.20	
Socialist (n = 19)	1708	4516	208	0.79	
Total (n = 83)	2057	7380	208	0.89	0.30

Source: Summers and Heston (1988).

Moreover, the variation within the four sets of politico-economic regimes is substantial. The eta-squared score indicates that the variation within the groups is larger than the variation between the groups. This finding is supported by the very high CV scores measuring the within-group variation. The socialist regimes and the capitalist-statist regimes tend to have a lower level of affluence when mean values are focused on. We also note that the maximum values in these two sets are high and that there are low-scoring countries in all four sets of politico-economic regimes.

During the 1970s and early 1980s the country mean average income measures rose, although not as rapidly as during the 1950s and 1960s. The increase was, however, weak among the capitalist-statist regimes, which began to lag behind. Actually, the average level of affluence among the capitalist-statist regimes was reduced in the early 1980s. The other major finding is the poor development in the socialist group of countries, which no longer kept pace with the group of capitalist or mixed capitalist regimes.

Table 7.3 Real GDP per capita in regime sets, 1985

	Mean	Max.	Min.	CV	Eta^2
Capitalist (n = 30)	3811	12532	254	1.01	
Capitalist-statist (n = 22)	2173	6437	210	0.73	
Mixed capitalist (n = 12)	9359	12623	5205	0.20	
Socialist (n = 20)	3009	8740	355	0.90	
Total (n = 84)	3984	12623	210	0.91	0.40

Source: Summers and Heston (1988).

The general finding is that the gap between the capitalist and mixed capitalist regimes on the one hand and the socialist and capitalist-statist regimes on the other hand has increased since the 1960s. Looking at country mean values, the mixed capitalist regimes in 1985 had a level of affluence three times those of the capitalist-statist and the socialist regimes, whereas the set of capitalist regimes displayed twice as high average income values as these two politico-economic regimes (Table 7.3). More specifically, it is found that politico-economic regimes that involve the state to a large extent controlling the actual operations of the economy do worse than politico-economic regimes which trust markets more.

Interestingly, the higher eta-squared statistic for the 1985 data indicates that politico-economic regime does matter somewhat. The within-group variation is only slightly larger than the between-group variation. The mixed capitalist regime does much better than the other systems, partly because it is to be found among rich countries. The socialist regimes, although they tend to have a higher level of affluence than the capitalist-statist regimes, cannot compete with the capitalist or mixed capitalist regimes. Thus, we may conclude that a socialist or capitalist-statist regime meant less economic affluence than a pure capitalist or mixed capitalist regime. The strong drive towards more markets at the end of the 1980s and early 1990s appears understandable given these performance data.

Economic growth

The gap between the set of socialist politico-economic systems and two of the capitalist types of system increased in terms of GDP per capita after 1960. Can we conclude that the rate of economic growth was persistently higher among these two types of capitalist regime than in the set of socialist regimes? No, there is too much variation between the countries within all three sets to permit any such general conclusion that capitalism always performed better than socialism with regard to yearly economic growth rates. Table 7.4 shows the data for 1980 to 1985.

Table 7.4 Economic growth among regime sets, 1980–5

	Mean	Max.	Min.	Eta²
Capitalist (n = 30)	0.2	11.5	−4.7	
Capitalist-statist (n = 22)	0.1	5.8	−4.9	
Mixed capitalist (n = 12)	1.3	2.3	0.1	
Socialist (n = 20)	0.5	8.5	−6.0	
Total (n = 84)	0.4	11.5	−6.0	0.02

Source: Summers and Heston (1988).

Any simple generalization about politico-economic systems fails to do justice to the real-world differences in average growth rates. There are examples of very high average growth rates among capitalist, capitalist-statist and socialist regimes, just as cases exist of very negative growth rates in the same categories of politico-economic regimes. We cannot say that generally speaking, capitalism all the time and everywhere did better than socialism in terms of economic growth. Some pure capitalist and capitalist-statist regimes did very badly for some time periods.

Inflation

It is possible to broaden the evaluation of various politico-economic regimes by bringing in additional economic evaluation criteria. Here we will look at inflation. The yearly rate of inflation has come to be regarded as a more and more important sign of stability in economic systems, as the disruptive consequences of hyperinflation are feared. Are there any systematic differences tied to the various types of politico-economic regimes in terms of average level of inflation in the early 1980s? Table 7.5 indicates how price stability varied in politico-economic regimes.

Table 7.5 Average rate of inflation 1980–5

	Mean	Max.	Min.	CV	Eta^2
Capitalist (n = 27)	11.2	36.4	1.2	0.80	
Capitalist-statist (n = 20)	75.7	569.1	3.7	1.84	
Mixed capitalist (n = 12)	7.7	14.2	3.2	0.41	
Socialist (n = 11)	15.5	45.1	2.4	0.84	
Total (n = 70)	29.7	569.1	1.2	2.68	0.02

Source: World Development Report (1987).

The overall finding is that it is not possible to trace a special pattern of inflation among the four categories or groups of politico-economic regimes, although the set of mixed capitalist systems is different. Hyperinflation has been a problem in mainly capitalist-statist regimes, but pure capitalist and socialist regimes have also experienced high levels of inflation. Let us turn to other evaluation criteria than simply economic developmental ones.

Human rights

Since there is no standard measure of democracy, we rely on indices that attempt to rank countries on the basis of various legal and political rights considerations. Here there are striking differences between the four politico-economic regimes, as the country variation around 1980 with regard to democracy is more tied to the between-group variation than was true of the economic evaluation criteria. The eta-squared score is much higher than noticed in the analysis of economic evaluation criteria (Table 7.6).

In the mid-1980s democratic political rights occurred mainly among the mixed capitalist regime type. Here we have a number of countries that scored very high on the Humana democracy index. The mean value for the capitalist or capitalist-statist regime is consistently lower, although these regime categories include countries that score high on the index: New Zealand, Australia and Japan among the capitalist regimes, and India in the category of capitalist-statist regimes. The democracy score among the three types of capitalistic regimes is higher than that of the socialist type of regime, but there exist some highly undemocratic regimes in the set of capitalist and capitalist-statist regimes.

Table 7.6 Democracy among regime sets, 1980

	Mean	Max.	Min.	CV	Eta^2
Capitalist (n = 26)	67.8	96	30	0.31	
Capitalist-statist (n = 22)	59.5	89	30	0.30	
Mixed capitalist (n = 12)	92.3	96	86	0.04	
Socialist (n = 20)	42.7	64	22	0.32	
Total (n = 80)	62.9	96	22	0.36	0.48

Note: The Humana index ranges from 0 to 100 and is based mainly on the occurrence of human rights, including political rights (Humana, 1983).

The major finding is that this political evaluation criterion does discriminate between the various politico-economic regimes. The capitalist-statist and socialist regime types displayed much lower values than the mixed capitalist. It is true that the capitalist regime scored higher than the socialist regime type on this measure, but this type also includes countries with low democracy scores; for example, Chile, Chad and Nigeria, not to speak of the Baby Tigers in South-East Asia.

Income inequality

There are a large number of potentially relevant outcome measures that may be employed for the evaluation of politico-economic regimes. Perhaps the extent of income inequality is one of the most sensitive evaluation criteria, because it has figured so prominently in the ideologies tied to the distinction between capitalism and socialism. Is it true, we may ask, that various politico-economic regimes promote income equality differently? Table 7.7 provides some clues to the problem of how and if politico-economic systems are characterized by different structures of income distribution. The data available for socialist regimes are meagre.

The eta-squared statistic of below 0.5 indicates that the variation within the four fundamental categories is larger than the variation between them. However, there is one major finding: it is not the case that a socialist regime resulted in the highest level of income equality, as the mixed capitalist regime type displayed lower scores on all but one of the statistics employed here. In the mixed capitalist systems a combination of economic affluence and political ambition to redistribute income has resulted in much lower levels of income inequality than in other types of politico-economic regimes. Not very surprisingly, income inequality tended to be sharp in most capitalist-statist and some pure capitalist countries.

Table 7.7 Income inequality, about 1975

	Mean	Max.	Min.	CV	Eta^2
Capitalist (n = 22)	52.7	72.0	39.2	0.18	
Capitalist-statist (n = 16)	56.2	66.6	44.5	0.13	
Mixed capitalist (n = 10)	40.9	46.5	37.0	0.09	
Socialist (n = 8)	45.7	61.1	30.7	0.22	
Total (n = 56)	50.6	72.0	30.7	0.16	0.33

Note: A top quintile index – income share of upper 20 per cent of the population – has been used to measure the extent of income inequality. A higher score implies more inequality in the distribution of income (Musgrave and Jarrett, 1979; Taylor and Jodice, 1983; Muller, 1985, 1988; Chan, 1989).

Summing up

The performance of politico-economic regimes may be measured by a comparative analysis based on economic, social and political evaluation criteria. The major institutional reforms initiated around 1990 may be seen as a search for a more effective politico-economic regime. What lessons could be learnt from the operation of four different politico-economic regimes during the post Second World War period up to the demise of the socialist systems? A first step towards a refined assessment of the politico-economic performance of various countries is to employ categories like capitalist, mixed capitalist, capitalist-statist and socialist regimes on the basis of how the state recognizes the institutions of private property and how much space there is for voluntary exchange in the allocation of resources.

The mixed capitalist tend to perform better on all evaluation criteria than the other regime types. The socialist and capitalist-statist regime types tend to lag behind the other two types of capitalist regimes on the evaluation criteria employed here, in particular the average level of affluence measured by the GDP per capita indicator. Politico-economic systems where markets are given a prominent role tend to do better than politico-economic systems where the state is heavily involved in directing the economy.

The failure of the socialist regime type to keep pace with the development rate among the two capitalist types of regime was apparent by 1970. One brand of capitalist regime – capitalist-statist – performs as badly as the socialist kind of regime. Yet there are straightforward examples of failure even among the decentralized capitalist regimes. What is the situation like in the early 1990s, with substantial pressures being mounted to spread the institutions of the market economy?

Politico-economic evaluation post-1989

The extensive institutional changes started in 1989 make it even more difficult to apply the politico-economic regime concepts. The shift from one regime to another may be a transparent move with a clear-cut transformation. Or countries attempting to change their economic institutions may partly fail, meaning that the country ends up having a mixture of institutions from the old and new regimes. Let us look around the world to see how things stand at the moment, employing two new sources offering classifications of politico-economic regimes in the 1990s. Following *Economic Freedom of the World 1975–1995* (Gwartney *et al.*, 1996) and 'The world survey of economic freedom' (Messick, 1996), we arrive at Table 7.8.

Table 7.8 Classification of politico-economic regimes after 1989

Capitalist	*Mixed*	*Capitalist-statist*	*Post-communist*
Argentina	Austria	Bangladesh	Afghanistan
Australia	Belgium	Bhutan	Albania
Bolivia	Denmark	Botswana	Algeria
Canada	Finland	Brazil	Angola
Chile	France	Burundi	Armenia
Colombia	Germany	Cameroon	Azerbaijan
Costa Rica	Greece	Central African Rep.	Belarus
Czech Republic	Iceland	Chad	Benin
Estonia	Ireland	Congo	Bosnia
Ghana	Israel	Côte d'Ivoire	Bulgaria
Guatemala	Italy	Dominican Rep.	Burkina Faso
Hong Kong	Netherlands	Ecuador	Cambodia
Jamaica	Norway	Egypt	China
Japan	Portugal	El Salvador	Croatia
South Korea	Spain	Gabon	Cuba
Luxembourg	Sweden	Guinea	Ethiopia
Malaysia		Haiti	Georgia
Mauritius		Honduras	Hungary
New Zealand		India	Kazakhstan
Panama		Indonesia	North Korea
Poland		Iran	Kyrgyzstan
Singapore		Iraq	Laos
South Africa		Jordan	Latvia
Switzerland		Kenya	Libya
Taiwan		Kuwait	Lithuania
Thailand		Lebanon	Macedonia
Trinidad		Lesotho	Moldova
United Kingdom		Liberia	Mongolia
Uruguay		Madagascar	Mozambique
USA		Malawi	Nicaragua
		Mali	Romania
		Mauritania	Russia
		Mexico	Slovak Rep.

Capitalist-statist	*Post-communist*
(cont.)	*(cont.)*
Morocco	Slovenia
Myanmar	Tajikistan
Namibia	Tanzania
Nepal	Turkmenia
Niger	Ukraine
Nigeria	Uzbekistan
Oman	Vietnam
Pakistan	Yugoslavia
Papua New Guinea	
Paraguay	
Peru	
Philippines	
Rwanda	
Saudi Arabia	
Senegal	
Sierra Leone	
Somalia	
Sri Lanka	
Sudan	
Syria	
Togo	
Tunisia	
Turkey	
Uganda	
United Arab Emirates	
Venezuela	
Yemen	
Zaire	
Zambia	
Zimbabwe	

Note: The classification is based upon Gwartney *et al.* (1996) and Messick (1996), who are not always in agreement as to how a country is to be classified.

According to the criteria offered by Gwartney *et al.* (1996) and Messick (1996), most of the countries of the world must be classified as either state-capitalist or post-communist. *Freedom Review* speaks of countries as free, partly free, mostly not free and not free – all in all 109 countries are ranked from 16 to 0. In *Economic Freedom of the World 1975–1995* there is first an area rating for four sectors of the economy and second a summary index ranging from 10 to 0, classifying 103 countries. There are some discrepancies between the two country rankings, as their correlation is $r = 0.71$ ($n = 62$). Using these two sources, we arrive at the following considerations, in which we indicate the economic regime of the country, stating also its population in millions of inhabitants.

The predominant orientation of the countries on the American continent towards some type of capitalist politico-economic regime is obvious in the 1990s, but are there regimes other than pure capitalism today? It is true that the only examples of a socialist politico-economic regime – Cuba (11 million) and possibly still Nicaragua (4.2) – are small states when compared with the giant capitalist nations in this hemisphere. As one may argue that there is hardly a real welfare state or a mixed capitalist regime in America, the basic division among the countries on the American continent is between two types of capitalist regimes, decentralized capitalist and capitalist-statist regimes. Besides Canada (28.5), the United States (264) belongs to the former category, where two Latin American countries could be placed in the 1990s: Argentina (34) and Chile (14). Costa Rica (3.4) and Panama (2.7) might be classified as market economies as well as, perhaps, Guatemala (11). The remaining countries in Central America (with the exception of Trinidad and Tobago (1.2)) belong to the state-capitalist set, although a few have moved towards the market economy: El Salvador (5.9), the Dominican Republic (8), Honduras (5.5). Despite institutional reforms in the early 1990s, most Latin American countries should still be classified as capitalist-statist, considering the importance of so-called parastatals in their economies. Here, we have two of the giant countries in Latin America: Mexico (94) and Brazil (161). A number of countries with fairly large populations enter into the same type of politico-economic systems – Venezuela (21), Peru (24), Ecuador (11), Bolivia (8), Paraguay (5.4) and Uruguay (3.2) – some of which have moved towards the market economy in the early 1990s, notably Bolivia, Uruguay and Colombia.

On the African continent one used to find a complex pattern of a blend of state-capitalist and socialist regimes, often existing side by side. Large-scale institutional changes have been attempted in the late 1980s and early 1990s, but it is difficult to assess how much has been accomplished in reality. Pressure to install the institutions of the market economy has come not only from the demise of the socialist economy but also from the IMF and World Bank side (structural adjustment policies) criticizing the capitalist-statist economy. When a socialist economy is dismantled, a country most often ends up in a capitalist-statist regime.

In the north there is Morocco (29), a capitalist-statist regime, coexisting with a number of more or less socialist regimes in Algeria (28.5), Libya (5.2), Egypt (62.4), Sudan (30) and Ethiopia (56). How these former socialist regimes are to be described today is not clear, as perhaps Libya has the only remaining socialist regime. Algeria moved more towards capitalism during the 1980s, as did Sudan. Tunisia (9) is difficult to place, Gastil suggesting that it belonged to the mixed capitalist type, which is not correct, as it is not a welfare state. Probably all these countries practice a state-capitalist regime, as there is much government intervention in the economy.

In West Africa the prevailing regime type is state-capitalism, reflecting how dominant the parastatals tend to be. Here we have the following countries: Senegal (9), Sierra Leone (4.7), Ivory Coast (15), Niger (9.3), Chad (5.6), Togo (4.4), Nigeria (101) and Cameroon (13.5). A few socialist-oriented regimes used to exist among these capitalist-oriented regimes – Guinea (6.5), Benin (5.5), Mali (9.4) and Burkina Faso (10.4) – but they have now changed their economic system. Ghana (17.8) is probably the only country that could qualify as a market regime today.

Moving to the Central and Southern parts of the African continent, the question is what has happened to the several socialist regimes, some of which used to adhere to the notion of an African version of socialism. On the socialist side we had the following regimes: Congo (2.5), Tanzania (29), Angola (10), Zambia (9.5), Zimbabwe (11), Mozambique (18) and Madagascar (14). These countries have moved towards more of a market economy, but the state involvement in the economy remains large by means of a few dominating parastatals, which do not need to be privatized when socialism is given up. The countries that have a politico-economic regime oriented towards a type of state-capitalism comprise the Central African Republic (3.2), Zaire (44), Malawi (9.8), Kenya (29) and Uganda (19.6). South Africa (45) has an advanced capitalist economy, emerging from the capitalist-statist regime that was practised under the Apartheid era. Like Botswana (1.4), it may qualify as a market economy, which is also true of the island of Mauritius. One must remember that several of the Central and Southern African countries have experienced civil war, destroying opportunities for economic growth.

The populous nations on the Asian continent (here including Australia and New Zealand) belong to the sets of capitalist or capitalist-state regimes with the exception of a few remaining socialist regimes. In the Middle East there are a number of capitalist-statist countries: Jordan (4.1), Saudi Arabia (18.8), United Arab Emirates (3), Oman (2.1), Yemen (14.7), Kuwait (1.8) and Iran (65). The classification of these countries is not unproblematic, as their persistent war involvement has had an impact, increasing state involvement in the economy. What remains of the socialist type in Syria (15.5) and Iraq (20.6) is not clear. How Israel (5.1) is to be described is an open question: mixed capitalist, capitalist-statist or market economy? In the Gulf states the state is heavily involved in the oil sector.

In East Asia we find the giant countries of the world, and they are socialist, capitalist or capitalist-statist. Thus, there is India (937), which used to be identified as capitalist-statist but has changed towards decentralized capitalism in the early 1990s. Pakistan (132), Sri Lanka (18.3) and Bangladesh (128) remain capitalist-statist, whereas Burma or Myanmar (45) is still a socialist regime. Examples of a capitalist politico-economic regime are to be found in Thailand (60.3), Malaysia (19.7), South Korea (45.6), Taiwan (21.5), Japan (126), Australia (18.3) and New Zealand (3.4), the last two countries moving towards the set of market economies and away from the welfare state regime.

Again, separating a capitalist regime from a capitalist-statist regime in this part of the world is not always easy. Thus it has been argued that capitalist Singapore (2.9) belongs to the mixed capitalist type, which is very debatable. Populous Indonesia (204) should be designated capitalist-statist, as should the Philippines (73). Whether the Baby Tigers really are examples of a decentralized market economy has been contested, with the exception of Hong Kong, which, though, is no state (Krugman, 1994). Into the set of socialist politico-economic regimes enter mainland China (1200), North Korea (24), Mongolia (2.5), Vietnam (74.4), Cambodia (10.6) and Laos (4.8). But in some of these countries extensive market reforms have been implemented which question the applicability of the socialist regime type.

It remains to look at politico-economic performance in the old world, here covering both Western and Eastern Europe, including Russia and Turkey. On the European continent in this wide sense, all the various politico-economic regime types used to be present. But now only parts remain of the command economy in the former communist countries. Socialism in the form of communism is of little relevance in Europe, but what kind of capitalism will replace socialism? It is far from easy to draw a sharp dividing line between the various kinds of capitalist regimes in Europe in the 1990s.

All countries with a strong welfare state combined with extensive market allocation should be counted in the set of mixed capitalist systems. The set of mixed capitalist regimes includes several small and a few large countries: Norway (4.3), Finland (5.1), Sweden (8.8), Denmark (5.2), Iceland (0.3), the Netherlands (15.5), Belgium (10.1), Ireland (3.5), Germany (81.4), Austria (8) and France (58.1). Perhaps one may argue that Italy (58.3) could be placed among the capitalist-statist regimes, but this applies only if the time period studied is the 1950s or 1960s. Equally debatable is the classification of Spain (39.4) and Portugal (10.6), which are here placed among the set of mixed capitalist regimes, as we refer to the early 1990s. Into the category of capitalist regimes we enter only Luxembourg (0.4 million), Switzerland (7.1) and, in the 1990s only, the United Kingdom (58.3). Turkey is a border case (63.4), as one could argue that Turkey could be placed among the capitalist-statist regimes.

Until 1989 the socialist regime type covered all of Eastern Europe, including the USSR. Thus a number of fairly populous socialist countries and one giant system existed. The command economies now belong to history, as all countries have moved away from this economic regime. Some have come close to the market regime, whereas others seem stuck in a state-capitalist type of regime. Here we have Poland (38.8), the Czech Republic (10.4), Slovakia (5.4), Hungary (10.3), Romania (23.2), Bulgaria (8.8), Yugoslavia (11.1), Slovenia (2.1), Croatia (4.7), Albania (3.4) and Russia (150). Today the Czech Republic and Estonia must be placed in the capitalist set, whereas things are far less clear in relation to the other Eastern European countries. Russia still operates a quasi-socialist economy, which is also true of the Ukraine (52) and of Uzbekistan (23), Kazakhstan (7.4) and Tajikistan (6.2). Poland and Slovenia have moved towards pure capitalism but a capitalist-statist regime seems to replace socialism in other parts of Eastern Europe, which is also true of the Baltic states.

Evaluation of politico-economic regimes in the 1990s

In the 1990s the traditional distinction between capitalism and socialism is even less relevant than before the system changes initiated in 1989. In order to understand the variation in politico-economic regimes we need to distinguish between three types of capitalist regimes, leaving the post-communist systems as a residual, where it is an open question in relation to several of them as to how they will transform themselves, i.e. which type of capitalist regime they will end up with.

As things now stand, the politico-economic regime with the best performance record is the mixed capitalist regime – the same finding as above. The average scores for the welfare states are very high on all evaluation dimensions except economic growth. Capitalist regimes do better on economic growth than the mixed economies, but their records on inflation, democracy and inequality are worse than those of the welfare states. The economic regimes where the state is much more involved – the state-capitalist and post-communist countries – do much worse on all evaluation criteria (Table 7.9).

One clearly observes the crisis for the state-capitalist systems and post-communist countries in the data in Table 7.9. The prominent place afforded the institutions of the market economy is understandable when one sees the huge differences in performance records between the two types of capitalist regimes which honour the market and the two types of politico-economic regime in which the state dominates over the market.

Table 7.9 Regime performance around 1990

	Affluence	Growth	Inflation	Democracy	Inequality
Capitalist	10716 (29)	2.1 (29)	28.6 (29)	77.8 (26)	11.2 (19)
Mixed	19889 (16)	1.9 (16)	6.4 (16)	93.3 (15)	5.9 (11)
Capitalist-statist	1521 (52)	–0.1 (57)	43.4 (56)	52.8 (45)	10.2 (21)
Post-communist	1288 (30)	–4.0 (29)	111.9 (30)	50.3 (18)	10.1 (4)
Mean	5880 (127)	–0.2 (131)	51.3 (131)	64.5 (104)	9.7 (55)
Eta^2	0.52	0.31	0.06	0.46	0.08

Sources: Affluence: GNP per capita 1994, World Bank (1996); growth 1985–94, World Bank (1996); inflation 1985–94, World Bank (1996); democracy 1991, Humana (1992); income inequality or ratio: UNDP (1994).

However, the eta-squared scores in Table 7.9 indicate that this is not the entire story, because there is more variation within the categories than between different categories, with the exception of affluence and possibly democracy. There are state-capitalist countries with a much better performance record than the average members of that category. Generally, the CV scores for each evaluation dimension indicate immense variation within the four categories.

One may also look at how the country classifications suggested in *Economic Freedom of the World 1975–1995* (Gwartney *et al.*, 1996) and *Freedom Review* (Messick, 1996) relate to the outcomes studied above. Table 7.10 shows the information, indicating the weight of free economic institutions.

Table 7.10 Economic freedom and politico-economic outcomes: correlations

	Affluence	Growth	Inflation	Democracy	Inequality
Economic freedom	0.69	0.57	–0.22	0.57	–0.11
index I	(92)	(97)	(96)	(85)	(52)
Economic freedom	0.65	0.25	–0.07	0.87	–0.10
index II	(72)	(75)	(76)	(69)	(40)

Note: Index I is from Gwartney *et al.* (1996); index II is from Messick (1996); sample numbers are in parentheses.

Conclusion

A classic question in political economy is the performance of different kinds of politico-economic regimes. The problem used to be framed as the contest between capitalism and socialism, but it was readily realized that this dichotomy was too blunt a tool for classifying the politico-economic regimes of the world. If two categories are not enough, then how many are?

One may employ alternative theories of the role of government in economic development in order to derive a classification of four types of politico-economic regimes: (a) decentralized capitalism (Adam Smith); (b) state-capitalism (Friedrich List); (c) command economy (Karl Marx); and (d) mixed economy or the welfare state (Adolf Wagner, John Maynard Keynes). It is not a straightforward task to apply the system categories derived from these alternative theories about the role of the state in economic development on to the real world, especially when the world changes rapidly, as after 1989.

The basic finding in the two evaluations made above, based upon different classifications of countries according to these four ideal types, is that the mixed economy does well on all evaluation criteria with the possible exception of economic growth. Decentralized capitalism seems to be more dynamic than the welfare states, but it does not always go together with high scores on democracy, low inflation and income equality. State-capitalist systems as well as post-communist countries face tremendous difficulties in their overall performance records, although there are exceptions. Is the nature of the economic institutions the only consideration that has a bearing upon the country variation in economic growth? We now turn to a more refined analysis of the political conditions for economic growth, testing whether the politico-economic system really matters that much when one takes other factors into account.

One may finally add that the mixed economies are in the process of increasing their private sector share. The call for privatization has been partly accepted by several welfare states, especially in infrastructure and in relation to certain public enterprises, but the mixed economies have not gone as far as the marketers wish. Public firms often remain in the form of public joint stock companies.

8 Politics and economic growth: the Olson model

Introduction

In the search for the determinants of economic development, it is argued that the traditional economic models of economic growth need to be supplemented or replaced by new ones that take into account the impact of political phenomena on the overall rate of change in the economy. According to one line of argument, the institutional fabric of the political system reduces the level of affluence as a function of the amount of institutional sclerosis (Olson, 1982). However, it remains an open question as to whether the addition of political variables really means anything to the understanding of the economic development of nations (Adelman and Morris, 1967, 1972; Lange and Garrett, 1985).

Economic growth used to be approached as an endogenous variable determined by exogenous economic variables together with one or two instrument variables manipulable by means of economic policy, either in the short run as in macroeconomic policy-making or in the long run as in the argument that the framing of an industrial policy is of crucial importance for a rapid process of economic growth (Zysman, 1983). *The Rise and Decline of Nations* by Mancur Olson (1982) marked a decisive break with this approach, as Olson argued that one political variable is of fundamental importance for economic growth, at least in rich countries: institutional sclerosis. Institutional sclerosis is related to a well known concept in political science, namely modernization or the point in time of the introduction of modernized leadership.

Once we move towards a political economy of economic growth, we need to integrate political variables with economic and social conditions that may have an impact on economic growth. What is the place of political variables such as public sector size in an integrated model of economic growth explaining the differences among the OECD countries? What about the empirical support for various political models of economic growth when a much larger set of countries is involved in the model estimation? Could the institutionalization hypothesis be of relevance for understanding economic growth in Third World countries as well (Bairoch, 1975; Reynolds, 1985)? Once one includes institutional factors, then one needs to take the kind of politico-economic regime into account.

Growth models: economic, social and political factors

There are a number of growth models in economic theory that predict economic change on the basis of economic variables: the savings and investment function, labour supply, capital–output ratio, technological change and trade or exports (Hahn and Matthews, 1964; Kuznets, 1965, 1966; Eltis, 1966; Hahn, 1971; Solow, 1988; Chaudhuri, 1989). These models have been broadened in developmental economics by the addition of social variables, such as employment, education or institutional variables (Hall, 1983). It is far from clear which variables are to be given major explanatory weight, as there is no agreement in the fields of economic growth theory or development economics about which factors are crucial in processes of economic progress (Thirlwall, 1986). According to one theme, the standard neo-classical growth model has limited applicability in the explanation of Third World economic development (Todaro, 1985; Syrquin, 1988).

A number of hypotheses have been put forward suggesting the factors that have an impact on growth rates in the long- and short-run perspectives (Kalecki, 1954; Johnson, 1958; Meade, 1961; Hahn and Matthews, 1964; Kemp, 1964; Södersten, 1965; Stiglitz and Uzawa, 1969; Hahn, 1971; Pasinetti, 1981). These include the following: (a) economic factors (labour, capital, technology, trade, level of affluence) (Harrod, 1939; Hicks, 1965; Kuznets, 1965, 1966, 1968); (b) social factors (agriculture, property rights) (Lewis, 1955; Meier, 1984); and (c) cultural factors (religion, traditionalism) (Myrdal, 1957; Thirlwall, 1986).

Where do we place political factors among the determinants of economic growth? Economic theory has concentrated on variables like labour, capital and technology (Ott *et al.*, 1975; Eltis, 1984; Chaudhuri, 1989; Scott, 1989), which, it seems, may be influenced by political decision-making. Thus the supply of labour might be augmented by policies that promote immigration, the availability of capital may depend on taxation rules and technological advance could be stimulated by research and development policies.

Two different types of model may be suggested in order to take the interaction between politics and economic growth into account. Politics may be singled out as a factor that, besides the traditional economic variables, conditions growth rates. Or politics may be modelled as a determinant of growth rates by means of its impact on the standard economic variables. Politics may explain what is left to explain after economic factors are considered, or politics may be conceived as a determinant of these very same economic variables.

Olson ventures that the institutional fabric of society is a missing link in traditional theories explaining economic growth. He argues that a crucial factor in explaining the rise and decline of nations such as the United Kingdom, Germany, France, Sweden, Switzerland and Japan is a politically very relevant factor: the structure of pressure groups at various levels of government. These so-called distributional coalitions reduce economic growth by pushing for their special interests, thus bringing about national decline.

Economic growth may be regarded as a public good characterized by a fundamental free rider problem. Since it benefits all indiscriminately but requires that each and everyone contributes, there is no individual incentive to supply the good. The stronger the distributional coalitions in a society, the less are the efforts to sustain a high level of economic growth, since it is in no one's interest to supply the good for every group if the others are free riders. It pays more to increase the share of the income going to the group than to make a sacrifice for the increase in overall income. If, on the other hand, there is a strong consensus that economic growth is to be pursued because it is more to the advantage of everyone, then there could be a long-run sustained growth process that would be of decisive importance for the economic development of the country.

The question of whether politics matters for the development of a nation may be approached in a broad way, as the search for the economic, social and political sources of economic development. Taking an inductive approach, a number of variables may be related to indicators of economic development. Theoretical guidance is to be found in the basic economic models of economic growth as well as in the public choice approach to the political sources of economic development (Eltis, 1966, 1984; Buchanan *et al.*, 1980; Gersovitz *et al.*, 1982; Little, 1982).

First, economic growth is assumed to be a function of the traditional economic variables: the levels and rates of change of investments, labour supply and trade (Stigliz and Uzawa, 1969; Sen, 1970; Kregel, 1972; Scott, 1989). Second, social factors may have an impact on economic growth, either directly or in terms of their impact on the economic variables (Chenery and Srinivasan, 1988). Third, political variables could be related to economic growth by means of their impact on the basic conditions for economic activity (Saunders, 1986; Weede, 1986; Castles, 1990, 1991). Thus we arrive at the following general model:

$$EG = f(EV, SV, PV)$$

where *EG* is economic growth, *EV* stands for economic variables, *SV* for social variables and *PV* for political variables. We now proceed to test various models consisting of these variables. First we examine economic growth between 1960 and 1980 in both rich and poor countries. Then we look at economic growth within the OECD countries. Finally we employ more recent data about the time period 1985 to 1994 to test the findings in the former analyses.

The abstract nature of the Olson model makes an empirical test of the theory a delicate business. Various tests may be devised, but it is far from clear what their import is. What could we reasonably expect if the Olson (1982) argument is true? It is possible to measure the variation in growth rates among the OECD nations for the post-Second World War period. If these data are employed to test the Olson theory we would expect to find that there is a country variation in economic growth and that some measure of the status and position of distributional coalitions would explain at least some of this variation.

It is far from clear how some of the concepts are to be measured or observed. What is a distributional coalition? How do we assess the influence and position of such an entity? What are the indicators on encompassing collective interests? Second, since economic growth is presumably affected by factors other than the structure of distributional coalitions, how can we devise a model that captures the interaction between all the relevant variables, allowing us to state the true partial impact of the institutional structure on economic development?

We face considerable variation in growth rates among the countries in our data sets. Some nations have experienced a high level of average growth, whereas others are characterized by a low level of economic development. Generally, growth rates were higher in the 1960s than in the 1970s. It should also be pointed out that there is considerable variation around the average values for each country. One needs to make a distinction between short-term growth theory and long-term growth theory. Economic growth is to a considerable extent a function of a particular year, which means that average growth rates are only part of the story. However, there tend to be consistent patterns of country variations when average growth rates are looked into (Table 8.1). Which are the explanatory factors?

Table 8.1 Percentage increase in GNP per capita 1960–80, 1965–90 (average yearly growth rates)

	1960–80	1965–90		1960–80	1965–90
Singapore	7.5	6.5	Netherlands	3.2	1.8
South Korea	7.0	7.1	Algeria	3.2	2.1
Japan	7.1	4.1	Cameroon	2.6	3.0
Iraq	5.3	–	Pakistan	2.8	2.5
Brazil	5.1	3.3	Philippines	2.8	1.3
Jordan	5.7	–	Kenya	2.7	1.9
Portugal	5.0	3.0	Australia	2.7	1.9
Tunisia	4.8	3.2	Mexico	2.6	2.8
Thailand	4.7	4.4	Sri Lanka	2.4	2.9
Malaysia	4.3	4.0	Morocco	2.5	2.3
Indonesia	4.0	4.5	United States	2.3	1.7
Ecuador	4.5	2.8	United Kingdom	2.2	2.0
Spain	4.5	2.4	Sweden	2.3	1.9
Austria	4.1	2.9	Malawi	2.9	0.9
Finland	4.0	3.2	Switzerland	1.9	1.4
Italy	3.6	3.0	New Zealand	1.8	1.1
Norway	3.5	3.4	India	1.4	1.9
Egypt	3.4	4.1	Chile	1.6	0.4
France	3.9	2.4	Venezuela	2.6	−1.0
Belgium	3.8	2.6	Tanzania	1.9	−0.2
Turkey	3.6	2.6	Argentina	2.2	−0.3
Dominican Rep.	3.4	2.3	El Salvador	1.6	−0.4
Canada	3.3	2.7	Bolivia	2.1	−0.7
Paraguay	3.2	4.6	Uruguay	1.4	0.8
Ireland	3.1	3.0	Ethiopia	1.4	−0.2
Colombia	3.0	2.3	Peru	1.1	−0.2
Nigeria	4.1	0.1	Zambia	0.2	−1.9
Germany (FR)	3.3	2.4	Zaire	0.2	−2.2
Denmark	3.3	2.1	Senegal	0.3	−0.6
Costa Rica	3.2	1.4	Madagascar	−0.5	−1.9

Source: World Development Report (1982, 1992).

Economic growth 1960 to 1980 in poor and rich countries

The first test of models of economic growth is based on data for roughly sixty nations during the period of 1960 to 1980. The selection of the countries is based

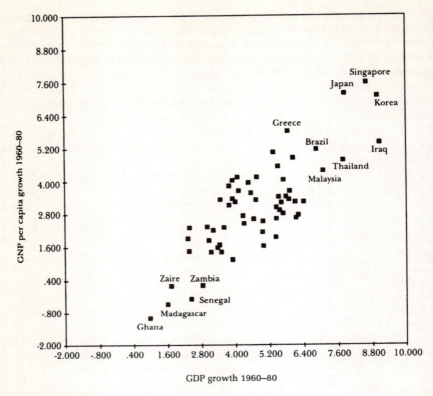

Figure 8.1 GDP growth and GNP per capita growth

on the idea that processes of economic development occur in both rich and poor countries, but that the mechanisms that explain these processes may differ. The set of rich countries includes the OECD nations and the set of poor nations covers a large number of Third World countries.

It could be argued that one should use overall GDP and not the GNP per capita measure when one studies economic development, because a strong increase in the population reduces growth rates when economic development is measured by the per capita indicator. However, there is a considerable covariation between the two measures ($r = 0.81$) (Figure 8.1).

Among the independent variables, we make a distinction between economic variables, social variables and political variables. The selection of the economic variables is based on the basic theories of economic development. Economic growth, according to the production function model, is the result of changes in capital formation, labour input and a residual consisting of productivity changes. Looking at economic growth from a wider perspective, other factors will be considered: social variables measuring industry structure, population changes and educational opportunities.

It may be predicted that the rate of change in agricultural employment is related to economic growth, as an increase in industrial employment would be conducive to economic growth in the Third World. Whether a decrease in industrial employment characterizes the process of economic development in the rich countries is an open question. Population growth could be assumed to drive down economic growth, whereas education would have the opposite effect. There is disagreement whether the impact of inequality in the distribution of incomes is positive or negative.

Political variables may be assumed to have an impact on economic growth directly or indirectly in terms of their effects on economic variables. A government dominated by left-wing ministers may be assumed to be in favour of public policies that are more oriented towards distribution of incomes than towards growth in affluence. It is interesting to inquire into whether democracies or authoritarian regimes accomplish more or less with regard to economic growth. We also include a variable for the extent of institutional sclerosis or modernization, following the hypothesis that the younger a nation is, the more it supports economic growth (Choi, 1983).

One may question the use of a cross-sectional approach to the analysis of economic growth, as a longitudinal perspective may be an alternative. However, if cross-sectional models are estimated on the basis of data consisting of average values for long-term periods, then the overall stability in the empirical information makes a cross-sectional approach more attractive (Jackman, 1985).

Economic factors

Several economic models are plausible. What does a certain level of economic development mean for growth rates over a decade or two (Horvat, 1973)? Is it the case that level of affluence in 1960 has any implications for growth rates during the 1960s and 1970s? On the one hand, it could be argued that only the rich countries can afford a high level of investment, which would guarantee high rates of economic development. On the other hand, there is the counter-argument that rich countries display a mature economy with low rates of economic growth, whereas it is truly in the interest of the developing nations to mobilize resources for a high level of investment. From a pure statistical point of view, it is easier to reach high growth rates when the level of affluence is low – the catch-up hypothesis. Figure 8.2 shows the relationship between level of affluence in 1960 and average growth rates between 1960 and 1980.

It is not the case that level of affluence determines potential growth or actual growth rates. We find considerable variation in growth rates among countries with a rather similar level of economic affluence, and it is certainly not the case that rich countries tend to have higher growth rates than poor countries. One may predict from looking at Figure 8.1 that the classification of rich and poor countries in 1960 is bound to change after a few decades owing to differential growth rates.

Table 8.2 reports on the test of models relating growth rates to various indicators of levels of economic activity, proportion of investments to GDP, percentage of workforce and proportion of exports to GDP.

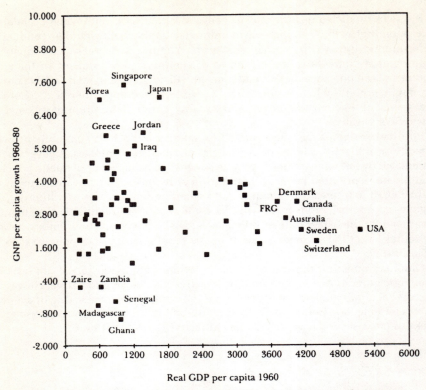

Figure 8.2 Real GDP per capita in 1960 and GNP per capita growth 1960–80

Table 8.2 Regression analysis: economic growth and levels of economic activity

	Total				Third World				OECD			
Predictors	Coeff.	Beta	r	t	Coeff.	Beta	r	t	Coeff.	Beta	r	t
GDInv.	0.16	0.48	0.52	4.03	0.14	0.38	0.46	2.05	0.18	0.55	0.46	2.75
Lab. force	0.02	0.07	0.14	0.61	0.01	0.01	−0.17	0.05	−0.02	−0.04	−0.09	−0.19
Export	0.01	0.09	0.23	0.73	0.02	0.21	0.36	1.26	−0.04	−0.42	−0.31	−2.12
Constant	−1.92				−0.90	−0.80			−0.15	1.31		0.24
R2	0.28				0.25				0.38			
R2A	0.24				0.19				0.27			

Note: $n = 61$ (total), $n = 40$ (Third World), $n = 21$ (OECD).

Sources: See Appendix 8.1., p. 171.

The emphasis in economic theory on a high level of investments as a condition for economic growth is amply supported in the model estimation. However, there is not much support for the other economic variables often adduced as crucial for economic expansion: level of labour force activity and level of exports. It seems that a high level of exports is not a necessary condition for economic growth, as some rich countries do not achieve high levels of economic growth although they have large exports. The fundamental place of a high level of investments is the same in rich countries as in Third World countries. On the other hand, we may look into the impact of the rate of change in a number of variables on economic growth. Here it is crucial to look at how increases in investments, labour force changes and exports relate to economic growth. Table 8.3 shows the findings of the test of such models.

Table 8.3 Regression analysis: economic growth and economic change

	Total				Third World				OECD			
Predictors	Coeff.	Beta	r	t	Coeff.	Beta	r	t	Coeff.	Beta	r	t
GDInv.	0.26	0.63	0.66	6.37	0.27	0.68	0.84	6.68	0.34	0.59	0.65	3.64
Lab. force	−0.45	−0.25	−0.03	−2.69	0.35	0.12	0.41	1.38	−0.48	−0.26	−0.15	−1.69
Export	0.14	0.37	0.65	4.17	0.08	0.22	0.62	2.24	0.20	0.39	0.66	2.47
Constant	1.50			4.30	−0.35			−0.62	1.10			1.68
R2	0.67				0.76				0.68			
R2A	0.65				0.74				0.62			

Note: $n = 61$ (total), $n = 40$ (Third World), $n = 21$ (OECD).

Sources: See Appendix 8.1.

Rapid increases in investments characterize countries with rapid economic growth, particularly in the Third World. The finding may be interpreted as indicating that economic growth processes are combined with heavy increases in the level of investments. Increases in the volume of exports also characterize processes of economic growth. Investment − level of and change in investments − is the key variable included in a pure economic model that, according to the empirical evidence, is of great importance.

The crucial importance of capital growth for economic development in the Third World appears in the data. An increase in the number of people employed has a positive impact on economic growth in Third World countries. In rich countries, economic growth leads to a reduction in the labour force. The importance of capital investments for economic growth, in particular in Third World countries, makes it crucial to look at the social and political sources of capital expenditures.

Social factors

Social factors may be relevant to the country variation in economic growth, as different social milieus or contexts may have different implications for basic parameters that determine economic growth, e.g. capital investments, labour input and technology. Thus, a transfer of parts of the workforce from agriculture to industry could raise productivity considerably, and higher levels of educational attainment may result in economic growth by increasing the quality of labour. What is the macro importance of these factors in our set of data? Table 8.4 shows the data.

Table 8.4 Regression analysis: economic growth and social structure

	Total				Third World				OECD			
Predictors	Coeff.	Beta	r	t	Coeff.	Beta	r	t	Coeff.	Beta	r	t
Secondary education	0.01	0.17	0.37	0.69	0.02	0.17	0.39	0.75	0.02	0.30	−0.00	0.94
Higher education	−0.00	−0.18	0.22	−0.97	−0.00	−0.05	0.24	−0.27	−0.00	−0.31	−0.22	−1.07
Agricultural change	0.03	0.42	0.44	2.07	0.04	0.42	0.43	2.29	−0.02	−0.20	−0.17	−0.72
Constant	1.80			4.73	1.25			2.37	3.96			2.61
$R2$	0.21				0.26				0.10			
$R2A$	0.17				0.20				0.00			

Note: $n = 61$ (total), $n = 40$ (Third World), $n = 21$ (OECD).

Sources: See Appendix 8.1.

Changes in agricultural employment have an impact on economic growth in the Third World nations. It is not the case that a reduction in industrial employment in rich countries leads to higher rates of economic growth. The level of education appears to be of limited importance, contrary to the human capital hypothesis. There is little indication of any general relationship between population growth and economic growth. The overall correlation between GDP growth and population growth tends to be positive, whereas the correlation between growth in GNP per capita and population growth tends to be negative, although these correlations are weak.

Political factors

It has been debated whether democracy affects economic growth positively or negatively (Weede, 1983, 1984a, b). This is a version of the theme of the strong state. An authoritarian regime would promote economic growth owing to its capacity to mobilize resources for investments. A similar line of argument has been suggested in a political hypothesis to the effect that left-wing governments promote economic growth (Whitely, 1980). Finally, there is the political hypothesis that a large public sector may have a net positive impact on economic growth, although some types of public expenditure reduce rather than enhance economic growth (Korpi, 1985a, b; Castles, 1990).

Political factors may affect economic growth by means of two mechanisms. On the one hand, specific policies conducted by governments for different periods of time are often conducive to a higher or lower rate of economic growth. On the other hand, the general political climate may be relevant for the economic factors that condition economic development. Tables 8.5 to 8.8 indicate that political factors are relevant for the explanation of the variation in average growth rates among nations. Let us begin with Tables 8.5 and 8.6.

Table 8.5 Regression analysis: economic growth and political structure

Predictors	Total				Third World				OECD			
	Coeff.	Beta	r	t	Coeff.	Beta	r	t	Coeff.	Beta	r	t
Institutional sclerosis	0.01	0.12	0.11	0.82	0.01	0.08	0.07	0.51	−0.06	−0.68	−0.70	−3.68
Democracy	−0.00	−0.02	0.04	−0.16	−0.01	−0.08	−0.06	−0.47	−0.00	−0.04	−0.33	−0.19
Constant	2.79			4.63	2.82			3.37	7.08			7.28
R2	0.01				0.01				0.49			
R2A	0.00				0.00				0.43			

Note: n = 61 (total), n = 40 (Third World), n = 21 (OECD).

Sources: See Appendix 8.1.

Table 8.6 Regression analysis: economic growth and political factors

Predictors	Total				Third World				OECD			
	Coeff.	Beta	r	t	Coeff.	Beta	r	t	Coeff.	Beta	r	t
Socialist government	−0.41	−0.22	−0.07	−1.38	−0.35	−0.14	−0.12	−0.85	−0.03	−0.02	−0.39	−0.08
Public expenditure	0.03	0.25	0.12	1.58	0.02	0.11	0.07	0.65	−0.06	−0.49	−0.50	−1.56
Constant	2.41			4.34	2.39			2.82	6.06			5.00
R2	0.05				0.02				0.25			
R2A	0.01				0.00				0.17			

Note: n = 61 (total), n = 40 (Third World), n = 21 (OECD).

Sources: See Appendix 8.1.

In the OECD set of countries it holds that the younger a nation the more rapid its rate of growth – institutional sclerosis as a negative determinant of economic growth, according to one interpretation. There is little or no support for the other political hypotheses. The nature of the regime – democratic or authoritarian – does not matter, and there is no indication of any link between socialist strength and high levels of economic growth. In addition, the direction of the impact of public expenditures seems to differ among rich and poor countries, if there is any impact at all.

It is interesting to look more closely at the impact of political factors on one crucial variable in economic growth, the investment function. Tables 8.7 and 8.8 report findings that only support the institutionalization hypothesis. Neither the hypothesis about democracy reducing investment leading to economic growth nor the hypothesis about left-wing governments enhancing investment promoting economic growth meets with empirical support.

The hypothesis that one political factor – institutional sclerosis – is related to economic growth is confirmed when the investments function is regressed on the political factors. The causal pattern is the same with regard to variation in investment and variation in economic growth. Institutional sclerosis makes a difference for economic growth, especially among the rich OECD countries.

Table 8.7 Regression analysis: investment growth and political factors

Predictors	Total				Third World				OECD			
	Coeff.	Beta	r	t	Coeff.	Beta	r	t	Coeff.	Beta	r	t
Institutional sclerosis	−0.03	−0.20	−0.29	−1.38	0.00	0.01	−0.01	0.04	−0.09	−0.65	−0.69	−3.45
Democracy	−0.03	−0.18	−0.28	−1.26	−0.02	−0.10	−0.10	−0.62	−0.01	−0.09	−0.37	−0.49
Constant	9.06			6.65	7.95			3.82	10.47			6.11
R2	0.11				0.01				0.48			
R2A	0.08				0.00				0.42			

Note: $n = 61$ (total), $n = 40$ (Third World), $n = 21$ (OECD).

Sources: See Appendix 8.1.

Table 8.8 Regression analysis: investment growth and political factors

Predictors	Total				Third World				OECD			
	Coeff.	Beta	r	t	Coeff.	Beta	r	t	Coeff.	Beta	r	t
Socialist government	−1.22	−0.28	−0.35	−1.82	−1.55	−0.25	−0.23	−1.53	−0.09	−0.04	−0.49	−0.15
Public expenditure	−0.04	−0.13	−0.29	−0.83	−0.05	0.10	0.03	0.59	−0.12	−0.58	−0.63	−2.11
Constant	8.26			6.54	6.71			3.24	9.51			4.98
R2	0.13				0.06				0.39			
R2A	0.10				0.01				0.33			

Note: $n = 61$ (total), $n = 40$ (Third World), $n = 21$ (OECD).

Sources: See Appendix 8.1.

Mixed models

The model tests reported so far show that some economic, social and political variables are relevant to the explanation of economic growth. Could it be the case that some of these factors cancel each other out? Perhaps the relationship between institutional sclerosis and economic growth is spurious, to be explained in terms of other factors? Tables 8.9 and 8.10 report the estimation of models that combine the factors that proved most relevant in earlier estimations of economic, social and political models. There can be no doubt about the importance of the crucial economic variable – capital investment – or changes in agriculture or education for economic development.

To sum up: there are a number of hypotheses that claim that political variables have an impact on average economic development. Testing of these hypotheses with regard to both rich and poor countries results in a note of warning. Only one political factor – institutional sclerosis – appears to be of importance in the explanation of economic growth. And the effect is particularly strong in rich countries. The basic role of investment is strongly underlined in the findings reported on here (Sommers and Suits, 1971), whereas there is little evidence of public sector expansion promoting economic growth.

Table 8.9 Regression analysis: economic growth: mixed model

Predictors	Total				Third World				OECD			
	Coeff.	Beta	r	t	Coeff.	Beta	r	t	Coeff.	Beta	r	t
GDInv. level	0.12	0.36	0.52	2.60	0.11	0.29	0.46	1.71	0.06	0.20	0.46	1.17
Prim. & second. education	0.02	0.29	0.37	1.44	0.03	0.25	0.39	1.36	0.03	0.41	−0.00	2.13
Agricultural change	0.02	0.25	0.44	1.18	0.03	0.25	0.50	1.29	−0.02	−0.20	−0.20	−1.08
Institutional sclerosis	−0.03	−0.40	0.11	−2.45	−0.02	−0.21	0.07	−1.35	−0.06	−0.75	−0.70	−4.04
Constant	0.16			0.18	−0.33			−0.28	4.61			2.77
R2	0.36				0.35				0.65			
R2A	0.32				0.27				0.56			

Note: n = 61 (total), n = 40 (Third World), n = 21 (OECD).

Sources: See Appendix 8.1.

Table 8.10 Regression analysis: economic growth: mixed model

Predictors	Total				Third World				OECD			
	Coeff.	Beta	r	t	Coeff.	Beta	r	t	Coeff.	Beta	r	t
GDInv. change	0.29	0.70	0.66	9.61	0.31	0.77	0.84	9.63	0.15	0.26	0.65	1.21
Secondary education	0.02	0.27	0.37	2.06	−0.00	−0.02	0.39	−0.17	0.03	0.40	−0.00	2.06
Agricultural change	0.03	0.42	0.44	3.41	0.03	0.34	0.50	3.55	−0.01	−0.07	−0.17	−0.36
Institutional sclerosis	−0.01	−0.17	0.11	−1.57	−0.01	−0.06	0.07	−0.66	−0.05	−0.67	−0.70	−3.03
Constant	−0.10			−0.30	−0.06			−0.19	4.50			2.63
R2	0.73				0.81				0.65			
R2A	0.71				0.78				0.57			

Note: n = 61 (total), n = 40 (Third World), n = 21 (OECD).

Sources: See Appendix 8.1.

Economic growth, it seems, is not determined by the level of affluence or the overall social structure. Economic growth is not predetermined by forces that cannot be influenced by political action. In the Third World, economic growth is closely tied up with overall investment behaviour, which may be affected by government. Perhaps in the rich countries economic growth is more related to institutional sclerosis. Let us test the Olson model in relation to OECD data.

Economic growth in rich countries 1960 to 1983

For the period between 1960 and 1983, the data about growth rates indicate that there is not only a country variation but also a variation over time. One would expect to find that economic growth rates differ more between nations than within nations over time. A simple analysis of variance may be employed to test this. As Table 8.11 shows, the test is negative: it is not the case that the yearly growth rates are more determined by country than by time, suggesting that the time variation is more pronounced than intra-nation differences.

Table 8.11 Analysis of variance of GDP growth rates 1961–83 by country and time

	GDP growth
Country (K = 24)	0.12 (0.00)
Year (K = 23)	0.35 (0.00)

Table 8.12 Average growth rates in the OECD nations: 1961–70, 1971–83, 1961–90 (real GDP), 1960–90

	Real GDP/capita		Real GDP		
	1960–81	1979–90	1961–70	1971–83	1979–90
Australia	2.5	1.6	5.2	2.9	3.1
Austria	3.7	2.1	4.8	3.1	2.3
Belgium	3.4	2.1	5.0	2.5	2.2
Canada	3.1	1.8	5.2	3.4	2.8
Denmark	2.7	1.8	4.6	2.2	1.9
FR Germany	3.0	1.7	4.6	2.2	2.0
Finland	3.7	2.9	5.0	3.3	3.4
France	3.6	1.7	5.6	2.8	2.1
Greece	5.0	1.0	7.7	3.7	1.5
Iceland	3.3	1.4	4.5	3.7	2.6
Ireland	3.1	3.1	4.3	3.9	3.4
Italy	3.5	2.2	5.7	2.3	2.4
Japan	6.4	3.5	10.7	4.6	4.1
Luxembourg	2.3	2.7	3.5	2.0	3.2
Netherlands	2.7	1.2	5.2	2.1	1.7
New Zealand	1.6	0.8	3.7	2.0	1.5
Norway	3.6	2.2	4.4	4.1	2.6
Portugal	4.9	2.3	6.4	4.1	2.9
Spain	4.2	2.3	7.4	3.2	2.8
Sweden	2.6	1.6	4.7	1.7	1.9
Switzerland	2.1	1.7	4.8	1.1	2.3
Turkey	2.9	2.3	5.7	5.5	4.8
United Kingdom	1.8	1.9	2.8	1.8	2.1
United States	2.2	1.6	3.9	2.6	2.6
Average	3.0	1.9	5.2	2.9	2.7

Note: Real GDP rates are based on OECD Economic Outlook nos 36 (1984) and 25 (1979); real GDP/capita growth rates are based on OECD Historical Statistics 1960–81 (1983), OECD Historical Statistics 1960–90 (1992).

It is worth emphasizing that the within-nation differences over time are far larger than the between-nation differences with regard to the yearly variation in growth rates. This finding is a warning against any theory that focuses on country as a crucial determinant of economic development. What about the long-run variation?

Even if the rate of economic growth alters from one year to another, which cannot be accounted for by the structure of political institutions but perhaps by political decision-making, it may still be the case that the average variation in growth rates displays a clear country identification. Table 8.12 shows various measures of the long-run variation in economic development.

By-passing the substantial yearly variations in growth rates, it is possible to identify a stable variation over time. Considering the first time period (1961–70), the average growth rate varies between 10.7 per cent (Japan) and 2.8 per cent (United Kingdom). The country variation is not as extensive during the second time period, as the difference between the maximum (Turkey at 5.5 per cent) and the minimum (Switzerland at 1.1 per cent) is lower. It must be emphasized that the structure of the country variation is only partly the same during the two time periods, as the correlation coefficient indicates ($r = 0.52$). This is again a warning against the attempt to identify a stable country variation during the post-war period. There is simply too much variation even between average growth rates over time. However, allowing for the substantial time variation, we may single out four sets of nations that differ in the average growth rate between 1961 and 1983:

1 Below 3.3 per cent: Denmark, West Germany, Luxembourg, New Zealand, Sweden, Switzerland, the United Kingdom and the United States.
2 From 3.3 to 3.9 per cent: Australia, Austria, Belgium, Italy, the Netherlands.
3 From 4.0 to 4.9 per cent: Canada, Finland, France, Iceland, Ireland and Norway.
4 Over 5.0 per cent: Greece, Japan, Portugal, Spain and Turkey.

How are we to account for this pattern of variation in average growth rates? Let us test a number of models that attempt to account for the long-run variation in economic growth. We will restrict our models by including politically relevant variables in order to search for evidence that indicates that politics matters. We ask if there is any evidence whatsoever for the theory that political factors have an impact on the average growth levels in advanced capitalist democracies.

Let us specify a data set including a number of indicators tapping some latent variables to be measured across the OECD nations during the post Second World War period, particularly since 1960. The data are based on indicators of variables that figure in major theories about the sources of a country variation in economic growth (Kormendi and Meguire, 1985; Castles, 1990, 1991) and comprise:

1 *Economic growth rates*: various indicators measuring economic performance, such as average growth rates for various periods of time in overall GDP and GDP per capita, allowing for the fact that the quality of the data is not always the same (OECD, 1979a, b, 1983a, b, 1984).
2 *Affluence*: the level of economic output as a starting point in, for example, 1957 measured by GNP per capita (Russett *et al.*, 1964). The catch-up hypothesis argues that the difference in average growth rates may be explained by the level of affluence at the starting point, richer countries growing less rapidly than less rich ones (Weede, 1986; Castles, 1991).
3 *Economic maturity*: it may be argued that high rates of economic growth should

be found in economies with a rapidly expanding secondary sector, whereas the coming of a tertiary sector would mean a slow-down in economic growth. The explanation for this hypothesis is that the potential for productivity increases is far less in the tertiary sector. Thus we include a measure of the size of the tertiary sector (OECD, *Historical Statistics*).

4   *Institutionalization*: an index developed by Choi which taps the length of the period for which a nation has had a political structure intact (Choi, 1983). The index has been extended to all OECD nations by additional estimates. It may be complemented by another measure of the age of a nation: a modernization index (Taylor and Hudson, 1972). However, it has been criticized as too simple for tapping institutional structure (Saunders, 1986; Castles, 1991).

5   *Structure of interest groups*: it is not easy to measure the structure of pressure groups or to come up with some index that expresses valid generalizations about each and every pressure group. We will focus on the structure of the trade unions: a unionization index (Kjellberg, 1983; Korpi, 1983; Miele, 1983; Therborn, 1984) and a centralization index (Heady, 1970).

6   *Corporatist interest mediation*: if trade union structure is not the only dimension in the nature of distributional coalitions, then perhaps the access of pressure groups to political power matters. Corporatist avenues to national decision-making may result in encompassing decision-making: two corporatization indexes (Wilensky, 1976; Schmitter, 1981).

7   *Consociationalism*: broad social decision-making would be conducive to encompassing social solutions. Thus we include some indicators that measure the amount of political competition in the composition of government: a consociationalism index (Lijphart, 1979) and an index of oversized cabinets (Lijphart, 1984).

8   *Party government*: it is natural to take the colour of government into account when looking at the trade-off between economic growth and redistribution. Presumably, a socialist government favours redistribution whereas non-socialist governments emphasize economic growth. However, there is the counter-argument that left-wing governments may find it easier to mobilize the population behind a policy favouring economic growth (Whitely, 1982). We measure the composition of governments in the following way: an index of socialist and bourgeois dominance (Schmidt, 1983b) and an index of government durability (Lijphart, 1984).

9   *Public policy*: pondering about the interaction between politics and economic growth, one cannot by-pass the impact of public policies on a long-run perspective. Since the dependent variable is the average growth rate, we test some hypotheses about the effect of long-run public policies, including the argument that a large public sector may promote economic growth (Korpi, 1985a, b; Castles, 1990). Thus we include measures of the size of the public sector since 1960 – total outlays, transfer payments and government consumption – since the impact of these various items of public expenditure may differ with regard to economic growth (OECD, *Historical Statistics*).

For modelling the relationship between political variables and average economic growth, some theoretical guidelines may be suggested. We single out economic performance as the dependent variable, but employ three different indicators: real GDP growth 1961–70; real GDP growth 1971–83; and real GDP per capita growth

1960–81. The substantial variation over time means that the estimates may vary depending on which indicator is used. It is reasonable to expect that the level of economic performance has an impact upon the rate of economic growth. The lower the starting point, the higher the rate of change if there is a process of economic growth. Political variables may have an impact upon economic performance over and above that of the level of economic performance.

We will now test the contribution of each political variable in a regression equation comprising, besides the wealth of nations, the particular political variable in question. Such a stepwise procedure, testing whether political factors mean anything over and above level of affluence, will be used in relation to all political variables.

Economic maturity

It is not quite clear how the level of economic performance relates to the rate of change in economic performance. One may argue that countries at a low level tend to display a low level of economic growth, as they are stuck in poor economic performance. The implication is that rich countries would tend to become even richer at a more rapid rate. Simon Kuznets argued along this line in his study of economic growth in a historical perspective (Kuznets, 1966, 1971). However, the opposite argument seems more plausible in relation to countries that have already reached a certain level of economic performance, as is true of the OECD countries. Here one would expect a negative relationship, i.e. that countries at a lower level of economic output tend to grow more rapidly than countries with a more mature economy – the catch-up hypothesis.

In order to test these two alternative hypotheses a simple regression was run, with economic level in 1957 predicting various measures of economic growth (Table 8.13). It appears that the second hypothesis is the correct one for the OECD nations, as there is a considerable connection between economic performance and rates of change in the direction suggested by this second hypothesis. A substantial portion of the variation in growth rates in the 1960s and the 1970s may be accounted for by the level of economic performance. High growth rates are to be found among nations at a low level of economic performance: Japan, Greece, Portugal, Spain and Turkey. However, this is hardly a complete explanation, as even the best model explains less than half of the variation. Thus a basic economic variable such as level of economic output is clearly relevant to the explanation of growth rates, but what is the contribution of political factors? We now add each of the political variables listed above to the simple model relating economic growth to level of economic affluence.

Table 8.13 Economic level and growth rates

	Coefficient	t	Beta wt	R^2	R^2A
(1) GDP growth 1961–70	−0.0016 GNP/cap. 1957	−3.16	−0.56	0.31	0.28
(2) GDP growth 1971–83	−0.0010 GNP/cap. 1957	−2.95	−0.53	0.28	0.25
(3) GNP/cap. growth 1960–81	−0.0012 GNP/cap. 1957	−3.87	−0.64	0.40	0.38

Institutionalization

The basic hypothesis in Olson (1982) states that the length of time of institutionalization has a negative impact on growth rates. How is institutionalization to be
measured? The concept of institutionalization is fairly similar to *modernization*,
as both refer to the emergence of a more or less constitutionally defined polity
based on an industrial economy and involving considerable portions of the citizens
in political life. What matters in the concept of institutionalization, according to
the Olson interpretation, is the length in time of unbroken institutionalization.
Thus, the occurrence of major societal disaster abolishing established institutions
is of crucial importance in this variable.

The index of institutionalization or institutional sclerosis developed by Choi is
fairly similar to a modernization measure identifying the years of consolidation of
a modernizing leadership. The correlation between the two measures is high, or
Pearson's r = -0.75. Institutionalization may have an impact on economic growth
either directly or in terms of its impact on level of economic performance. Since
institutionalization refers to an extended period of time, it may have an impact on
both level and rate of change in economic performance. We will test a model
comprising both institutional sclerosis and economic level.

Table 8.14 Institutionalization, economic level and growth rates

	Coefficient	t	Beta wt	R^2	R^2A
(1) GDP growth 1961–70	−0.0001 GNP/cap. 1957	−0.14	−0.04	0.45	0.40
	−0.0570 Institutional	−2.33	−0.64		
(2) GND growth 1971–83	−0.0002 GNP/cap. 1957	−0.47	−0.12	0.51	0.46
	−0.0466 Institutional	−3.09	−0.81		
(3) GNP/cap. growth 1960–81	−0.0004 GNP/cap. 1957	−0.83	−0.22	0.50	0.45
	−0.0309 Institutional	−1.94	−0.51		

Table 8.15 Economic maturity, institutionalization, economic level and growth
rates

	Coefficient	t	Beta wt	R^2	R^2A
(1) GDP growth 1961–70	−0.0007 GNP/cap. 1957	−0.93	−0.26	0.54	0.47
	−0.0762 Institutional	−3.04	−0.86		
	0.0878 Service sector	1.93	0.51		
(2) GDP growth 1971–83	0.0003 GNP/cap. 1957	0.57	0.16	0.51	0.44
	−0.0440 Institutional	−2.62	−0.76		
	−0.0107 Service sector	−0.39	−0.10		
(3) GNP/cap. growth 1960–81	−0.0009 GNP/cap. 1957	−1.72	−0.46	0.59	0.53
	−0.0457 Institutional	−2.84	−0.76		
	0.0635 Service sector	2.20	0.56		

A model that includes institutionalization in addition to economic performance is more helpful than a simple economic equation. The parameter estimated indicates that institutionalization is more important than economic level. Table 8.14 indicates a positive corroboration of the basic argument in Olson (1982): political institutions matter in relation to the average growth rates of nations. The model must fit very well. It may be argued that institutionalization merely measures another economic dimension, the economic maturity of the economy. Testing a model including an index of economic maturity – size of the third sector – does not change the findings, however (Table 8.15).

It seems to be the case that the way in which the severe methodological problems involved in the test of the Olson hypothesis are resolved has an impact on the findings (Saunders, 1986).

Unionization

Although the argument in Olson (1982) concerns all kinds of distributional coalitions, it is possible to test some implications concerning the impact of trade unions on economic growth. It is often believed that the mere existence of trade unions has a negative impact on economic growth. Olson adheres to this standard assumption, but qualifies it by adding the reverse hypothesis that encompassing trade unions promote economic growth. What is the relationship between trade unionization and economic growth in advanced capitalist societies? We will test a model that predicts economic growth by means of trade union organization, besides the general level of economic performance (Table 8.16).

It appears that the contribution of trade union organization to economic growth is slight when the level of economic performance is taken into account. Although there is an overall negative relationship between trade unionization and economic growth, as well as an overall positive relationship between trade union centralization and economic growth, these partial relations are not very strong. The argument about distributional coalitions implies that the relationship between trade union density and economic growth constitutes a U-shaped curve. Testing this implication for various time periods, we may establish that there is little confirmation of this hypothesis, except for the 1960s if the analysis also includes Spain and Portugal with their high unionization within an authoritarian state system. It could be the case that trade union organization has a more clear negative impact on economic growth, but that its partial impact will only be revealed in more complex models.

It has been argued that trade union strength is only one political factor that is of crucial importance in a politico-economic perspective. Thus we find in the literature a number of hypotheses about the implications of corporatism, consociationalism and the type of party government (Castles, 1982; Wildavsky, 1985). The question we pose is whether these factors are equally valid for predicting the variation in growth rates. Therefore, we test a number of models predicting various measures of economic growth by means of economic level plus one institutional factor at a time. Table 8.17 reports only a few of these models, namely the models with the best fit.

Table 8.16 Unionization, institutionalization, economic level and growth rates

	Coefficient	t	Beta wt	R^2	R^2A
(1) GDP growth 1961–70	−0.0002 GNP/cap. 1957	−0.25	−0.07	0.46	0.38
($n = 24$)	−0.0544 Institutional	−2.11	−0.61		
	−0.0063 Union 1960s	−0.41	−0.07		
(2) GDP growth 1971–83	0.0002 GNP/cap. 1957	0.42	0.11	0.51	0.44
($n = 24$)	−0.0458 Institutional	−2.90	−0.79		
	−0.0020 Union 1970s	−0.22	−0.04		
(3) GNP/cap. growth 1960–81	−0.0005 GNP/cap. 1957	−0.97	−0.26	0.52	0.45
($n = 24$)	−0.0273 Institutional	−1.67	−0.45		
	−0.0091 Unions 1970s	−0.99	−0.16		
(4) GNP growth 1961–70	0.0001 GNP/cap. 1957	0.16	0.05	0.52	0.36
($n = 13$)	−0.0323 Institutional	−2.22	−0.69		
	0.0016 Union centraliz.	0.93	0.22		
(5) GDP growth 1971–83	0.0003 GNP/cap. 1957	0.57	0.22	0.28	0.04
($n = 13$)	−0.0305 Institutional	−1.71	−0.65		
	0.0116 Union centraliz.	0.06	0.02		
(6) GDP/cap. growth 1960–81	0.0000 GNP/cap.	0.08	0.02	0.76	0.68
($n = 13$)	−0.0313 Institutional	−3.73	−0.82		
	0.0104 Union centraliz.	1.46	0.24		

Note: Two indices are employed to tap trade union organization (membership) as well as centralization (influence). The two indices do not coincide and the selection of different points of time for the measurement of the variable results in alternative estimates of the impact of the variable depending on the number of cases involved.

Table 8.17 Institutional factors, institutionalization, economic level and growth rates

	Coefficient	t	Beta wt	R^2	R^2A
(1) GDP growth 1961–70	−0.0004 GNP/cap. 1957	−0.50	−0.14	0.52	0.43
($n = 20$)	−0.0503 Institutional	−1.19	−0.52		
	−0.6187 Socialist domin.	−2.02	−0.38		
(2) GDP growth 1971–83	0.0002 GNP/cap. 1957	0.41	0.13	0.39	0.27
($n = 20$)	−0.0397 Institutional	−2.28	−0.70		
	−0.1075 Socialist domin.	−0.53	−0.11		
(3) GNP/cap. growth 1960–81	−0.0002 GNP/cap. 1957	−0.42	−0.11	0.59	0.51
($n = 20$)	−0.0431 Institutional	−2.68	−0.67		
	−0.1478 Socialist domin.	−0.79	−0.14		
(4) GNP growth 1971–83	−0.0002 GNP/cap. 1957	−0.19	−0.05	0.54	0.44
($n = 19$)	−0.0368 Institutional	−2.30	−0.60		
	−0.0129 Oversized cab.	−2.14	−0.38		

The finding is that adding other political factors, such as corporatism, consociationalism or type of party government, results in very minor changes in the basic explanatory power of the economic variable. It is clearly the case that economic level matters more for growth rates than these political variables. It may be pointed out that corporatist institutions may benefit economic growth, whereas socialist dominance in party governments tends to have the opposite effect, as predicted in the standard assumption about socialist governments favouring redistribution. However, it is not possible to corroborate any strong hypothesis about the contribution of these political factors to economic growth.

Public policy variables

According to mainstream economic theory, an increase in public expenditure has two opposite consequences on economic growth. Whereas spending on collective and semi-collective goods would be conducive to economic growth adding to the infrastructure of society, an increase in transfer payments would have a negative impact, favouring distribution before growth. Perhaps the variation between the OECD countries in terms of average growth rates could be accounted for by means of the variation in basic public sector dimensions: total outlays, final government consumption and social transfer payments. According to one hypothesis, public expenditures display an overall positive relationship with economic growth (Korpi, 1986; Castles, 1990). We test three models predicting economic growth by a combination of economic, institutional and policy variables (Table 8.18).

The finding is that political institutions matter more than public policies for economic growth rates. Adding various indicators of the size of the public sector does not change the finding that institutional sclerosis is the best single predictor of average economic growth. The relationships between various policy dimensions and economic growth are hardly strong, but the direction of the interaction is negative, contrary to the hypothesis that on the whole, public expenditure, in particular final government consumption, tends to promote economic growth (Korpi, 1985a, b). A large public sector, whatever its composition, does not appear to be conducive to economic growth.

Summary

Looking beyond economic theory and the standard growth models, we have searched for the non-economic factors that condition economic development in rich countries. Testing the argument in Olson (1982), we find that the length of time of institutionalization matters very much for understanding of the variation in long-run growth rates in the period 1960 to 1980, the amount of institutional sclerosis driving down average economic growth. Yet we must ask if we can detect the same effect in data about economic growth in the past decade. Let us move to a test of the models that have figured above by using data about economic growth between 1985 and 1994. Can we detect the same stable relationships between political variables and economic factors, or are there structural shift points?

Table 8.18 Public policy, institutionalization, economic level and growth rates

	Coefficient	t	Beta wt	R^2	R^2A
(1) GDP growth 1961–70	–0.0000 GNP/cap. 1957	–0.00	–0.01	0.48	0.41
(n = 20)	–0.0467 Institutional	–1.79	–0.53		
	–0.1279 Gov. fin. cons.	–1.07	–0.22		
(2) GDP growth 1971–83	0.0002 GNP/cap. 1957	0.46	0.12	0.51	0.44
(n = 20)	–0.0469 Institutional	–2.86	–0.81		
	0.0025 Gov. fin. cons.	0.05	0.01		
(3) GNP growth 1961–70	0.0002 GNP/cap. 1957	0.24	0.07	0.46	0.38
(n = 19)	–0.0527 Institutional	–1.98	–0.59		
	0.0295 Social sec. trans.	0.47	0.08		
(4) GNP growth 1971–83	0.0001 GNP/cap. 1957	0.19	0.05	0.61	0.55
(n = 19)	–0.0359 Institutional	–2.46	–0.62		
	–0.0660 Social sec. trans.	–2.24	–0.34		
(5) GNP growth 1961–70	–0.0003 GNP/cap. 1957	–0.37	–0.10	0.54	0.47
(n = 19)	–0.0378 Institutional	–1.52	–0.43		
	–0.0880 Total outlays	–1.98	–0.35		
(6) GNP growth 1971–83	0.0001 GNP/cap. 1957	0.21	0.05	0.54	0.47
(n = 19)	–0.0378 Institutional	–2.28	–0.66		
	–0.0220 Total outlays	–1.22	–0.22		
(7) GNP/cap. growth 1960–81	–0.0004 GNP/cap. 1957	–0.86	–0.24	0.50	0.42
(n = 19)	–0.0284 Institutional	–1.56	–0.47		
	–0.0082 Total outlays	–0.32	–0.06		

Note: The public policy variables refer to averages for the following periods: 1960–7, 1974–81 and 1960–81 respectively; some data have been estimated for New Zealand.

The Olson model concentrates upon one factor: institutional sclerosis. How is it to be measured? Choi suggested a time indicator for institutional sclerosis, i.e. the length of time of an uninterrupted process of institutionalization. But countries do not remain on a continuous evolution of institution formation. Countries could conceivably break with the past and reduce sclerosis, for instance by competition policy, privatization and marketization. One may also employ the Black indicator on the year of introduction of modernized leadership, but it is open to the same criticism. On the Choi index, high scores stand for much sclerosis whereas on Black's index, high scores stand for late modernization.

Table 8.19 Economic growth 1985–94 (annual rates)

OECD		Third World		Post-communist	
Ireland	5.2	Thailand	8.2	China	6.9
Portugal	4.0	South Korea	7.8	Mozambique	3.5
Japan	3.2	Singapore	6.9	Laos	2.1
Spain	2.7	Botswana	6.6	Tanzania	1.1
Austria	2.3	Chile	6.2	Poland	0.9
Belgium	2.3	Indonesia	6.0	Burkina Faso	−0.2
Germany	1.9	Malaysia	5.7	Ethiopia	−0.6
Netherlands	1.9	Mauritius	5.6	Benin	−0.8
Italy	1.8	Hong Kong	5.3	Angola	−0.9
France	1.7	Namibia	3.4	Hungary	−0.9
Turkey	1.5	Uganda	3.0	Turkmenistan	−1.5
Norway	1.4	Uruguay	3.0	Belorus	−1.7
UK	1.4	India	2.9	Algeria	−2.4
Denmark	1.3	Costa Rica	2.8	Uzbekistan	−2.4
Greece	1.3	Nepal	2.2	Bulgaria	−3.2
USA	1.3	Bangladesh	2.1	Slovakia	−3.3
Luxembourg	1.3	Dominican Rep.	2.1	Russia	−4.4
Australia	1.2	Papua New Guinea	2.1	Ukraine	−5.1
New Zealand	0.5	Argentina	1.9	Kyrgyzstan	−5.4
Switzerland	0.5	Bolivia	1.9	Albania	−6.0
Canada	0.4	Colombia	1.9	Romania	−6.2
Iceland	0.3	Philippines	1.8	Latvia	−6.2
Sweden	0.0	Tunisia	1.8	Nicaragua	−6.4
Finland	−0.3	Morocco	1.1	Estonia	−6.4
		Ecuador	1.0	Kazakhstan	−6.5
Mean	1.6	Paraguay	1.0	Lithuania	−7.8
CV	0.77	Chad	0.9	Tajikistan	−11.7
		Guatemala	0.9		
		Mali	0.9	Mean	−3.8
		Mexico	0.6	CV	1.36
		Oman	0.6		
		Venezuela	0.6		
		Lesotho	0.5		
		Mauritania	0.2		
		United Arab Em.	0.2		
		Kenya	0.0		
		Panama	0.0		
		Honduras	−0.1		
		Mean	0.6		
		CV	5.3		

Source: World Bank (1996).

Politics and economic growth 1985 to 1994

Searching for the political conditions for economic development, we have thus far been able partly to confirm the Olson model. In explaining the country variation in average economic growth rates between 1960 and 1980 among OECD countries, it is impossible to by-pass institutional sclerosis. But in relation to the interpretation of the country variation in growth rates among both rich and poor countries, other factors than institutional sclerosis, such as investments, play a larger role. How do things stand when we look at the most recent data about economic growth?

Table 8.19 gives the country variation in growth rates between 1985 and 1994, where countries are classified as OECD, Third World and post-communist, and ranked according to average growth rate.

We can see that economic growth rates vary tremendously between countries. Not only is the difference between the minimum and maximum scores tremendous, but it is also the case that clusters of countries perform very differently. Thus, economic growth in the former command economies has been dismal with the exception of China. Economic growth among Third World countries varies in an extreme fashion, from countries with huge negative growth rates to countries with highly positive growth scores. Finally, among the OECD countries (excluding Mexico) the variation is not that large, as most countries have had a rather meagre growth rate during this time period, although the difference between Ireland and Portugal on the one hand and Sweden and Finland on the other hand is a substantial 4 or 5 per cent per year.

Which factors help us to understand this variation in economic development during the past decade? Which are the common factors behind the fast growing countries, and are there any common variables which the slow growing countries share? Let us test a few models discussed above relating to underlying factors such as: (a) institutional sclerosis; (b) public sector size; (c) economic system; (d) investments; (e) openness of the economy. We will employ three country samples, one for the OECD countries, one for the Third World countries and one for all countries, including the post-communist countries.

Table 8.20 reports regression analyses on factors related to economic growth, holding GDP constant, according to the maturity hypothesis or the catch-up model.

It is possible to proceed to a conclusive evaluation on the basis of the findings in Table 8.20. The Olson model, pinpointing institutional sclerosis, is of little relevance for understanding economic development in the past decade. This is all the more astonishing, as the model was quite useful in relation to the interpretation of economic growth between 1960 and 1980. What is of crucial importance is instead another institutional factor; the degree of economic freedom in the overall regime governing transactions. Perhaps one should look for another indicator of institutional sclerosis, since the one adopted here – length of time of uninterrupted institutionalization – has little relevance with regard to the time period 1985 to 1994. Countries may change their institutional patterns whether they have a long tradition or not.

Table 8.20 Regression analysis: economic growth 1985–94

	All Countries			OECD			Third World		
	Coeff.	t	r	Coeff.	t	r	Coeff.	t	r
LNRGDP80	0.47	1.43	0.17	−1.59	−2.15	−0.44	0.50	1.25	0.17
Sclerosis	0.00	0.12	0.07	−0.00	−0.39	0.14	−0.00	−0.41	−0.04
R^2A	0.01			0.12			0.00		
LNRGDP80	0.72	2.70	0.17	−0.81	−1.34	−0.44	0.90	2.14	0.17
Govcon92	−0.11	−2.41	−0.25	−0.15	−2.82	−0.56	−0.13	−2.28	−0.23
R^2A	0.08			0.31			0.11		
LNRGDP80	−0.89	−2.57	0.17	−2.68	−3.18	−0.44	−0.52	−1.07	0.17
Ecfr95	1.41	6.71	0.57	0.69	2.10	−0.03	1.48	5.59	0.60
R^2A	0.35			0.27			0.36		
LNRGDP80	−0.05	−0.16	0.17	−2.22	−2.45	−0.44	0.26	0.66	0.17
Ecfree	−0.67	−2.52	−0.48	−0.84	−1.18	0.16	−0.63	−1.52	−0.26
R^2A	0.06			0.17			0.02		
LNRGDP80	0.12	0.36	0.17	−1.35	−1.93	−0.44	0.08	0.19	0.17
Inv6085	0.08	1.82	0.26	−0.01	−0.19	−0.15	0.11	1.89	0.26
R^2A	0.05			0.10			0.04		
LNRGDP80	0.27	1.13	0.17	−1.23	−1.92	−0.44	−0.37	−1.10	0.17
Inv95	0.17	5.49	0.37	0.08	1.37	0.36	0.27	6.70	0.57
R^2A	0.22			0.19			0.40		
LNRGDP80	0.37	1.45	0.17	−1.58	−2.47	−0.44	0.38	0.95	0.17
Open80	0.01	1.41	0.16	0.01	1.15	0.14	0.01	1.44	0.21
R^2A	0.03			0.17			0.03		
LNRGDP80	0.65	3.12	0.17	−1.31	−1.80	−0.44	1.08	3.51	0.17
GDI8093	0.43	9.32	0.53	0.03	0.26	0.22	0.40	7.88	0.70
R^2A	0.50			0.10			0.54		
LNRGDP80	−0.06	−0.23	0.17	−2.57	−2.59	−0.44	0.58	1.61	0.17
Ecfr95	0.73	4.06	0.57	0.64	1.77	−0.03	0.72	3.51	0.60
GDI8093	0.39	8.54	0.53	0.00	0.00	0.22	0.39	8.37	0.70
R^2A	0.67			0.19			0.74		

Note: n varies from 86 to 114 for all, from 21 to 24 for OECD and from 56 to 76 for the Third World. Economic growth 1985–94, World Bank (1996); LNRGDP80 (the natural logarithm of real GDP 1980), Summers and Heston (1994); Sclerosis (institutional sclerosis), Black (1966); Govcon92 (general government consumption expenditure/GDP), UNDP (1995); ECFR95 (degree of economic freedom 1995), Gwartney *et al.* (1996); ECFREE (degree of economic freedom), Wright (1982); INV6085 (investments as a percentage of GDP on average, 1960–85), Mankiew *et al.* (1992); INV95 (investments as a percentage of GDP 1994), World Bank (1995b, 1996); OPEN80 (openness of the economy 1980), Summers and Heston (1994); GDI8093 (average annual growth rate of gross domestic investment 1980–93), World Bank (1995a).

The crucial importance of investment is again apparent in the data. It is not the level of investment that is critical, but the yearly growth in investment, as predicted in a conventional accelerator model. It is most interesting to observe once again that economic growth in rich countries is less sensitive to investment, which remains the key factor in the Third World and the post-communist world. Economic growth in the OECD world has a different background, which will be analysed in Chapter 12.

Conclusion

The Olson hypothesis about a relationship between institutional sclerosis and economic growth has attracted a lot of attention. It has been argued that there are severe measurement problems involved in the Olson hypothesis (Saunders, 1986; Weede, 1986; Castles, 1990), particularly with regard to the indicator on institutional sclerosis. Although the Olson hypothesis has stimulated several attempts to test the theory empirically, it is difficult to make an overall assessment of the empirical evaluation. It has been argued that the theory has met with empirical corroboration, but also that there are severe counter-instances (Mueller, 1983; *International Studies Quarterly*, 1983). Moreover, it has been claimed that the theory is very difficult to test, as it is problematic to measure institutional sclerosis.

Yet we have applied the Olson model when interpreting economic growth data, first for the 1960 to 1980 period, and then for the time period 1985 to 1994. By measuring the length of time of uninterrupted modern institutions – institutional longevity – we have measured one aspect of institutional sclerosis. There are two major findings. When institutional sclerosis matters, we are talking about the variation in growth rates in rich countries, and almost exclusively with regard to the time period 1960 to 1980. In relation to these countries and with regard to this time period, institutional sclerosis really matters. However, this is only a partial corroboration of the model.

The second major finding is that economic growth in poor countries is driven by, on the one hand, the economic regime and, on the other hand, investment. As predicted by standard economic growth theory, a yearly increase in investment has a profound impact upon average growth rates. Typical for the time period 1985 to 1994 is that countries with a decentralized market economy perform better than the other kinds of politico-economic regimes. Perhaps it is in pure capitalism that we find the least degree of institutional sclerosis, meaning that the Olson factor should be measured in a totally different manner.

In any case, it seems that variations in average economic growth rates have a complex background in behavioural and institutional factors, among which institutional sclerosis is only one. Economic growth varies very much, and it is not always the case that the same countries do well or badly from one year to another. We end with an analysis of variance of economic growth rates for 1985 to 1994, showing that time and space explain little (Table 8.21).

Table 8.21 Analysis of variance of GDP growth rates 1985–94 by country and time

GDP growth

	GDP growth
Country ($n = 24$)	0.11 (0.25)
Time ($n = 10$)	0.20 (0.00)

Note: The eta-squared statistic has been computed for the OECD countries where the number of cases is 24 × 10 = 240. The larger the eta coefficient (between 0 and 1), the more the total variation is explained by the category.

Source: OECD (1985, 1995a).

Appendix 8.1 Sources of predictors for Tables 8.2–8.10

GDInv. level: Gross Domestic Investment in per cent of GDP 1960, 1965, 1970, 1977, 1980	World Bank, 1983
GDInv. change: Growth in Gross Domestic Investment 1960–80	World Bank, 1983
Labour force: male labour force participation rate 1960, 1980	World Bank, 1983
Export: export in per cent of GDP 1960,1980	World Bank, 1983
Primary education	World Bank, 1983
Secondary education: enrolment 1960, 1980	World Bank, 1983
Higher education: enrolment 1975	Taylor, 1981
Agricultural change: change in agricultural employment 1960–80	World Bank, 1984
Institutional sclerosis	Choi, 1983; Taylor and Hudson, 1972
Democracy *c*. 1965	Bollen, 1980
Socialist government: post-Second World War	Schmidt, 1983b; Delury, 1983
Public expenditure in per cent of GDP *c*. 1977	IMF, 1982

9 Third World policy choice: growth or redistribution?

Introduction

The basic outcome characteristic of a Third World country is poverty. Third World countries may have different kinds of political institutions, ranging from right-wing authoritarian to left-wing authoritarian regimes, with a few democracies in between, such as Costa Rica, Botswana and India. It is true that Third World countries are not equally poor. There is a considerable range of variation from the countries that face the threat of mass famine and those that have a real opportunity to catch up with some of the countries in the First World. However, the overall predicament of Third World countries is the economic condition of low average GDP per capita scores.

Since mass poverty sets the tone for life in a country, the critical policy problem in a Third World country is what can be done about it. What kinds of economic policy should government pursue in order to improve upon the plight of the masses: growth and/or redistribution? One assumption is already made when this question is phrased in this manner, namely that the political elite in the country is committed to benevolent purposes. In some Third World countries governments have other objectives than furthering the interests of those governed. Here, we start from an assumption of benevolent political elites.

Our case is the Republic of South Africa (RSA), for which country the assumption is not out of place. The RSA is an interesting case for several reasons, both economic and political. Now, the government of the RSA faces several critical policy choices (Schrire, 1990, 1992), one of which is growth versus redistribution (*Financial Times*, 2 May 1995). Theoretically, we will draw upon the implications of the Kuznets curve, discussed in Chapter 3.

The problem

Poverty may coexist with huge income differentials. In some Third World countries a small portion of the population holds sway over a large share of national income and wealth. Where income inequality is huge, the question of redistribution arises. In other Third World countries poverty is shared by all, which implies that redistributive issues have little policy relevance. The RSA is characterized by sharp income inequalities.

Poverty in this country may be counteracted by either of two strategies: economic growth or income and wealth redistribution. Which strategy is the best one?

Economic policies may be evaluated on different grounds. On the one hand, there are criteria that belong under the efficiency umbrella, or all the kinds of criteria one may use to enquire about effectiveness and efficiency. On the other hand, we have criteria related to practical expediency or to what is politically acceptable. Economic efficiency versus political feasibility may imply very different economic policies, because the former types of policies may be politically unacceptable and the latter types of policies may be economically counterproductive. Usually, the conflict between economic efficiency and political expediency shows up in a confrontation between short-term goals and long-term goals, at least with regard to economic policy-making.

Here the focus is upon one objective: to combat poverty. The critical question concerns the choice of a strategy to achieve that objective in the most efficient way. Looking first at efficiency, we end up discussing political feasibility. We should point out that poverty will be approached in terms of the GDP per capita indicator, which is a limitation, as poverty involves many other things than purchasing power. In addition, we make the assumption that there are two real policy alternatives, in the sense that it is possible for a country like South Africa to enter a process of sustained economic growth and that redistribution can take place. One may argue that these alternatives have a low degree of likelihood for various reasons, meaning that economic growth in the RSA is going to be low whatever policy steps are taken, and that income redistribution would be resisted to such a degree as to make it virtually impossible. Yet let us make the above assumptions, or more specifically that the RSA has the potential of a sustained economic growth rate of 5 per cent.

The distinction between economic growth and redistributive policies follows Musgrave's framework, separating between the allocative branch and the redistributive branch of government (Musgrave, 1959; Musgrave and Musgrave, 1986). Redistribution covers not only money transfers but also redistribution in kind, i.e. the provision of goods and services to people virtually free of charge for the purpose of equity. Economic growth policies lead to an increase in total output in the economy and are motivated by efficiency.

Whether redistributive policies take the form of cash transfers or the provision of goods and services without user fees, they have to be financed in principle by taxation, raising revenues from the affluent or wealthy income strata. This type of taxation may also in itself promote more equality in society, which has been a traditional concern in considerations of equity. Below we will not specify whether it is a matter of redistribution in money or in kind, but we will assume that any kind of redistribution is paid for by means of some kind of tax scheme levelled upon those who can pay; for instance, by means of a tax on income. In the South African debate one is well aware of the trade-off between redistribution and economic growth (see Schrire, 1992; also Wilson and Ramphele, 1989; Moll *et al.*, 1991).

A naive model

In order to combat poverty, a Third World country has to accomplish growth in the national income that is higher than the increase in the population. Thus, we have the first condition:

$$dY > dP \tag{1}$$

where Y is national income and P is population.

It is a well known fact that the population of South Africa is growing very rapidly, which makes it imperative that the rate of growth in the economy picks up, simply for the rather modest objective of maintaining average income. The second condition refers to the distribution of the gains from a sustained process of economic growth, because if the additional income generated by economic growth is not distributed to the poor, then poverty may remain the same while the extent of skewedness in the income distribution simply increases. Thus, we have that:

Income inequality must not increase $\tag{2}$

The basic model requirement here is that the gains for a long period of economic growth are shared by all. The contribution from economic growth to counteracting poverty will be much higher the more the gains are distributed to the low income groups. Finally, we have to start from one point in time, meaning that national income will have a fixed value, N^*, and we have to specify the time horizon, in this case roughly two decades. We make no assumptions about discounting, but assume that one rand tomorrow has the same utility as one rand today. Thus,

$$N = N^*, \; T0 = 1992, \tag{3a}$$

and

$$dY/Y = 5 \text{ per cent up to } T18 = 2010. \tag{3b}$$

These three assumptions, (1) to (3), will now be applied to data about the South African economy and society, in order to calculate what the growth option implies and what the redistributive option entails. We will focus on the distribution of income and not wealth. Redistributing wealth as a stock is much more difficult to accomplish without major economic or social problems. Moreover, it may be argued that the implications of wealth distribution are to some extent taken into account in the data about income distribution, since the yearly rent on capital is an income flow.

Household income

It is well known that the distribution of income and wealth is highly skewed in the RSA, although the available and most recent data are not entirely first-class. This reflects large differences in wages and income from the ownership of capital and land. What is distinctive of the RSA is not only the extreme income differentials but also the fact that they coincide with ethnic differences. One of the most interesting policy questions in the RSA is the impact of the dissolution of the Apartheid system on the class system, especially when the economy, as now, moves towards a rather steady and fairly strong growth path.

National income in 1992 amounted to some 325 billion rand, which can first be divided between the major aggregates shown in Table 9.1. One US dollar was equivalent to 3.5 rand.

Table 9.1 GDP in RSA in 1992 (million rand)

Public consumption expenditure	69700
Gross domestic saving	53203
Private consumption expenditure	203407
Other items	10000
Total	326300

Source: Race Relations Survey (1994/5).

What government can redistribute is the sum of the GDP that goes to private consumption expenditure. Gross domestic savings are needed for investment if any rate of economic growth is to be at all possible. Gross savings include depreciation costs for existing physical capital. Similarly, the costs for government at various levels have to be covered, including public goods and infrastructure, which both enhance economic growth. Finally, the RSA has a negative capital flow in relation to the external world, which must be covered in order for the RSA to be able to operate in the international capital markets.

In 1992 the average income per capita in the RSA was 8160 rand which is simply the total national income divided by the population – 40 million people at that time. However, the real distribution of purchasing power is totally different, because not all the national income can be distributed for private consumption and the actual distribution of income to households follows ethnic lines to a very high extent.

A major concern has been the unequal income distribution. Table 9.2 shows the distribution of household income for various groups, stating both the mean household income before tax and the share of the total group income of the respective decile.

Table 9.2 Distribution of pre-tax income around 1993 (percentage shares)

Decile	African		Coloured		Asian		White		All	
	Mean	Share	Mean	Share	Mean	Share	Mean	Share	Mean	Share
1	831	0.6	3172	1.1	6592	1.1	10262	1.0	1161	0.4
2	2841	2.1	7547	2.5	14790	2.6	27940	2.8	3638	1.1
3	4264	3.2	11136	3.7	21511	3.7	42570	4.3	5422	1.7
4	5596	4.2	15185	5.0	28505	4.9	54477	5.5	7618	2.4
5	7274	5.4	19947	6.6	38692	6.7	66878	6.8	10481	3.3
6	9227	6.9	26726	8.9	48018	8.3	80025	8.1	14895	4.6
7	12139	9.1	33410	11.1	57486	10.0	95621	9.7	21780	6.8
8	16365	12.2	41161	13.7	73911	12.8	117672	12.0	34947	10.9
9	23673	17.6	53649	17.8	97376	16.9	152016	15.4	60571	18.8
10	51919	38.7	88966	29.6	189839	32.9	333462	34.2	161242	50.1

Source: A Profile of Poverty, Inequality and Human Development in South Africa. Human Science Research Council, 1995.

Since income inequality in South Africa is among the most pronounced in the world, one may argue that there is scope for redistributing money either by transfer payments or by redistribution in kind. An expert on the distribution of income in South Africa, Mike McGrath, estimates the Gini-coefficient for RSA to be as high as 0.68 – clearly the highest Gini-score in the world. Calculation of the Gini-score from Table 9.2 results in a somewhat lower score, 0.63. McGrath (in Whiteford, Posel and Keletwang, 1995) concludes that redistributive policies should be introduced.

However, data on the distribution of income are only one side of the story. The redistribution option has to take into account a number of additional factors. First, redistribution can only be done with regard to after-tax income, because parts of the national income must be used to cover the costs of vital government functions, such as the provision of public goods. Table 9.3 shows monthly household after-tax income data.

Table 9.3 Monthly household after-tax income 1993

Income group (R/month)	African proportion	Asian prop.	Coloured prop.	White prop.
1–499	34.5	3.7	17.0	1.5
500–799	18.6	4.5	10.1	2.2
800–1399	28.4	19.2	22.6	6.5
1400–2499	11.8	20.0	20.9	12.0
2500–3999	4.3	21.7	16.4	18.7
4000–5999	1.5	18.0	7.9	21.1
6000–7999	0.4	8.8	3.4	16.0
8000+	0.3	4.0	1.6	22.0
Average	996	3261	2050	5602

Source: Race Relations Survey (1994/5: 493).

Data on the distribution of after-tax household income in the RSA have been collected by the South African Advertising Research Foundation. The information is published in the yearly handbook Race Relations Survey, which gives after-tax income data for households, broken down for the four major groups: white, coloured, Asians and blacks.

The available data on the distribution of income can be used to allot most of the national income item for private consumption expenditure to households. Actually, the sum of 175 billion rand corresponds almost completely with the item remuneration to employees in the national income statistics in the RSA, which lists 179 billion rand for 1992.

Second, one must be aware of the fact that the distribution of income in the RSA has two components, the between-ethnic-groups dimension and the within-ethnic-groups dimension. Although considerable income differences exist within the four major ethnic groups, it remains true that the between-ethnic-group differences are larger than the within-ethnic-group differences. Table 9.4 shows the average data for 1992 on monthly and yearly bases.

Table 9.4 Household after-tax income by groups 1992 (rand)

	White	Coloured	Asian	Black
Monthly income	5160	1800	2900	900
Yearly income	62000	21500	34500	11000
Number of households (1000s)	1630	580	180	5000
Total income (billions)	101	12.5	6.2	55

Source: *Race Relations Survey* (1994/5).

The white community as a whole has about twice as much income as the black community, although it is far smaller. One must note that the average size of a black household is far larger than that of a white household: 3.2 members in a white household, 5.2 members in a coloured household, 4.8 members in an Asian household and 5.9 members in a black household.

The income profile of white households is entirely different from that of the households in the other ethnic communities, although it should also be pointed out that there are poor white households. The implication is clearly that redistribution in South Africa entails increasing the taxation on rather few medium and high income white households and distributing the money to numerous black households with far more members than the white households.

A majority of the white households earn more than 4000 rand per month while five-sixths of the black households have to live on less than 1400 rand per month. Asian households are doing relatively better than black and coloured households on average. The Department of National Health and Population Development calculates the 1992 per capita after-tax monthly incomes (at 1990 prices) for blacks, coloureds, Asians and whites at 160, 270, 470 and 1300 rand respectively, which is in agreement with the data given above.

Third, any redistributive policy bringing down the level of income inequality would have to involve substantial lump sums from the high and middle income white households, since they are the only ones that earn enough money to be extensively taxed. Is this politically feasible, even if it were rational from an economic point of view?

Projections

Economic policy-making oriented towards the amelioration of mass poverty in the RSA has to take two major parameters into account. First is the overall trend in population growth and second is the potential of the economy to follow a steady growth path. The government can do little to influence the first parameter, but the second parameter is sensitive to the framing of economic policies – short-term as well as long-term ones. It is true that the RSA has a population policy, but it is not likely that the government can do much about the projected rapid population growth for the next twenty years.

The future population growth figures for the African continent are projected to be at a very high level, which also applies to the RSA. Whereas these growth rates will cause famine in some African countries, they will constitute a major challenge to the RSA. If poverty is not to increase, then the average growth rate in the economy must at least be higher than the average population increase. Table 9.5 shows data about the projected increase in population.

Table 9.5 Projected population growth 1990–2010 (in millions)

	Whole RSA	Whites	Coloureds	Asians	Blacks
1990	39	5	3.2	1	30.3
2010	64	5.5	4.3	1.2	53

Source: Race Relations Survey (1994).

These projections about the population increase in the next two decades involve almost a doubling of the population of the RSA. This will create tremendous pressure on the labour market, where the rate of unemployment is already high, especially in the densely populated black townships. In order for the level of unemployment to stay the same, there has to be economic growth, with an attendant increase in employment for the large groups of mainly young blacks entering the economically active population. One cannot make any strict connections between the rate of growth in the economy and the increase in employment, as Table 9.6 shows.

Table 9.6 RSA: economic growth and increase in employment 1960–89

Years	GDP growth (%)	Employment increase (%)
1960–9	5.6	2.6
1970–9	3.3	1.7
1980–9	2.0	1.0

Source: Race Relations Survey (1993).

If these relationships between economic growth figures and employment increase rates are predicting the future, it seems unavoidable that unemployment will go up in the RSA.

It may be mentioned that the structure of the South African economy is entirely different from that of the other countries on the African continent. The RSA is a highly industrialized and urbanized country, where the majority of the population does not, as in other African countries, live in rural areas, trying to survive on the basis of inefficient agriculture. The heart of the economy is the mining and industrial sectors, while the agricultural sector is large enough to support the entire population with relatively inexpensive food. The economy is divided into three sectors: those employed in the formal sector, those working in the informal sector and the unemployed, where the borderline between the informal economy and those unemployed is blurred.

How long would it take for the RSA to double its national income? It depends. One must distinguish between an absolute doubling of GDP and a doubling of GDP per capita, because when population growth is projected to reach such high rates, even high expansion rates for the economy may be required just to maintain average living standards. Let us assume that the economy of the RSA has the potential of a 5 per cent yearly growth rate. What would it mean for the absolute level of GDP and the GDP per capita? Table 9.7 shows the data.

Table 9.7 Projected economic growth rate: 5 per cent per year

	GDP (billion rand)	Population (millions)	GDP per capita (rand)
1992	327	40	8160
2010	787	64	12300

Given the assumption of a 5 per cent growth rate, the RSA would nearly double its national income within 18 years, which would involve a not inconsiderable increase in the relative average income, i.e. GDP per capita. It would rise by 50 per cent, which is a quite substantial figure given the projected drastic increase in the overall population. Should the population growth number turn out to be overestimated, then the increase in relative income could only be even more substantial. The impact upon poverty of a sustained process of economic growth of 5 per cent per year will depend upon how the rise in total income is distributed among the households in the various ethnic communities. What about the redistribution option?

Redistribution alternatives

What can be redistributed is not the entire GDP but only the part of it that ends up as private consumption expenditure. In any society that wishes to have a decent future, there must be public expenditure and investment. One may question the division of the national income in the RSA between wages and profit, as the share of the latter seems to be higher than is usual. However, a considerable portion of the national income must be set aside for savings, which result in investment. Without the latter there can be no economic growth.

What can be redistributed is a portion of the income of groups with a higher than average income. In the RSA that would imply redistributing income from white households to non-white households or black households. What would a policy of income redistribution mean practically in the RSA, in the short term and the long term? Let us give a few examples.

Example 1: Take 10 per cent from White to Coloured and Black Households

Short-term perspective
What would it imply to redistribute in general from the white households to the non-white households? The average white household has an after-tax income of 62000 rand and there are 1.63 million white households comprising on average 3.2 persons. Suppose that one decides on a redistributive policy that will

redistribute 10 per cent of white household income to the households in the other three communities. What would be the consequences in the short term?

Ten per cent of the average white household income means 6200 rand and, since there are 1.63 million white households, the total available sum to redistribute would amount to about 10 billion rand, assuming no losses in national income due to redistributive taxation. Since there are some 5.6 million coloured and black households, a 10 per cent income redistribution would give each of these households 1800 rand, which, given the large size of these households, would mean some 310 rand per person per year or less than 1 rand per day.

Long-term perspective
One may have different opinions about the impact of redistribution upon the size of the cake that is to be divided. Redistribution may lower total national income by hurting the incentive system, or it may increase national income by provoking a larger work effort in order to counteract the loss of income owing to taxation. We will not bring up this contested issue here, because we will only take the projected increase in the population into account. Suppose that national income is neither reduced nor increased owing to the 10 per cent redistribution.

Since the projected growth in population involves a tremendous expansion of the black population, the 10 per cent redistribution of white household income would by the year 2000 mean about 1000 rand per coloured and black household or 200 rand per person per year. Around 2010 it would mean less than 0.5 rand per day per person. Although the overall efficiency of such a redistributional policy appears low, there is one major difficulty. A portion of the white households live close to poverty, meaning that a 10 per cent reduction in their incomes would be difficult to make. Let us take another redistribution example.

Example 2: Take 10 Billion Rand from Rich White to Black and Coloured Households

There are some 900 000 white households that earn more than 48 000 rand. In order to get hold of 10 billion rand the state would have to withhold some 11 000 rand from each of these households. The redistributive effect would be the same in the short-run perspective and the long-run perspective. However, redistributing 11 000 rand away from white households means a substantial decrease in the living standard of the rich white community. It is impossible not to bring up the question of feasibility in relation to such a redistributive policy. Let us, before we discuss feasibility, look at a third and less drastic proposal.

Example 3: Take 2000 Rand from Each Middle and Rich White Household to Each Poor Black Household

Such a redistribution would assemble some 3 billion rand, given the existence of roughly 1.5 million white households above the cut-off point for low income households. Since there are some 4.3 million poor black households below the same income line, they would receive almost 700 rand per household per year, which boils down to 0.3 rand per person per day.

The conclusion that redistribution is inferior to economic growth as a method for improving the lot of the many poor in the RSA appears to be the reasonable policy interpretation of these numerical examples. Yet economic policy-making need not be either pure growth or pure redistribution. An economic policy oriented towards the improvement of the predicament of the poor could employ some mixed strategy, involving modest redistribution with a high rate of economic growth.

In any case, the potential contribution of a sustained process of economic growth to income equality is much larger than the impact of various redistributional schemes. In relation to the African situation, characterized by tremendous population growth, the only road ahead is the growth option. A combination of slow economic growth with considerable redistribution would result in a predicament where almost everyone was poor.

Feasibility

Any discussion about the feasibility of an economic policy directed towards poverty would have to take into account both the general problems involved in the redistribution–growth trade-off and the special circumstances of the country concerned. One may be optimistic in relation to the future prospects of the RSA but sceptical about the possibilities of resolving some of the main difficulties in the redistribution–growth trade-off. Let us start with the present predicament of the political economy of the RSA.

State finance as well as the structure of the economy have an impact upon what economic policies may achieve. The South African economy is a truly modern one, highly industrialized and comprising advanced economic institutions such as the stock exchange in Johannesburg (Nattrass, 1981; Nattrass and Ardington, 1990; Du Toit, 1992). Its performance deteriorated during the end of the Apartheid regime, as reflected in declining rates of economic growth as well as in increasing capital flight abroad. The economic decline of the RSA was attended by a sharp depreciation of its currency, the rand. It is an open question whether economic decline in the RSA was due to internal factors connected with the Apartheid system or whether the external boycott of the RSA was the major contributor. Clearly, the blockade had repercussions for economic life, increasingly as time went by. However, at the same time the economic nationalist policies of the Apartheid regime, underlining import substitution, also weakened the economy. Labour relations remained very tense under the discrimination regime (Bendix, 1989; Barker, 1992).

After the fall of the Apartheid system the private sector has picked up, with economic growth projections rising to 3 per cent in the short-run perspective (*Financial Times*, 18 July 1994). Investments have gone up as the economy has been opened up to foreign capital. However, the political situation in the RSA is still not considered stable enough for a major investment drive, as basic constitutional issues remain unresolved. It may be argued that the RSA economy remains very much focused upon mining and gold. The Johannesburg stock index has risen sharply since the political transition.

Yet redistribution must come from taxation. Thus, we need to look at state finances when considering the feasibility of the redistribution option. The limits on what the government can do derive not only from the private sector economy but also from the shape of the state finances. Here the situation is not entirely bright, because the state of the RSA is already in great debt.

Total public expenditure stood in 1995 at about 30 per cent of GDP, which means some 150 billion rand. Total income is only 120 billion rand, which entails a deficit spending of about 6 per cent of GDP – a high figure not only for a Third World country but also for the advanced economies. A prolonged period of deficit spending has resulted in a rather substantial state debt, which now stands at about 45 per cent of GDP. Deficit spending on this scale must mean that the rand cannot appreciate against other major currencies, at least not until the budget is balanced. But to balance the budget would require sharp increases in taxation, which would leave even less space for redistribution. What is feasible is to change the structure of the state budget somewhat, since military spending accounts for a high 10 per cent of total expenditure.

Whereas the state budget is not in balance, it is a strength of the South African economy that it has almost achieved external balance. Exports amount to some 80 billion rand and imports are somewhat lower, at 75 billion rand, meaning that there is a surplus on the trade account. The RSA has an open economy, with the impex indicator scoring a high 45 per cent. However, there is at the same time a deficit on the current account owing to a heavy flow of capital from the RSA. It is a major objective of economic policy to halt and possibly reverse the outflow of capital by, for instance, more foreign investment. Again, here we have a restraint on possible redistribution policies. Since foreign liabilities (95 billion rand) are greater than foreign assets (64 billion rand), the government cannot afford to engage in a redistribution policy that further aggravates the deficit on the current account. The running costs on its foreign liabilities take a substantial part of the income from exports.

It is difficult to see any real opportunity for a radical policy of redistribution. The tax rates already levied are not enough to balance the budget. The average tax rate on the rich white households is already almost 50 per cent. In addition, there is now a lot of demand for policies other than simply income redistribution.

A major policy effort has been launched in housing, where the key issue is not income redistribution but redistribution in kind, i.e. the provision of certain goods and services targeted for deprived groups. If the new government places a high priority upon redistribution in kind in other policy areas as well, such as education, health and social care for the elderly, then there is not going to be much money left over for true income redistribution.

Finally, one may bring up the whole question of political feasibility, as distinct from economic feasibility. Whereas the latter basically relates to the well known efficiency–equity trade-off (Okun, 1975), the former is less well known and has not been modelled in any precise way. How much redistribution are the high income earners going to accept before they react? Will there really be a strong enough redistributive coalition to initiate a radical policy of redistribution? Should a black bourgeoisie emerge, what is the likelihood that it will support radical redistribution?

One must remember that the new government presented its first budget in the spring of 1995. At the same time that this budget proposal was made public, the government abolished one of the characteristic features of the Apartheid economy, the dual exchange system. The distinction between the financial and commercial rand was a tool for controlling capital flows into and out of South Africa, although it never worked perfectly. The distance between the two currencies was at times as large as 30 per cent barring inlanders from transferring money out of South Africa. The reform is part of the general opening up of the South African economy to the external world, removing restrictions to trade and financial flows. However, it is attended by uncertainties about whether the rand is overvalued, which, again, sets limits to what the government can do in terms of redistribution. The RSA can hardly cope with large increases in debt, whether external or internal, because it would reduce the economic growth prospects.

The financial rand was a special investment currency available only to foreigners and designed to protect South Africa's foreign reserves against capital withdrawals triggered by political instability. The demise of the financial rand has been regarded as a condition for more foreign investments in the RSA, but the double concerns about international investor confidence and internal capital flight have made the government hesitant about getting rid of this currency. One should observe that the very tight restrictions on residents taking money out of the RSA were not abolished when the unified rand made its debut in March 1995.

The first budget of a non-racist government favoured the growth option (*Financial Times*, 2 May 1995). At the same time, government spending was to be restrained in order to drop the fiscal deficit from 6.4 per cent of GDP to 5.8 per cent, and there will be increased spending in education, housing and health, meaning more redistribution in kind. Total public expenditures for 1995–6 was estimated at some 150 billion rand, with as much as 38 billion rand as the borrowing requirement. One must bear in mind that the economy of the RSA has a strong inflationary bent, which may be fuelled by too much public expenditure at a time when the real resources in the economy are still not abundant, given an estimated growth rate of 2.7 per cent for 1995–6 (*Financial Times*, 3 October 1996). Again, the interpretation of the economic realities speaks for the growth option.

Conclusion

It is true that economic policy-making involves a number of different issues, but many of them relate to the crucial dilemma: growth or redistribution. Third World countries handle this policy dilemma in a number of ways, trading off growth measures against distributional considerations in various policy mixes. The South-East Asian model implies a strong preference for the growth option, with the hope that the short-term sacrifices caused by a heavy commitment to economic growth policies will be more than compensated by long-term gains in the form of a higher level of affluence for all. In several Third World countries, economic policies have failed in the sense that poverty has increased, mainly owing to population growth outpacing any increase in GDP.

The international attention paid to the RSA derives from the fact that the country is both similar to and different from the South-East Asian tigers. The basic difference is the commitment to democracy, which makes it all the more imperative that the RSA does not fail in its ambitions to reduce poverty in one part of the African continent, where in general mass poverty is highly visible. The RSA is similar to the NICs in South-East Asia in its economic potential, because it has the natural resources, the labour and the economic institutions that are necessary for a sustained process of economic expansion. What in the RSA could be a major restriction on the possibility of achieving a high rate of economic growth over a longer period of time is the lack of labour force with advanced training, especially in management and engineering.

There are two major impediments to the making of an economic success story out of the RSA, namely political instability and redistributional zest. Whereas the probability of political stability is difficult to estimate, the consequences of a redistributional policy emphasis are not difficult to calculate. Given the projected population growth for the RSA, any policy that does not give first priority to economic growth will result in increased poverty.

Poverty is a chief feature of Third World countries. What policies should governments in these countries pursue in order to combat poverty? This policy choice is critical for Third World governments, often facing a society with sharp income inequalities among various groups. It has been argued that redistribution is what is needed, but it may be shown, however, that the growth option is superior to redistributive policies. Actually, the same policy alternatives – economic growth versus redistribution – are relevant for the rich countries too. There the debate concerns the pros and cons of two alternative politico-economic regimes: welfare states versus welfare societies. Typical of the former is large-scale redistribution. We look at the outcomes in the following chapters, and Chapter 10 deals with the conditions that raise public expenditure, of which redistribution is one kind.

Part III

Developmental Ideals

---

10   State or market?: the Wilensky model

Introduction

State and market are the two principal methods for the allocation of scarce resources to human needs and wants. If a nation favours public resource allocation it will end up with a large public sector, whereas if it trusts the market the private sector will tend to be larger than the public sector (Hirschman, 1982). Nations differ quite considerably in their principal choice between state and market. How are we to account for the various ways of combining state and market as allocative mechanisms? This problem is related to the basic question in comparative public policy of how to explain the policy variation between various kinds of nations, as measured by the amount of resources allocated by means of the public budget. Here we will first take a broad look at public finance variations between various countries all over the world, and then examine the differences in the OECD set of countries.

The distinction between public and private is made in different ways in the world. Some nations trust public resource allocation, whereas other nations emphasize the private sector and market allocation. What are the sources of these differences? In the 1970s and 1980s the policy determinant literature searched for models that would explain the variation in public expenditures. One seminal work was Harold Wilensky's *The Welfare State and Equality* from 1975, which focused upon economic resources and modernization. The contrary theory argued that politics mattered, especially the strength of the left in state and society. Below we will assess the policy determinant debate with regard to the country variation in public expenditure, suggesting a new factor that seems to be essential when we look at public expenditure in the 1990s.

Does politics matter?

The first attempts to account for the tremendous public sector growth in rich countries took the form of *demand* theories, suggesting that: socio-economic development of necessity requires public resource allocation (Wagner's law); increasing affluence implies larger budgets (Wilensky's first law); the dominance of the left in society or government means budget expansion replacing market mechanisms (Schmidt's law); a strong position for the right in government is a negative determinant (Castles's law); collectivist ideologies promote public sector expansion (Wilensky's second law); sudden social shocks necessitate budgetary shift points towards much higher levels of public spending (Peacock's and Wiseman's law); technological development pushes industrial societies more towards the public sector to balance the private sector (Galbraith's law); welfare spending by the neighbouring state implies a demand for welfare programmes at home (Tarschys's law); the increasing openness of the economies of the rich countries of the world creates a demand for budgetary stabilization of the erratic fluctuations of markets (Cameron's law); and all political systems, whether capitalist or socialist, face the same policy demands for public programmes (Pryor's law).

The second stage in the debate about public sector growth was *supply*-oriented. Here we find the hypotheses that: budget-making must mean oversupply (Niskanen's law); public spending involves bureaucratic waste (Tullock's law); public sector growth is a function of bureau size maximization (Downs's law); public sector productivity is negative, claiming more resources every year for the 'same' output (Baumol's law); budget-making rests upon fiscal illusions about the relation between cost and benefit (Oates's law); budget-making is asymmetrical, meaning that those benefiting from public sector expansion are strategically stronger than those that have to pay (Kristensen's law); public officials, whether politicians or bureaucrats, are motivated by a private interest function tied to the size of the budget; and it is difficult to close the gap between benefit and cost in the public sector (Wicksell's law).

It used to be considered that political structures mattered very much. The interest of political scientists was focused upon the structure of the state, classifying political systems as democratic, authoritarian, modern and traditional in one popular scheme. The properties of the structure of the public organization of society had a value in themselves, because some structures were regarded as better than others. The reorientation of political science after the Second World War meant that outputs have been considered more interesting than structural properties. However, the basic problem remains of how structure is related to output. The literature on comparative public policy has identified a number of determinants of policy outputs (Tarschys, 1975; Ashford, 1978; Dye and Gray, 1980), but so far there is no agreement on the *relative weight* of politics or political institutions as a determinant of public policy in relation to, for example, economic factors (Borcherding, 1977, 1984; Wildavsky, 1986).

This predicament may partly be a reflection of severe methodological problems. It has been argued that a simple cross-sectional approach is bound to be inadequate, as the impact of politics would take some time to become visible in policy outputs (Sharpe and Newton, 1984). On the other hand, a longitudinal approach means that our conclusion may be affected by sudden changes and by the fact that we restrict ourselves to countries with an abundance of data. Policies survive their originators and they are inherited by all, even the opponents of the policy in question. Given the fact of policy inertia and the difficulty of changing past commitments, how could policies matter longitudinally? Let us remember the Jackman insistence that cross-sectional and longitudinal approaches are not always comparable. Cross-sectional analyses are particularly suitable for structural analyses of highly aggregate variables (Jackman, 1985).

From a theoretical point of view, we argue that politics matters in relation to the fundamental choice of mechanism of allocation, between public resource allocation and market. These two forms for the making of collective choice can only be substituted to a certain extent. In relation to the so-called pure public goods, there are no alternatives to choose from. This implies that politics should matter far less in relation to military expenditure than in relation to welfare spending where there is a real choice between state and market. It may be the case that it is difficult to pin down why politics matters for the detailed variation in various kinds of expenditure, but we argue that politics is a crucial determinant of the basic choice between state and market. Thus, we expect to find that the total civilian public sector will be large and that overall welfare spending will be high in countries where the left is strong in various ways. However, politics enters into a context of policy-making, which includes other factors that must be taken into account (Danziger, 1978).

Policy-determinant models

According to one seminal theme, *economic* factors are of crucial importance for public policy-making (Wilensky, 1975). A higher level of affluence is supposed to result in more public spending, as the supply of, as well as the demand for, public policies increases with more abundant resources – *Wagner's law* (Wildavsky, 1985). This does not imply that the higher the economic growth the larger the public sector, only that nations that are more affluent will display a distinction between the public and the private that is different from that of poor nations. In terms of economic growth there is the counter-Wagner law, claiming that rapid economic growth cannot be combined with rapid public sector expansion. Economic hypotheses about the variation in public spending focus on either supply factors or demand factors (Borcherding, 1977, 1984). Some emphasize some special economic variable, like the openness of the economy (Cameron, 1978).

According to another seminal theme, slow, broad social change accounts for a reorientation of the distinction between the public and the private. As stated above, it is argued that *social structure* factors such as modernization or urbanization imply more public spending for both indivisible and divisible goods and services. In a similar vein, it is argued that broad demographic changes result in a demand for public policies. According to one hypothesis, the relative proportion of the elderly has a definitive impact on various types of welfare spending (Wilensky, 1975).

A different hypothesis states the contrary: that rapid social change accounts for public sector expansion. External shocks like war or social upheaval have the result that public expenditure jumps to a substantially higher level, where it tends to remain – the *displacement hypothesis* (Peacock and Wiseman, 1961).

A third set of hypotheses focus on the impact of *politics* on the distinction between public and private. On the one hand, it has been argued that the political power of parties of the right is a decisive negative determinant of the size of the public sector (Castles, 1978, 1982). On the other hand, a different argument is that the strength of the position of parties of the left is conducive to public budget-making (Schmidt, 1982). A variety of indicators may be employed to measure the position of the left, implying that there is a large number of hypotheses about the implications of politics, some referring to leftist governments, others to trade union power or more generally to the power division between the left and the right in society, and still others to the relevance of various types of regimes (Weede, 1983;

Cameron, 1984). In addition to the party effect hypothesis, one may also include here the *demonstration hypothesis*, which argues that countries take over policies from other countries as partners in a policy diffusion process.

It seems relevant to include *institutionalization* as an independent variable. It denotes the time span of modern leadership in a polity. It is a different variable from modernization, which refers to material well-being. It could be the case that institutionalization matters more than other political variables. According to the argument about institutional sclerosis, we may expect to find extensive policy-making in nations with a long and unbroken tradition of modern public institutions resulting in various kinds of policies that hamper the free operation of the market (Olson, 1982).

Since the publication of *The Welfare State and Equality* (Wilensky, 1975), there has been an ongoing debate about the determinants of national public policies. Wilensky's emphasis on economic factors was derived from an analysis covering both rich and poor countries. However, many of the later findings have been confined to the rich non-communist countries, pointing to the relevance of political factors (Schmidt, 1982). It is interesting to go back to the first more comprehensive approach and cover as many different nations as possible considering the availability of data. Is it then really true that affluence or modernization is such a powerful determinant of public policy-making? Is it really the case that political institutions or political parties matter little when the sample of countries is made as broad as possible? We will test this for before and after 1989.

The set of countries included in the analysis cannot be considered an entirely representative sample of the universe of discourse. However, an attempt has been made to cover three different regimes on a broad basis: advanced capitalist systems in the form of OECD countries, communist systems as they existed up to the 1989 upheaval in Eastern Europe and developing countries – both LDCs and NICs.

In the literature, models of determinants of public expenditures have been estimated mainly on OECD data (Swank, 1984). It is interesting to inquire into what the findings are when a much larger set of country data is used. First, we estimate a number of regression models by a comparative analysis that includes at most 78 countries: the 24 OECD countries, 8 communist systems and 46 Third World countries, selected on the basis of the availability of data. Let us present the findings under each separate dependent variable.

Size of public expenditure around the world *circa* 1975

The theoretical considerations presented above point us to look for indicators that measure a few latent variables. Considering the existing data sources and the ambition to cover a large set of countries, the following indicators are included in the analysis.

- *Public expenditure*: measures of the total civilian public sector are included (e.g. total non-military outlay/GDP), as are indicators of sub-aggregates (e.g. defence expenditure, education and health expenditures). The reliability of the data may be questioned for some nations, which also applies to the indicators listed below. The data on public expenditures for the communist countries appear to be most uncertain. We have calculated a ratio between total public budget and net material product, which is not identical to GDP, to arrive at a measure comparable to total civilian outlays of general government; the data for these countries have, with the exception for Romania, been taken from *Europa Yearbook*. They roughly refer to the mid-1970s.

- *Economy*: level of economic affluence (GNP per capita) in 1975, economic growth between 1960 and 1977, and the structure of employment in agriculture in 1977.
- *Openness of the economy*: an index measuring the size of exports and imports in relation to GNP.
- *Modernization*: the level of modernization may be measured by two kinds of indicators; one refers to material aspects (energy consumption, radio or TV licences, telephones), while the other stands for health (life expectancy for males, proportion of physicians, infant mortality). Broad demographic changes may be described by indicators such as population density and the proportion of the population in major cities.
- *Politics and political structures*: a set of democratically oriented nations may be identified by means of a human rights index for the late 1970s, and a democracy index for 1960 and 1965. In order to identify a set of communist regimes, an index of the strength of the communist parties is employed, which also allows us to classify political systems as to the extent of radicalism. Moreover, we use two other indices of the strength of the left: an index of the strength of socialist parties and an index of the dominance of the left in governments over the past decades.
- *Social structure*: refers to a set of indicators that tap the variation in social structure between nations, such as ethnic or religious fragmentation and proportion of Catholics and Muslims.
- *Institutionalization*: an index measuring the introduction of modern leadership and modern political institutions.
- *Shock events*: the occurrence of events such as war, social protest and domestic violence may be described by three separate indices.

The regression analysis presented in Table 10.1 gives a number of estimates for three sets of nations, from the most inclusive, consisting of 78 countries, to the small set of 24 OECD countries. The models fit quite well, as the R^2 values indicate.

Wealth and modernity are clearly a source of policy-making. The state must have a certain amount of resources in order to employ public resource allocation for purposes other than those entailed in the minimal state. Public policy-making beyond the provision of pure collective goods is to be found in an economy with abundant resources. In poor countries the state will be smaller than the market.

The implication of wealth and modernity is clear when it is a matter of comparing all types of nations. The picture is more ambiguous when we look at the really rich nations. It seems as if there is a limit to the opportunities that affluence creates for public resource allocation. Once a nation has passed a certain threshold in terms of affluence, public policy-making become less relevant. Most interestingly, a high rate of economic growth is negatively associated with total civilian outlays in the set of rich nations.

Table 10.1 Determinants of total civilian general government outlays

	(n = 78)		(n = 70)		(n = 24)	
Predictors	Beta-wt	t	Beta-wt	t	Beta-wt	t
GNP/cap. 1975	0.13	0.80	0.40	2.17	0.04	0.27
Modernization: health aspects	0.35	2.32	0.07	0.36	0.23	1.90
Economic growth 1960–77	−0.02	−0.25	−0.07	−0.73	−0.16	−1.23
Impex index	0.16	2.05	0.24	2.77	0.34	2.65
Proportion living in cities >100 000	−0.14	−1.58	−0.19	−1.90	−0.27	−1.94
Social heterogeneity	0.05	0.58	−0.09	−0.86	0.04	0.28
War experience	0.05	0.65	0.16	1.82	−0.04	−0.40
Left dominance in government	0.36	3.91	0.17	1.84	0.35	2.95
Democracy index	−0.21	−2.13	0.11	0.93	0.13	1.02
Time of institutionalization	−0.27	−2.13	−0.19	−1.32	−0.09	−0.76
R^2	0.66		0.79		0.92	
$R^2 A$	0.61		0.63		0.85	

Sources: Total civil general government outlays, Taylor and Hudson (1972) and IMF (1982); GNP per capita 1975, Taylor (1981); modernization, health aspects, Taylor (1981); economic growth, 1960–77, World Bank (1980b); impex index, Taylor (1981); proportion living in cities > 100 000, Taylor (1981); social heterogeneity, Taylor and Hudson (1972); war experience, Weede (1984a); left dominance in government, Banks (1978), Delury (1983); democracy index, Humana (1983); time of institutionalization, Taylor and Hudson (1972).

There can be no doubt about the importance of the political dimension for the overall structuring of the distinction between the public and the private. Whatever the set of nations studied, the position of the left within government or society has an impact on the division between state and market as long as we are not trying to account for the narrow variation in the welfare states of Western Europe. It is not only the case that public resource allocation is the only mechanism employed in those systems where the left has a hegemonic position; it also applies that the stronger the left is in non-communist regimes, the larger the public sector. The hypothesis about the impact of institutionalization receives support. The longer a nation has been engaged in nation-building, the more the state tends to be engaged in extensive policy-making.

The displacement effect hypothesis is not confirmed, but the impex hypothesis is clearly corroborated. Speaking generally, it is not the case that affluence is the major variable. While it is true that economic resources matter, as predicted in Wagner's law and the openness of the economy hypothesis, it is far from being the crucial variable. Politics does matter.

Education is a kind of good that tends to be more in demand the more affluence there is. However, this does not mean that there have to be policy programmes providing this good. Affluence also means that citizens have a larger capacity to make their own choices, suggesting that they may use the market to provide themselves with education opportunities. We may expect to find that wealth or modernity explain part of the variation in education expenditure, but only a part. The findings in Table 10.2 confirm this interpretation.

Table 10.2 Determinants of general government educational expenditures

Predictors	($n = 78$)		($n = 70$)		($n = 24$)	
	Beta-wt	t	Beta-wt	t	Beta-wt	t
GNP/cap. 1975	0.55	2.71	0.59	2.73	0.28	1.20
Modernization: health aspects	−0.18	−0.92	−0.22	−1.02	−0.37	−1.69
Economic growth 1960–77	−0.18	−1.76	−0.03	−0.25	0.20	0.84
Impex index	0.16	1.66	0.07	0.68	0.23	1.00
Proportion living in cities						
>100 000	0.00	0.05	−0.02	−0.20	0.14	0.56
Social heterogeneity	0.02	0.21	0.09	0.71	0.33	1.31
War experience	0.20	2.05	0.18	1.73	0.06	0.33
Left dominance in government	0.34	2.90	0.30	2.76	0.52	2.38
Democracy index	0.21	1.63	0.24	1.68	0.34	1.42
Time of institutionalization	0.14	0.86	0.09	0.53	−0.01	−0.06
R^2	0.45		0.50		0.72	
R^2A	0.37		0.42		0.51	

Sources: Educational expenditure/GDP, Sivard (1980), Taylor (1981); see also Table 10.1.

Poor nations cannot afford to operate extensive programmes in the field of education. Rich nations, on the other hand, face a choice between public and private, as they can afford to allocate resources to various kinds of education. Which mechanism of allocation is resorted to, depends on other factors, of which politics appears to be the most relevant one. The position of the left matters very much in relation to public spending for education. It is also the case that democratically structured nations favour public education systems.

The provision of health tends to be larger in richer countries than in poorer ones, but this does not imply that affluence implies public spending for health. Health may be provided for privately in terms of market operations. The results presented in Table 10.3 confirm this hypothesis.

Wealth and modernity have a positive impact on health policy-making, up to a certain level. Once there is a certain level of public provision of health services, other factors will determine whether there will be public or private provision. Most important is politics, the left favouring public resource allocation.

It may be believed that military spending is more favoured in authoritarian or communist systems than in democratic ones. Table 10.4 shows that this is not the case when the data for the 1970s are examined.

Table 10.3 Determinants of general government health expenditures

	($n = 78$)		($n = 70$)		($n = 24$)	
Predictors	Beta-wt	t	Beta-wt	t	Beta-wt	t
GNP/cap. 1975	0.32	1.84	0.28	1.50	−0.22	−0.76
Modernization: health aspects	0.14	0.88	0.15	0.80	0.35	1.28
Economic growth 1960–77	−0.13	−1.48	−0.05	−0.58	−0.26	−0.89
Impex index	0.01	0.15	−0.04	−0.43	−0.02	−0.07
Proportion living in cities >100 000	0.12	1.25	0.12	1.22	0.26	0.84
Social heterogeneity	0.07	0.80	0.13	1.21	0.28	0.90
War experience	−0.02	−0.21	−0.03	−0.35	−0.07	−0.31
Left dominance in government	0.30	3.07	0.27	2.82	0.46	1.68
Democracy index	0.13	1.25	0.12	0.98	0.04	0.13
Time of institutionalization	−0.11	−0.80	−0.16	−1.09	0.17	0.61
R^2	0.61		0.63		0.57	
R^2A	0.55		0.57		0.23	

Sources: Health expenditure/GDP, Sivard (1980), Taylor (1981); see also Table 10.1.

Table 10.4 Determinants of military expenditures

	($n = 78$)		($n = 70$)		($n = 24$)	
Predictors	Beta-wt	t	Beta-wt	t	Beta-wt	t
GNP/cap. 1975	−0.12	−0.59	−0.21	−0.99	−0.37	−1.50
Modernization: health aspects	0.41	2.25	0.58	2.66	0.15	0.66
Economic growth 1960–77	0.15	1.56	0.14	1.29	0.16	0.65
Impex index	0.05	0.55	0.05	0.53	−0.43	−1.76
Proportion living in cities >100 000	0.02	0.18	0.01	0.11	−0.34	−1.29
Social heterogeneity	0.15	1.39	0.21	1.75	0.10	0.38
War experience	0.62	6.46	0.60	5.87	0.60	3.10
Left dominance in government	0.22	1.97	0.28	2.58	0.28	1.20
Democracy index	−0.05	−0.38	−0.19	−1.32	0.01	0.05
Time of institutionalization	0.35	2.21	0.34	1.98	−0.36	−1.55
R^2	0.49		0.50		0.69	
R^2A	0.41		0.42		0.45	

Sources: Defence expenditure/GDP: Sivard (1980), Taylor (1981); see also Table 10.1.

What matters with regard to military effort is war experience. Countries that have this kind of experience emphasize military spending. Wealth and modernity have a limited impact, indicating that the richer a nation is, the more resources there are available for such purposes, but still the most important determinant is the actual experience of war.

Now, do these findings stand up when we look at the evidence from data about the 1990s?

Size of public expenditure around the world *circa* 1994

In the social sciences one has to be constantly aware of the problem of structural variability (Westlund and Lane, 1983). One employs correlations between variables in order to identify structural connections between factors. Yet the evidence from one data set about structural links may be different from what evidence from other data suggests. The same thing applies to the findings from regression analyses. To what extent does the information about the public sector size in the 1990s corroborate the findings reported upon above? Let us look at the country variation first, before we test policy determinant models.

Table 10.5 shows the basic difference between three kinds of countries in terms of size of public expenditure in 1980 and 1992, i.e. two measurement points of time before and after the 1989 system changes.

Table 10.5 Public expenditure 1980 and 1992 as a percentage of GDP

	Total expenditure	Government consumption	Military expenditure	Education expenditure	Health expenditure
1980					
OECD	45.9 ($n = 15$)	17.8 ($n = 22$)	2.7 ($n = 24$)	5.6 ($n = 24$)	4.8 ($n = 24$)
Third World	31.0 ($n = 31$)	15.4 ($n = 74$)	4.5 ($n = 91$)	4.2 ($n = 93$)	1.6 ($n = 92$)
Communist	41.7 ($n = 2$)	11.8 ($n = 4$)	4.6 ($n = 9$)	4.1 ($n = 8$)	3.5 ($n = 9$)
Mean	36.1 ($n = 48$)	15.8 ($n = 100$)	4.2 ($n = 124$)	4.5 ($n = 125$)	2.4 ($n = 125$)
1992					
OECD	46.8 ($n = 24$)	18.6 ($n = 21$)	2.4 ($n = 24$)	5.3 ($n = 23$)	5.9 ($n = 24$)
Third World	25.7 ($n = 60$)	14.6 ($n = 73$)	5.2 ($n = 89$)	4.1 ($n = 70$)	2.2 ($n = 70$)
Post-communist	49.2 ($n = 3$)	17.1 ($n = 13$)	2.7 ($n = 17$)	4.9 ($n = 4$)	4.6 ($n = 19$)
Mean	32.3 ($n = 87$)	15.7 ($n = 107$)	4.3 ($n = 130$)	4.5 ($n = 97$)	3.4 ($n = 113$)

Sources: Total expenditure 1980; IMF (1984); military expenditure 1980, Sivard (1983); educational expenditure 1980, Sivard (1983); health expenditure 1980, Sivard (1983); total expenditure 1992, IMF (1994); military expenditure 1992, UNDP (1995); educational expenditure 1992, UNDP (1995); health expenditure 1992, UNDP (1995).

Measuring the size of the public sector in a command economy is notoriously difficult, since the state in practice dominates society completely, meaning that the private–public distinction loses its import. What has happened in the post-communist countries is an expansion of the public sector together with a reduction in public expenditures, a process that the figures in Table 10.5 fail to identify. Outside of the command economies, public expenditure is one proper measure of the size of the public sector, but within the communist systems the public sector is much larger than public expenditure, as the state controls the entire economy, owning the capital.

Public expenditure as a percentage of GDP is slightly higher among the rich countries, whereas things are ambiguous with regard to the Third World countries, as the figures for the 1980s are based on a small sample. It may be of interest to look at the developments between 1980 and 1992 for the countries for which data are available (Table 10.6).

Table 10.6 Public sector size: total expenditure 1980 and 1992

	1980	1992		1980	1992
Argentina	30.4	16.9	Malawi	39.2	25.0
Australia	36.9	41.2	Malaysia	39.8	31.5
Austria	51.0	54.0	Mexico	23.2	33.4
Belgium	56.4	54.1	Myanmar	15.9	11.3
Brazil	30.7	38.5	Norway	55.8	56.7
Central African Rep.	22.3	–	Oman	42.1	43.0
Chile	28.1	29.1	Panama	33.2	21.2
Colombia	16.6	15.3	Paraguay	11.3	13.8
Costa Rica	25.9	23.9	Romania	49.1	41.4
Dominican Rep.	56.6	10.8	Singapore	24.2	19.4
Ecuador	17.2	14.7	South Africa	28.9	34.1
Finland	39.9	45.3	Spain	31.1	43.8
France	44.7	51.5	Sri Lanka	43.2	26.9
Germany	49.7	48.4	Sweden	64.5	65.0
Greece	36.8	33.6	Switzerland	37.0	39.5
Guatemala	15.8	11.7	Thailand	20.0	16.8
India	27.1	30.0	Tunisia	35.7	31.9
Indonesia	24.5	20.0	UK	48.3	47.4
Iran	38.2	18.6	USA	36.0	39.1
Ireland	56.2	53.0	Uruguay	24.3	28.8
Israel	63.7	52.2	Yemen	41.9	31.4
Kenya	31.2	28.0	Yugoslavia	34.3	–
Kuwait	34.4	–	Zaire	29.0	15.3
Luxembourg	44.0	57.6	Zimbabwe	46.7	45.5

Source: IMF (1984, 1994).

Among Third World countries one can observe both increases and decreases. Some countries have moved in the same direction as the rich countries, i.e. more public expenditure and a larger public sector. But one can also observe the other process, involving a substantial reduction in public expenditures. Countries that have reduced their public sector include, among others, Argentina, Dominican Republic, Ecuador, Guatemala, Indonesia, Kenya, Malaysia and Thailand – all countries that have attempted to move out of the state-capitalist regime and towards decentralized capitalism. However, we also find Third World countries that have increased their public expenditures; for instance, Brazil, India, Mexico, Paraguay and Uruguay. These developments have resulted in an enormous variation among Third World countries (Table 10.7).

Table 10.7 Public sector size 1992: Third World countries

	Expenditure			Expenditure	
	Total	Health		Total	Health
Argentina	16.9	2.5	Niger	–	3.4
Bhutan	42.4	–	Nigeria	–	1.2
Bolivia	35.4	2.4	Oman	43.0	–
Botswana	35.4	–	Pakistan	24.3	1.8
Brazil	38.5	2.8	Panama	31.2	–
Cambodia	19.2	1.0	Papua New Guinea	32.3	2.8
Chad	31.3	4.7	Paraguay	13.8	1.2
Chile	29.1	3.4	Peru	12.9	1.9
Colombia	15.3	1.8	Philippines	20.0	1.0
Ecuador	14.7	–	Rwanda	25.3	1.9
Egypt	39.3	1.0	Saudi Arabia	–	3.1
El Salvador	11.1	2.6	Senegal	–	2.3
Ethiopia	26.7	2.3	Sierra Leone	21.9	1.7
Gabon	30.4	–	Singapore	19.4	1.1
Ghana	16.6	1.7	Somalia	–	0.9
India	30.0	1.3	South Africa	34.1	3.2
Indonesia	20.0	0.7	Sri Lanka	26.9	1.8
Iran	18.6	1.5	Sudan	–	0.5
Israel	52.5	–	Syria	23.1	0.4
Jordan	33.4	1.8	Tanzania	–	3.2
Kenya	28.0	2.7	Thailand	16.8	1.1
Korea, South	17.0	2.7	Trinidad	31.9	–
Malawi	25.0	2.9	Uganda	–	1.6
Malaysia	31.5	1.3	United Arab Emirates	12.1	–
Mauritius	25.5	–	Uruguay	28.8	2.5
Mexico	33.4	1.6	Venezuela	20.0	2.0
Morocco	28.7	0.9	Vietnam	–	1.1
Myanmar	11.3	–	Yemen	31.4	1.5
Namibia	44.3	–	Zaire	15.3	0.8
Nepal	18.3	2.2	Zambia	21.7	2.2
Nicaragua	30.0	6.7	Zimbabwe	45.5	3.2

Sources: IMF (1994), UNDP (1995).

What is the relevance today of the Wilensky model when the set of Third World countries contains so much variation with regard to the size of public expenditure? Since the rich countries also vary tremendously in the size of their public sectors (Chapter 12), one must question the validity of affluence or modernization as the basic determinant of policy differences. One should raise the same question in relation to the problem of political determinants. There is such a substantial country variation among both the rich and poor countries that it seems far-fetched that the position of the left in society or government could account for all the variation. This is especially true when ideological distance between the right and the left has lost some of its import owing to the dismantling of the communist regimes. Perhaps there is some other factor at work here: neither affluence or modernization nor politics when it comes to accounting for public policies, as measured by public expenditures.

The variation in education expenditure is much too small to allow for a statistical treatment. When the country variation is so small, macro variables will not be able to explain much. Military expenditure, however, varies considerably. Table 10.8 lists the major military spenders in the world.

Table 10.8 Countries with high military and educational expenditure

High military expenditure				High educational expenditure			
OECD		Third World		OECD		Third World	
USA	5.3	Angola	35.5	Norway	6.8	Zimbabwe	10.6
Greece	5.6	Ethiopia	20.1	Canada	6.7	Algeria	9.1
UK	4.0	Iraq	21.1	Sweden	6.5	Kenya	6.8
Turkey	4.7	North Korea	25.7	Finland	6.1	Saudi Arabia	6.1
France	3.4	Oman	17.5	France	6.1	Cuba	6.6
Norway	3.3	Syria	16.6	Iceland	6.0	Botswana	8.4
Portugal	2.9	Sudan	15.8	New Zealand	5.8	Congo	5.6
Australia	2.4	Saudi Arabia	11.8	Luxembourg	5.8	Mozambique	6.3
Germany	2.4	Jordan	11.2	Netherlands	5.6	Morocco	5.5
Netherlands	2.4	Israel	11.1	USA	5.5	Egypt	6.7
Sweden	2.5	Vietnam	11.0	UK	5.3	Gabon	5.7

Source: UNDP (1995).

Given a variation like the one for military expenditures and the one for educational expenditures in Table 10.8 one may expect that the pattern of policy determinants will be entirely different. When Third World countries consider that they can afford public expenditures, they opt very often for educational spending. The level of education spending as a percentage of GDP is not very different in rich and poor countries. Among the rich countries, almost all allot 5 per cent or more to public education.

We now turn to a regression analysis of the expenditure variation, where we focus upon the differences among the OECD and Third World countries. Thus, we exclude the set of post-communist countries, as they are still in the process of bringing down their public sectors, searching for a new public–private mix. Table 10.9 has all the regressions.

The major finding in Table 10.9 is the evidence that points at democracy as a key factor for understanding the public–private sector mix and how it varies around the world. It is not the case that either modernization (GDP per capita) or politics (left) are key variables. Democracy is more relevant than the standard factors listed in the policy determination literature. It drives up public expenditure in general, especially health care expenditure, and drives down military spending.

Table 10.9 Regression analysis of public expenditures: OECD and Third World

	Coeff.	Beta wt	t
Total expenditure 1992			
LNRGDP	2.14	0.14	0.89
Open80	0.02	0.06	0.65
Left	1.26	0.13	1.28
Demo91	0.30	0.44	3.00
Inst	−0.03	−0.12	−0.79
R^2A	0.50	($n = 70$)	
Military expenditure 1992			
LNRGDP	2.68	0.66	6.02
Open80	0.01	0.09	1.07
War	−0.12	−0.02	−0.17
Left	0.04	0.01	0.13
Demo91	−0.17	−0.95	−7.74
R^2A	0.48	($n = 81$)	
Educational expenditure 1992			
LNRGDP	0.45	0.27	1.53
Open80	0.00	0.06	0.45
Left	0.15	0.12	0.84
Demo91	0.02	0.20	1.03
Inst	0.00	0.19	0.91
R^2A	0.10	($n = 70$)	
Health expenditure 1992			
LNRGDP	0.51	0.25	1.95
Open80	−0.00	−0.03	−0.34
Left	0.02	0.02	0.21
Demo91	0.04	0.45	3.95
Inst	−0.01	−0.21	−1.53
R^2A	0.67	($n = 73$)	

Sources: LNRGDP (in real gross domestic product per capita), Summers and Heston (1994); OPEN80 (export plus import as a percentage of GDP), Summers and Heston (1994); war (occurrence of war or armed conflict in 1989–94), Wallensteen and Sollenberg (1995); left (from 0 (non-socialist) to 4 (socialist) dominance in government), Encyclopaedia Britannica (1995); demo91 (democracy score 1991 from 0 to 10), Humana (1992); inst (institutionalization, i.e. the year of introduction of modernized leadership in a country), Black (1966).

In democratic states it is evidently the case that politicians face strong pressure to enhance citizens' well-being by increasing civilian expenditure and holding back military spending – this is the demand side interpretation of this finding. An equally plausible supply side interpretation may be made, focusing upon how politicians may resort to employing public expenditure items in order to enhance their popularity with the electorate. In any case, democracy means a larger public sector on the civilian side, whereas an authoritarian regime implies more military spending.

Conclusion

State or market in a country is a real choice when national public policy-making moves beyond the provision of pure public goods. And this choice opportunity becomes an actuality when nations have been modernized to such an extent that the state has large extractive capacities. Economic development and institutionalization of state structures open up the possibility of extensive public policy-making – so far, Wilensky is right. But the Wilensky mechanism seems to have lost much of its explanatory force, as the variation in public sector size has become more complex and some countries have initiated public sector retrenchment.

Although it is true that as nations modernize, resources become available for civil public expenditure, one must ask whether this possibility also becomes a reality in terms of a large public sector. As nations modernize their economy and social structure and institutionalize their public bodies, they face the basic choice between public resource allocation and market operations as the mechanism for allocating scarce resources to semi-public or private goods. And politics mattered very much for the way that choice was resolved in the 1970s. This applies in particular in relation to non-military expenditure, which in advanced economies mainly refers to semi-public or private goods.

Politics, as the left versus the right, used to matter for the *fundamental choice* between public resource allocation and market operations. Yet public resource allocation is only necessary in relation to pure public goods. It may or may not be an efficient mechanism of allocation in relation to semi-public goods, depending upon the circumstances. However, it is inferior to market operations when it is a question of allocation of private goods. Pure public goods will consume a smaller relative proportion of the resources as GDP grows when the economy is modernized. The tendency for public resource allocation to expand as a function of the modernization of the economy expresses a decision to trust one mechanism of allocation more than the other – and this decision is based more on *political considerations* than simply *economic determinism*. These preferences for public expenditure may be reversed when markets are given a more prominent role. Thus, public sector growth is not inevitable, as the findings above show.

The most interesting finding here is that democracy is a powerful explanatory factor when it comes to public expenditure in the 1990s. The more democratic a country, the larger the public sector tends to be. Public expenditure, especially on health care, is driven up by democratic politics. Economic resources constitute a necessary condition for public expenditure, but they do not make up a sufficient condition. In the 1970s it was the position of the left that was critical; now it is democracy.

Public resource allocation is resorted to as nations grow richer and more modern, but there is a limit to the attractiveness of the state. In several countries the relevance of the market increases, as citizens may wish to emphasize exit more than voice

(Hirschman, 1970). In developing countries, public resource allocation may be the more attractive alternative owing to the non-existence of markets or the need for political control, but there is a limit to the usefulness of this mechanism of collective choice. Technical considerations may give public resource allocation an advantage in relation to certain semi-public goods, but the attractiveness of public resource allocation is founded on culture, meaning that the spread of a market ideology can reverse processes of public sector growth. There used to be extensive policy-making where the left had a strong tradition of participation in government. However, now the public sector is considered a part of democratic politics. Military expenditure has a different set of conditions, where war involvement is prominent, but here too we find the role of democratic politics in the 1990s, this time in depressing expenditure.

In order to interpret the finding that democracy matters for public expenditure, one must consult Alexis de Tocqueville's *Democracy in America* (1835–40) where this link is first suggested. De Tocqueville actually predicts the coming of the Schumpeterian tax state in democratic societies due to the strong push towards equality which big government would promote, in de Tocqueville's analysis.

11 The Swedish disease and the Scandinavian model

Introduction

In the political economy literature, the phrase 'Dutch disease' is a well known expression. It stands for a certain type of economic problem that is home made and cannot be blamed on the international economy. The difficulties in the Swedish economy are also home made, but of a different type. The purpose of this chapter is to identify the cause of the decline of the Swedish model, which was basically an attempt at combining a complete welfare state with an efficient advanced economy.

A search for an explanation of the decline of the Swedish model has to start from an examination of the model itself, because it comprises a profound contradiction that proved more and more difficult to reconcile. The Swedish disease, which ultimately explains the dramatic fall of the Swedish welfare state, is the failure to combine and balance the public and private sectors in such a way that a proper trade-off between efficiency and equity can be maintained. One may begin by illuminating the difficulties of the Swedish public sector with a comparison with the other Scandinavian countries.

This chapter examines the crisis of the Swedish public sector against the background of the declining economic performance of the country's economy. It argues that the root cause of the Swedish difficulties is the imbalance between its public and private sectors. And it shows that Danish and Norwegian public administration never succumbed to the Swedish excesses in inefficient public spending, many tax wedges and extravagant deficit financing.

The Scandinavian or the Swedish model?

In the literature mention is made of either the Swedish model or the Scandinavian model. It stands for a combination of the private and public sectors that distinguishes the Nordic countries, meaning large public expenditure together with an advanced economy harbouring so-called capitalist institutions. The Scandinavian model is an attempt to combine an efficient market economy with extensive public administration. Denmark and Norway have succeeded but Sweden has failed. Why?

The four Nordic countries – Denmark, Finland, Norway and Sweden – are comprehensive welfare states. A fully scaled welfare state includes a mixed economy with welfare programmes based upon universalistic criteria. Using the Musgrave distinction between three branches of government, the Scandinavian model consists of the following policy commitments:

1   *The allocative branch*: about 25 per cent of GDP is allocated to the provision of a number of services that are almost free, such as education, health care and social care, as well as law and order and roads. Welfare services are mainly provided by the local government system, which includes so-called primary and secondary communes.
2   *The redistributive branch*: about 25 per cent of GDP is redistributed in terms of generous transfer programmes, including pensions, child allowances, unemployment benefits and sickness benefits. The level of compensation ranges from 75 to 100 per cent, depending on the programme, the country and the time period.
3   *The stabilization branch*: the promotion of full employment by a number of programmes, such as public works and fully financed retraining schemes. Whereas the macroeconomic regime used to be orthodox Keynesianism, more attention is given to fighting inflation today.

The Scandinavian model implies that the duties of government are extensive in all three branches of government, and in consequence the Nordic countries have the highest public expenditure and the largest number of public employees in the OECD set of countries in relation to the private sector. Public administration is important in the Nordic countries, because such a large portion of the GDP is channelled through the public household. Denmark and Norway have managed well to combine such a large public sector with an efficient private sector economy, whereas Sweden and Finland faced tremendous difficulties in the early 1990s. It seems that Finland's problem is essentially owing to the loss of exports to the Soviet Union, but no improvement is yet in sight for the Swedes. Why?

The delicate balance between efficiency concerns and equity considerations that any comprehensive welfare state must respect was upset in Sweden, because Sweden took matters in all three branches of government further than Norway and Denmark.

Sweden has operated a special version of the Scandinavian welfare state model. The so-called Swedish model was a set of institutions for governing the economy that emerged out of the Great Depression and the new macroeconomic theories of the Stockholm School of Economics (Jonung, 1990). It worked well until 1970, when the model began to disintegrate. Table 11.1 lists the key features of the Swedish model, both as it worked ideally before 1970 and as it operated after 1970.

Some have interpreted the Swedish model as corporatism, since it comprised few encompassing interest organizations in hierarchical interest intermediation and policy agreement. Others look upon it as a compromise model, because the elites from the socialist and non-socialist camps by means of piecemeal social engineering built a fully fledged welfare state. Both interpretations underline centralized decision-making and implementation by means of strong and rather independent bureaus or state agencies in Stockholm. Why did the Swedish model first perform well from 1935 to 1970 and then collapse, leading to economic disaster

for the country? What is at fault, we argue, is the imbalance between the public
and the private sectors.

Table 11.1 The Swedish model 1935–95

Pre-1970 regime	*Post-1970 regime*
1 Growth emphasis	1 Emphasis on redistribution
2 Low nominal wage increases	2 High nominal wage increases
3 Private sector priority	3 Public sector priority
4 Few strikes	4 High strike activity
5 Low inflation	5 High inflation
6 Full employment	6 High unemployment
7 Steady growth rates	7 Extreme economic volatility

Public–private sector imbalance

Total public sector outlays now stand at 70 per cent, which is far in excess of the
average of 42 per cent for OECD and 50 per cent for OECD Europe, which is the
result of the exceptional public sector growth process, mainly since 1970. Sweden
now has the largest public sector among the OECD countries, without any other
country approaching this. In 1960, total outlays stood at 31 per cent of GDP, which
at that time was in line with the OECD average of 28 per cent and the OECD Europe
figure of 31.3 per cent.

The expansion of the public sector in Sweden involves sharply increased outlays
on three items: (a) public resource allocation; (b) social security expenditures; (c)
interest payments on the state debt and subsidies. The first category comprises the
enormous expansion of local government, responsible for the delivery of a number
of welfare services, whereas the second category covers transfer payments in
Swedish welfare – the redistributive state (Table 11.2).

Table 11.2 Public expenditure: consumption and transfer payments (% of GDP)

	Public consumption		Transfer payments	Total public outlays/GDP
	National gov.	*Local gov.*		
1960	8	10	8	29
1970	8	14	12	37
1980	9	20	19	57
1990	10	22	21	59
1995	11	24	24	70

Sources: OECD National Accounts; Finansplanen 1995–6.

In the 1960s the exceptional public sector expansion process is initiated as a
growth in public resource allocation, as there is a considerable increase in public
consumption, i.e. in the provision of goods and services that are almost free of

charge. Around 1980 the next growth process starts, as there is a sharp increase in transfer payments. Since 1990, the fastest growing item in the public household has been interest payments on the state debt. Sweden expects that its state debt will keep growing until 1998, with a peak at almost 100 per cent of GDP. The deficit was still an astonishing 10 per cent of GDP in 1995.

Public sector expansion has not been a continuous, smooth process. Instead, we see two major jumps in overall public expenditure, one occurring in the 1970s and the other in the early 1990s, i.e. during periods of severe economic recession. The public sector has literally driven out the private sector (Table 11.3).

Table 11.3 Employment 1960–90 (millions)

	Public sector		Public enterprises	Private sector	Total
	State	Local gov.			
1960	266	150	170	2658	3244
1970	353	407	188	2462	3410
1980	281	1080	303	2200	3860
1990	242	1275	295	2293	4105

Source: Statistical Yearbook of Sweden.

There has been steady growth in the total number of those gainfully employed, adding some one million over the past thirty years. However, all the increase has taken place within the public sector. The almost phenomenal growth of local government employment, in municipalities and county councils, reflects to only a minor extent a transfer of state officials to the local government sector. The expansion of local government employment was incredibly wide in the 1970s and the 1980s and first abated in 1993.

Private sector employment has been reduced not only relatively speaking but also in absolute numbers, despite the one million increase in employment. The decline in private sector employment involves a considerable reduction in agricultural employment, from some 450 000 in 1960 to roughly 150 000. This means that there has actually been a small decrease in employment in the basis of the Swedish economy, namely manufacturing and mining: from 1 150 000 in 1960 to 1 000 000 in 1990, despite the one million addition to the workforce during the same time. Private sector employment constituted 80 per cent of all employment in 1960, but amounted to only 56 per cent in 1990. If private employees are more productive than public employees in general, then the overall level of affluence of Sweden could only possibly develop in one direction.

Public sector allocation: efficient?

The Achilles' heel of the Swedish public sector is the large local government part of it. It has expanded in an astonishing way since 1960, including both the 286 communes at the local level and the 23 county councils at the regional level, all with directly elected boards of politicians. The high priority given to the decentralization philosophy since 1975 has made local government the sole provider of a large number of services. Local governments have big budgets and are run as formal organizations with a huge number of employees, working either in authorities or public agencies or in joint-stock companies owned by the local governments. But are they cost-effective?

Local governments fund their activities by means of taxation, user fees and state grants. From a constitutional point of view, local governments have been granted autonomy, but Sweden remains a unitary state where all competencies are ultimately derived from legislation in the Riksdag. Local governments levy a proportional tax on income, the rate of which they may decide for themselves within national government recommendations.

The national government began relying heavily on local governments to provide welfare services in the 1960s, obligating them to supply at certain quality levels a lot of goods and services, while at the same time paying in part for costs by means of general and special state grants. The emphasis upon decentralization has, however, resulted in much less steering from the national government, confining itself to framework legislation and block grants.

The question about efficiency in local government operations can be looked at from either a macro or a micro perspective. Micro analyses of various programmes have shown that there is a productivity problem, as several programmes display a negative productivity trend over many years (Murray, 1987), amounting to about a 2 per cent negative trend yearly during some time periods. What could such a process (reminiscent of the Baumol disease phenomenon) result in from a macro perspective? Let us compare the efficiency of the local government sectors in the four Nordic countries.

The local government systems in Denmark, Finland, Norway and Sweden are basically comparable. It is true that there are differences both organizationally and in terms of functions, but they are minor, owing to the strong convergence process in policy-making between these countries. There has been considerable policy diffusion over the years, meaning that all adhere to the Scandinavian model, with its emphasis upon large local government that handles the core services of a fully fledged welfare state. In Finland there are no regional governments, as local government cooperative corporations take charge of health care among other things. It is also true that the actual division of competencies between communes and county councils differs slightly between Denmark, Norway and Sweden, but the basic organizational framework is the same in all four countries. Table 11.4 presents data on total costs and total personnel for the entire local government sector in the four Nordic countries.

The cost and personnel differences between Sweden on the one hand and Denmark, Finland and Norway on the other are striking, to say the least. The Swedish local government sector is far larger than the local government sectors in the other countries, even when one holds population constant. What roughly ten local government employees do in Denmark, Finland and Norway takes almost fifteen employees in the Swedish local government sector. The total additional cost for Swedish local government is over one hundred billion Swedish krona, or 10 000 to 15 000 krona per capita, which is as large a sum as the entire public sector deficit in Sweden. Table 11.5 shows that the cost disadvantage of Swedish communes was aggravated during the 1980s, in particular in relation to Danish communes.

Table 11.4 Costs and personnel in local government in 1991

Population (millions)	Total cost (billions)	Cost per capita	Employees (thousands)	Employees per 1000
Denmark (5.2)	225 DK	43300 DK	595000	114
Finland (5.1)	130 FM	25500 FM	446000	88
Norway (4.3)	150 NK	35000 NK	470000	109
Sweden (8.7)	462 SK	53000 SK	1229000	141

Note: The total cost figures are in local currency at billions whereas the employee numbers are in thousands. In 1990 the Swedish krona stood 10 per cent higher than the Norwegian krone but 10 per cent lower than the Danish krone, whereas the Finnish mark was much stronger than the Swedish krona, or about 1 mark = 1.4 krona.

Table 11.5 Total primary local government costs per capita 1983–90

	Norway	Sweden	Denmark
1983	9798	14360	14744
1984	11038	15720	15422
1985	12194	17368	16621
1986	13601	18667	16909
1987	15458	20352	18896
1988	16662	21327	19773
1989	17862	23097	20851
1990	18204	25744	21720

Note: All costs are expressed in Norwegian krone and have been standardized by removing differences in accounting practices and functions.

Table 11.6 Total costs per capita in primary local governments of different sizes

	Norway	Sweden
< 1000	37280	–
1001–2000	29990	–
2001–3000	22930	–
3001–5000	20590	27110
5001–10000	19370	23400
10 001–14000	18470	22350
14 001–20000	18450	22690
20 001–35000	18930	23720
35 001–60000	18500	25580
> 60 000	22840	29250

Note: All costs are expressed in Norwegian krone.

It is not possible to argue that service quality is much higher in Swedish communes than in Danish ones. But it is often claimed that Norwegian communes have lower per capita costs in their communes because service standards are far lower than Swedish norms. However, the characteristic feature of Norwegian communes is the immense cost differences between the small and large communes (Table 11.6).

The problem in the Norwegian local government structure is the many and very costly small communes, mainly paid for by state grants. The large communes in Norway are much more cost effective than the corresponding Swedish communes. This observation applies in particular to the large urban areas, including the cities. Only with regard to day care services is there systematic evidence that service quality is higher in Sweden than in Norway. But the crux of the matter is of course that the Swedish public sector, including the communes, has a quantity and quality that the country cannot pay for. The Norwegian public sector is fully financed in every detail. Not only is the state budget balanced, but Norway has a state debt of zero when the large state assets are included in calculation of the overall net state debt. The Swedish state's liabilities are far in excess of its assets. Sweden used to be much wealthier than Norway, and the change cannot only be attributed to the economic revenue that Norway has earned from its oil and natural gas resources. The strong public sector emphasis has been attended by increasingly worse overall economic performance – the problem of excess burdens.

Economic performance

Between 1913 and 1950, the average economic growth rate was highest in Sweden among the Western European countries. After the Second World War, average growth rates were an impressive 3 per cent per year. For several reasons the high rates of economic development began to decline in the 1970s. In the 1980s and early 1990s, there were even a few years with a negative economic growth rate of about 2 per cent per year.

Table 11.7 presents data about economic development since 1970. Growth rates have been consistently lower in Sweden than in most other Western European countries, particularly during the past decade. It is important to note that the decline was initiated long before the most recent depression in the world economy, and that Sweden has consistently performed below the OECD average performance records.

Table 11.7 Economic growth in Sweden 1970–93

	1970–93	1970–77	1978–86	1987–93
Sweden	1.5	1.7	2.1	0.1
OECD	2.8	3.8	2.5	2.3
OECD Europe	2.3	2.5	2.0	2.3

Source: OECD Economic Outlook, June 1993.

While the European economy returned to a higher gear in 1995, the growth rate predictions for Sweden remain more pessimistic than for the OECD in general. The Swedish growth crisis has set off a debate about the factors that may account for the seminal decline: too much investment in the housing sector and too little in growth-generating infrastructure, weak entrepreneurship, too small wage differentials, and wage rigidities between various sectors in the economy, and too little investment in human capital (Henrekson et al., 1994; Freeman et al., 1995).

Table 11.8 State debt, budget deficit and foreign debt (current prices in billion Swedish krona)

	Budget deficit	State debt	Foreign debt	GDP
1960	0.5	20	–	76
1970	4	31	+15	172
1980	43	192	50	528
1990	+3	583	580	1340
1995	171	1470	836	1580

Sources: Statistical Yearbook of Sweden; Finansplanen 1995/6.

The most conspicuous expression of the crisis of the Swedish welfare state is the huge deficit on the state budget (Table 11.8). Table 11.8 indicates the incapacity of the Swedish state to pay for all its public sector programmes. Deficit spending on a large scale began in 1976, which shows up in the drastic expansion of the accumulated state debt. Although there were a few years in the 1980s when the state budget was balanced, during most years since 1976 there have been deficits. In the early 1990s any kind of control over the size of the yearly deficits was lost. The deficit moved up to 15 per cent of GDP in 1994. The accumulated state debt is now almost 100 per cent of GDP, whereas in 1975 it was less than 25 per cent.

Interest payments on the state debt are the single largest item on the national budget, amounting to over 100 billion Swedish krona. Local governments do not regularly engage in deficit spending, but several large local governments have had increasing difficulties in balancing their books. For example, the cities of Gothenburg and Malmö have faced problems in financing large capital investments by means of foreign borrowing.

In addition, Sweden has indebted itself heavily abroad. The accumulated foreign debt for both the public and private sectors is more than 50 per cent of GDP. The foreign debt exploded during the 1980s, when both the state and private organizations borrowed heavily abroad. At present, 500 billion krona of the 1500 billion in state debt is placed outside Sweden. Table 11.9 shows the value of the krona in relation to a few major currencies since the deficit period was initiated.

The depreciation of the krona is only to a limited extent intentional, because Sweden only devalued its currency a couple of times in the late 1970s and in 1982. In 1991, Sweden was forced to leave the krona to float freely, which led to a dramatic depreciation of around 25 per cent, which was further accentuated in 1995.

Table 11.9 The value of the krona against major currencies

	US dollar	Yen	Pound sterling	Deutschmark	Danish krone
1960	5.2	–	14.5	1.24	0.75
1970	5.2	–	12.4	1.42	0.69
1980	4.2	1.9	9.9	2.33	0.75
1990	5.9	4.1	10.6	3.67	0.96
1995	7.6	7.5	11.8	4.81	1.24

Note: The table states how many Swedish krona it takes to buy one unit of the foreign currency.

Source: Statistical Yearbook of Sweden.

The failure to maintain a stable currency reflects macroeconomic difficulties. The preference for a highly discretionary regime, involving many policy reversals, adding to the uncertainties from external shocks, has been typical of Swedish macroeconomic policy-making. There has been a belief in demand management in a short-term perspective (Bergman and Jonung, 1994). When the Swedish model worked at its best, it delivered low levels of unemployment and inflation. However, the performance record deteriorated rapidly in the 1990s (Table 11.10).

Table 11.10 Unemployment and inflation

	Open unemployment (per cent per year)	Yearly inflation (per cent)
1960–9	1.8	4.1
1970–9	2.3	9.2
1980–9	2.3	7.8
1990–5	6	4.6

Sources: Statistical Yearbook of Sweden; Finansplanen 1995–6.

The recession in the early 1990s resulted in levels of unemployment that Sweden had not experienced since the 1930s. When open unemployment hit a high 8 per cent in 1993, total unemployment went up to almost 12 per cent, given the traditional policy of the government to retrain the unemployed within various schemes. Some 4 per cent of the labour force was engaged in retraining programmes in the early 1990s, which is very costly for the state. Such a high level of unemployment completely wiped out all kinds of wage-induced inflationary pressures, inflation dropping to some 2 per cent in 1994.

The persistently low unemployment figures made it possible for the trade unions to carry through considerable nominal wage increases in the 1970s and 1980s. However, these huge nominal wage increases did not increase real wages. Instead, they caused recurrent cost crises for Swedish enterprises. The market share of the private sector in Sweden has been declining since the early 1970s, when wage inflation started to pick up. Table 11.11 gives a few relative indicators on private sector performance, including real wages (Jakobsson and Jagren, 1993).

Table 11.11 Performance indicators, the private sector 1970–90 (relative trends)

	1970	1975	1980	1985	1990
Absolute wages	100	103	110	115	140
Relative wages	100	105	97	70	81
Market shares	100	90	80	78	70
Productivity	100	100	95	92	85
Investments	100	120	100	120	150

Note: The trends are expressed in terms of the 1970 scores which have been set to 100 per cent. Absolute wages are inflation-adjusted money wages, whereas relative wages add the depreciation of the Swedish krona. The productivity level in 1970 refers to Swedish productivity in relation to the average level in the OECD countries. Investments include only the domestic economy.

Source: Jakobsson and Jagren (1993: 73–95).

The combined effect of high nominal wage increases, rapid inflation and several currency depreciations has left Swedish workers with lower relative wages. The decline is substantial, involving an almost 20 per cent reduction in real wages in comparison with neighbouring industrial countries. Sweden has had the lowest increase in factor productivity among the advanced industrial economies.

Despite lower relative wages, Swedish firms have lost substantial international market shares. The decline of Swedish manufacture involves a reduction from 3.6 per cent of total OECD output in 1965 to 2.8 per cent in 1990 – a 25 per cent reduction. Swedish firms have invested and expanded abroad, but this has not resulted in huge spin-off effects at home (Isaksson, 1993). Although private investment has increased as a percentage of GDP from 14 to 18 per cent between 1950 and 1990, this has not been enough, owing to the relative decline in the overall role of the private sector. Let us look at incentive compatibility.

Redistribution: equity?

The preference for public income redistribution has meant that the Swedish transfer state has grown tremendously over a very short time, owing to very generous entitlements. It was not until the major economic crisis in 1991 that the rules about entitlements were reformed, but costs in the many transfer programmes are still growing as a percentage of GDP. There is still, despite the huge budget deficits, an ambition to secure for everyone a 90 per cent income maintenance protection against all risks. This redistributive ambition has hurt the incentive system in the economy, making employment in the private sector less and less attractive when such a scheme is combined with a heavy expansion of employment opportunities in the public sector.

When the Swedish model worked effectively, i.e. up to 1975, it delivered a proper balance between the private and the public sector, between a capitalist market economy and a welfare state with socialist ambitions. The trade-off was a compromise which all the major players supported for pragmatic reasons. Behind the successful compromise politics in Sweden stood a firm growth coalition, consisting of the employers' association (SAF), the Landsorganisationen (LO, the trade union for blue-collar workers) and the Social Democratic Party, supported not only by the centre parties but also by the Conservative Party (Rustow, 1955).

When the Swedish model operated at its best, there were few strikes or lockouts. Wage bargaining involved two key players, the LO on the blue-collar workers' side and the SAF on the employers' side. However, with the expansion of the public sector, this highly centralized pattern could not be maintained. Instead, wage negotiations involved several actors, not only white-collar workers but also public employees and central and local governments. The petrification of the bargaining system, which made opportunistic strategies much more attractive, reflects the transformation of the occupational structure. There are now simply too many veto players for any sustainable cut-back policy to emerge that would make an economic policy on the deficit and the debt credible.

The erosion of the Swedish model was caused by the coming to power in the 1970s of a different kind of coalition, a distributional coalition which cared only for the distribution of the gains of the economy, not economic growth. Actually, only the SAF argued for the growth alternative in economic policy-making, all the other major players favouring distribution. They favoured public resource allocation, because it implied that everyone would have the same and equal access to vital goods and services. They engaged in heavy redistribution, channelling money from various groups to other groups in an ever more complex system, compensating for all kinds of income losses that people suffered.

A sign of the redistributive ambition is the phenomenal increase in the number of persons with a complete or partial disability pension. In 1995, 10 per cent of the labour force was given a disability pension, or some 400 000 people. Table 11.12 shows that in the early 1990s redistributional state, transfer payments remained at a very high level, still increasing absolutely though not relatively as a percentage of GDP.

Table 11.12 Transfer payments 1990–5 (billion krona)

	1990	1991	1992	1993	1994	1995
Unemployment	11	22	46	57	56	48
Sickness	45	43	32	30	29	28
Pensions	154	173	186	192	204	214
Family and youth	67	79	85	91	96	99
Total	277	317	349	370	385	389

There are two problems in relation to the transfer programmes. On the one hand, there is the gigantic size of the transfers, amounting to 33 per cent of GDP when one includes the transfer programmes not rendered in Table 11.12 (housing, agriculture, EU membership). This is surely the most expensive transfer state in the world.

On the other hand, there is the problem of deficit financing. The transfer state is far from fully financed, with the result that Sweden runs the largest current state budget deficit in the OECD set of countries. Interest payments are the single most expensive item on the national budget, soaring to 8 per cent of GDP in 1996. This has driven up interest rates to levels that are far higher than those in neighbouring countries, such as Norway, Denmark and Germany.

It is sometimes claimed that the deficit is not so worrying, because there is a large surplus in the national social insurance funds. However, even considering the consolidated public sector, there are heavy deficits each year. And one must recall that these funds are earmarked for pension outlays. Actually, there is for the first time a fear among many men and women that the state will not be able to deliver upon its pension promises in the future (Ståhlberg, 1995).

Conclusion

The decline of Swedish economic performance is now a known fact. Data on economic growth, the depreciation of the krona and high unemployment have been reported in international news media time and again in connection with the delivery of various rescue packages by Swedish politicians. What is missing is an explanation of the Swedish decline. From having been recognized as a model example for other countries, Sweden is now placed in the set of weak currency countries and its famous model is now often referred to as a warning case.

The Swedish developments involved the public sector driving out the private sector. This was true of both public resource allocation and public income redistribution. The allocative state and the redistributive state were at their maximum in the Swedish welfare state, although a market economy of some sort was retained.

The preference for public resource allocation instead of markets meant that almost all types of education, health care and social care were allocated by the state and financed by taxation, where the burden of provision fell upon the local government system. The almost phenomenal increase in the number of local government employees testified to the fact that any private provision of these goods and services was ruled out. This was a very risky strategy, given the probability of inefficiency in the administrative state owing to strategic interaction and opportunistic behaviour. The productivity measurements of budget allocation between 1960 and 1980 at both national and local government levels revealed profound efficiency problems (Murray, 1987). It should be pointed out that Sweden moved to reform its welfare state in the mid 1990s, and its economic difficulties have eased considerably.

An examination of one welfare state – Sweden – suggests that this type of politico-economic regime may run into severe difficulties involving bad outcomes. Can one generalize from the Swedish case? Is there a risk of the Swedish disease occurring among the other welfare states? Chapter 12 weighs the pros and cons of two ideals for a rich society, the welfare state model and the welfare society model.

12   Welfare states or welfare societies?

Introduction

A much debated theme in the political economy literature is the pros and cons of
the welfare states, or the politico-economic regimes which employ budget allocation
and income redistribution to a large extent in order to complement market
operations. In a sense the welfare states belong to the set of market economies, but
at the same time they are different from decentralized capitalism. After the Second
World War it seemed for a few decades as if there was convergence towards the so-
called mixed economy, with a large tax state as one of the pillars of society and the
market economy as the other pillar. However, the 1980s and 1990s have witnessed
a steady advance of the principles of the market economy in the form of the so-
called welfare societies or decentralized capitalism, where public expenditure is
being kept low or has been reduced.

A few countries have switched from the welfare state format to the ideal of a
welfare society, such as Australia, New Zealand and Canada. The United Kingdom
under the Thatcher government remodelled the British welfare state on the basis
of market ideals, whereas the debate about the future of the American welfare state
became intense when the Republicans won the 1994 elections to Congress. What
is at stake here? Can we speak of a crisis of the welfare state? Is the welfare state
no longer performing as it did in the heyday of Keynesian macroeconomics? Could
it be the case that large public expenditure is counterproductive, meaning that it
worsens state performance on outcomes? This is the basic question in this chapter.

A welfare state is a politico-economic regime where the state is active in the
economy without extensive ownership, which results in a mixed economy instead
of the system of decentralized capitalism, where markets prevail and there is less
redistribution. The welfare state is active, with public resource allocation, transfer
payments and policies that promote full employment. What are the difficulties of
the welfare states, which – it is argued – constitute a case for a revival of the market
economy? When we speak of the welfare state, the universe of discourse is the set
of OECD countries. Let us look at public sector growth.

Public sector growth

A seminal trend in the development of the politico-economic regimes in the so-
called Western world is the growth of the state, particularly since 1945. In all

so-called advanced capitalist countries there is a seminal process of government budget expansion measured in terms of resources mobilized by the public sector as a percentage of GDP. The growth of the welfare state has been particularly strong in the major Western European countries. Table 12.1 shows data about the growth of what Joseph Schumpeter in 1918 called the 'tax state' (Schumpeter, 1989).

Table 12.1 General government: current receipts as a percentage of GDP 1950–92

	1950	1955	1960	1965	1970	1975	1980	1985	1990	1992
Austria	27.9	29.5	31.4	36.1	39.7	42.9	46.0	47.7	46.6	48.4
Belgium	24.2	24.0	26.7	30.7	35.2	40.4	43.2	46.5	49.5	49.5
Denmark	21.7	25.7	27.6	31.4	41.7	46.2	52.2	57.0	55.9	57.5
Finland	30.3	30.2	31.6	33.5	34.9	38.8	37.8	40.5	40.8	53.2
France	32.6	33.0	34.1	37.7	39.0	40.3	45.6	48.5	46.4	46.3
Germany	31.6	34.7	36.0	36.2	38.5	42.7	44.6	45.4	43.2	45.1
Greece	15.5	18.2	20.4	23.4	26.8	27.4	30.5	34.9	34.2	40.1
Iceland	27.6	26.9	36.4	29.0	31.8	35.6	32.1	33.4	34.3	37.8
Ireland	23.4	23.8	24.6	28.0	35.3	35.2	41.7	44.3	40.3	40.1
Italy	21.0	26.2	29.8	31.6	30.4	31.2	37.4	37.5	42.3	44.0
Luxembourg	31.7	30.0	32.5	35.2	35.0	49.0	51.5	53.0	–	–
Netherlands	33.0	28.9	33.4	36.8	44.5	53.2	55.0	54.4	51.9	54.0
Norway	29.6	30.8	34.5	37.7	43.5	49.6	54.0	56.1	56.3	55.3
Portugal	20.0	19.1	17.6	20.4	24.3	24.8	31.5	35.9	37.6	–
Spain	–	–	18.1	19.3	22.5	24.4	30.0	33.2	37.9	40.2
Sweden	26.2	32.7	35.0	42.0	47.0	50.7	56.7	59.4	63.8	59.2
Switzerland	25.5	24.0	25.4	25.4	26.5	32.1	32.8	34.4	34.1	34.5
Turkey	–	–	–	19.9	23.7	–	–	–	–	–
UK	33.5	30.4	29.6	32.8	40.7	40.8	40.9	43.7	39.5	38.0
Canada	24.1	26.0	28.0	30.6	35.2	36.9	37.2	38.8	42.1	43.5
USA	24.0	25.0	27.5	27.3	30.3	30.5	32.8	31.1	31.9	31.5
Japan	21.9	19.9	20.7	20.8	20.7	24.0	28.0	31.2	34.6	33.8
Australia	–	–	25.4	27.3	27.8	31.0	33.4	33.7	35.2	33.1

Note: Current receipts consist mainly of direct and indirect taxes, and social security contributions paid by employers and employees. General government consists of all departments, offices, organizations and other bodies which are agents or instruments of the central, state or local public authorities. Data for New Zealand are not available.

Sources: Lane *et al.* (1991), OECD (1993, 1995b).

The public sector in the OECD countries grew from a level of about 20 per cent of GDP at the end of the Second World War to roughly 50 per cent or more in some countries in the early 1990s. One may say that the exceptional growth process was brought to a halt in the mid-1980s, but it should be pointed out that there has been a slight increase in tax revenues in the past decade. Is there a magic number that would definitely seal off public sector growth? Hardly, since when tax revenues are not enough governments may use deficit spending. We must look at the expenditure side, and not only at the income side of the public household.

The public sector in the rich countries is larger than the data about receipts in Table 12.1 indicate, as it has become more and more common to engage in deficit spending. Table 12.2 shows that current disbursements tend to be larger than current receipts.

Table 12.2 General government: current disbursements as a percentage of GDP

	1950	1955	1960	1965	1970	1975	1980	1985	1990	1992
Austria	21.2	23.0	25.4	28.9	33.1	38.6	42.7	45.2	44.7	46.4
Belgium	25.5	23.8	27.8	29.8	33.0	41.2	48.1	52.3	53.6	54.3
Denmark	18.0	21.4	21.7	25.9	34.6	43.5	52.2	56.7	56.5	58.8
Finland	19.7	20.7	21.9	25.8	28.9	32.2	34.3	37.7	37.5	56.9
France	26.7	29.8	30.2	32.9	34.7	39.2	43.1	49.4	45.7	48.7
Germany	28.3	27.0	28.2	30.4	32.6	43.4	42.8	43.4	42.5	44.3
Greece	19.6	16.3	17.8	21.3	22.4	26.7	30.4	45.3	49.6	48.9
Iceland	19.9	20.0	23.4	20.6	21.7	28.3	25.0	28.3	31.1	34.8
Ireland	22.9	23.4	24.5	27.6	34.2	42.0	48.3	50.4	41.9	41.7
Italy	20.7	24.6	26.6	30.9	30.2	38.3	41.4	44.1	48.8	51.9
Luxembourg	22.5	26.9	25.5	29.7	28.6	41.3	45.7	47.8	–	–
Netherlands	23.9	25.5	28.0	33.0	40.2	51.1	54.2	55.2	54.0	55.5
Norway	21.9	24.4	28.0	31.9	36.5	41.8	45.1	44.0	56.3	57.7
Portugal	16.3	15.9	15.2	17.7	19.5	27.2	33.8	39.4	39.4	–
Spain	–	–	13.7	15.8	18.8	21.2	29.4	34.7	36.9	40.7
Sweden	23.5	26.4	28.7	31.9	37.2	44.9	57.1	60.8	58.5	64.3
Switzerland	19.4	18.5	19.1	21.3	21.3	28.8	29.3	30.9	30.9	34.9
Turkey	–	–	–	15.5	16.4	–	–	–	–	–
UK	30.1	28.8	29.3	30.5	33.2	41.0	42.3	44.9	38.2	42.1
Canada	19.2	23.4	26.6	26.4	32.2	36.8	37.7	43.8	44.9	49.4
USA	20.0	22.5	25.0	25.2	30.3	33.6	33.5	35.3	35.1	36.6
Japan	14.6	15.5	13.6	14.7	14.0	20.9	25.4	26.9	26.2	26.0
Australia	–	–	18.9	21.6	21.8	27.6	30.4	35.5	34.7	36.9

Note: Current disbursements consist of final consumption expenditure, interest on the public debt, subsidies and social security transfers to households. General government consists of all departments, offices, organizations and other bodies which are agents or instruments of the central, state or local public authorities. Data for New Zealand are not available.

Source: See Table 12.1.

As the distance between the maximum scores – Sweden's 64 per cent and Denmark's 59 per cent – and the minimum scores – Japan's 26 per cent and Switzerland's 35 per cent – is immense, one has to pose the question of what drives up public spending. On the one hand, there seem to exist almost irresistable forces that increase public expenditure. A number of countries have tried to roll back the size of the public sector, but they manage to only maintain the same level – see the UK, the USA and Australia. Countries like Spain and Portugal have augmented their public sector rapidly after system transformation. Even in Japan and

Switzerland the public household is growing. On the other hand, there are considerable differences even among the mixed economies, as some of these countries stay under the 50 per cent barrier whereas others move towards the 60 per cent limit. Why one choice and not another of a public–private sector mix, if countries can choose?

There are two problems involved in the theories explaining public sector expansion in the OECD countries. On the one hand, we want to know why there is this general growth in the tax state in the rich, advanced capitalist countries. On the other hand, we need to explain why the public sector has grown in such a different manner in various countries. Whereas the tax state has expanded from 24 to 60 per cent in Sweden, the increase in the tax state in Switzerland is only from 19 to 34 per cent.

There is a whole literature on the determinants of welfare state expansion, discussing whether public expenditure growth is driven by the Wagner–Wilensky mechanism, i.e. affluence, or whether politics matters for policy-making. It is a typical feature of this discussion about expenditure or policy determinants that it is possible to identify a whole set of factors that could be conducive to public sector growth, but that it is difficult to exclude any of them, as every factor may be relevant in at least some country (Lybeck, 1986; Lybeck and Henrekson, 1988).

What we will analyse here is not the factors that explain the emergence of the welfare state, as we will focus upon the outcomes of the welfare state. The relevant question now, when the welfare state model is challenged by the market economy, is whether the welfare state is conducive to a negative performance profile for the countries that adhere to this model. In evaluating the outcomes of the welfare state, we will look at economic growth, unemployment, inflation and income equality. First, though, we wish to point out that the public sector in the rich countries can have alternative profiles relating to how countries position themselves with regard to public resource allocation, income redistribution and deficit spending.

Two types of public–private mix

Table 12.3 presents a perspective on the country variation in general government public finance items by dividing the public household into two different components: final government consumption and general government transfer payments. It includes all the OECD countries (except Mexico and Czechoslovakia), as we wish to enquire into whether the welfare states differ on these items from the welfare societies. How large is the variation between those countries that have low allocative or redistributive expenditure and those that have large costs for these public expenditure items?

Among the big welfare states, one may distinguish first those that have large allocative expenditure and large redistributive expenditure. Second, we identify those that mainly have large transfer payments. Third, we have a set of countries which are low on both allocative and redistributive expenditure, when military expenditure has been taken out. Table 12.4 contains a classification of the three types of public sector.

Table 12.3 Allocative and redistributive welfare expenditures/GDP

| | Government final consumption | | Social security transfers | |
	1990	1992	1990	1992
Austria	21.8	18.4	19.9	20.3
Belgium	14.5	14.7	22.2	24.0
Denmark	25.2	25.7	18.5	19.7
Finland	21.1	24.8	11.0	23.7
France	17.9	18.8	21.5	22.4
Germany	18.4	17.9	15.9	14.8
Greece	21.1	19.7	14.8	15.3
Iceland	18.8	20.2	5.5	6.7
Ireland	15.7	16.1	15.8	15.3
Italy	17.4	17.6	18.4	19.3
Netherlands	14.5	14.5	26.1	26.5
Norway	21.1	21.5	19.5	20.5
Portugal	16.7	–	12.4	–
Spain	15.5	17.0	15.9	17.6
Sweden	27.2	27.9	20.8	23.4
Switzerland	13.4	14.3	13.6	15.9
UK	20.0	22.2	12.8	14.3
Canada	20.2	21.9	12.9	15.8
USA	17.9	17.7	11.3	13.1
Japan	9.1	9.3	12.0	11.5
Australia	17.7	18.4	11.0	11.3

Note: Government final consumption consists of expenditure on goods and services for public administration, defence, health and education. Social security transfers consist of social security benefits, social assistance grants, unfunded employee pension and welfare benefits, and transfers to private non-profit institutions serving households. The deficit is current receipts minus current disbursements. Data for Luxembourg, Turkey and New Zealand are not available.

Source: See Table 12.1.

There are, one may suggest, two kinds of welfare states, the allocative and the redistributive ones. To a limited extent these are the same countries; for instance, the Scandinavian countries score high in both. The redistributive welfare state offers a larger space for markets than allocative welfare states, where government is responsible for the supply of numerous services. Transfer payments in the form of cash contributions to individuals play a major role in the redistributive welfare state. The critical question is whether it matters whether a country has one or the other kind of welfare state or adheres to the welfare society ideal – matters, that is, for social and economic outcomes such as unemployment, economic growth and inflation, as well as income equality. Before we examine these outcomes, upon which so much emphasis is usually placed, we will look at a third aspect of the public household: the gap between revenue and outlay, or deficit spending.

Table 12.4 Types of societies: public–private sector mixes around 1990

Welfare states		Welfare societies
Allocative	*Redistributive*	
Austria	Austria	Ireland
Denmark	Denmark	Portugal
Finland	Finland	Spain
France	France	Switzerland
Germany	Italy	Turkey
Greece	Luxembourg	USA
Iceland	Netherlands	Japan
Luxembourg	Norway	Australia
Norway	Sweden	New Zealand
Sweden	Belgium	
UK		
Canada		

Note: Allocative welfare states use about 18 per cent or more of the GDP for general government consumption; redistributive welfare states employ 18 per cent or more on social security payments.

Deficits

During the past decade deficit spending has become a typical aspect of public households. There appears to be a real break with traditional budgetary principles in the OECD countries – what James Buchanan (1986) has referred to as the breakdown of Victorian fiscal norms. It cannot be doubted that deficit spending has entered the public budget and forms a most important means for the financing of considerable portions of state expenditure. Our question here is whether the welfare states differ in terms of deficit spending from the welfare societies. The problem of the size of deficit spending has for a long time been considered a highly relevant one, not only for Third World nations where huge public debts cause constant anxiety about political bankruptcy and political instability, but also for rich nations. Why?

Deficit spending – it is argued – has taken on such proportions that strong political intervention is called for in the form of a constitutional amendment or a general spending limit. Presumably, deficit spending is resorted to because it is an acceptable means to some desired end, such as the provision of public goods, the redistribution of income or full employment. However, the criticisms of public borrowing state not only that is not a proper means to desirable ends but that these ends too are questionable. The attempt to find decision mechanisms that will curb government deficit spending coincides with a general hesitance about public spending. Whereas public sector budget-making used to be defended on grounds of social efficiency and equity, the new theory of public choice argues that public budgets involve worse allocation failures than the standard market imperfections (Niskanen, 1971; Brennan and Buchanan, 1980). Deficit spending would, if left uncontrolled, be conducive not only to public sector inefficiencies but also to inequities, besides being an improper tool in the first place as a way to raise public revenues. How extensive is deficit spending in welfare states and welfare societies?

Public debt is as old as the public household (Webber and Wildavsky, 1986). The new criticism of public borrowing is not directed at the phenomenon *per se*; only when it is used for the purpose of deficit spending is public borrowing condemned, because it is neither an acceptable instrument for financing public outlays nor conducive to a rational choice between the public and the private sectors. Public borrowing is considered bad when part of deficit spending or the underbalancing of the public budget, because either it is an unproper means (*the means argument*) or it does not result in good outcomes (*the ends argument*). The classical theory of public finance contains a number of guidelines as to decisions about public borrowing and public debt which are not questioned in the criticism of budgetary deficits.

The new phenomenon of massive deficit spending not only opens up the possibility of a fundamental shift from private sector to public sector, but, it is argued, also accounts for the emergence of stagflation: high unemployment with

Table 12.5 Deficit spending/GDP: central government 1950–92

	1950	1955	1960	1965	1970	1975	1980	1985	1990	1992
Austria	0.9	4.0	3.2	3.2	2.3	−0.5	0.0	−0.7	−0.2	−0.1
Belgium	−1.3	−0.2	−2.0	−0.3	0.8	−1.6	−3.9	−6.7	−4.3	−5.2
Denmark	−	−	4.7	4.3	6.0	0.2	−2.7	−1.7	−2.0	−2.8
Finland	−	−	6.8	4.8	5.1	3.3	1.5	1.7	2.6	−5.8
France	−	−	2.8	3.7	2.9	−0.2	0.9	−2.2	−0.4	−2.7
Germany	0.8	3.9	2.9	2.0	2.9	−0.6	0.4	0.6	−0.9	0.1
Greece	−5.6	0.7	1.3	0.3	1.8	−2.1	−2.1	−8.3	−14.3	−9.7
Iceland	6.4	4.7	10.3	5.2	7.2	2.8	4.8	3.2	1.2	1.2
Ireland	0.3	0.5	−0.1	0.5	1.5	−5.6	−5.6	−5.5	−0.8	−1.1
Italy	−0.2	0.6	2.7	0.5	0.4	−2.6	−4.7	−7.5	−6.8	−9.0
Luxembourg	5.8	1.7	4.0	2.8	4.0	5.6	4.0	4.0	−	−
Netherlands	−	2.3	4.1	3.4	3.5	2.0	0.7	−1.6	−2.3	−2.3
Norway	5.8	4.3	4.5	3.8	4.5	5.9	7.6	−2.3	2.6	−0.4
Portugal	1.8	1.2	1.2	1.2	2.1	−2.5	−2.6	−4.8	0.3	−
Spain	−	−	−	3.1	2.6	2.3	0.3	−2.2	0.0	0.0
Sweden	2.1	3.3	5.1	4.2	3.9	1.5	−5.3	−4.5	2.3	−8.9
Switzerland	−	−	3.3	2.6	1.7	0.7	0.5	0.5	0.8	0.0
Turkey	−	−	−	1.4	4.8	−	−	−	−	−
UK	2.3	1.6	0.1	2.1	7.4	−1.3	−1.3	−1.2	1.4	−3.1
Canada	3.2	0.6	0.0	1.5	0.6	−1.7	−3.1	−6.0	−3.6	−3.9
USA	3.2	1.0	0.6	−0.1	−2.0	−3.7	−1.8	−4.9	−4.1	−5.2
Japan	−	−	8.3	5.7	2.3	−1.2	−2.0	−1.5	1.5	−0.1
Australia	−	−	5.0	4.1	4.6	1.2	1.6	−0.5	0.0	−2.7

Note: Data for New Zealand are not available. Negative figures indicate deficits.

Sources: Lane *et al.* (1991), OECD (1993, 1995).

high levels of inflation. It is assumed that the higher the levels of deficit spending, the larger the public sector, the more unemployment and the higher the inflation; or the more deficit spending, the larger the growth in public expenditure, unemployment and inflation (Buchanan and Wagner, 1977; Wagner and Tollison, 1982). As these propositions play a major role in the criticism of public borrowing, we will scrutinize them in an empirical test in relation to the OECD countries: (a) the larger the budgetary deficit, the larger the public sector or the larger the public expenditure; (b) the larger the budgetary deficit, the larger the unemployment; (c) the larger the budgetary deficit, the larger the inflation rate; (d) the more deficit spending, the lower the rate of growth in the economy.

During the 1970s, 1980s and early 1990s, governments resorted to deficit spending to an extent not previously experienced. The direction of change in the OECD countries has been towards less and less budgetary surplus and more and more budgetary deficit. One may observe this at two levels. First there is the central or national government deficit; second is the general govenment deficit, i.e. for the entire public household. Table 12.5 gives information for central government, for which the huge pension outlays are sometimes, but not always, included.

Table 12.6 Deficit spending/GDP: general government 1950–92

	1950	1955	1960	1965	1970	1975	1980	1985	1990	1992
Austria	6.7	6.5	6.0	7.3	6.6	4.3	3.3	2.5	1.9	2.0
Belgium	−1.3	0.1	−1.2	0.8	2.2	−0.7	−4.9	−5.8	−4.0	−4.8
Denmark	3.7	4.3	5.8	5.5	7.1	2.6	0.0	0.3	−0.6	−1.3
Finland	10.6	9.5	9.7	7.8	6.0	6.6	3.5	2.8	3.4	−3.7
France	5.9	3.2	3.8	4.8	4.3	1.1	2.5	−0.9	0.7	−2.4
Germany	3.3	7.8	7.7	5.8	5.8	−0.7	1.8	2.0	0.6	0.8
Greece	−4.1	1.9	2.5	2.1	4.4	0.7	0.1	−10.5	−15.4	−8.8
Iceland	7.7	6.9	13.1	8.5	10.1	7.2	7.1	5.1	3.2	3.0
Ireland	0.5	0.4	0.1	0.4	1.1	−6.7	−6.7	−6.1	−1.6	−1.6
Italy	0.3	1.6	3.2	0.7	0.2	−7.1	−4.0	−6.6	−6.5	−7.9
Luxembourg	9.2	3.1	7.0	5.6	6.4	7.6	5.7	5.2	–	–
Netherlands	9.1	3.4	5.4	3.8	4.3	2.1	0.8	−0.8	−2.1	−1.5
Norway	7.7	6.4	6.5	5.8	7.0	7.8	8.9	12.1	0.0	−2.4
Portugal	3.7	3.2	2.3	2.6	4.8	−2.5	−2.3	−3.5	−1.8	–
Spain	–	–	4.4	3.5	3.8	3.1	0.6	−1.5	1.1	−0.4
Sweden	2.7	6.3	6.3	10.2	9.9	5.8	−0.4	−1.4	5.3	−5.1
Switzerland	6.1	5.5	6.4	4.1	5.2	3.3	3.6	3.5	3.2	−0.4
Turkey	–	–	–	4.4	7.2	–	–	–	–	–
UK	3.4	1.6	0.3	2.3	7.6	−0.3	−1.4	−1.2	1.3	−4.1
Canada	4.9	2.6	1.5	4.3	3.0	0.1	−0.5	−5.0	−2.7	−5.9
USA	4.0	2.5	2.5	2.1	0.0	−3.1	−0.7	−4.2	−3.2	−5.0
Japan	7.3	4.4	7.1	6.1	6.7	3.2	2.6	4.3	8.4	7.8
Australia	–	–	6.5	6.7	5.9	3.4	3.0	−1.8	0.5	−3.8

Note: See Table 12.5. Current receipts – current disbursements = deficit.

Sources: Lane *et al.* (1991), OECD (1993, 1995).

Most conspicuous is the drive towards deficit spending at the national government level, but it is also true that total public sector surpluses which used to be quite substantial have been reduced considerably in most nations. It is often argued that national government deficits are acceptable in the short run but not in the long run, while general government deficits are much more difficult to handle, even in the short-term perspective. Countries that have a general government deficit also have a central government deficit, but the reverse is certainly not always true. Table 12.6 gives figures for total public sector deficits.

In 1970, only the USA had no total public sector surpluses, but in the 1980s quite a number of democracies could not balance total public sector expenditure and revenue: Ireland, Belgium, Portugal, Greece, Denmark, the United Kingdom, Sweden, and the USA and Canada, for example. Not surprisingly, even more countries failed to balance their general government budget, which was rather a common phenomenon in 1970. Between 1970 and the 1990s the trend towards deficit spending is striking as all nations have moved towards smaller surpluses or larger deficits at both levels of government. If deficit spending is a major problem, then it has to be faced by some welfare states – Sweden, Belgium and Italy – as well as by some welfare societies – the USA, Australia and Portugal. It is not the case that only welfare states have to struggle with huge yearly deficits, which result in a large accumulated state debt. But how dangerous is deficit spending? Does deficit spending lead to bad outcomes?

The criticism of public borrowing argues that deficit spending is an improper means that is conducive to an improper growth in public expenditures. Deficit spending feeds on a fiscal illusion and results in a choice between private and public spending that is neither intended nor desirable (Buchanan and Wagner, 1977). It misleads democratic decision-making, as it creates the fiscal illusion that benefits may be enjoyed without paying the cost. Is it true that deficit spending is typical of welfare states more than welfare societies? Is it correct that deficit spending goes together with unemployment, inflation and low economic growth? Table 12.7 suggests a clue to the last question.

Deficit spending at the national or general government level is strongly and persistently connected with only one of the outcomes identified above, i.e. unemployment. The relationship is probably that high levels of unemployment call for deficit spending owing to the increased costs of unemployment benefits and falling tax revenues accompanying a rise in unemployment. Rising unemployment costs also entail larger public expenditure, which accounts for the negative association between deficits and current disbursements. However, it is far from always the case that deficit spending reduces economic growth or results in higher inflation. Only in the 1990s do we see a clear negative connection between deficits and inflation.

Yet one can see in the evidence from the early 1990s a firm corroboration of the negative theory of public deficits, as the larger the surpluses the better the growth rate, the lower the unemployment and the lower the rate of inflation. Clearly, deficit spending is conducive to larger public expenditure overall. Why, then, is deficit spending accepted?

Table 12.7 Correlations between deficits and outcomes

	Current disbursements (years)	GDP growth (five-year averages)	Unemployment (five-year averages)	Inflation (five-year averages)
		General government deficit		
1965	−0.00	−0.18	−0.40	0.29
1970	−0.12	0.18	−0.62	0.34
1975	−0.09	−0.21	−0.72	0.01
1980	−0.29	0.38	−0.72	0.14
1985	−0.27	0.03	−0.61	−0.12
1990	−0.39	−0.11	−0.32	−0.62
1992	−0.53	0.28	−0.42	−0.42
		Central government deficit		
1965	−0.11	0.01	−0.55	0.42
1970	0.21	0.11	−0.49	0.43
1975	0.09	−0.30	−0.58	0.01
1980	−0.13	0.29	−0.50	0.19
1985	−0.38	0.26	−0.52	−0.05
1990	−0.39	−0.03	−0.23	−0.61
1992	−0.49	0.46	−0.24	−0.50

Sources: Tables 12.2, 12.5, 12.6, 12.10, 12.11, 12.12.

Basically, the negative theory of deficit spending looks at deficits from the perspective of the tax payer, who cannot calculate the relationship between advantages and costs if budgets are not balanced. In the short run, the financing of public expenditure by borrowing means that individual choice between public goods and private goods is systematically biased in favour of the consumption of the former. Assuming a standard choice situation, the democratic citizen has a set of preferences for the mix of public goods and private goods that may be represented by indifference curves, and budget restriction allows for the consumption of X units of public goods and Y units of private goods in a balanced budget account, so we can see how deficit spending might result in irresponsible behaviour. At first, the price of public goods will be reduced, which will result in more of both public and private goods. Then, the price of public goods will go up, meaning that the citizen will get less after-tax money for private spending. In the long run there will be an unintended shift from private allocation to public allocation. Since spending on public goods is characterized by a large degree of inertia, the true price of the allocation of public goods will be reflected in tax increases, which the citizen cannot withdraw from. In the end he or she will end up worse off than had the relationship between benefit and cost been clear. This amounts to a fiscal illusion, as the movement is based upon false premises: the move to deficit spending reduces the cost of public goods provision only in the short run, but it simultaneously sets off a higher demand for public goods, which is illusory.

From the perspective of the politician/bureaucrat, the possibility of deficit spending opens up promising expectations in the short run. If the utility of the politician/bureaucrat is a function of budget size, then it is easy to show that the move to deficit spending allows the supply of larger quantities of public goods. Assuming normal demand and supply curves, the restriction of budgetary balance means that the amount of public goods allocated is fixed, whereas the employment of deficit spending allows the politician/bureaucrat to expand budget size to a higher level of provision. Deficit spending is less costly supply. In the long run, the real supply capacity of the politician/bureaucrat is the same as before, which means that there will be an oversupply of public goods. Again, there is a fiscal illusion, as the politician/bureaucrat is led to supply a quantity of public goods that he or she cannot pay for in the long run. Combining the two types of fiscal illusion – one on the demand side and the other on the supply side of the public sector – the situation may be even worse. Is this the explanation of big government among the welfare states?

These forces, if operative over the whole political economy, will result not only in public sector growth in the short run, but also in a reduction in the relative size of the private sector in the long run. Public expenditure has grown at a faster rate than GDP among the welfare states, meaning that politics is driving the market, but is this a function of deficit spending? The empirical analysis indicates that the variation in public expenditure levels or growth rates is to a small extent a function of the variation in deficit spending.

Existing budgetary practices imply that budget-making in the public sector is a building-up process. Actors and programmes place their demands for appropriations, which are squeezed down to some total, requiring a mix of finance decisions. The proposal that decisions on expenditure should be made simultaneously with decisions on finance is not often followed in actual public resource allocation. A constitutional amendment concerning the balancing of the budget does not accomplish an individual quid pro quo in public resource allocation; nor does it introduce a break down of budget-making. Individual rationality, in the sense that each citizen knows the tax price of each public good, is not achieved, because the balance requirement refers only to totals or the aggregation of public goods into a single expenditure and taxation decision. The norm that government must balance its books does not imply that income will determine outputs, as the option is still open to government to raise taxes as the public budget grows. Budgetary balance is not a sufficient condition for individual rationality in public goods spending; nor is it a sufficient condition for halting public expenditure growth.

Is it ever possible to make individual choices as to the mix of public and private goods on the basis of a rational calculation of costs and benefits? If this is individual accountability, then is it possible with regard to the decision about the optimal size of public goods? The simple requirement that expenditure must be covered by revenue does not allow a citizen to calculate what various programmes cost; nor does the abolition of deficit spending help the citizen to calculate the benefits from public goods. The requirement of budgetary balance is a *collective* decision rule, while the notion of individual rationality in equating the costs and benefits is not. The connection between the two principles is not straightforward. The introduction of a ban on deficit spending certainly does not mean that individuals will find that they make optimal choices about costs and benefits concerning the allocation of private and public goods. Balanced budgets do not imply that the taxes each citizen pays match the benefits from public goods provision.

Although the normative appeal of a system of financing the public sector based on the benefit principle still attracts serious attention, a positive understanding of the way revenues are raised in modern public finance systems cannot be based on these assumptions. The split between expenditure decisions and revenue decisions is such a pervasive property of public budget-making that it has to be incorporated in a theory of deficit spending. Revenue decisions have a logic of their own apart from the logic of expenditure decisions. In particular, we must take into account the possibility that expenditure decisions and revenue decisions do not match, i.e. that the conflict between the output and input sides of the public budget forces the budget-makers to engage in deficit spending to an extent that is not called for if the need for collective capital formation is to be fulfilled or if macroeconomic objectives are consulted.

Generally, politicians face a probability function of being re-elected that depends upon their capacity to supply public goods in the wide sense of the word, including impure public goods and so-called merit goods. The shape of the probability function may not be fully known to the politicians in power; for reasons of simplicity it may be drawn asymptotically, expressing the fact that the allocation of public goods has a decreasing marginal impact upon the probability of being elected.

In a competitive democracy the government can increase the probability of staying in power by spending more on popular programmes; there is a limit to such policies, because some groups may not place a high value upon public resource allocation or public goods, or the satisfaction of one set of clients may not be in agreement with the satisfaction of another set. Moreover, the probability function may include other arguments as well. In any case, if the provision of public goods is low, the government will no doubt stand a small chance of being re-elected. It may increase the probability of staying in power by expenditure decisions oriented to powerful groups of citizens, though there is a limit to how much expenditure may affect the probability of being re-elected.

Budgets have to be paid for in the public household. Taxation, however, has the opposite impact upon the probability function, as it decreases the probability of staying in power, the higher the taxes are raised. In the public household citizens want more for less, which contradicts the benefit rule. The relationship between the probability of being re-elected and the amount of resource mobilized by means of taxation is clearly negative; the probability function may be drawn as a linear negative function of the amount of tax revenue. Assume now that the expenditure decision resulting in a budget of size S means that revenue of size S also has to be collected, which drastically reduces the probability of being re-elected. The resort to deficit spending is the only way out of this dilemma.

The fundamental asymmetry between expenditure and taxation implies that benefits and costs cannot be equalized in analogy with the workings of the private economy. Though the public budget has to be paid for like any budget, it does not have to be financed on a micro basis with each and every expenditure item having its special source of revenue. The public budget is financed as a whole, which means that a sum of expenditure decisions looks for a general revenue decision. The two may not be in agreement and it may not be *feasible* to bring the two together, or their combination may not be *desirable*. The decline in the capacity of taxation to raise revenues may not simply express the growing concern of politicians to raise taxes in order to meet expenditure demands, it may also reflect the incapacity of taxation as a revenue instrument.

Table 12.8 Deficits/GDP 1950–92

		Welfare states				Welfare societies		
		Mean	Min.	Max.		Mean	Min.	Max.
GGDEF50	(n = 15)	4.65	−4.1	10.6	(n = 5)	4.32	0.5	7.3
GGDEF55	(n = 15)	4.35	0.1	9.5	(n = 5)	3.20	0.4	5.5
GGDEF60	(n = 15)	5.17	−1.2	13.1	(n = 7)	4.19	0.1	7.1
GGDEF65	(n = 15)	5.02	0.7	10.2	(n = 8)	3.74	0.4	6.7
GGDEF70	(n = 15)	5.66	0.2	10.1	(n = 8)	4.34	0.0	7.2
GGDEF75	(n = 15)	2.47	−7.1	7.8	(n = 7)	0.10	−6.7	3.4
GGDEF80	(n = 15)	1.50	−4.9	8.9	(n = 7)	0.01	−6.7	3.6
GGDEF85	(n = 15)	−0.15	−10.5	12.1	(n = 7)	−1.33	−6.1	4.3
GGDEF90	(n = 14)	−1.06	−15.4	5.3	(n = 7)	0.94	−3.2	8.4
GGDEF92	(n = 14)	−3.01	−8.8	3.0	(n = 6)	−0.57	−5.0	7.8
CGDEF50	(n = 11)	1.84	−5.6	6.4	(n = 3)	1.77	0.3	3.2
CGDEF55	(n = 12)	2.29	−0.2	4.7	(n = 3)	0.90	0.5	1.2
CGDEF60	(n = 15)	3.37	−2.0	10.3	(n = 6)	3.05	−0.1	8.3
CGDEF65	(n = 15)	2.77	−0.3	5.2	(n = 8)	2.31	−0.1	5.7
CGDEF70	(n = 15)	3.55	0.4	7.4	(n = 8)	2.20	−2.0	4.8
CGDEF75	(n = 15)	0.71	−2.6	5.9	(n = 7)	−1.26	−5.6	2.3
CGDEF80	(n = 15)	−0.21	−5.3	7.6	(n = 7)	−1.37	−5.6	1.6
CGDEF85	(n = 15)	−2.21	−8.3	4.0	(n = 7)	−2.70	−5.5	0.5
CGDEF90	(n = 14)	−1.76	−14.3	2.6	(n = 7)	−0.33	−4.1	1.5
CGDEF92	(n = 14)	−3.76	−9.7	1.2	(n = 6)	−1.52	−5.2	0.0

Note: GGDEF50 is general government deficit in 1950, etc.; CGDEF50 is central government deficit in 1950, etc.

Sources: Lane *et al.* (1991), OECD (1993, 1995).

With governments confronted with a decline in the growth of tax revenues owing to rapidly increasing costs in taxation – output restriction and tax evasion – deficit spending may not only constitute an opportunity for government but may also represent the best collective choice, given the asymmetry between the demand for public expenditure as expressed by voting and the willingness to pay as expressed in taxation behaviour. Not only is it very difficult to engage in substantive cutback policies when the expansion of revenues begins to decline; it may also be socially non-desirable to opt for a balanced budget owing to increasing taxation costs. Deficit spending may not be the main stimulus of public expenditure, but a rational reaction to the logic of revenue collection.

The increase in deficit spending during the past decade in the welfare states has resulted in a new criticism of public borrowing, demanding that the public household budget should be balanced on a yearly basis. It is argued that deficit spending is a major malady that is conducive to fiscal irresponsibility and excessive public sector growth. Constitutional reform is recommended as a tool to implement the balanced budget idea. Is the new criticism of deficit spending correct? Empirically, there is actually partial support for the general statements about the negative effects of deficit spending if data for the OECD nations during the past decade, when deficit spending took on huge proportions, are consulted.

Are deficits larger in the welfare states than in the welfare societies? Table 12.8 supplies the answer.

One cannot claim that welfare states are more prone to engage in deficit spending than welfare societies. The evidence in Table 12.8 indicates that welfare societies have made more deficit spending than welfare states on average, except in the early 1990s, when clearly welfare states displays a worse performance than welfare societies. Table 12.9, correlating deficits with welfare regime, confirms this impression.

Table 12.9 Correlations between welfare regimes and deficits

WS		WS		WS		WS	
GGDEF50	−0.04	GGDEF75	−0.27	CGDEF50	−0.01	CGDEF75	−0.33
GGDEF55	−0.20	GGDEF80	−0.19	CGDEF55	−0.36	CGDEF80	−0.17
GGDEF60	−0.14	GGDEF85	−0.11	CGDEF60	−0.05	CGDEF85	−0.07
GGDEF65	−0.24	GGDEF90	0.20	CGDEF65	−0.13	CGDEF90	0.18
GGDEF70	−0.24	GGDEF92	0.30	CGDEF70	−0.30	CGDEF92	0.32

Note: GGDEF = general government deficit; CGDEF = central government deficit; WS = welfare state (= 0); welfare society (= 1).

When welfare state regimes is evaluated against welfare societies, much more than deficits is involved. The critical question in this debate is whether the characteristic that is typical of the welfare states – high public expenditure – promotes beneficial outcomes in general, such as economic growth, low inflation and unemployment and income equality. Can we find any evidence from the early 1990s that large public allocative or redistributive expenditure is harmful to these politico-economic outcomes?

Politico-economic outcomes

When one looks at outcomes in the literature on the political economy of the advanced capitalist countries, then one often employs the so-called misery index, consisting of inflation and unemployment. The difficulty is that these two indices may cancel each other out, which is the reason why we prefer to look at the two outcomes separately. There is, of course, no natural set of outcomes to which one must stick. However, it seems evident that economic growth and income equality should be added to the list of outcomes when one examines the OECD countries. We begin with economic growth.

Economic growth

The expansion of economic output is considered a contribution to well-being because it makes a higher standard of living possible. The size of the cake to be divided among the stakeholders of society increases, but it is an open question how the cake is to be divided between, for example, labour and capital. A process of sustained economic growth can within a decade or two result in a doubling of economic output. How affluence is divided among the groups in society is measured by the indices on income inequality. Table 12.10 only reports on the expansion of total output.

Three things stand out clearly when one examines Table 12.10: first, there is a general decline in the average growth rates in almost all the country economies, reflecting the notion of a slowdown of economic growth when affluence reaches high levels (maturity hypothesis); second, some of the less affluent countries have done rather better than the already rich countries (the catch-up hypothesis); third, there are considerable variations between the OECD countries in each five-year interval, but it is not the case that the countries with high growth rates or with meagre growth rates are the same for each five-year period.

Economic growth reflects the ups and downs in the world economy as well as country-specific events, such as the choice of unsuccessful economic policies or the failure in adaptation to internationalization or globalization. One may list the winners in the 1960s and 1970s as Austria, France, Germany, Greece, Ireland, Norway, Portugal, Turkey, Canada and Japan. In the 1980s and early 1990s the list of the top scorers would contain Ireland, Norway, Turkey, the USA and Australia. Is the variation in economic growth related to the size of the public sector, or more specifically to either the allocative or redistributive welfare state?

Although economic growth in the 1990s is substantially lower than in the 1960s – the maturity effect – a Western European growth problem can be seen in Table 12.10. Countries such as Sweden, Finland, France, Italy, Spain, Portugal, Belgium and Switzerland have not done well. Oil revenues have no doubt helped Norway, Denmark and the UK, but what explains the meagre results in the other countries? Finland lost its trade with the USSR, Sweden suffered from its high taxes – excess burden, or tax wedges – Italy could not stabilize its public debt and its currency and France did not open up its economy to competition in time. Spain and Portugal expanded their public sector too quickly. The Swiss case is most difficult to explain, as Switzerland has low public expenditure, stable currency and low debt. It is probably a case of overprotection of internal markets, plus the fact that labour market flexibility has been reduced.

Economic growth used to be a policy goal, because it brought jobs with it. What we have witnessed in the early 1990s is that economic growth does not necessarily reduce unemployment, which has become a major problem in some of the OECD countries.

Table 12.10 Economic growth: five-year averages 1965–94

	1965–9	1970–4	1975–9	1980–4	1985–9	1990–4
Austria	4.46	5.44	2.76	1.42	2.66	2.30
Belgium	4.30	5.08	1.82	1.50	2.50	1.60
Denmark	4.20	2.54	2.48	1.72	2.00	1.88
Finland	4.36	5.38	2.34	3.32	4.08	−1.58
France	5.20	5.12	3.12	1.46	3.10	1.20
Germany	4.28	3.50	3.04	0.96	2.62	2.92
Greece	7.52	5.54	5.26	1.10	2.54	0.80
Iceland	2.16	7.78	3.36	2.82	3.66	0.60
Ireland	4.46	4.46	4.66	2.58	3.56	4.74
Italy	5.82	4.24	2.36	1.72	3.12	1.00
Luxembourg	3.62	5.42	0.98	2.10	4.60	2.30
Netherlands	5.20	4.72	2.32	0.68	2.76	2.26
Norway	4.44	4.22	4.84	3.14	2.26	3.14
Portugal	6.02	7.20	3.56	1.24	4.96	1.44
Spain	6.68	6.16	1.88	1.28	4.26	1.50
Sweden	3.58	3.38	1.54	1.70	2.40	−0.30
Switzerland	3.60	3.64	−0.68	1.54	3.08	0.48
Turkey	6.16	7.02	5.50	3.56	4.62	3.44
UK	2.50	2.80	1.96	0.84	4.02	0.80
Canada	5.60	5.28	3.34	2.30	3.94	1.12
USA	4.34	2.62	3.34	1.84	3.12	2.02
Japan	10.32	6.20	4.60	3.48	4.52	2.10
Australia	5.52	4.62	2.78	2.76	3.94	2.14
New Zealand	3.22	4.80	−0.60	3.92	0.90	1.22

Source: Real GDP growth: OECD (1985, 1995).

Unemployment

The sharp increase in unemployment in most countries can be seen in Table 12.11. It is true that a few countries remain at very low levels, but several face two digit numbers in the 1990s.

Although the long-term trend is a sharp increase in unemployment, it is still the case that a few countries manage with very little unemployment: Switzerland and Japan – welfare societies – as well as Iceland and Austria – welfare states. One may note that unemployment has been reduced in the USA during the past decade, when unemployment has shot up in Western Europe. In some countries unemployment has reached 15 per cent or more: Spain, Ireland, Finland and Italy. The increase in unemployment reflects the slowdown in economic growth at the same time that there is no longer any automatic link between economic growth and employment. The correlation between economic growth and unemployment is generally very weak at the macro level: 0.28 (1965–9), -0.03 (1970–4), 0.36 (1975–9), -0.32 (1980–4), 0.10 (1985–9) and 0.02 (1990–4).

In the political economy literature there has been much debate about a connection between unemployment and the price level. The well known Philips curve predicts that low inflation can only be achieved by means of high levels of unemployment and vice versa. When we turn to the inflation numbers, we observe that inflation has come down rather drastically in the past decade, while unemployment has shot up, especially in the welfare states.

Table 12.11 Unemployment as a percentage of total labour force: five-year averages

	1965–9	1970–4	1975–9	1980–4	1985–9	1990–4
Austria	1.86	1.18	1.92	2.88	3.44	3.78
Belgium	2.24	2.18	6.36	11.28	10.96	10.64
Denmark	1.22	1.42	6.56	9.30	8.50	11.12
Finland	2.48	2.12	4.98	5.12	4.70	12.10
France	2.04	2.70	4.88	7.92	10.10	10.50
Germany	0.94	1.06	3.70	5.98	7.56	7.82
Greece	5.22	2.70	1.92	5.72	7.56	8.54
Iceland	1.54	0.68	0.20	0.74	0.86	3.06
Ireland	4.92	5.70	8.08	11.62	16.30	14.64
Italy	5.50	5.68	6.82	11.62	16.30	14.64
Luxembourg	–	–	0.60	1.26	1.58	1.82
Netherlands	1.06	1.88	5.34	7.98	8.06	6.20
Norway	0.90	1.24	1.84	2.60	2.96	5.60
Portugal	2.50	2.34	6.84	7.92	7.06	5.10
Spain	2.58	2.82	5.72	16.10	19.96	19.58
Sweden	1.80	2.24	1.86	2.86	2.20	5.22
Switzerland	–	–	0.42	0.56	0.68	2.66
Turkey	10.08	6.34	8.58	7.50	8.04	8.64
UK	1.68	2.48	4.58	8.90	9.14	8.68
Canada	3.90	5.74	7.54	9.86	8.84	10.28
USA	3.74	5.28	6.92	8.32	6.24	6.50
Japan	1.22	1.28	2.04	2.38	2.62	2.36
Australia	1.74	2.20	5.52	7.52	7.46	9.56
New Zealand	0.28	0.22	0.88	3.84	4.86	9.20

Source: OECD (1985, 1995).

Inflation

In the late 1970s and early 1980s it was not unusual for countries to have inflation rates around or above 10 per cent. In the 1990s, such a high rate of inflation is very unusual, as only Turkey displays signs of hyperflation (Table 12.12). Inflation has come down considerably, with Greece as the major exception.

Inflation is highly subdued in the 1990s, with only Greece, Turkey and Portugal displaying considerable price instability. One notes, though, that inflation varies considerably from one country to another. Several countries had less than 3 per cent inflation per year in the early 1990s: e.g. Denmark, France, Japan and New Zealand.

Table 12.12 Inflation: five-year averages (consumer prices)

	1965–9	1970–4	1975–9	1980–4	1985–9	1990–4
Austria	3.42	6.50	5.70	5.50	2.16	3.44
Belgium	3.54	6.68	7.62	7.30	2.42	2.84
Denmark	6.58	8.56	9.86	9.46	4.34	2.08
Finland	5.16	8.80	12.04	9.72	4.92	3.32
France	3.76	7.58	10.14	11.16	3.58	2.56
Germany	2.62	5.62	4.20	4.56	1.28	3.30
Greece	2.48	10.58	14.08	21.78	17.18	16.22
Iceland	11.70	18.68	40.20	55.08	23.78	6.38
Ireland	4.66	10.84	14.68	14.98	3.72	2.66
Italy	2.92	9.08	15.54	16.48	6.18	5.40
Luxembourg	2.74	6.02	6.96	7.62	1.82	3.16
Netherlands	4.90	7.30	6.74	5.02	0.70	2.86
Norway	3.72	8.18	8.56	10.12	6.58	2.70
Portugal	4.90	12.84	22.66	22.66	12.62	9.08
Spain	6.58	9.88	18.92	13.60	6.88	5.56
Sweden	4.06	7.40	9.74	10.26	5.60	5.78
Switzerland	3.40	7.08	2.88	4.40	2.14	3.90
Turkey	7.48	16.04	38.00	51.74	51.10	73.76
UK	4.26	9.62	15.64	9.62	5.26	4.64
Canada	3.66	5.90	8.88	8.70	4.32	2.78
USA	3.40	6.14	8.08	7.48	3.60	3.64
Japan	5.24	10.90	7.32	3.90	1.14	2.02
Australia	3.14	8.08	11.58	9.00	7.82	3.04
New Zealand	4.16	8.62	14.32	12.42	11.28	2.54

Source: OECD (1988, 1995a, b).

Is there evidence of a Philips curve in the data on unemployment and inflation
in the 1980s and 1990s? One would assume that the correlation between inflation
and unemployment is negative, countries with high unemployment having little
inflation. However, this is not so, despite the fact that unemployment has shot up
and inflation fallen back – a characteristic which applies to almost all countries.
It is not the case that on the country level unemployment goes together with little
inflation, as we can observe all kinds of combinations. The correlation between
inflation and unemployment is almost zero: 0.07 (1965–9), 0.06 (1970–4), 0.17
(1975–9), –0.07 (1980–4), –0.03 (1985–9) and 0.02 (1990–4).

Income equality

Measures of income equality are not as easily accessible as information about the
other outcomes described above. Typically, one faces difficult problems about
indicator validity and reliability when one sets out to compare various countries.
A rough picture is given in Table 12.13, which contains income information based
upon two indicators, the share of income of the lowest 40 per cent of households
– 'low' – and the income of the highest 20 per cent of households in relation to that
of the lowest 20 per cent) – 'ratio'.

Table 12.13 Income inequality about 1990

	Low	Ratio
Belgium	21.6	4.6
Denmark	17.4	7.1
Finland	18.4	6.0
France	18.4	6.5
Germany	19.5	5.7
Italy	18.8	6.0
Netherlands	20.1	5.6
Norway	19.0	5.9
Spain	19.4	5.8
Sweden	21.2	4.6
Switzerland	16.9	8.6
UK	17.3	6.8
Canada	17.5	7.1
USA	15.7	8.9
Japan	21.9	4.3
Australia	15.5	9.6
New Zealand	15.9	8.8

Note: Data for Austria, Greece, Iceland, Ireland, Luxembourg, Portugal and Turkey are not available. See also Table 3.3.

Source: *UNDP* (1994).

One can observe the outline of a country variation in income inequality. High scores for the share of income of the lowest 20 per cent of the income earners as well as low ratios between the shares of the top income earners and the bottom income earners are to be found among the welfare states: Scandinavia, Finland, Germany and Belgium. One welfare society also displays much income equality, i.e. Japan, but the characteristic feature is that the welfare societies have larger income inequality than the welfare states, whether the allocative or redistributive versions. Thus, the USA, Australia and New Zealand display income inequalities to a much larger extent than France, Germany and Italy.

Switzerland as a welfare society scores high on income inequality. Actually, Switzerland is an interesting case on all outcome measures, as they tend to have extreme values. In particular, development over time has meant that Switzerland faces difficulties, as it is no longer doing as well as it used to do on growth, inflation and unemployment.

Table 12.14 contains other measures of income inequality, which corroborate the overall picture that welfare states have lower income inequality than welfare societies. These measures consist of various estimates of household income, either pre-tax or after-tax, where higher scores indicate more income inequality. They testify to the difficulties in measuring income distribution, as they only partly correlate with each other and with the two chief measures employed here: low and ratio.

We find the same country variation in these different measures which use different kinds of information and alternative indices of income inequality. It has been widely discussed whether income inequalities promote or hinder economic growth and employment. We find the following correlations between income inequality and economic growth for the OECD countries where data are available: growth 1965–80, $r = 0.64$; growth 1985–94, $r = 0.46$. Note that the correlation is positive, meaning that growth goes with a more equal distribution of income – a finding worth a deeper analysis. It amounts to a corroboration of the Kuznets curve with regard to this country selection. One may speculate about the causal direction of the association, but Kuznets would have argued that economic growth is conducive to income inequality although one could argue the other way around that income inequality hinders economic growth. The correlation for ratio is: economic growth 1965–80, $r = -0.67$; economic growth 1980–95, $r = -0.40$.

Table 12.14 Income inequality in the 1980s: other measures

	TOP2070	SIMP1	SIMP2	MUS	AHLU	PAUK	MUL1	MUL2	MUL3	MUL4
Austria	–	44	37	–	–	–	–	–	0.37	44.0
Belgium	–	40	34	–	–	–	40	0.30	0.30	39.8
Denmark	44	43	37	48	43	0.37	–	–	–	–
Finland	50	–	–	49	49	0.46	–	–	–	–
France	46	47	39	54	54	0.50	46	0.38	0.38	46.4
Germany	45	45	37	53	46	0.45	45	0.36	0.36	45.2
Greece	–	–	–	50	–	0.38	–	–	–	–
Iceland	–	–	–	–	–	–	–	–	–	–
Ireland	39	39	30	–	–	–	39	0.30	0.30	39.4
Italy	–	47	38	48	–	0.40	47	0.38	0.38	46.5
Luxembourg	–	–	–	–	–	–	–	–	–	–
Netherlands	37	40	30	49	49	0.42	40	0.30	0.30	40.0
Norway	41	37	30	41	41	0.35	37	0.30	0.30	37.3
Portugal	56	49	40	–	–	–	49	0.40	0.40	49.1
Spain	44	45	36	46	45	–	45	0.36	0.36	45.2
Sweden	37	41	34	44	43	0.39	37	0.29	0.29	37.0
Switzerland	–	46	40	–	–	–	–	–	–	–
Turkey	57	59	52	61	61	–	59	0.49	0.49	58.6
UK	–	40	31	39	39	0.38	39	0.31	0.31	39.2
Canada	40	41	34	40	40	–	41	0.34	0.34	41.0
USA	43	45	41	39	39	0.34	43	0.36	0.36	42.8
Japan	46	43	33	40	44	0.39	41	0.30	0.30	41.0
Australia	–	42	35	39	39	0.30	43	0.34	0.34	43.0
New Zealand	41	42	35	42	41	–	41	0.31	0.31	41.4

Note: These various income distribution measures state either the income share of the top quintile or the Gini-index score.

Sources: World Bank (1991); Simpson (1990); Musgrave and Jarret (1979); Ahluwalia (1976a); Paukert (1973); Muller (1985, 1988).

Welfare state failure?

Given the evidence above about different country performance in terms of politico-economic outcomes, can we conclude that the size of the public sector matters? The argument that public expenditures are conducive to policy failure has been launched in a consistent manner by scholars connected with Chicago School Economics. The main function of the state is to maintain law and order, protecting the freedom and validity of contracts, as well as the price level (Friedman, 1962; Friedman and Friedman, 1980; Stigler, 1988; Posner, 1992). When governments take on other tasks, there will be a process of public sector expansion which is not conducive to economic performance. Can we find any evidence for these effects in our data about growth, unemployment and inflation for the OECD countries?

Table 12.15 reports on a number of correlations between, on the one hand, two measures of the size of welfare state expenditure, allocative versus redistributive expenditure as percentages of GDP, and, on the other hand, a set of outcome measures.

Table 12.15 Public expenditure and outcomes: government final consumption

	Real GDP (averages)	Unemployment (averages)	Inflation (averages)
1965	−0.38	−0.09	−0.42
1970	−0.66	0.17	−0.42
1975	0.00	0.31	−0.37
1980	−0.12	0.05	−0.09
1985	−0.50	−0.07	0.12
1990	−0.30	0.04	0.18
1992	−0.44	0.12	0.15

Table 12.16 Public expenditure and outcomes: social security transfers

	Real GDP (averages)	Unemployment (averages)	Inflation (averages)
1965	−0.30	−0.39	−0.41
1970	−0.34	−0.29	−0.52
1975	−0.24	0.04	−0.36
1980	−0.44	0.14	−0.47
1985	−0.36	0.22	−0.56
1990	0.24	0.15	−0.20
1992	−0.17	0.22	−0.18

There is one clear finding in Table 12.15 which corroborates the theory about welfare state failure: large allocative expenditures drag down the average growth rate. In relation to unemployment and inflation there is no transparent finding, which is a little surprising, as one would expect large allocative expenditure to reduce unemployment and increase inflation. Evidently, it is not possible to increase employment by high allocative expenditure, at least not in the long run. What about the impact of large redistributive expenditure (Table 12.16)?

Transfer payments seem to decrease economic growth, increase unemployment and lead to higher rates of inflation, but the connections are not strong, although the direction or sign of relationships is in accordance with the theory about welfare state failure.

Perhaps economic growth is the most critical of the outcomes studied here. If there is a process of long-term economic growth, then it would be more likely that the misery index will display low values, meaning that unemployment and inflation will be low – at least in the long run. We face a considerable variation in economic growth among the OECD countries, but the country pattern is not stable over time. Countries move up and down in the league of top and bottom scorers. Let us test a model of economic growth that focuses upon the impact of high public expenditure upon economic growth (Table 12.17).

Table 12.17 Economic growth in OECD countries: regression analysis

	1965–9			1970–4		
	Coeff.	Beta	t	Coeff.	Beta	t
Level of affluence	−0.00	−0.45	−2.55	−0.00	−0.50	−3.13
Large public sector	−0.07	−0.25	−1.41	−0.08	−0.44	−2.66
Trade union membership	−0.04	−0.37	−2.32	0.01	0.12	0.80
R^2A	0.47 ($n = 23$)			0.55 ($n = 23$)		

	1975–9			1985–9		
	Coeff.	Beta	t	Coeff.	Beta	t
Level of affluence	−0.00	−0.61	−2.83	−0.00	−0.31	−1.63
Large public sector	0.01	0.04	0.21	−0.05	−0.56	−2.96
Trade union membership	−0.01	−0.13	−0.64	0.00	0.01	0.03
R^2A	0.22 ($n = 22$)			0.29 ($n = 22$)		

Sources: Level of affluence, Summers and Heston (1994); large public sector, Table 12.2; trade union membership, OECD (1994).

Table 12.18 Variation in economic growth rates 1965–94: correlations

	1965–9	1970–4	1975–9	1980–4	1985–9	1990–4
1965–9	1.0000	0.3567	0.5170	0.0950	0.3468	0.1688
1970–4		1.0000	0.3240	0.3164	0.5063	−0.0031
1975–9			1.0000	0.1535	0.3084	0.4445
1980–4				1.0000	0.0634	0.0815
1985–9					1.0000	0.0324
1990–4						1.0000

Table 12.19 Economic growth: inflation and public expenditure (correlations)

	Inflation	Public expenditure
1965–9	−0.12	−0.53
1970–4	0.66	−0.61
1975–9	0.34	−0.16
1980–4	0.31	−0.33
1985–9	0.24	−0.55
1990–4	0.24	0.08

The findings support the hypothesis that a large public sector drives down the growth rate. But an even stronger effect is that of the level of affluence, which, in accordance with the catch-up and maturity hypotheses, also drives down economic growth. The hypothesis that trade union strength – here trade union density in terms of membership (OECD, 1994) – is negative for economic growth can only be corroborated for the first time period. If we examine economic growth between 1965 and 1980, the clearest effect is the Barro model prediction that less affluent countries tend to catch up (Barro, 1991). However, economic growth differs a great deal from one period to another. In the data for the 1980s and the 1990s the above models do not explain much. It has not been possible to substantiate the idea that deficits play a major role in explaining growth rates.

Table 12.18 contains correlations between the economic growth data for six time periods. Countries move up and down the growth ratings, scoring high during some periods and low during other periods. This means that it is difficult to find constant explanatory factors. One such, however, is the size of the public sector (Table 12.19).

The connection between total public outlays and economic growth is consistently a negative one, for all time periods except the early 1990s. This must mean that the welfare states face a growth problem. On the other hand, the connection with inflation is not in accordance with expectations, at least in the short run.

We end by looking at the determinants of long-term economic growth, covering the entire time period 1965 to 1994. Which effect is strongest: level of affluence or public sector size? Table 12.20 shows the answer.

Table 12.20 Regression analyses: economic growth 1965–94

	Coeff.	Beta wt	t		Coeff.	Beta wt	t
GDP6090	−0.00	−0.37	−2.05	RGDPCH60	−0.00	−0.46	−2.68
GGCU6590	−0.03	−0.33	−1.88	GGCU65	−0.04	−0.27	−1.68
SCLER	0.00	0.32	1.70	SCLER	0.00	0.23	1.34
R^2A		0.45 ($n = 21$)		R^2A		0.59 ($n = 23$)	

Note: GDP6090 = gross domestic product 1960 to 1990; GGCU6590 = general government current outlays 1965 to 1990; SCLER = institutional sclerosis; RGDPCH60 = real GDP per capita 1960; GGCU65 = general government current outlays 1965.

The impact of affluence is slightly more pronounced than that of total public sector size, but the direction of causality is clear. High public expenditure tends to reduce economic growth, meaning that the welfare states have a profound growth problem. Interestingly, the impact of institutionalization – Olson's factor – is weaker than the two others.

Conclusion

Welfare states or welfare societies? This is a critical debate in the 1990s on the size of the public sector, very much initiated by the Chicago School of Economics (Barro, 1990; Attfield *et al.*, 1992; Barr, 1994), which favours the welfare society model. But what are the outcomes? Do welfare societies perform better than welfare states?

According to one theory, welfare states are prone to engage in deficit spending, which worsens outcomes. However, only the evidence for the early 1990s supports this theory. Welfare societies also display deficit spending and deficits, but they do not appear to be extremely detrimental to economic growth, as they more reflect the state of the economy – high unemployment – than drive economic development.

Yet welfare states appear to have a growth problem, independent of deficit spending problems. In explanations of economic growth in the OECD countries, the size of public expenditure cannot be by-passed, although growth rates vary in an almost unpredictable fashion. A number of factors have been suggested in order to explain the variations in growth rates among the OECD countries: inflation, deficits, institutional sclerosis, economic maturity and public sector size. We find that the catch-up effect is real, but that high public expenditure is a negative, producing the excess burden problem or the occurrence of tax wedges. Thus, welfare societies may be more vibrant than welfare states.

Conclusion

In the twelve chapters that make up this book a number of findings have been stated, testifying to the diversity of the concerns of comparative political economy. As political economy studies the interrelationships between politics and economics, a lot of things must be covered even if one looks at only one country. After all, politics and economics dominate much human activity. Taking a comparative approach, broadening the range of countries examined to include over one hundred cases means that the descriptive task becomes immense.

However, focusing the examination of the wealth of country-specific data upon the evaluation of a few specific models that have played a major role in the social sciences gives direction to this task. These key models are broad enough to allow us to include a lot of information about a large set of countries and at the same time they entail middle-range hypotheses, meaning that they are strictly capable of falsification in relation to the data assembled for this particular set of countries. The models focused on in this book all deal with how the state relates to the market, the interaction between the public and the private sectors, and government intervention in the economy. What do all the findings in the separate chapters add up to ?

First, in political economy one must move away from talking in terms of simple dichotomies as if there could only be confrontation between politics and economics, the state and the market or government and capitalism. It is not either/or but both. The antagonistic perspective on the relationship between the public and the private sectors derives much of its appeal from the Great Debate in the 1930s when the adherents of the market economy or pure capitalism (von Mises, Hayek) clashed with the protagonists of socialism or the planned economy (Barone, Lange) – see Hayek (1935) and Lange and Taylor (1964). The strong emergence of Chicago School economics during recent decades has to some extent fuelled this confrontation image of government versus capitalism or politics against markets (Friedman, 1962 ; Friedman and Friedman, 1980), which is also typical of the marxist tradition in political economy (Esping-Andersen, 1985).

Yet what one observes all over the world is the reciprocity between the public and the private sectors. The key problem in political economy is to model the interdependencies and the interpenetration of politics and economics. This task has become even more relevant given the virtual disappearance of the planned economy. There is no alternative to a capitalist economy, realistically speaking, but a market economy may relate to the state in many different ways. We approach this interaction between politics and economics by examining on the one hand, models that claim that economic conditions have a major impact upon political matters and on the other hand, models that state that politics shape economics.

The adherents of the market economy never denied that however large a scope was provided for the operation of competitive markets in solving allocative problems, there would always be a need for state intervention. A market economy – pure capitalism – requires a machine for the implementation of contracts – how else could voluntary exchange work? This is the same problem as Walras's auctioneer. In order to get the market process started, someone from outside must begin the process of *tatonnement* suggesting and revising prices on a trial and error basis in order to reach the competitive equilibrium. The auctioneer, like the state, has to be there before the market interaction begins and is furthermore needed all the time in order to govern and implement contractual validity. Once one recognizes that the state as the legal order plays a profound role in making the market economy possible, as discussed in the law and economics literature (Posner, 1992), then one realizes that the auctioneer in Walrasian economics is only a tiny aspect of all the questions about state intervention in the economy, which may concern not only the presuppositions of the market economy (voluntary exchange) but may also extend to include the kind of law that the state provides (Posner, 1992) and the sectors of the economy where government is active (Hollingsworth et al., 1994).

Moreover, the perspective of state intervention for purposes of efficiency or justice is only one side of the political economy coin, the other side being the heavy influence of economic factors upon politics and public policies. In the literature discussing the sources of democracy and the welfare state economic development or as it is also called 'capitalist development' (Rueschemeyer et al., 1992) figures prominently either in the form of the level of affluence or the rate of change of affluence, i.e. economic growth. Both sides of the coin need to be taken into account when modelling as politics and economics, state and market, government and capitalism all interrelate.

Political economy, or the study of the mix of state and market, would benefit from going back to its roots among the few scholars who realized early on that the industrial revolution meant not only a new economic system but also different functions for the state. Economic development changed not only the structure of society with regard to employment and urbanization; it also entailed a new role for the government in the economy. Economic development could call for government to take action either before or after events, but in no way was economic development something to be handled only by the 'invisible hand'. Three scholars stand out as particularly important when it comes to conceptualizing the interdependency between state and market, or government and capitalism: Adolf Wagner, Gustav Schmoller and Werner Sombart. All three of them studied and taught both politics and economics, and the former two even held university chairs in *Staatswissenschaften* (political science).

The reputation of these three pioneers in political economy was overshadowed by the fact that they propagated certain ideas that were soon to be denounced as untenable. Schmoller and Sombart rejected the methodology of mainstream economic analysis – the neo-classical school of Menger, Walras, Marshall and Wicksell – favouring instead a historical approach. All three believed in a kind of social conservatism that tended to be undemocratic and hostile to liberalism. Yet their ideas about political economy are worth returning to and their relevance in understanding present-day political economy needs to be emphasized, as nowhere is the economy handed over to the 'invisible hand'. State intervention ranges from supplying the legal foundations for contractual relationships (Posner, 1992), over governance of the entire process of economic development (Wade, 1990) and state regulation of certain sectors of the economy (Hall, 1986), to comprehensive income redistribution interference which has market outcomes (Atkinson, 1996). Capitalist development and state intervention go hand in hand, although this involves friction and tension. Schmoller, Wagner and Sombart seem to have been the first to recognize this dialectical interaction between politics and economics, economic development being conducive to state intervention, which in turn has an impact on economic development.

The German political economists met in the so-called Verein für Sozialpolitik (Association for Social Welfare Policy), that was founded in 1872 and directed by Schmoller from 1890, and attracted both political scientists and economists with an interest in understanding the tasks of social policy in a capitalist economy. It is true that Schmoller (1838-1917) argued the case for state intervention from a paternalistic point of view, calling for state intervention in order to prevent social unrest – (*Kathedersozialismus*), but his analysis of economic development revealed a profound insight into the social and political consequences of capitalist processes of change. The economic system could not be separated from society and any consideration of economic change also involved moral questions of justice, although Schmoller himself strongly favoured Prussian values over liberalism.

Few would defend the position that Schmoller took in the famous *Methodenstreit* with Menger about the usefulness of abstract models in the interpretation of data, Schmoller favouring radical historicism. However, Schmoller's underlining of the importance of case studies, of which he conducted several himself, led him to recognize the broader social and political implications of economic change, and these insights could be used for modelling politico-economic interdependencies. Schumpeter deplored the Historical School in Germany, accusing it of hindering the advance of abstract modelling. However true this negative verdict may be in relation to the concerns of economic theory in general, it is not quite justified in relation to political economy, where case studies are necessary to unravel the complex links between the state and the market.

Adolf Wagner (1835-1917) showed convincingly that political economy could interpret its data by means of generalizations, for instance in the well-known Wagner's law about the need for state intervention when capitalist development picks up speed. Wagner's law is a brilliant example of an abstract model in political economy and it has retained its relevance in interpreting today's realities. Wagner's law belongs to the set of middle-range hypotheses that are often very fruitful in social science research, because they can easily be tested and thus govern empirical research. Perhaps it is the best achievement of German political economy, combining cameralism with historicism. In any case, it remains a basic tool in the analysis of public expenditure in rich and poor countries.

Wagner adhered to *Katherdersozialismus* but rejected the methodological teachings of the Historical School. His *Finanzwissenschaft* (1871–2) went beyond the mainstream cameralistic standpoints that were typical of *Staatswissenschaften* around 1900, to integrate many findings about the impact of capitalism upon politics, especially public policies. Wagner identified a moden role for the state when the economy transformed itself from an agrarian concern to an industrial one. Such a major social transformation could not, argued Wagner, leave government untouched. The responsibilities of the state would expand alongside economic development, calling for social and fiscal policies. Capitalism meant economic progress but at the same time social problems, which the state could contribute towards solving, if a modern system of public finance and taxation was introduced.

Wagner's argument was both a prediction and a moral commitment, as he forsaw that as it evolved at great speed, capitalism would call for state intervention in terms of public transport and infrastructure, but he also wished government to engage in progressive income taxation and use inheritance taxes to enhance 'justice in the economic system' – the goal of the Verein. Public sector expansion was thus necessary, both as a functional necessity in relation to the needs of the economy and as a moral obligation in relation to distributive justice, especially against the unearned gains of capitalism. Wagner's political economy retains a surprising freshness, combining an attempt at abstract modelling with a profound insight into the realities of politico-economic interdependencies.

Wagner looked first and foremost at the role of government in a period when economic development changed society tremendously. He emphasized the analysis of the fiscal and expenditure functions of the state in capitalist development. Sombart worked the other way round, focusing upon the path in time of capitalism, or Western economic development, but he also arrived at the observation of an increasing role for the state in the economy. Yet with Sombart we come to the other side of the coin, the private sector or capitalism.

Werner Sombart (1863-1941) published his major work, *Der Moderne Kapitalismus*, in several editions, the latest one appearing complete in 1927 in three volumes. Sombart was chiefly concerned with interpreting the development over time of market economy, or capitalism. He traced Western-type capitalism back to the thirteenth century, when the capitalist entrepreneurs appeared on a large scale, the period of early capitalism (*Frühkapitalismus*) lasting until the industrial revolution, i.e. until the middle of the seventeenth century. Sombart called the capitalism of the industrial economy *Hochkapitalismus* (high capitalism) in order to emphasize that during this stage capitalism not only blossomed but also began to dominate society in the form of an institutionally complex economic system involving for instance the use of joint-stock companies and mass production enterprises. No doubt Sombart anticipated some of the ideas of institutional economics, such as Veblen's and Commons's ideas in the United States in the early twentieth century, although an exact definition of 'capitalism' has never been accomplished (Hoover, 1968).

However, what is most interesting from the perspective of political economy is Sombart's insights into the limits of the market economy, especially in the period which he called *Spätkapitalismus* (late capitalism), that he dated from 1914 with the outbreak of the First World War. Much has been written about Sombart's ideas about late capitalism (Appel, 1992). It seems as if Sombart believed that capitalism would somehow go into decline after 1914, calling for an increased role for agriculture, if not a movement towards economic autarchy. Some link these erroneous predictions to Sombart's political views, which during the 1930s put him in the conservative, if not the fascist camp.

This is not the place to engage in an interpretation of Sombart. Suffice it to say that major predictions about the market economy have often been wrong. The Marxian analysis, which Sombart started out from, is well known but the unfortunate analysis by Schumpeter, launched after Sombart, is also worth mentioning. Schumpeter claimed in 1942 that 'Marx's vision was right', that 'the capitalist system showed a tendency towards self-destruction' and that 'the capitalist process not only destroys its own institutional framework but it also creates the conditions for another', i.e. socialism (Schumpeter, 1965: 162). As we have seen in the various chapters in this book, capitalism is very much alive as we approach the year 2000, whereas there are only a handful of countries where socialism is practised. What is crucial is the distinction between various types of contemporary capitalist economy, where it is necessary to take into account the role of the state in the economy. We have listed three kinds of state-market mixes, based upon the models of Adam Smith, List and Keynes, which are highly relevant to the interpretation of capitalism today.

The interesting thing with Sombart's concept of late capitalism is not that his prediction may have been seriously wrong, but that he clearly saw that government intervention in the economy took on such proportions after the First World War that high capitalism underwent a basic transformation. Let us follow the argument in his article 'Capitalism' (Sombart, 1930). Capitalism as an economic system involves, says Sombart, characteristic constellations of three elements: (A) spirit, (B) form and (C) technology.

(A) The spirit of capitalism – its economic outlook – contains three components : acquisition, competition and rationality. This is the driving mechanism inherent in the capitalist form, which is responsible for its unrelenting character. (B) The form of capitalism is basically its typical institutions: economic individualism, exchange, occupational specialization and functional separation, which result in the characteristic division between the owners of capital and the wage earners. (C) The technology of capitalism is the search for the improvement and perfection of productivity, involving the large-scale use of scientific and mechanistic means of production. At the heart of capitalism is the entrepreneur, whose activity in the period of high capitalism takes the form of the capitalistic enterprise – 'It represents the form through which an independant existence is granted to business as such' (Sombart, 1930: 200).

Sombart's general analysis, which in some ways anticipates Oliver Williamson (Williamson, 1985), is linked up with his developmental notions of capitalist evolution. Late capitalism is distinguished not only by the spread of industrialism 'to every corner of the world' (Sombart, 1930 : 206), i.e. the placement of Gerschenkron's 'late developers' into a capitalist world economy. What is even more characteristic is that in the industrialized countries non-capitalist undertakings expand: there are '"mixed" public–private undertakings, state and communal public works, cooperative enterprises' (Sombart, 1930: 207). Finally, in late capitalism 'the economic process as a whole has changed also' (Sombart, 1930: 207). Sombart states:

> What used to be a matter of spontaneous, natural development is fast becoming a system of external regulations ... Thus regulation of economic life through the market mechanism ... is gradually disappearing. It is being superseded by the price regulation of combinations or even of the government; by wage regulation of the trade unions, who pay little attention to the market conditions; by indirect regulation of the geographic distribution of industry through the intervention of the central and local governments, who disregard the natural rationality in the existing situation. (Sombart, 1930: 207–8)

Sombart here clearly makes a correct prediction about the coming of a mixed economy in Western Europe, or the taming of capitalism by means of the welfare state. He even anticipates the Keynesian position in the *General Theory* of 1936:

> Public authorities have intervened to offset the business fluctuations by withholding orders in periods of prosperity and granting them more generously in periods of depression; this policy will play an increasingly important role. 'Stabilization of business' seems to be both the slogan and the accomplishment of this period. (Sombart, 1930: 208)

In late capitalism government is more present than in high capitalism – here Sombart is no doubt correct, but he underestimated the ability of the market economy to flourish under various schemes of interaction with the state -- the growth and expansion of managerial capitalism (Chandler, 1990). The market economy, especially in its export-oriented version, has kept expanding and integrating almost all the countries of the globe into a world economy, but even in its pure Chicago-style version of a market economy (Friedman, 1962) there is government intervention on a fairly large scale, as the private sector cannot operate without a public sector of some sort.

Yet the state-market interaction is still a very prominent feature of all countries in the world. Economic factors have a profound impact upon politics, as we discussed when testing models of the conditions for democracy and public sector size or government expenditure. Political conditions also impact upon economic predicaments, as seen in the test of models concerning economic growth and income distribution.

The interdependencies between the private and the public sectors, between capitalism and government, may be structured differently, as outlined in the models of politico-economic regimes. Here, we have used four regime types: Adam Smith's (1723–1790) decentralized capitalism or the pure market economy, Friedrich List's (1789–1846) state-capitalism or economic nationalism, John Maynard Keynes's (1883–1946) welfare state or the mixed economy and Karl Marx's (1818–1883) command economy or Communism, which are still highly relevant for understanding politico-economic outcomes in the world today.

The great contestation in the future concerns the challenge of the market economy in relation to state-capitalism and to the welfare state. Will the role of government in these two different politico-economic regimes be reduced as the marketers demand? Will decentralized capitalism prevail in the twenty-first century? We believe not. The public sector will be pruned but not dismantled.

References

Adelman, I. and Morris, C.T. (1967) *Society, Politics and Economic Development*, Baltimore, Johns Hopkins University Press (revised edn, 1973).

Adelman, I. and Morris, C.T. (1972) 'The measurement of institutional characteristics of nations: methodological considerations', *Journal of Development Studies*, **8**, 3, 111–35.

Adelman, I. and Robinson, S. (1989) 'Income distribution and development', in Chenery, H. and Srinivasan, T.N. (eds), *Handbook of Development Economics, vol. II.*

Ahluwalia, M. (1976a) 'Income distribution and development: some stylized facts', *American Economic Review*, **66**, 2, 128–35.

Ahluwalia, M. (1976b) 'Inequality, poverty and development', *Journal of Development Economics*, **3**, 4, 307–42.

Ahluwalia, M.S., Carter, G. and Chenery, H.B. (1978) 'Growth and poverty in developing countries', *Journal of Development Economics*, **6**, 299–341.

Akerloff, G. (1970) 'The market for lemons: qualitative uncertainty and the market mechanism', *Quarterly Journal of Economics*, **84**, 488–500.

Albrow, M. (1970) *Bureaucracy*, London, Macmillan.

Alchian, A.A. (1988) 'Uncertainty, Evolution and Economic Theory', in Barney, J.B. and Ouchi, W.G. (eds) *Organizational Economics*, San Francisco, Jossey-Bass.

Alexeev, M. and Gaddy, C.G. (1993) 'Income distribution in the USSR in the 1980s', *Review of Income and Wealth*, **39**, 23–36.

Almond, G.A. (1970) *Political Development: Essays in Heuristic Theory*, Boston, Little, Brown.

Almond, G.A. and Coleman, J. (eds) (1960) *The Politics of Developing Areas*, Princeton, NJ, Princeton University Press.

Almond, G.A., Flanagan, S.C. and Nundt, R.J. (eds) (1973) *Crisis, Choice, and Change: Historical Studies of Political Development*, Boston, Little, Brown.

Almond, G.A. and Powell, G.B. (1966) *Comparative Politics: a Developmental Approach*, Boston, Little, Brown.

Alt, J. and Crystal, A.K. (1983) *Political Economics*, Berkeley, University of California Press.

Anckar, D. and Ståhlberg, K. (1980) 'Assessing the impact of politics', *Scandinavian Political Studies*, **3**, 191–208.

Appel, M. (1992) *Werner Sombart, Theoretiker und Historiker des modernen Kapitalismus*, Marburg, Metropolis.

Apter, D.E. (1965) *The Politics of Modernization*, Chicago, University of Chicago Press.

Apter, D.E. (1971) *Choice and the Politics of Allocation*, New Haven, CT, Yale University Press.

Apter, D.E. (1977) *Introduction to Political Analysis*, Cambridge, MA, Winthrop.

Apter, D.E. and Andrain, C. (1968), 'Comparative government: developing new nations', in Irish, M.D. (ed.), *Political Science: Advance of the Discipline*, Englewood Cliffs, NJ, Prentice-Hall, 82–126.

Arat, Z.F. (1991) *Democracy and Human Rights in Developing Countries*, Boulder, CO, Lynne Rienner.

Arrow, K.J. (1963) *Social Choice and Individual Values*, New York, Wiley.

Arrow, K.J. (1983) *General Equilibrium*, Oxford, Basil Blackwell.

Arrow, K.J. and Hurwicz, L. (1960) 'Decentralization and computation in resource allocation', in Pfouts, T. (ed.), *Essays in Economics and Econometrics in Honour of Harold Hotelling*, Chapel Hill, University of North Carolina Press.

Arrow, K.J. and Scitovsky, T. (eds) (1972) *Readings in Welfare Economics*, London, Allen and Unwin.

Ashford, D. E. (ed.) (1978) *Comparing Public Policies: New Concepts and Methods*, Beverly Hills, Sage.

Åslund, A. (1989) *Gorbachev's Struggle for Economic Reform: the Soviet Reform Process, 1985–88*, London, Pinter.

Atkinson, A.B. (1989) *The Economics of Inequality*, Oxford, Clarendon Press (2nd edition 1996, Oxford: Oxford University Press).

Atkinson, A.B. and Stiglitz, J.E. (1980) *Lectures on Public Economics*, Maidenhead, McGraw-Hill.

Attfield, C.L.F., Demery, D. and Duck, N.W. (1992) *Rational Expectations in Macroeconomics*, Oxford, Blackwell.

Auerbach, A.J. and Feldstein, M. (eds) (1985) *Handbook of Public Economics, vol. 1*, Amsterdam, North-Holland.

Auerbach, A.J. and Feldstein, M. (eds) (1987) *Handbook of Public Economics, vol. 2*, Amsterdam, North-Holland.

Bain, G.S. and Price, R. (1980) *Profiles of Union Growth*, Oxford, Blackwell.

Bairoch, P. (1975) *The Economic Development of the Third World since 1900*, Berkeley, University of California Press.

Balassa, B. (1989) *Comparative Advantage, Trade Policy and Economic Development*, London, Harvester Wheatsheaf.

Balassa, B. (1991) *Economic Policies in the Pacific Area Developing Countries*, London, Macmillan.

Banks, A.S. (1971) *Cross-polity Time-series Data*, Cambridge, MA, MIT Press.

Banks, A.S. (1972a) 'Correlates of democratic performance', *Comparative Politics*, **4**, 217–30.

Banks, A.S. (1972b) 'Political characteristics of nation-states: a longitudinal summary', *Journal of Politics*, **34**, 246–57.

Banks, A.S. (1974) 'Industrialization and development: a longitudinal analysis' *Economic Development and Cultural Change*, **22**, 320-37.

Banks, A.S. (ed.) (1978) *Political Handbook of the World: 1978*, New York, McGraw-Hill.

Banks, A.S. (1994) *Cross-national Time-series Data Archive*, Binghampton, NY, Center for Social Analysis, State University of New York at Binghampton.

Banks, D.L. (1989) 'Patterns of oppression: an exploratory analysis of human-rights data', *Journal of the American Statistical Association*, **84**, 674–81.

Banster, N. (1972) 'Development indicators: an introduction', *Journal of Development Studies*, **8**, 1–20.

Bardhan, P. (1984) *The Political Economy of Development in India*, Oxford, Blackwell.

Bardhan, P. (1988) 'Alternative approaches to development economics', in Chenery, H. and Srinivasan, T.N. (eds), *Handbook of Development Economics, vol. I.*

Barker, F. (1992) *The South African Labour Marker: Critical Issues for Transition*, Pretoria, J.L. van Schaik.

Barone, E. (1935) 'The ministry of production in a collectivist state' in Hayek, F.A. von (ed.), *Collectivist Economic Planning*, London, Routledge and Kegan Paul.

Barr, N. (1994) *The Economics of the Welfare State*, Oxford, Oxford University Press.

Barrett, D.B. (ed.) (1982) *World Christian Encyclopaedia: a Comparative Study of Churches and Religions in the Modern World, AD 1900–2000*, Nairobi, Oxford University Press.

Barro, R.J. (1990) *Macroeconomic Policy*, Cambridge, MA, Harvard University Press.

Barro, R.J. (1991) 'Economic growth in a cross section of countries', *Quarterly Journal of Economics*, **56**, 407–43.

Barry, B. (1970) *Sociologists, Economists and Democracy*, London, Collier-Macmillan.

Barsh, R.L. (1992) 'Democratization and development', *Human Rights Quarterly*, **14**, 120–34.

Barsh, R.L. (1993) 'Measuring human rights: problems of methodology and purpose', *Human Rights Quarterly*, **15**, 87–121.

Basu, D.K. and Sisson, R. (eds) (1986) *Social and Economic Development in India*, New Delhi, Sage.

Bator, F.M. (1958) 'The anatomy of market failure', *Quarterly Journal of Economics*, **72**, 351–79.

Baumol, W.J. (1965) *Welfare Economics and the Theory of the State*, Cambridge, MA, Harvard University Press.

Bebler, A. and Seroka, J. (eds) (1989) *Contemporary Political Systems: Classifications and Typologies*, Boulder, CO, Lynne Rienner.

Bell, D. (1973) *The Coming of Post-industrial Society*, New York, Basic Books.

Bendix, S. (1989) *Industrial Relations in South Africa*, Cape Town, Juta.

Ben-Dor, G. (1975) 'Institutionalization and political development: a conceptual and theoretical analysis', *Comparative Studies in Society and History*, **17**, 309–25.

Benjamin, R.W. (1972) *Patterns of Political Development*, New York, McKay.

Bergman, M. and Jonung, L. (1994) *Svenskt och Internationellt Konjunkturbeteende*, Stockholm, Finansdepartementet (Bilaga 13 till Långtidsutredningen).

Bergson, A. (1981) *Welfare, Planning and Employment*, Cambridge, MA, MIT Press.

Bergson, A. and Levine, H.S. (eds) (1983) *The Soviet Economy: toward the Year 2000*, London, Allen and Unwin.

Berry, B.J.L. (1966) 'By what categories may a state be characterized?', *Economic Development and Cultural Change*, **15**, 91–3.

Beyme, K. von (1982) *Parteien in westlichen Demokratien*, Munich, Piper.

Bhagwati, J.N. and Ruggie, J.G. (eds) (1984) *Power, Passions and Purpose: Prospects for North–South Negotiations*. Cambridge, MA, MIT Press.

Bhalla, S.J. (1994) 'Freedom and economic growth: a virtious cycle?', Paper Presented at the Nobel Symposium on Democracy's Victory and Crisis, Uppsala University, Sweden, 27–30 August.

Bigsten, A. (1987) 'Growth and equity in some African and Asian countries', Stockholm, SIDA (unpublished manuscript).

Bill, J.A. and Hardgrave, R.L. (1973) *Comparative Politics: the Quest for Theory*, Columbus, OH, Merrill.

Binder, A.S., Solow, R.M., Breat, G.F., Steiner, P.O. and Netzer, D. (1974) *The Economics of Public Finance*, Washington, DC, Brookings.

Binder, L. (1972) 'Political development in the Middle East', in Desai, A.R. (ed.), *Essays on Modernization of Underdeveloped Societies*, New York, Humanities Press.

Binder, L. (1986) 'The natural history of development theory', *Comparative Studies of Society and History*, **28**, 3–33.

Binder, L., Coleman, J.S., La Palombara, J., Pye, L.W., Verba, S. and Weiner, M. (1971) *Crises and Sequences in Political Development*, Princeton, NJ, Princeton University Press.

Black, C. (1966) *The Dynamics of Modernization*, New York, Harper and Row.

Bliss, C. (1989) 'Trade and development', in Chenery, H. and Srinivasan, T.N. (eds), *Handbook of Development Economics, vol. II*.

Blondel, J. (1969) *An Introduction to Comparative Government*, London, Weidenfeld and Nicolson.

Bohm, P. (1986) *Social Efficiency: a Concise Introduction to Welfare Economics*, London, Macmillan.

Bollen, K.A. (1979) 'Political democracy and the timing of development', *American Sociological Review*, **44**, 572–87.

Bollen, K.A. (1980) 'Issues in the comparative measurement of political democracy', *American Sociological Review*, **45**, 370–90.

Bollen, K.A. (1986) 'Political rights and political liberties in nations: an evaluation of human rights measures, 1950 to 1984', *Human Rights Quarterly*, **8**, 567–91.

Bollen, K.A. (1990) 'Political democracy: conceptual and measurement traps', *Studies in Comparative International Development*, **25**, 7–24.

Bollen, K.A. (1993) 'Liberal democracy: validity and method factors in cross-national measures', *American Journal of Political Science*, **37**, 1207–30.

Bollen, K.A. and Grandjean, J. (1981) 'The dimension(s) of democracy: further issues in the measurement and effects of political democracy', *American Sociological Review*, **46**, 651–9.

Bollen, K.A. and Jackman, R.W. (1985) 'Political democracy and the size distribution of income', *American Sociological Review*, **50**, 438–57.

Bollen, K.A. and Jackman, R.W. (1989) 'Democracy, stability and dichotomies', *American Sociological Review*, **54**, 612–21.

Borcherding, T.E. (1977) *Budgets and Bureaucrats: the Sources of Government Growth*, Durham, NC, Duke University Press.

Borcherding, T.E. (1984) 'A survey of empirical studies about causes of the growth of government', paper presented to the Nobel Symposium on the Growth of Government, Stockholm.

Boström, M. (1989) 'Political waves in Latin America, 1940-1988', *Ibero-Americana: Nordic Journal of Latin American Studies*, **19**, 1, 3–19.

Brandt Report (1980) *North–South: a Programme for Survival*. London: Pan Books.

Brennan, G. and Buchanan, J.M. (1980) *The Power to Tax: Analytical Foundations of a Fiscal Constitution*, Cambridge, Cambridge University Press.

Bromley, D.W. (1989) *Economic Interests and Institutions*, Oxford, Blackwell.

Brown, C.W. and Jackson, P.M. (1978) *Public Sector Economics*, Oxford, Martin Robertson.

Brown, M.B. (1985) *Models in Political Economy: a Guide to the Arguments*, Boulder, CO, Lynne Rienner.

Brunner, R.D. and Brewer, G.D. (1971) *Organized Complexity: Empirical Theories of Political Development*, New York, Free Press.

Brus, W. and Laski, K. (1990) *From Marx to the Market: Socialism in Search of an Economic System*, Oxford, Clarendon Press.

Buchanan, A. (1985) *Ethics, Efficiency and the Market*, Oxford, Clarendon Press.

Buchanan, J.M. (1967) *Public Finance in Democratic Process*, Chapel Hill, University of North Carolina Press.

Buchanan, J.M. (1977) *Freedom in Constitutional Contract*, College Station, Texas A & M University Press.

Buchanan, J.M. (1986) *Liberty, Market and State: Political Economy in the 80s*, London, Harvester Wheatsheaf.

Buchanan, J.M. and Flowers, M.R. (1980) *The Public Finances*, Homewood, IL, Irwin-Dorsey.

Buchanan, J.M., Tollison, R.D. and Tullock, G. (eds) (1980) *Toward a Theory of the Rent-seeking Society*, College Station, Texas A & M University Press.

Buchanan, J.M. and Wagner, R.E. (1977) *Democracy in Deficit: the Political Legacy of Lord Keynes*, New York, Academic Press.

Budge, I. and Farlie, D.J. (1981) 'Predicting regime change: a cross-national investigation with aggregate data 1950-1980', *Quality and Quantity*, **15**, 335–64.

Burkhart, R.E. and Lewis-Beck, M. (1994) 'Comparative democracy: the economic development thesis', *American Political Science Review*, **88**, 4, 903–10.

Caiden, N. and Wildavsky, A. (1974) *Planning and Budgeting in Poor Countries*, New York, Wiley.

Cairncross, A. and Puri, M. (eds) (1976) *Employment, Income Distribution and Development Strategy*, London, Macmillan.

Cameron, D.R. (1974) 'Toward a theory of political mobilization', *Journal of Politics*, **36**, 138–71.

Cameron, D. (1978) 'The Expansion of the Public Economy: a comparative analysis', *American Political Science Review*, **72**, 1243–61.

Cameron, D.R. (1984) 'Impact of political institutions on public sector expansion', paper presented to the Nobel Symposium on the Growth of Government, Stockholm.

Cantori, L.T. and Ziegler, A. (eds) (1988) *Comparative Politics in the Post-behavioural Era*, Boulder, CO, Lynne Rienner.

Castles, F.G. (1978) *The Social Democratic Image of Society: a Study of the Achievements and Origins of Scandinavian Social Democracy in Comparative Perspective*, London, Routledge and Kegan Paul.

Castles, F.G. (ed.) (1982) *The Impact of Parties: Politics and Policies in Democratic Capitalist States*, London, Sage.

Castles, F.G. (1986) 'Whatever happened to the communist welfare state?', *Studies in Comparative Communism*, **19**, 213–26.

Castles, F.G. (1989) 'Big government in weak states', Canberra: Centre for Economic Policy Research, Discussion Paper no. 209.

Castles, F. (1990) 'The impact of government spending on medium-term economic growth in the OECD 1960–85', *Journal of Theoretical Politics*, **2**, 173–204.

Castles, F. (1991) 'Democratic politics, war and catch-up: Olson's thesis and long-term economic growth in the English-speaking nations of advanced capitalism', *Journal of Theoretical Politics*, **3**, 5–25.

Castles, F.G., Lehner, F. and Schmidt, M.G. (1988) 'Comparative public policy analysis: problems, progress and prospects', in Castles, F.G. (ed.) *Managing Mixed Economies*, Berlin, Walter de Gruyter, 197–223.

Cave, M. and Hare, P. (1983) *Alternative Approaches to Economic Planning*, London, Macmillan.

Caves, R.E. and Jones, R.W. (1985) *World Trade and Payments*, Boston, Little, Brown.

Chacholiades, M. (1985) *International Trade: Theory and Policy*, London, McGraw-Hill.

Chan, S. (1989) 'Income distribution and war trauma: a cross-national analysis', *Western Political Quarterly*, **42**, 263–81.

Chandler, A.D. (1990) *Scale and Scope. The Dynamics of Industrial Capitalism*, Cambridge, Belknap Press.

Chaudhuri, P. (1989) *The Economic Theory of Growth*, Brighton, Harvester Wheatsheaf.

Chenery, H.B. (1983) 'Interaction between theory and observation in development', *World Development*, **11**, 10, 853–62.

Chenery, H.B., Robinson, S. and Syrquin, M. (1986) *Industrialization and Growth*, Oxford, Oxford University Press.

Chenery, H. and Srinivasan, T.N. (eds) (1988) *Handbook of Development Economics, Vol. I*, Amsterdam, North-Holland.

Chenery, H. and Srinivasan, T.N. (eds) (1989) *Handbook of Development Economics, Vol. II*, Amsterdam, North-Holland.

Chenery, H.B. and Taylor, L. (1968) 'Development patterns: among countries and over time', *Review of Economics and Statistics*, **50**, 391–416.

Chilcote, R.H. and Johnson, D.L. (eds) (1983) *Theories of Development*, Beverly Hills, CA, Sage.

Choi, K. (1983) 'A statistical test of Olson's model', in Mueller, D. (ed.) *The Political Economy of Growth*, New Haven, CT, Yale University Press, 57–78.

Choksi, A.M. and Papageorghiou, D. (eds) (1986) *Economic Liberalization in Developing Countries*, Oxford, Blackwell.

Chowdhury, A. and Iyanatul, I. (1993) *The Newly Industrialising Economies of East Asia*, London, Routledge.

Clapham, C. (1985) *Third World Politics: an Introduction*, London, Croom Helm.

Clark, J. and Wildavsky, A. (1990) *The Moral Collapse of Communism*, San Francisco, ICS Press.

Claude, R.P. (1975) 'Comparative civil liberties: the state of the art', *Policy Studies Journal*, **4**, 175–80.

Cockcroft, J.D., Frank, A.G. and Johnson, D.L. (eds) (1972) *Dependence and Under-development*, New York, Anchor Books.

Cohen, S.S. (1977) *Modern Capitalist Planning: the French Model*, Berkeley, University of California Press.

Coleman, J.S. (ed.) (1965) *Education and Political Development*, Princeton, NJ, Princeton University Press.

Coleman, J.S. (1968) 'Modernization: political aspects', in Sills, D.L. (ed.) *International Encyclopedia of the Social Sciences, Vol. 10*, New York, Free Press, 395–402.

Collier, D. (1978) 'Industrial modernization and political change: a Latin American perspective', *World Politics*, **30**, 593–614.

Collier, D. (ed.) (1979) *The New Authoritarianism in Latin America*, Princeton, NJ, Princeton University Press.

Coppedge, M. and Reinicke, W.H. (1990) 'Measuring polyarchy', *Studies in Comparative International Development*, **25**, 51–72.

Coulter, P. (1971) 'Democratic political development: a systemic model based on regulative policy', *Development and Change*, **3**, 25–61.

Cutright, P. (1963) 'National political development: measurement and analysis', *American Sociological Review*, **28**, 253–64.

Dahl, R.A. (1947) 'The science of public administration: three problems', *Public Administration Review*, **7**, 1, 1–11.

Dahl, R.A. (1971) *Polyarchy*, New Haven, CT, Yale University Press.

Dahl, R.A. (1985) *A Preface to an Economic Theory of Democracy*, Cambridge, Polity Press.

Dahl, R.A. and Lindblom, C.E. (1953) *Politics, Economics and Welfare*, New York, Harper and Row.

Dalton, G. (1974) *Economic Systems and Society*, Harmondsworth, Penguin.

Danziger, J.N. (1978) *Making Budgets: Public Resource Allocation*, Beverly Hills, CA, Sage.

DasGupta, P. and Weale, M. (1992) 'On measuring the quality of life', *World Development*, **20**, 119–31.

Davis, H. and Scase, R. (1985) *Western Capitalism and State Socialism*, Oxford, Blackwell.

Day, A.J. and Degenhardt, H.W. (1980) *Political Parties of the World: a Keesing's Reference Publication*, Harlow, Longman.

Debreu, G. (1959) *Theory of Value*, New York, Wiley.

de Carvalho, J.A.M. and Wood, C.H. (1980) 'Morality, income distribution and rural-urban residence in Brazil', *Population and Development Review*, **4**, 3, 405–20.

Delury, G.E. (ed.) (1983) *World Encyclopedia of Political Systems*, Harlow, Longman.

Derbyshire, J.D. and Derbyshire, I. (1989) *Political Systems of the World*, Edinburgh, Chambers.

de Schweinitz, K. (1964) *Industrialization and Democracy*, Glencoe, IL, Free Press.

Deutsch, K.W. (1961) 'Social mobilization and political development', *American Political Science Review*, **55**, 493–514.

Diamant, A. (1966) 'The nature of political development' in Finkle, J. and Gable, W. (eds) *Political Development and Social Change*, New York, Wiley, 91–6.

Diamond, L. (1992) 'Economic development and democracy reconsidered', *American Behavioral Scientist*, **35**, 450–99.

Diamond, L., Linz, J. and Lipset, S.M. (eds) (1988) *Democracy in Developing Countries, vol. 2, Africa*, Boulder, CO, Lynne Rienner.

Diamond, L., Linz, J. and Lipset, S.M. (eds) (1989a) *Democracy in Developing Countries, vol. 3, Asia*, Boulder, CO, Lynne Rienner.

Diamond, L., Linz, J. and Lipset, S.M. (eds) (1989b) *Democracy in Developing Countries, vol. 4, Latin America*, Boulder, CO, Lynne Rienner.

Dick, G.W. (1974) 'Authoritarian versus nonauthoritarian approaches to economic development', *Journal of Political Economy*, **82**, 817–27.

Dobb, M. (1940) *Political Economy and Capitalism*, London, Routledge and Kegan Paul.

Doel, J. van den (1979) *Democracy and Welfare Economics*, Cambridge, Cambridge University Press.

Dowrick, S. and Nguyen, D.T. (1987) 'OECD economic growth in the post-war period: a test of the convergence hypothesis', Canberra, Centre for Economic Policy Research, Discussion Paper no. 181.

Doyal, L. and Gough, I. (1991) *A Theory of Human Need*, Basingstoke, Macmillan.

Drewnowski, J. (1961) 'The economic theory of socialism: a suggestion for reconsideration', *Journal of Political Economy*, **69**, 341–54.

Dunleavy, P. and O'Leary, B. (1987) *Theories of the State*. London, Macmillan.

Dunsire, A. (1973) *Administration*, London, Martin Robertson.

Dye, T. (1966) *Politics, Economics and the Public*, Chicago, Rand-McNally.

Dye, T.R. and Gray, V. (eds) (1980) *The Determinants of Public Policy*, Lexington, MA, Lexington Books.

Dye, T.R. and Zeigler, H. (1988) 'Socialism and equality in crossnational perspective', *Political Science and Politics*, **21**, 45–56.

Dyker, D.A. (1976) *The Soviet Economy*, London, Crosby Lockwood Staples.

Dyker, D.A. (1985) *The Future of the Soviet Planning System*, Cambridge, Cambridge University Press.

Easton, D. (1965) *A Systems Analysis of Political Life*, New York, Wiley.

Eatwell, J., Milgate, M. and Newman, P. (eds) (1987a) *The New Palgrave: a Dictionary of Economics*, London, Macmillan.

Eatwell, J., Milgate, M. and Newman, P. (eds) (1987b) *The Invisible Hand*, London, Macmillan.

Eatwell, J., Milgate, M. and Newman, P. (eds) (1989a) *General Equilibrium*, London, Macmillan.

Eatwell, J., Milgate, M. and Newman, P. (eds) (1989b) *Allocation, Information and Markets*, London, Macmillan.

Eatwell, J., Milgate, M. and Newman, P. (eds) (1990) *Problems of the Planned Economy*, London, Macmillan.

Eckstein, A. (1958) 'Individualism and the role of the state in economic growth', *Economic Development and Cultural Change*, **6**, 81–7.

Eckstein, A. (ed.) (1971) *Comparison of Economic Systems: Theoretical and Methodological Approaches*, Berkeley, University of California Press.

Eckstein, H. (1966) *Division and Cohesion in Democracy: a Study of Norway*, Princeton, NJ, Princeton University Press.

Eckstein, H. (1971) *The Evaluation of Political Performance: Problems and Dimensions*, Beverly Hills, CA, Sage.

Eckstein, H. (1982) 'The idea of political development: from dignity to efficiency', *World Politics*, **34**, 451–86.

Economist Atlas (1989) London, Hutchinson.

Eidem, R. and Viotti, S. (1978) *Economic Systems*, London, Martin Robertson.

Eisenstadt, S.N. (1962) 'Initial institutional patterns of political modernization', *Civilizations*, **12**, 461–72.

Eisenstadt, S.N. (1964a) 'Political modernization: some comparative notes', *International Journal of Comparative Sociology*, **5**, 3–24.

Eisenstadt, S.N. (1964b) 'Breakdowns of modernization', *Economic Development and Cultural Change*, **12**, 345–67.

Eisenstadt, S.N. (1966) *Modernization*, Englewood Cliffs, NJ, Prentice Hall.

Eisenstadt, S.N. (1973) *Tradition, Change and Modernity*, New York, Wiley.

Ellman, M. (1979) *Socialist Planning*, Cambridge, Cambridge University Press.

Eltis, W.A. (1966) *Economic Growth: Analysis and Policy*, London, Hutchinson.

Eltis, W.A. (1984) *The Classical Theory of Economic Growth*, London, Macmillan.

Emerson, R. (1960) 'Nationalism and political development', *Journal of Politics*, **22**, 3–28.

Encyclopaedia Britannica (1995) *Britannica Book of the Year: Britannica World Data*, Chicago: Encyclopaedia Britannica.

Esping-Andersen, G. (1985) *Politics against Markets*, Princeton, NJ, Princeton University Press.

Esping-Andersen, G. (1991) *The Three Worlds of Welfare Capitalism*, Cambridge, Polity Press.

Estes, R.J. (1984) *The Social Progress of Nations*, New York, Praeger.

Estrin, S. (1983) *Self-management: Economic Theory and Yugoslav Practice*, Cambridge, Cambridge University Press.

Etzioni, A. (1988) *The Moral Dimension*, New York, Free Press.

Europa Yearbook (1978) London, Europa Publications.

Flanigan, W. and Fogelman, E. (1971) 'Patterns of political development and democratization: a quantitative analysis', in Gillespie, J.V. and Nesvold, B.A. (eds) *Macro-quantitative Analysis: Conflict, Development and Democratization*, Beverly Hills, CA, Sage, 441–73.

Flora, P. and Heidenheimer, A.J. (eds) (1981) *The Development of the Welfare States in Europe and America*, New Brunswick, NJ, Transaction Books.

Foltz, W.J. (1981) 'Modernization and nation-building: the social mobilization model reconsidered', in Merritt, R.L. and Russett, B.M. (eds) *From National Development to Global Community*, London, Allen and Unwin, 25–45.

Frank, A.G. (1967) *Capitalism and Underdevelopment in Latin America: Historical Studies of Chile and Brazil*, New York, Monthly Review Press.

Freedom House (1992) *Freedom in the World: Political Rights and Civil Liberties 1991–1992*, New York, Freedom House.

Freedom House (1993) 'The comparative survey of freedom: 1993', *Freedom Review*, **24**, 1, 3–22.

Freeman, R.B., Swedenborg, B. and Topel, R. (1995) *Välfärdsstat i Omvandling*. Stockholm: SNS.

Frey, B. (1978) *Modern Political Economy*, London, Macmillan.

Friedman, M. (1962) *Capitalism and Freedom*, Chicago, University of Chicago Press.

Friedman, M. and Friedman, R. (1980) *Free to Choose*, New York, Harcourt Brace Jovanovich.

Galbraith, J.K. (1962) *The Affluent Society*, Boston, Houghton Mifflin.

Galbraith, J.K. (1969) *The New Industrial State*, Harmondsworth, Pelican.

Gastil, R.D. (ed.) (1987) *Political Rights and Civil Liberties 1986-1987*, New York, Greenwood Press.

Gastil, R.D. (1990) 'The comparative survey of freedom: experiences and suggestions', *Studies in Comparative International Development*, **25**, 25–50.

Gerschenkron, A. (1962) *Economic Backwardness in Historical Perspective*, Cambridge, Harvard University Press.

Gersovitz, M.F., Diaz-Alejandro, C.F., Ranis, G. and Rozenzweig, M.R. (eds) (1982) *The Theory and Experience of Economic Development: Essays in Honor of Sir W. Arthur Lewis*, London, Allen and Unwin.

Goldsmith, A. (1985) 'Democracy, political stability and economic growth in developing countries: some evidence on Olson's theory of distributional coalitions', *Comparative Political Studies*, **18**, 517–31.

Goodwin, R.M. (1982) *Essays in Economic Dynamics*, London, Macmillan.

Gregory, P.R. and Stuart, R.C. (1989) *Comparative Economic Systems*, Boston, Houghton Mifflin.

Grew, R. (ed.) (1978) *Crises of Political Development in Europe and the United States*, Princeton, NJ, Princeton University Press.

Grier, K.B. and Tullock, G. (1989) 'An empirical analysis of cross-national economic growth, 1951–80', *Journal of Monetary Economics*, **24**, 259–76.

Griffith-Jones, S. (ed.) (1988) *Managing World Debt*, London, Harvester Wheatsheaf.

Groth, A.J. (1971) *Comparative Politics: a Distributive Approach*, New York, Macmillan.

Gurr, T.R. (1974) 'Persistence and change in political systems, 1800–1971', *American Political Science Review*, **68**, 1482–504.

Gurr, T.R. (1990) *Polity II: Political Structures and Regime Change, 1800–1986* (Computer file), Boulder, CO, Center for Comparative Politics (producer), 1989, Ann Arbor, MI, Inter-university Consortium for Political and Social Research (distributor), 1990.

Gurr, T.R. and McClelland, M. (1971) *Political Performance: a Twelve-nation Study*, Beverly Hills, CA, Sage.

Gwartney, J., Lawson, R. and Block, W. (1996) *Economic Freedom of the World 1975–1995*, Vancouver, Fraser Institute.

Hadenius, A. (1992) *Democracy and Development*, Cambridge, Cambridge University Press.

Hahn, F.H. (1971) *Readings in the Theory of Economic Growth*, London, Macmillan.

Hahn, F.H. and Matthews, R.C.O. (1964) 'The theory of economic growth: a survey', *The Economic Journal*, **74**, 779–902.

Hall, P. (1983) *Growth and Development: an Economic Analysis*, Oxford, Martin Robertson.

Hall, P.A. (1986) *Governing the Economy: the Politics of State Intervention in Britain and France*, Oxford, Oxford University Press.

Hamberg, D. (1971) *Models of Economic Growth*, New York, Harper and Row.

Hanson, J.L. (1974) *A Dictionary of Economics and Commerce*, London, Macdonald and Evans.

Harff, B. (1984) *Genocide and Human Rights: International, Legal and Political Issues*, Denver, CO, University of Denver.

Harrod, R.R. (1939) 'An essay in dynamic theory', *Economic Journal*, **49**, 14–33.

Haug, M.R. (1967) 'Social and cultural pluralism as a concept in social system analysis', *American Journal of Sociology*, **73**, 294–304.

Hayek, F.A. von (ed.) (1935) *Collectivist Economic Planning*, London, Routledge and Kegan Paul.

Hayek, F.A. von (1940) 'Socialist calculation: the competitive solution', *Economica*, **VII**, 125–49.

Hayek, F.A. von (1945) 'The use of knowledge in society', *American Economic Review*, **XXXV**, 519–30.

Head, J.G. (1974) *Public Goods and Public Welfare*, Durham, NC, Duke University Press.

Heady, B. (1970) 'Trade unions and national wage policies', *Journal of Politics*, **32**, 407–39.

Heady, F. (1979) *Public Administration: a Comparative Perspective*, New York, Dekker.

Heal, G.M. (1973) *The Theory of Economic Planning*, Amsterdam, North-Holland.

Heap, S.H. (1989) *Rationality in Economics*, Oxford, Blackwell.

Hedström, P. (1986) 'From political sociology to political economy', in Himmelstrand, U. (ed.) *Sociology: from Crisis to Science, Vol. 1*, London, Sage, 173–89.

Heidenheimer, A.J., Heclo, H. and Adams, C.J. (1983) *Comparative Public Policy: the Politics of Social Choice in Europe and America*, London, Macmillan.

Helliwell, J.F. (1994) 'Empirical linkages between democracy and economic growth', *British Journal of Political Science*, **24**, 225–48.

Henrekson, M., Jonung, L. and Stymne, J. (1994) 'Economic growth and the Swedish model', Stockholm, School of Economics (unpublished).

Hewitt, C. (1977) 'The effect of political democracy and social democracy on equality in industrial societies: a cross-national comparison', *American Sociological Review*, **42**, 450–64.

Hibbs, D.A. (1987) *The American Political Economy: Macroeconomics and Electoral Politics*, Cambridge, Harvard University Press.

Hibbs, D.A. and Fassbender, H. (eds) (1981) *Contemporary Political Economy*, Amsterdam, North-Holland.

Hicks, J. R. (1965) *Capital and Growth*, Oxford, Clarendon Press.

Higgott, R.A. (1980) 'From modernization theory to public policy: continuity and change in the political science of development', *Studies in Comparative International Development*, **15**, 26–50.

Higgott, R.A. (1983) *Political Development Theory*, London, Croom Helm.

Hirschman, A. (1958) *Strategy of Economic Development*, New Haven, CT, Yale University Press.

Hirschman, A.O. (1970) *Exit, Voice and Loyalty: Responses to Decline in Firms, Organizations and States*, Cambridge, MA, Harvard University Press.

Hirschman, A.O. (1971) *A Bias For Hope: Essays on Development and Latin America*, New Haven, CT, Yale University Press.

Hirschman, A.O. (1982) *Shifting Involvements: Private Interests and Public Action*, Princeton, NJ, Princeton University Press.

Hofferbert, R. (1974) *The Study of Public Policy*, Indianapolis, Bobbs-Merrill.

Hollingsworth, J.R., Schmitter, P.C. and Streeck, W. (eds) (1994) *Governing Capitalist Economies*, Oxford, Oxford University Press.

Hoover, C.B. (1968) 'Capitalism', in *International Encyclopedia of the Social Sciences*, vol. 2, New York, Macmillan and Free Press.

Hopkins, R.F. (1969) 'Aggregate data and the study of political development', *Journal of Politics*, **31**, 71–94.

Horvat, B. (1973) 'The relation between rate of growth and level of development', *Journal of Development Studies*, **10**, 382–94.

Hozelitz, B.F. (1957) 'Economic growth and development: noneconomic factors in economic development', *American Economic Review*, **47**, 28–41.

Humana, C. (1983) *World Human Rights Guide*, London, Hutchinson.

Humana, C. (1986) *World Human Rights Guide*, 2nd edn, London, Economist Publications.

Humana, C. (1992) *World Human Rights Guide*, 3rd edn, New York, Oxford University Press.

Huntington, S.P. (1965) 'Political development and political decay', *World Politics*, **17**, 386–430.

Huntington, S.P. (1968) *Political Order in Changing Societies*, New Haven, CT, Yale University Press.

Huntington, S.P. (1971) 'The change to change: modernization, development and politics', *Comparative Politics*, **3**, 283–322.

Huntington, S.P. (1984) 'Will more countries become democratic?', *Political Science Quarterly*, **99**, 193–218.

Huntington, S.P. (1991) *The Third Wave: Democratization in the Late Twentieth Century*, Norman, University of Oklahoma Press.

Huntington, S.P. and Dominguez, J.I. (1975) 'Political development' in Greenstein, F.I. and Polsby, N.W. (eds) *Handbook of Political Science, Vol. 3, Macropolitical Theory*, Reading, MA, Addison-Wesley, 1–114.

IMF (1982) *Government Finance Statistics Yearbook*, Washington, DC, International Monetary Fund.

IMF (1984) *Government Finance Statistics Yearbook 1984*, Washington, DC, International Monetary Fund.

IMF (1994) *Government Finance Statistics Yearbook 1994*, Washington, DC, International Monetary Fund.

Inkeles, A. (1993) 'Industrialization, modernization and the quality of life', *International Journal of Comparative Sociology*, **34**, 1–23.

Inman, R.P. (1987) 'Markets, governments and the role of the "new" political economy', in Auerbach, A.J. and Feldstein, M. (eds) *Handbook of Public Economics, vol. 2*, Amsterdam, North-Holland, 647–778.

International Studies Quarterly (1983) Special Issue on M. Olson (1982) *The Rise and Decline of Nations*.

Isaksson, M. (1993) 'De svenska direktinvesteringarna i ett internationellt perspektiv', *SOU*, **16**, 47–66.

Jackman, R.W. (1973) 'On the relation of economic development to democratic performance', *American Journal of Political Science*, **17**, 611–21.

Jackman, R.W. (1974) 'Political democracy and equality: comparative analysis', *American Sociological Review*, **39**, 29–45.

Jackman, R.W. (1975) *Politics and Social Equality: a Comparative Analysis*, New York, Wiley.

Jackman, R.W. (1985) 'Cross-national statistical research and the study of comparative politics', *American Journal of Political Science*, **29**, 161–82.

Jakobsson, U. and Jagren, L. (1993) 'Den underliggande konkurrenskraften', *SOU*, **16**, 67–108.

Janda, K. (1980) *Political Parties: a cross-national Survey*, New York, Free Press.

Johansen, L. (1977) *Public Economics*, Amsterdam, North-Holland.

Johansen, L. (1977–8) *Lectures on Macroeconomic Planning I–II*, Amsterdam, North-Holland.

Johansen, L. (1979) 'The Bargaining Society and the Inefficiency of Bargaining', *Kyklos*, **32**, 497–522.

Johnson, C. (ed.) (1984) *The Industrial Policy Debate*, San Francisco, Jossey-Bass.

Johnson, H. (1958) *International Trade and Economic Growth*, London, Allen and Unwin.

Johnson, H.G. (1975) *Technology and Economic Interdependence*, London, Macmillan.

Jones, R.W. and Kenen, P.B. (eds) (1984) *Handbook of International Economics*, Amsterdam, North-Holland.

Jonung, L. (ed.) (1990) *Swedish Economic Thought: Explorations and Advances*, London, Routledge.

Kahn, H. and Wiener, A. (1967) *The Year 2000*, London, Macmillan.

Kalecki, M. (1954) *Theory of Economic Dynamics*, London, Allen and Unwin.

Katzenstein, P. (1985) *Small States in World Markets*, Ithaca, NY, Cornell University Press.

Kjellberg, A. (1983) *Facklig organisering i tolv länder*, Lund, Arkiv.

Kmenta, J. (1971) *Elements of Econometrics*, New York, Macmillan.

Kormendi, R.C. and Meguire, P.G. (1985) 'Macroeconomic determinants of growth: cross-country evidence', *Journal of Monetary Economics*, **16**, 141–63.

Kornai, J. (1980) *Economics of Shortage*, Amsterdam, North-Holland.

Kornai, J. (1986) *Contradictions and Dilemmas. Studies on the Socialist Economy and Society*, Cambridge, MA, MIT Press.

Kornai, J. and Liptak, T. (1962) 'A mathematical investigation of some economic effects of profit sharing', *Econometrica*, **30**, 140–61.

Korpi, W. (1983) *The Democratic Class Struggle*, London, Routledge and Kegan Paul.

Korpi, W. (1985a) 'Economic growth and the welfare state: leaky bucket or irrigation system', *European Sociological Review*, **1**, 97–118.

Korpi, W. (1985b) 'Economic growth and the welfare state: a comparative study of 18 OECD countries', *Labour and Society*, **10**, 2, 195–209.

Kregel, J.A. (1972) *The Theory of Economic Growth*, London, Macmillan.

Kreuger, A.O. (1978) *Liberalization Attempts and Consequences*, New York, National Bureau of Economic Research.

Kristensen, O.P. (1987) *Vaeksten i den offentlig sektor*, Copenhagen, Munksgaard.

Krugman, P. (1994) 'The myth of Asia's miracle', *Foreign Affairs*, **73**, 6, 62–78.

Kuhnle, S. (1990) 'Den skandinaviske velferdsmodellen – skandinavisk?, velferd?, modell?', in Hovdum, A.R., Kuhnle, S. and Stokke, L. (eds), *Visjoner om Velferdssamfunnet*, Bergen, Alma Mater.

Kuhnle, S. and Solheim, L. (1991) *Velferdsstaten: Vekst og Omstilling*, Oslo, Tano.

Kuznets, S. (1955) 'Economic growth and income inequality', *American Economic Review*, **45**, 18–25.

Kuznets, S. (1965) *Economic Growth and Structure*, New York, Norton.

Kuznets, S. (1966) *Modern Economic Growth*, New Haven, CT, Yale University Press.

Kuznets, S. (1968) *Toward a Theory of Economic Growth*, New York, Norton.

Kuznets, S. (1971) *Economic Growth of Nations: Total Output and Production Structure*, Cambridge, MA, Harvard University Press.

Laband, D.L. (1984) 'Is there a relationship between economic conditions and political structure?', *Public Choice*, **42**, 27–37.

Lachman, L.M. (1986) *The Market as an Economic Process*, Oxford, Blackwell.

Laffer, A.B. (1978) 'Taxation, GNP, and potential GNP', in *Proceedings of the Business and Economics Statistics Section*, Washington, DC, American Statistical Association.

Laffer, A.B. (1981) 'Government exactions and revenue deficiencies', *Cato Journal*, **1**, 1.

Lal, D. (1983) *The Poverty of 'Development Economics'*, London, Institute of Economic Affairs.

Lane, J.E. (ed.) (1985) *State and Market*, London, Sage.

Lane, J.E. (ed.) (1987) *Bureaucracy and Public Choice*, London, Sage.

Lane, J.E. (ed.) (1991) *Understanding the Swedish Model*, London, Frank Cass.

Lane, J.E., McKay, D. and Newton, K. (1991) *Political Data Handbook: OECD Countries*, Oxford, Oxford University Press.

Lange, O. (1936–7) 'On the economic theory of socialism', *Review of Economic Studies*, **4**, 53–71, 123–42.

Lange, O. (1942) 'The foundations of welfare economics', in Arrow, K.J. and Scitovsky, T. (1969) (eds) *Readings in Welfare Economics*, London, Allen and Unwin, 26-38.

Lange, O. and Taylor, F.M. (1964) *On the Economic Theory of Socialism*, Minneapolis, University of Minnesota Press.

Lange, P. and Garrett, G. (1985) 'The politics of growth: strategic interaction and economic performance in the advanced industrial democracies, 1974–1980', *Journal of Politics*, **47**, 729–827.

LaPalombara, J. (ed.) (1967) *Bureaucracy and Political Development*, Princeton, NJ, Princeton University Press.

LaPalombara, J. and Weiner, M. (eds) (1967) *Political Parties and Political Development*, Princeton, NJ, Princeton University Press.

Larkey, P., Stolp, L. and Winer, M. (1981) 'Theorizing about the growth of government: a research assessment', *Journal of Public Policy*, **2**, 157–220.

Lauterbach, A. (1989) *The Odyssey of Rationality*, Munich, Accedo Verlagsgesellschaft.

Layard, P.R.B. and Walters, A.A. (1978) *Microeconomic Theory*, New York, McGraw-Hill.

Leeman, J.W. (ed.) (1963) *Capitalism, Market Socialism and Central Planning*, Boston, Houghton Mifflin.

Leftwich, A. (1990) 'Politics and development studies', in Leftwich, A. (ed.), *New Developments in Political Science*, London, Edward Elgar.

Le Grand, J. and Estrin, S. (eds) (1989) *Market Socialism*, Oxford, Clarendon.

Lenski, G. (1963) *The Religious Factor: a Sociological Study of Religion's Impact on Politics, Economics and Family Life*, Garden City, NY, Doubleday.

Lenski, G. (1966) *Power and Privilege*, New York, McGraw-Hill.

Lerner, A.P. (1944) *The Economics of Control*, New York, Macmillan.

Lerner, D. (1958) *The Passing of Traditional Society: Modernizing the Middle East*, New York, Free Press.

Lerner, D. (1968) 'Modernization: social aspects', in Sills, D.L. (ed.), *International Encyclopedia of the Social Sciences, Vol. 10*, New York, Free Press, 386–95.

Levine, R. and Renelt, D. (1992) 'A sensitivity analysis of cross-country growth regressions', *American Economic Review*, **82**, 942–63.

Levy, M.J. (1952) *The Structure of Society*, Princeton, NJ, Princeton University Press.

Levy, M.J. (1966) *Modernization and the Structure of Societies*, Princeton, NJ, Princeton University Press.

Lewis, S.R. (1989) 'Primary exporting countries', in Chenery, H. and Srinivasan, T.N. (eds), *Handbook of Development Economics*, vol. II.

Lewis, W.A. (1955) *The Theory of Economic Growth*, London, Allen and Unwin.

Lewis, W.A. (1988) 'The roots of development theory', in Chenery, H. and Srinivasan, T.N. (eds), *Handbook of Development Economics, vol. I.*

Lijphart, A. (1968) 'Typologies of democratic systems', *Comparative Political Studies*, 1, 3–44.

Lijphart, A. (1977) *Democracy in Plural Societies*, New Haven, CT, Yale University Press.

Lijphart, A. (1979) 'Consociationalism and federation: conceptual and empirical links', *Canadian Journal of Political Science*, 21, 499–515.

Lijphart, A. (1984) *Democracies: Patterns of Majoritarian and Consensus Government in Twenty-one Countries*, New Haven, CT, Yale University Press.

Lind, N.C. (1993) 'A compound index of national development', *Social Indicators Research*, 28, 267–84.

Lindbeck, A. (1977) *The Political Economy of the New Left: an Outsider's View*, New York, Harper and Row.

Lindbeck, A., Petersson, O., Swedenborg, B., Persson, T., Sandmo, A. and Thygesen, N. (1993) *Nya Villkor för Ekonomi och Politik: Ekonomikommissionens Förslag*, Stockholm, Allmänna Förlaget.

Lindbeck, A., Petersson, O., Swedenborg, B., Persson, T., Sandmo, A. and Thygesen, N. (1994) *Turning Sweden Around*, Cambridge, MA, MIT Press.

Lindblom, C. (1977) *Politics and Markets*, New York, Basic Books.

Lindblom, C. (1988) *Democracy and Market System*, Oslo, Norwegian University Press.

Linz, J.J. (1975) 'Totalitarian and Authoritarian Regimes', in Greenstein, F.I. and Polsby, N.W. (eds), *Handbook of Political Science, Vol. 3, Macropolitical Theory*, Reading, MA, Addison-Wesley, 175–411.

Linz, J.J. and Stepan, A. (eds) (1978) *The Breakdown of Democratic Regimes*, Baltimore, Johns Hopkins University Press.

Lippincott, B.E. (ed.) (1938) *On the Economic Theory of Socialism*, Minneapolis, University of Minnesota Press.

Lipset, S.M. (1959) 'Some social requisites of democracy: economic development and political legitimacy', *American Political Science Review*, 53, 69–105.

Lipset, S.M. (1960) *Political Man: the Social Bases of Politics*, Garden City, NY, Doubleday.

Lipset, S.M. (1963) *Political Man*, London, Heinemann.

Lipset, S.M. (1994) 'The social requisites of democracy revisited', *American Sociological Review*, 88, 4, 903–10.

Lipset, S.M., Seong, K.-Y. and Torres, J.C. (1993) 'A comparative analysis of the social requisites of democracy', *International Social Science Journal*, 45, 2, 155–75.

List, F. (1983) *The Natural System of Political Economy*, London, Frank Cass (originally published 1837).

Little, I.M. (1982) *Economic Development: Theory, Policy, and International Relations*, New York, Basic Books.

Little, I.M.D., Scitovsky, T. and Scott, M. (1970) *Industry and Trade in Some Developing Countries*, Oxford, Oxford University Press.

Loewenberg, G. and Patterson, S.C. (1979) *Comparing Legislatures*, Boston, Little and Brown.

Lybeck, J. (1986) *The Growth of Government in Developed Economies*, London, Gower.

Lybeck, J.A. and Henrekson, M. (eds) (1988) *Explaining the Growth of Government*, Amsterdam, North-Holland.

Lydall, H. (1986) *Yugoslav Socialism*, Oxford, Clarendon Press.

McAuley, A. (1979) *Economic Welfare in the Soviet Union*, London, Allen and Unwin.

McCormick, B.J. (1988) *The World Economy: Patterns of Growth and Change*, Deddington, Philip Allan.

Mackie, T.T. and Rose, R. (1982) *The International Almanack of Electoral History*, London, Macmillan.

Macridis, R.C. (1955) *The Study of Comparative Government*, New York, Random House.

Maddison, A. (1995) *Monitoring the World Economy 1820–1992*, Paris, OECD.

Madsen, H.J. (1978) 'Poetics', Aarhus, Institute of Political Science (mimeo).

Madsen, E.S. and Paldam, M. (1978) *Economic and Political Data for the Main OECD-countries 1948–1975*. Aarhus, Institute of Economics.

Malinvaud, E. (1967) 'Decentralized procedures for planning', in Malinvaud, E. and Bacharach, M.O.L. (eds), *Activity Analysis in the Theory of Growth and Planning*, New York, Macmillan and Co.

Mandel, E. (1986) 'A critique of market socialism', *New Left Review*, **159**, 5–37.

Mankiew, N.G., Romer, D. and Weil, D.N. (1992) 'A contribution to the empirics of economic growth', *Quarterly Journal of Economics*, **57**, 407–37.

March, J.G. and Olsen, J.P. (1984) 'The new institutionalism: organizational factors in political life', *American Political Science Review*, **78**, 734–49.

March, J.G. and Olsen, J.P. (1989) *Rediscovering Institutions: the Organizational Basis of Politics*, New York, Free Press.

Mareshwari, S.R. (1968) *Indian Administration*, New Delhi, Orient Longman.

Mareshwari, S.R. (1984) *Rural Development in India*, New Delhi, Sage.

Margolis, J. and Guitton, H. (eds) (1969) *Public Economics: an Analysis of Public Production and Consumption and Their Relations to the Private Sector*, London, Macmillan.

Matheson, D.K. (1979) *Ideology, Political Action and the Finnish Working Class*, Helsinki, Societas Scientarium Fennica.

Mathur, A. (1983) 'Regional development and income disparities in India: a sectorial analysis', *Economic Development and Cultural Change*, **31**, 475–505.

Meade, J.E. (1961) *A Neo-classical Theory of Economic Growth*, Oxford, Oxford University Press.

Meier, G.M. (ed.) (1984) *Leading Issues in Economic Development*, New York, Oxford University Press.

Messick, R.E. (1996) 'The world survey of economic freedom', *Freedom Review*, **27**, 2, 7–17.

Miele, S. (ed.) (1983) *Internationales Gewerkschaftshandbuch*, Opladen, Leeske und Budrich.

Milner, H. (1990) *Sweden: Social Democracy in Practice*, Oxford, Oxford University Press.

Milner, H. (1994) *Social Democracy and Rational Choice*, London, Routledge.

Mises, L. von (1936) *Socialism: an Economic and Sociological Analysis*, London, Cape.

Mishan, E.J. (1981) *Introduction to Normative Economics*, Oxford, Oxford University Press.

Moll, T.C., Nattrass, N. and Loots, L. (1991) *Redistribution: How Can It Work in South Africa?* Cape Town, David Philip.

Montias, J.M. (1976) *The Structure of Economic Systems*, New Haven, CT, Yale University Press.

Moore, B. (1966) *Social Origins of Dictatorship and Democracy*, Harmondsworth, Pelican.

Morishima, M. (1964) *Equilibrium, Stability and Growth*, Oxford, Clarendon Press.

Morris, C.T. and Adelman, I. (1980) 'The religious factor in economic development', *World Development*, **8**, 491–501.

Morris, M.D. (1979) *Measuring the Conditions of the World's Poor: the Physical Quality of Life Index*, New York, Pergamon Press.

Mueller, D.C. (ed.) (1983) *The Political Economy of Growth*, New Haven, CT, Yale University Press.

Mueller, D.C. (1986) *The Modern Corporation*, London, Harvester Wheatsheaf.

Mueller, D.C. (1989) *Public Choice II*, 2nd edn, Cambridge, Cambridge University Press.

Muller, E. (1985) 'Income inequality, regime repressiveness and political violence', *American Sociological Review*, **50**, 47–61.

Muller, E. (1988) 'Democracy, economic development, and income inequality', *American Sociological Review*, **53**, 50–68.

Murray, R. (1987) 'Productivity measurements in bureaucratic organizations', in Lane, J.E. (ed.), *Bureaucracy and Public Choice*, London, Sage.

Musgrave, R.A. (1959) *Theory of Public Finance*, New York, McGraw-Hill.

Musgrave, R.A. and Jarrett, P. (1979) 'International redistribution', *Kyklos*, **32**, 541–58.

Musgrave, R.A. and Musgrave, P. (1980) *Public Finance in Theory and Practice*, New York, McGraw-Hill.

Musgrave, R.A. and Peacock, A.T. (eds) (1967) *Classics in the Theory of Public Finance*, New York, St Martin's Press.

Myrdal, G. (1957) *Economic Theory and Underdeveloped Regions*, London, Duckworth.

Myrdal, G. (1961) '"Value-loaded" concepts', in Hegeland, H. (ed.), *Money, Growth, and Methodology and Other Essays in Honor of Johan Åkerman*, Lund, Gleerup.

Myrdal, G. (1968) *Asian Drama I–III*, New York, Pantheon Books.

Myrdal, G. (1970) *Objectivity in Social Research*, London, Duckworth.

Mytelka, L.K. (1979) *Regional Development in a Global Economy*, New Haven, CT, Yale University Press.

Nash, M. (1959) 'Some social and cultural aspects of economic development', *Economic Development and Cultural Change*, **7**, 137–50.

Nath, S.K. (1969) *A Reappraisal of Welfare Economics*, London, Routledge and Kegan Paul.

Nattrass, J. (1981) *The South African Economy. Its Growth and Change*, Cape Town, Oxford University Press.

Nattrass, N. and Ardington, E. (eds) (1990) *The Political Economy of South Africa*, Cape Town, Oxford University Press.

Nettl, J.P. (1967) *Political Mobilization: a Sociological Analysis of Methods and Concepts*, New York, Basic Books.

Neubauer, D.E. (1967) 'Some conditions of democracy', *American Political Science Review*, **61**, 1002–9.

Niskanen, W.E. (1971) *Bureaucracy and Representative Government*, Chicago, Aldine Publishing Company.

Nove, A. (1983) *The Economics of Feasible Socialism*, London, Allen and Unwin.

Nove, A. (1986) *The Soviet Economic System*, Boston, Allen and Unwin.

Nove, A. (1987) *An Economic History of the USSR*, 3rd edn, London, Unwin Heinemann.

Nurkse, R. (1961) *Equilibrium and Growth in the World Economy*, Cambridge, MA, Harvard University Press.

Oates, W.E. (1972) *Fiscal Federalism*, New York, Harcourt Brace Jovanovich.

O'Brien, D.C. (1972) 'Modernization, order, and the erosion of a democratic ideal: American political science 1960–70', *Journal of Development Studies*, **8**, 4, 351–78.

Ocampo, J.F. and Johnson, D.L. (1972) 'The concept of political development', in Cockcroft, J.D. *et al.* (eds), *Dependence and Underdevelopment: Latin America's Political Economy*, Garden City, NY, Doubleday, 399–424.

O'Donnell, G. (1973) *Modernization and Bureaucratic- authoritarianism: Studies in South American Politics*, Berkeley, CA, Institute of International Studies.

O'Donnell, G. (1988) *Bureaucratic Authoritarianism: Argentina 1966–1973 in Comparative Perspective*, Berkeley, University of California Press.

O'Donnell, G. *et al.* (eds) (1986) *Transitions from Authoritarian Rule: Prospects for Democracy*, Baltimore, Johns Hopkins University Press.

O'Donnell, G. and Schmitter, P.C. (1986) *Transitions from Authoritarian Rule: Tentative Conclusions about Uncertain Democracies*, Baltimore, Johns Hopkins University Press.

OECD (1968) *National Accounts 1950–1968*, Paris, OECD.

OECD (1979a) *Economic Outlook*, Paris, OECD.

OECD (1979b) *National Accounts 1960–1977*, Paris, OECD.

OECD (1983a) *Historical Statistics 1960–1981*, Paris, OECD.

OECD (1983b) *National Accounts 1964–1981*, Paris, OECD.

OECD (1984) *Economic Outlook*, Paris, OECD.

OECD (1985) *Economic Outlook*, Paris, OECD.

OECD (1987) *National Accounts 1973–1985*, Paris, OECD.

OECD (1988) *Labour Force Statistics 1966–1986*, Paris, OECD.

OECD (1993) *National Accounts 1979–1991*, Paris, OECD.

OECD (1994) *Employment Outlook*, Paris, OECD.

OECD (1995a) *Economic Outlook*, Paris, OECD.

OECD (1995b) *National Accounts 1981–1993*, Paris, OECD.

OECD (1995c) *Labour Force Statistics 1973–1993*, Paris, OECD.

Okimoto, D.I. (1989) *Between MITI and the Market: Japanese Industrial Policy for High Technology*, Stanford, Stanford University Press.

Okun, A.M. (1975) *Equality and Efficiency*, Washington, DC, Brookings.

Olsen, M.E. (1968) 'Multivariate analysis of national political development', *American Sociological Review*, **33**, 699–712.

Olsen, M.E. (1982) 'Linkages between socioeconomic modernization and national political development', *Journal of Political and Military Sociology*, **10**, 41–69.

Olson, M. (1965) *The Logic of Collective Action*, Cambridge, MA, Harvard University Press.

Olson, M. (1982) *The Rise and Decline of Nations: Economic Growth, Stagflation and Social Rigidities*, New Haven, CT, Yale University Press.

Olson, M. (1983) 'The political economy of comparative growth rates', in Mueller, D. (ed.), *Political Economy of Growth*, New Haven, CT, and London, Yale University Press.

Olson, M. (1990) *How Bright are the Northern Lights? Some Questions about Sweden*, Lund University, Institute of Economic Research.

Olson, M. (1993) 'Dictatorship, democracy, and development', *American Political Science Review*, **87**, 567–76.

Olson, M. (1996) 'Big bills left on the sidewalk: Why some nations are rich, and others poor', *Journal of Economic Perspectives*, **10**, 23–4.

Organski, A.F.K. (1965) *Stages of Political Development*, New York, Knopf.

Ott, D.J., Ott, A.F. and Yoo, J. (1975) *Macroeconomic Theory*, New York, McGraw-Hill.

Öyen, E. (ed.) (1990) *Comparative Methodology*, London, Sage.

Pack, H. (1988) 'Industrialisation and trade', in Chenery, H. and Srinivasan, T.N. (eds), *Handbook of Development Economics, vol. I.*

Page, E.G. (1985) *Political Authority and Bureaucratic Power*, Brighton, Harvester Press.

Paldam, M. (1990) 'How robust is the vote function? a comparative study of 197 elections in the OECD area 1948–85', in Lafay, J.D., Lewis-Beck, M. and Norpoth, H. (eds), *Economics and Elections in the United States and Western Europe*, Ann Arbor, University of Michigan Press.

Paldam, M. (1991a) 'Politics matters after all (1): a comparative test of Alesina's theory of partisan cycles', in Thygesen, N., Velupillai, K. and Zambelli, S. (eds), *Business Cycles: Theories, Evidence and Analysis*, Basingstoke, Macmillan.

Paldam, M. (1991b) 'Politics matters after all (2): a comparative test of Hibb's theory of partisan cycles', in Hillman, A.L. (eds), *Markets and Politicians: Politicized Economic Choice*, Boston, Kluwer.

Palgrave, R.H.I. (1899) *Dictionary of Political Economy*, London, Macmillan.

Park, T. (1973) 'Measuring the dynamic patterns of development: the case of Asia 1949–1968', *Multivariate Behavioral Research*, **8**, 227–51.

Parsons, T. (1951) *The Social System*, New York, Free Press.

Parsons, T., and Shils, E. (eds) (1951) *Towards a General Theory of Action*, New York, Harper and Row.

Parsons, T. and Smelser, N. (1956) *Economy and Society*, London, Routledge and Kegan Paul.

Pasinetti, L. (1981) *Structural Change and Economic Growth*, Cambridge, Cambridge University Press.

Paukert, F. (1973) 'Income distribution at different levels of development: a survey of evidence', *International Labour Review*, **108**, 97–125.

Payne, J.L. (1989) *Why Nations Arm*, Oxford, Blackwell.

Peacock, A. (1979) *The Economic Analysis of Government and Related Themes*, Oxford, Martin Robertson.

Peacock, A. and Wiseman, J. (1961) *The Growth of Public Expenditure in the United Kingdom*, Princeton, NJ, Princeton University Press.

Peacock, A. and Wiseman, J. (1979) 'Approaches to the analysis of government expenditure growth', *Public Finance Quarterly*, **7**, 3–23.

Perlmutter, A. (1981) *Modern Authoritarianism: a Comparative Institutional Analysis*, New Haven, CT, Yale University Press.

Perry, C.S. (1980) 'Political contestations in nations: 1960, 1963, 1967 and 1970', *Journal of Political and Military Sociology*, **8**, 161–74.

Peters, B.G. and Heisler, M.O. (1983) 'Thinking about public sector growth', in Taylor, C.L. (ed.), *Why Governments Grow: Measuring Public Sector Size*, Beverly Hills, CA, Sage.

Petersson, O. (1990) *Demokrati och Makt i Sverige*, Stockholm, Allmänna Förlaget.

Phelps, E.S. (ed.) (1962) *The Goal of Economic Growth*, New York, Norton.

Phillips, A. (1978) 'The concept of "development"', *Review of African Political Economy*, **8**, 7–20.

Pindyck, R.S. and Rubinfeld, D.L. (1981) *Econometric Models and Economic Forecasts*, New York, McGraw-Hill.

Portes, A. (1976) 'On the sociology of national development: theories and issues', *American Journal of Sociology*, **82**, 55–85.

Posner, R.A. (1992) *Economic Analysis of Law*, Boston, Little, Brown.

Pourgerami, A. (1988) 'The political economy of development: a cross-national causality test development–democracy–growth hypothesis', *Public Choice*, **58**, 123–41.

Pourgerami, A. (1989) 'The political economy of development: an empirical examination of the wealth theory of democracy', (mimeo) Bakerfield, California State University, Dept of Economics.

Pourgerami, A. (1991) *Development and Democracy in the Third World*, Boulder, CO, Westview Press.

Pride, R.A. (1970) *Origins of Democracy: a Cross-national Study of Mobilization, Party Systems, and Democratic Stability*, Beverly Hills, CA, Sage.

Pryor, F.L. (1968) *Public Expenditures in Communist and Capitalist Nations*, London, Allen and Unwin.

Przeworski, A. (1975) 'Institutionlization of voting patterns, or is mobilization the source of decay?', *American Political Science Review*, **69**, 49–67.

Przeworski, A. (1987) 'Methods of cross-national research, 1970–83: an overview', in Dierkes, M. (ed.) *Comparative Policy Research: Learning from Experience*, Aldershot, Gower, 31–49.

Przeworski, A. (1992) 'The neoliberal fallacy', *Journal of Democracy*, **3**, 33, 45–59.

Przeworski, A. and Limongi, F. (1993) 'Political regimes and economic growth', *Journal of Economic Perspectives*, **7**, 51–69.

Przeworski, A. and Teune, H. (1970) *The Logic of Comparative Social Inquiry*, New York, Wiley.

Pye, L.W. (1958) 'Administrators, agitators, and brokers', *Public Opinion Quarterly*, **22**, 342–8.

Pye, L.W. (1966) *Aspects of Political Development*, Boston, Little, Brown.

Pye, L.W. (1987) 'Political Development', in Bogdanor, V. (ed.) *The Blackwell Encyclopedia of Political Institutions*, Oxford, Blackwell.

Pye, L.W. (ed.) (1967) *Communications and Political Development*, Princeton, NJ, Princeton University Press.

Pye, L.W. and Verba, S. (eds) (1969) *Political Culture and Political Development*, Princeton, NJ, Princeton University Press.

Ranis, G. (1975) 'Equity and growth: new dimensions of development', *Journal of Conflict Resolution*, **19**, 558–68.

Rawls, J. (1971) *A Theory of Justice*, Cambridge, MA, Harvard University Press.

Reconstruction and Development Programme (1995) *Key Indicators of Poverty in South Africa*, Cape Town, Office of the Reconstruction and Development Programme.

Reynolds, L.G. (1975) 'Agriculture in development theory: an overview', in L.G. Reynolds (ed.), *Agriculture in Development Theory*, New Haven, CT, and London, Yale University Press.

Reynolds, L.G. (1985) *Economic Growth in the Third World*, 1850–1980, New Haven, CT, Yale University Press.

Ricketts, M. (1987) *The Economics of Business Enterprise*, Brighton, Harvester Wheatsheaf.

Riggs, F.W. (1957) 'Agraria and industria: toward a typology of comparative administration', in Siffin, W.J. (ed.), *Toward a Comparative Study of Public Administration*, Bloomington, Indiana University Press, 23–116.

Riggs, F. (1964) *Administration in Developing Countries*, Boston, Houghton Mifflin.

Riggs, F.W. (1967) 'The theory of political development', in Charlesworth, J.C. (ed.), *Contemporary Political Analysis*, New York, Free Press.

Riggs, F.W. (1984) 'Development', in Sartori, G. (ed.), *Social Science Concepts*, Beverly Hills, CA, Sage, 125–203.

Robbins, L.C. (1934) *The Great Depression*, London, Macmillan.

Rokkan, S. *et al.* (1970) *Citizens, Elections, Parties: Approaches to the Comparative Study of the Process of Development*, Oslo, Universitetsforlaget.

Rose, R. (1973) 'Comparing public policy: an overview', *European Journal of Political Research*, 1, 67–94.

Rose, R. (1984) *Understanding Big Government*, London, Sage.

Rose, R. (1985) 'Getting by in three economies: the resources of the official, unofficial and domestic economies', in Lane, J.-E. (ed.), *State and Market*, London, Sage.

Rose, R. (1989) *Ordinary People in Public Policy*, London, Sage.

Rosen, H. (1988) *Public Finance*, Homewood, IL, Irwin.

Rostow, W.W. (1960) *The Stages of Economic Growth: a Non-communist Manifesto*, Cambridge, Cambridge University Press.

Rostow, W.W. (1971) *Politics and the Stages of Growth*, Cambridge, Cambridge University Press.

Roth, G. (1975) 'Socio-historical model and developmental theory', *American Sociological Review*, 40, 148–57.

Rothschild, K.W. (1989) 'Political Economy or Economics? Some terminological and normative considerations', *European Journal of Political Economy*, 5, 1, 1–12.

Rubinson, R. and Quinlan, D. (1977) 'Democracy and social equality: a reanalysis', *American Sociological Review*, 42, 611–23.

Rueschemeyer, D., Stephens, E.H. and Stephens, J.D. (1992) *Capitalist Development and Democracy*, Cambridge, Polity Press.

Russett, B., Alker, H., Deutsch, K.W. and Lasswell, H.D. (1964) *World Handbook of Political and Social Indicators*, New Haven, CT, Yale University Press.

Rustow, D.A. (1955) *The Politics of Compromise: a Study of Parties and Cabinet Governments in Sweden*, Princeton, NJ, Princeton University Press.

Rustow, D.A. (1967) *A World of Nations: Problems of Political Modernization*, Washington, DC, The Brookings Institution.

Rustow, D.A. (1970) 'Transitions to democracy: toward a dynamic model', *Comparative Politics*, 2, 337–63.

Rustow, D.A. and Ward, R.E. (1964) 'Introduction', in Ward, R.E. and Rustow, D.A. (eds), *Political Modernization in Japan and Turkey*, Princeton, NJ, Princeton University Press.

Samuelson, P. (1971) *Foundations of Economic Analysis*, Cambridge, MA, Harvard University Press.

Sandbrook, R. (1976) 'The "crisis" in political development theory', *Journal of Development Studies*, **12**, 165–85.

Sartori, G. (1969) 'From the sociology of politics to political sociology', in Lipset, S.M. (ed.), *Politics and the Social Sciences*, New York, Oxford University Press, 65–100.

Sartori, G. (1976) *Parties and Party Systems: a Framework for Analysis*, Cambridge, Cambridge University Press.

Saunders, P. (1986) 'What can we learn from international comparison of public sector size and economic performance', *European Sociological Review*, **2**, 52–60.

Sawyer, J.A. (1989) *Macroeconomic Theory*, Brighton, Harvester Wheatsheaf.

Scalapino, R.A. (1964) 'Environmental and foreign contributions: Japan', in Ward, R.E. and Rustow, D.A. (eds), *Political Modernization in Japan and Turkey*, Princeton, NJ, Princeton University Press.

Schmidt, M.G. (1982) *Wohlfahrtsstaatliche Politik unter bürgerlichen und sozialdemokratischen Regierungen: ein internationaler Vergleich*, Frankfurt, Campus.

Schmidt, M.G. (ed.) (1983a) *Westliche Industrie Gesellschaften: Wirtschaft, Gesellschaft, Politik*, Munich, Piper.

Schmidt, M.G. (1983b) 'The welfare state and the economy in periods of economic crisis: a comparative study of twenty-three OECD nations', *European Journal of Political Research*, **11**, 1–26.

Schmitter, P.C. (1981) 'Interest intermediation and regime governability in contemporary western Europe and North America', in Berger, S. (ed.), *Organizing Interests in Western Europe*, Cambridge, Cambridge University Press, 285–327.

Schneider, F. (1989) 'Political economy or economics? A comment', *European Journal of Political Economy*, **5**, 1.

Schrire, R. (ed.) (1990) *Critical Choices for South Africa: an Agenda for the 1990s*, Cape Town, Oxford University Press.

Schrire, R. (ed.) (1992) *Wealth or Poverty? Critical Choices for South Africa*, Cape Town, Oxford University Press.

Schumpeter, J. (1944) *Capitalism, Socialism and Democracy*, London, Allen and Unwin.

Schumpeter, J.A. (1989) *Essays on Entrepreneurs, Innovations, Business Cycles and the Evolution of Capitalism*, New Brunswick, Transaction Publishers.

Scott, M.F. (1989) *A New View of Economic Growth*, Oxford, Clarendon Press.

Scully, G.W. (1988) 'The institutional framework of economic development', *Journal of Political Economy*, **96**, 652–62.

Scully, G.W. (1992) *Constitutional Environments and Economic Growth*, Princeton, NJ, Princeton University Press.

Scully, G.W. and Slottje, D.J. (1991) 'Ranking economic liberty across countries', *Public Choice*, **69**, 121–52.

Sen, A.K. (ed.) (1970) *Penguin Modern Readings: Growth Economics*, Harmondsworth, Penguin.

Sen, A. (1988) 'The concept of development', in Chenery, H. and Srinivasan, T.N. (eds) *Handbook of Development Economics*, Amsterdam, North-Holland.

Share, D. (1987) 'Transitions to democracy and transition through transaction', *Comparative Political Studies*, **19**, 525–48.

Sharkansky, I. (1969) *The Politics of Taxing and Spending*, Indianapolis, Bobbs-Merril.

Sharpe, L.J. and Newton, K. (1984) *Does Politics Matter?* Oxford, Clarendon Press.

Sigelman, L. (1971) *Modernization and the Political System: a Critique and Preliminary Empirical Analysis*, Beverly Hills, CA, Sage.

Sigelman, L. and Gadbois, G.H. (1983) 'Contemporary comparative politics: an inventory and assessment', *Comparative Political Studies*, **16**, 275–305.

Simpson, M. (1990) 'Political rights and income inequality: a cross-national test', *American Sociological Review*, **55**, 682–93.

Singer, J.D. and Small, M. (1966) 'The composition and status ordering of the international system: 1815–1940', *World Politics*, **18**, 236–82.

Singleton, F. and Carter, B. (1982) *The Economy of Yugoslavia*, London, Croom Helm.

Sirowy, L. and Inkeles, A. (1990) 'The effects of democracy on economic growth and inequality: a review', *Studies in Comparative International Development*, **25**, 126–57.

Sivard, R.L. (1980) *World Military and Social Expenditures 1980*, Leesburg, VA, World Priorities.

Sivard, R.L. (1983) *World Military and Social Expenditures 1983: an Annual Report on World Priorities*, Washington, DC, World Priorities.

Slottje, D.J. (1991) 'Measuring the quality of life across countries', *Review of Economics and Statistics*, **73**, 684–93.

Slottje, D.J., Scully, D.W., Hirschberg, J.G. and Hays, K.J. (1991) *Measuring the Quality of Lifes Across Countries: a Multidimensional Analysis*, Boulder, CO, Westview Press.

Smith, A. (1962–4) *The Wealth of Nations*, 2 vols, London, Everyman's Library.

Smith, A.K. (1969) 'Socio-economic development and political democracy: a causal analysis', *Midwest Journal of Political Science*, **13**, 95–125.

Södersten, B. (1965) *A Study of Economic Growth and International Trade*, Stockholm, Almqvist and Wicksell.

Solow, R.M. (1988) *Growth Theory*, Oxford, Oxford University Press.

Sombart, W. (1916–1927) *Der moderne Kapitalismus*, 3 vols, Munich and Leipzig, Duncker and Humblot.

Sombart, W. (1930) 'Capitalism' in *Encyclopedia of the Social Sciences*, vol. 3, London, Macmillan, 195–208.

Sommers, P.M. and Suits, D.B. (1971) 'A cross-section model of economic growth', *Review of Economics and Statistics*, **53**, 121–8.

Sørensen, G. (1992) *Democracy and Authoritarianism: Consequences for Economic Development*, Aarhus, Institute of Political Science.

South African Institute of Race Relations (1990–) *Race Relations Survey*, Johannesburg, South African Institute of Race Relations.

Spindler, Z.A. (1991) 'Liberty and development: a further empirical perspective', *Public Choice*, **69**, 197–210.

Spulber, D.F. (1989) *Regulation and Markets*, Cambridge, MA, MIT Press.

Spulber, N. (1969) *The Soviet Economy. Structure, Principles, Problems*, New York, Norton.

Staar, R.F. (1981) 'Checklist of communist parties and fronts, 1980', *Problems of Communism*, **30**, 2, 88–92.

Ståhlberg, A.-C. (1995) *Våra Pensionssystem*, Stockholm, SNS.

Staniland, M. (1985) *What Is Political Economy? A Study of Social Theory and Underdevelopment*, New Haven, CT, Yale University Press.

Stigler, G. (1966) *The Theory of Price*, New York, Macmillan.

Stigler, G. (1988) *Chicago Studies in Regulation*, Chicago, Chicago University Press.

Stiglitz, J.E. (1988) *Economics of the Public Sector*, New York, Norton.

Stiglitz, J.E. and Uzawa, H. (1969) *Readings in the Modern Theory of Economic Growth*, Cambridge, MA, MIT Press.

Streeten, P. (1972) *The Frontiers of Development Studies*, London, Macmillan.

Summers, R. and Heston, A. (1984) 'Improved international comparisons of real product and its composition, 1950–80 [mark 3]', *Review of Income and Wealth*, **30**, 207–62.

Summers, R. and Heston, A. (1988) 'A new set of international comparisons of real product and price levels estimates for 130 countries, 1950–1985 [mark 4]', *Review of Income and Wealth*, **34**, 1–25.

Summers, R. and Heston, A. (1991) 'The Penn World Table (mark 5): an expanded set of international comparisons, 1950–1988', *Quarterly Journal of Economics*, **56**, May, 1–41.

Summers, R. and Heston, A. (1994) Penn World Tables, mark 5.6, Internet: http://nber.harvard.edu/pwt56.html (May 1996).

Sutton, F.X. (1963) 'Social theory and comparative politics', in Eckstein, H. and Apter, D. (eds), *Comparative Politics: a Reader*, New York, Free Press, 67–81.

Swank, D.H. (1984) 'The political economy of state domestic spending in eighteen advanced capitalist democracies, 1960–1980', paper presented to the 1984 APSA Meeting, Washington.

Syrquin, M. (1988) 'Patterns of structural change', in Chenery, H. and Srinivasan, T.N. (eds), *Handbook of Development Economics, vol. I*.

Szentes, T. (1983) *The Political Economy of Underdevelopment*, Budapest, Akadémiai Kiadó.

Tarschys, D. (1975) 'The growth of public expenditures: nine modes of explanation', *Scandinavian Political Studies*, **10**, 9–31.

Taylor, C.L. (1972) 'Indicators of political development', *Journal of Development Studies*, **8**, 3, 103–9.

Taylor, C.L. (1981) *Codebook to World Handbook of Political and Social Indicators, vol. I, Aggregate Data*, 3rd edn, West Berlin, IIVG.

Taylor, C.L. and Hudson, M. (1972) *World Handbook of Political and Social Indicators*, 2nd edn, New Haven, CT, Yale University Press.

Taylor, C.L. and Jodice, D. (1981) *Codebook to World Handbook of Political and Social Indicators, vol. II, Political Events Data*, 3rd edn, West Berlin, IIVG.

Taylor, C.L. and Jodice, D. (1983) *World Handbook of Political and Social Indicators*, 3rd edn, New Haven, CT, Yale University Press.

Taylor, J.G. (1979) *From Modernization to Modes of Production: a Critique of the Sociologies of Development and Underdevelopment*, Atlantic Highlands, NJ, Humanities Press.

Taylor, L. and Arida, P. (1988) 'Long-run income distribution and growth', in Chenery, H. and Srinivasan, T.N. (eds), *Handbook of Development Economics, vol. I*.

Taylor, P.A.S. (1966) *A New Dictionary of Economics*, London, Routledge and Kegan Paul.

Taylor, P.J. (1987) 'The poverty of international comparisons: some methodological lessons from world-system analysis', *Studies in Comparative International Development*, **22**, 12–39.

Terlouw, C.P. (1989) 'World-system theory and regional geography: a preliminary exploration of the context of regional geography', *Tijdschrift voor Economische en Sociale Geografie*, **80**, 206–21.

Therborn, G. (1984) 'The prospects of labour and the transformation of advanced capitalism', *New Left Review*, **145**, 5–38.

Thirlwall, A.P. (1983) *Growth and Development: with Special Reference to Developing Economies*, London, Macmillan (4th edn, 1986).

Tilly, C. (ed.) (1975) *The Formation of Nation States in Western Europe*, Princeton, NJ, Princeton University Press.

Tilly, C. (1978) *From Mobilization to Revolution*, Reading, MA, Addison-Wesley.

Tilton, T. (1990) *The Political Theory of Swedish Social Democracy*, Oxford, Oxford University Press.

Tinbergen, J. (1952) *On the Theory of Economic Policy*, Amsterdam, North-Holland.

Tinbergen, J. (1967) *Economic Policy: Principles and Design*, Amsterdam, North-Holland.

Todaro, M.P. (1985) *Economic Development in the Third World*, New York, Longman.

Tocqueville, A. de (1990) *Democracy in America, I-II*, New York, Vintage. (First published 1835–40.)

Toye, J. (1987) *Dilemmas of Development*, Oxford, Blackwell.

Tufte, E. (1978) *Political Control of the Economy*, Princeton, Princeton University Press.

United Nations Development Programme (1990) *Human Development Report 1990*, New York, Oxford University Press.

United Nations Development Programme (1993) *Human Development Report 1993*, New York, Oxford University Press.

United Nations Development Programme (1994) *Human Development Report 1994*, New York, Oxford University Press.

United Nations Development Programme (1995) *Human Development Report 1995*, New York, Oxford University Press.

Usher, D. (1981) *The Economic Prerequisite to Democracy*, Oxford, Blackwell.

Vanat, J. (1972) *The General Theory of Labor-managed Economies*, Ithaca, NY, Cornell University Press.

Vanhanen, T. (1984) *The Emergence of Democracy: a Comparative Study of 119 States, 1850–1979*, Helsinki, Societas Scientiarum Fennica.

Vanhanen, T. (1990) *The Process of Democratization: a Comparative Study of 147 States, 1980–88*, New York, Crane Russak.

Vanhanen, T. (1992) *Strategies of Democratization*, Washington, DC, Crane Russak.

Varian, H. (1984) *Microeconomic Analysis*, New York, Norton.

Verma, S.P. and Sharma, S.K. (1984) *Development Administration*, New Delhi, Indian Institute of Public Administration.

Von Vorys, K. (1973) 'Toward a concept of development', in Masannat, G.S. (ed.), *The Dynamics of Modernization*, Pacific Palisades, CA, Goodyear.

Vorhies, F. and Glahe, F. (1988) 'Political liberty and social development: an empirical investigation', *Public Choice*, **58**, 45–71.

Wade, R. (1990) *Governing the Market: Economic Theory and the Role of Government in East Asian Industrialization*, Princeton, NJ, Princeton University Press.

Wagner, A. (1877–1901) *Finanzwissenschaft*, 4 vols, Leipzig and Heidelberg, Winter.

Wagner, R.E. and Tollison, R.D. (1982) *Balanced Budgets, Fiscal Responsibility and the Constitution*, Washington, DC, Cato Institute.

Wallensteen, P. and Sollenberg, M. (1995) 'After the cold war: emerging patterns of armed conflict 1989–94', *Journal of Peace Research*, **32**, 345–60.

Wallerstein, I. (1974) *The Modern World-system: Capitalist Agriculture and the Origins of the European World-economy in the Sixteenth Century*, New York, Academic Press.

Wallerstein, I. (1977) 'Rural economy in modern world society', *Studies in Comparative International Development*, **12**, 29–40.

Wallerstein, I. (1979) *The Capitalist World-economy*, Cambridge, Cambridge University Press.

Ward, R.E. and Rustow, D.A. (eds) (1968) *Political Modernization in Japan and Turkey*, Princeton, NJ, Princeton University Press.

Webber, C. and Wildavsky, A. (1986) *A History of Taxation and Expenditure in the Western World*, New York, Simon and Schuster.

Weber, M. (1949) *The Methodology of the Social Sciences*, Glencoe, IL, Free Press.

Weede, E. (1980) 'Beyond misspecification in sociological analysis of income inequality', *American Sociological Review*, **45**, 497–501.

Weede, E. (1983) 'The impact of democracy on economic growth: some evidence from cross-national analysis', *Kyklos*, **36**, 21–39.

Weede, E. (1984a) 'Democracy and war involvement', *Journal of Conflict Resolution*, **28**, 649–64.

Weede, E. (1984b) 'Political democracy, state strength and economic growth in LDCs: a cross-national analysis', *Review of International Studies*, **10**, 297–312.

Weede, E. (1986) 'Catch-up, distributional coalitions and government as determinants of economic growth and decline in industrialized democracies', *British Journal of Sociology*, **37**, 194–220.

Weede, E. (1993) 'The impact of democracy or repressiveness on the quality of life, income distribution and economic growth rates', *International Sociology*, **8**, 177–95.

Weiner, M. (1965) 'Political integration and political development', *Annals of the American Academy of Political and Social Science*, **358**, 52–63.

Weiner, M. and Huntington, S.P. (eds) (1987) *Understanding Political Development*, Boston, Little, Brown.

Wesson, R. (ed.) (1987) *Democracy: a Worldwide Survey*, New York, Praeger.

Westlund, A. and Lane, J.E. (1983) 'The relevance of the concept of structural variability to the social sciences', *Quality and Quantity*, **17**, 189–201.

Whiteford, A., Posel, D. and Keletwang, T. (1995) 'A profile of poverty, inequality and human development', Pretoria, Human Sciences Research Council (unpublished).

Whiteley, P. (ed.) (1980) *Models of Political Economy*, London, Sage.

Whiteley, P. (1982) 'The political economy of economic growth', *European Journal of Political Research*, **11**, 197–213.

Whiteley, P. (1986) *Political Control of the Macroeconomy: The Political Economy of Public Policy Making*, London, Sage.

Wiarda, H.J. (1983) 'Toward a non ethnocentric theory of development: alternative conceptions from the Third World', *Journal of Developing Areas*, **17**, 433–52.

Wildavsky, A. (1973) 'If planning is everything, then maybe it is nothing', *Policy Sciences*, **4**, 127–53.

Wildavsky, A. (1979) *Speaking Truth to Power: the Art and Craft of Policy Analysis*, Boston, Little, Brown.

Wildavsky, A. (1980) *How to Limit Government Spending*, Berkeley, University of California Press.

Wildavsky, A. (1984) *The Politics of the Budgetary Process*, Boston: Little, Brown.

Wildavsky, A. (1985) 'The logic of public sector growth', in Lane, J.-E. (ed.), *State and Market*, London, Sage.

Wildavsky, A. (1986) *Budgeting: a Comparative Theory of the Budgetary Process*, 2nd edn, New Brunswick, NJ, Transaction.

Wildavsky, A. (1988) *The New Politics of the Budgetary Process*, Boston, Scott, Foresman and Company.

Wilensky, H. (1975) *The Welfare State and Equality*, Berkeley, University of California Press.

Wilensky, H. (1976) *The 'New Corporatism', Centralization and the Welfare State*, Beverly Hills, CA, Sage.

Williamson, O.E. (1975) *Markets and Hierarchies: Analysis and Antitrust Implications*, New York, Free Press.

Williamson, O.E. (1985) *The Economic Institutions of Capitalism*, New York, The Free Press.

Williamson, O.E. (1986) *Economic Organization: Firms, Market and Policy Control*, Brighton, Harvester Wheatsheaf.

Wilson, F. and Ramphele, M. (1989) *Uprooting Poverty: the South African Challenge*, Cape Town, David Philip.

Wittman, D. (1989) 'Why democracies produce efficient results', *Journal of Political Economy*, **97**, 1395–424.

Wolf, C. (1988) *Markets or Governments*, Cambridge, MA, MIT Press.

World Bank (yearly from 1978) *World Development Report*, New York, Oxford University Press.

World Bank (1980a) *World Bank Atlas*, Washington, DC, World Bank.

World Bank (1980b) *World Tables 1980*, 2nd edn, Baltimore, Johns Hopkins University Press.

World Bank (1983) *World Development Report 1983*, New York, Oxford University Press.

World Bank (1984) *World Tables*, 3rd edn, Baltimore, Johns Hopkins University Press.

World Bank (1991a) *World Development Report 1991*, New York, Oxford University Press.

World Bank (1991b) *Social Indicators of Development 1990*, Baltimore, Johns Hopkins University Press.

World Bank (1995a) *World Development Report 1995*, New York, Oxford University Press.

World Bank (1995b) *World Bank Atlas 1995*, Washington, DC, World Bank.

World Bank (1996) *World Bank Atlas 1996*, Washington, DC, World Bank.

Wright, D.M. (1947) *The Economics of Disturbance*, New York, Macmillan.

Wright, L.M. (1982) 'A comparative survey of economic freedoms', in Gastil, R.D. (ed.), *Freedom in the World: Political Rights and Civil Liberties*, 1982, Westport, CT, Greenwood Press, 51–90.

Yarbrough, B.Y. and Yarbrough, R.M. (1988) *The World Economy*, Chicago, Dryden Press.

Yotopoulos, P.A. and Nugent, J.B. (1976) *Economics of Development: Empirical Investigations*, New York, Harper and Row.

Zaleski, E. (1980) *Stalinist Planning for Economic Growth*, London, Allen and Unwin.

Zysman, J. (1983) *Governments, Markets and Finance*, Ithaca, NY, Cornell University Press.

Index

Adelman, Irma 9, 16, 62
affluence 5, 9, 44, 191,
  236–7
  and democracy 11–12,
    89
  and development 54–6
  distribution 48–53, 59
  and economic growth
    42–3, 59
  and HDI 59–60
  levels 133–5
    1950 and *1990* 28–39,
    42–3, 59
  OECD 159
  and policy-making 190,
    191, 192–3
  and purchasing power
    parity 41
  and quality of life
    28–39, 46–7, 59–60
  regimes compared 144
  and trade 56–9
Africa
  affluence levels 28–42
  democracy 76, 77, 79,
    94, 95
  economic growth 39, 96
  economic systems
    141–2
  GDP growth rates 55;
    1900–92 40;
    1950 28, 30;
    1960 31;
    1970 32, 33;
    1980 34, 35;
    1990 36;
    1992 36, 38
  GNP growth rates 38, 54
  human development
    scores 97
  income inequality 48,
    49, 98, 100
  institutionalization 81–2
  military effort 79, 80
  polity capacity 78
  population 55
  protest 83–4

purchasing power
  parities 41
quality of life 47
trade 57
violence 84–5
see also countries
agriculture 6, 67, 154
Albania 143
Algeria 31, 32, 33, 55, 56,
  79, 141
allocation, resources
  budget 110–11, 120–5,
    126–8, 225
  competitive socialist
    model 115–18, 119
  efficiency 111–15,
    205–8
  expenditure 234
  market, as method
    110–13, 128, 187–201
  mechanisms 109–28,
    187–9, 200–1
  public 187–190, 191–6,
    200–1, 205–8, 213
    see also public
      expenditure
  in welfare states 217–19
    Scandinavia 203,
    205–8, 213
Almond, Gabriel A. 22,
  63–4, 70
Americas
  democracy 94, 95
  economic growth 96
  human development 97
  income equality 98
  see also Latin America;
    United States
Angola 31, 32, 33, 82, 141
apartheid 174, 181, 182–3
Apter, David E. 20, 22, 67
Argentina 29, 34, 37, 41,
  141
Arrow, K.J. 116
Asia
  affluence levels 28–44,
    47

democracy 76, 77, 79,
  94, 95
economic growth 96
economic systems 142
GDP
  growth rates 38–41,
    55
  per capita 28, 30–6,
    38, 40
GNP growth rates 38, 54
human development 47,
  97, 100
income inequality 48,
  49, 98
institutionalization 81–2
military effort 79, 80
polity capacity 78
population 55
protest 83–4
purchasing power
  parities 41
trade 57
violence 84–5
see also countries
auctions 239
Australia 29, 37, 41, 136,
  142, 214, 216, 232
Austria 143, 228, 229, 230
authoritarian regimes 62,
  89, 154, 163, 172, 200

Baby Tigers 137, 142
Balassa, Bela 56
Bangladesh 142
Barro, R.J. 3, 60, 236, 237
Barsh, R.L. 91
Baumol, W.J. 188
Belgium 56, 82, 143, 221,
  222, 232
Benin 141
Benjamin, R.W. 21
Binder, A.S. 22, 70
Bolivia 141
Bollen, K.A. 62, 93, 94
Botswana 39, 82, 142, 172
Brazil 39, 50, 53, 141
Brunner, R.D. 70